Social-Emotional Curriculum With Gifted and Talented Students

The *Critical Issues in Equity and Excellence in Gifted Education* Series

Social-Emotional Curriculum

With Gifted and Talented Students

Edited by
Joyce L. VanTassel-Baska, Ed.D.
Tracy L. Cross, Ph.D.,
and **F. Richard Olenchak, Ph.D.**

Prufrock Press Inc.
Waco, Texas

a service publication of

NATIONAL ASSOCIATION FOR
Gifted Children

Library of Congress Cataloging-in-Publication Data

Social-emotional curriculum with gifted and talented students / edited by Joyce L. VanTassel-Baska, Tracy L. Cross and F. Richard Olenchak.
   p. cm.—(Critical issues in equity and excellence in gifted education series)
  Includes bibliographical references.
  ISBN-13: 978-1-59363-349-3 (pbk.)
  ISBN-10: 1-59363-349-1 (pbk.)
  1. Gifted children—Education—United States—Curricula. 2. Social interaction—Study and teaching—United States. 3. Social skills in children—Study and teaching—United States. 4. Curriculum planning—United States. I. VanTassel-Baska, Joyce. II. Cross, Tracy L. III. Olenchak, F. Richard, 1960–.
  LC3993.9.S627 2009
  371.95′3—dc22
                          2008034174

Printed in the United States of America.

At the time of this book's publication, all facts and figures cited are the most current available. All telephone numbers, addresses, and Web site URLs are accurate and active. All publications, organizations, Web sites, and other resources exist as described in the book, and all have been verified. The authors and Prufrock Press Inc. make no warranty or guarantee concerning the information and materials given out by organizations or content found at Web sites, and we are not responsible for any changes that occur after this book's publication. If you find an error, please contact Prufrock Press Inc.

Prufrock Press Inc.
P.O. Box 8813
Waco, TX 76714-8813
Phone: (800) 998-2208
Fax: (800) 240-0333
http://www.prufrock.com

Dedication

To my family, Lee and Ariel, who continue to
support and inspire.
—Joyce VanTassel-Baska

To Pam, Lawren, and those whose love supports me through
trials of health and identity.
—F. Richard Olenchak

Acknowledgements

I would like to acknowledge the support of Bronwyn
MacFarlane for her assistance in the revision stages of this
manuscript. Her work was deeply appreciated.
—Joyce VanTassel-Baska

I would like to thank Jennifer R. Cross and A. Dawn Frazier
for their invaluable assistance with this book.
—Tracy L. Cross

I would like to thank Andrius Dzedulionis for his assistance in
the development of this book.
—F. Richard Olenchak

Contents

1. Introduction   1
   Joyce VanTassel-Baska

2. Theories to Guide Affective Curriculum Development   11
   Sidney M. Moon

3. Creating a Life: Orchestrating a Symphony of Self,   41
   a Work Always in Progress
   F. Richard Olenchak

4. Operation Houndstooth: A Positive Perspective   79
   on Developing Social Intelligence
   Joseph S. Renzulli

5. Affective Curriculum and Instruction for Gifted Learners   113
   Joyce VanTassel-Baska

6. Counseling Gifted Students From Non-White Racial Groups: 133
   Conceptual Perspectives and Practical Suggestions
   Kwong-Liem Karl Kwan and Wayne J. Hilson, Jr.

7. Addressing Social-Emotional and Curricular Needs   **153**
   of Gifted African American Adolescents
      Norma L. Day-Vines, James M. Patton, Chwee G. Quek,
      & Susannah Wood

8. Focusing on Where They Are: A Clinical Perspective   **193**
      Jean Sunde Peterson

9. The Role of the Arts in the Socioemotional   **227**
   Development of the Gifted
      Joyce VanTassel-Baska, Brandy L. E. Buckingham, & Ariel Baska

10. Guiding Gifted Teenagers to Self-Understanding   **259**
    Through Biography
       Thomas P. Hébert

11. Discussion Groups as a Component of Affective   **289**
    Curriculum for Gifted Students
       Jean Sunde Peterson, George Betts, & Terry Bradley

12. Preventing Suicide Among Students With Gifts and Talents   **321**
       Tracy L. Cross, Andrea D. Frazier, & Samantha M. McKay

13. Professional Development for Promoting   **345**
    the Social and Emotional Development of Gifted Children
       Elissa F. Brown

14. Creating Gifted Lives: Concluding Thoughts   **361**
       Tracy L. Cross, Joyce L. VanTassel-Baska, & F. Richard
       Olenchak

About the Editors   373

About the Authors   375

List of Tables

1.1 Standards for Preparation of Gifted Education   4
     Teachers Focusing on Social-Emotional Needs
     of Students (NAGC and Council for Exceptional
     Children, 2006, p. 1–3, 5)

7.1 Web References and Resources for Multicultural Education 183

9.1 Applying and Integrating Standards Into Gifted Curriculum 247

13.1 An Action Plan for Understanding Needed Changes in   351
     Professional Development.

13.2 Traditional and Alternative Modes of Delivery   356
     for Professional Development

List of Figures

3.1. Bull's Eye Model for Affective Development   57

4.1. Operation Houndstooth Intervention Theory   82

4.2. Graphic representation of Operation Houndstooth Theory   88

4.3. Operation Houndstooth Intervention Theory   101

9.1. The counseling process   237

9.2. Overlapping processes and outcomes for the use   239
     of the arts and counseling to assist social-emotional
     development

9.3. Sample visual arts standards   246

CHAPTER 1

Introduction

Joyce VanTassel-Baska

This book has been a long time in coming together. In 2003, a group of several of the contributors gathered in Houston for a weekend of discussion and planning under the leadership of Rick Olenchak, then president of the National Association for Gifted Children (NAGC). We worked diligently to produce outlines and then first drafts for several chapters. We also identified others whom we felt could make a strong contribution to the book. We continued to stay in touch by e-mail and critique each other's work over the next year. We have now chosen to reenergize the project with a broadened group of contributors and an expanded editorship model as well. The book now represents a more timely focus on different curriculum directions that offer affective support. It also provides a strong contribution to our field on a topic often not discussed—how can teachers help gifted students develop their social and emotional selves in the context of standards and assessment-driven school environments?

The book comprises 12 chapters, each of which offers a unique perspective on social-emotional curriculum. What binds the book together is the powerful theme of meaning-making, in other words, helping gifted students make sense of the big ideas in life including their own identity and the processes by which personal growth and development occur. It is a book that has content that is valid for both educators and counselors; even though the processes may vary based on their areas of skilled training. Why do we feel the book is important enough to have in a series on equity and excellence? Because this book offers guidance and counsel to all who work with the gifted and gets to the heart of their concerns.

By working through the layers of self that we all bring to this thing called life, gifted students can come to know they are not alone, whether through reading about a protagonist in a novel suffering similar angst or a biography of an eminent individual who demonstrated similar struggles and came out on the other side. They can begin to express their emotions rather than repress them through the process of discussion or the engagement in the arts. They can come to understand their different selves as individuals and as individuals in various groups, realizing that they present distinctive selves based on context and relationships. They can face the problems that most gifted students encounter at some stage of their growing into early adulthood—confronting perfectionism, developing important relationships, dealing with sensitivity and their own intensity, and channeling their concerns about the world into worthwhile service projects and careers. Yet, gifted students often cannot do these things unaided. They need a wise teacher or counselor who will guide them in the right direction, listen to their fears, and reassure and nurture them when they need support.

This book is intended to provide those wise friends and mentors with the support they need to do that work. The editors hope the chapters herein can sustain an ongoing program of socioemotional guidance throughout the school years, from kindergarten through high school. We hope that schools will realize the importance of providing a social-emotional curriculum and provide professional development for their teachers in this area, based on the Gifted Education Teacher Standards, passed by the National Council for Accreditation of Teacher Education (NCATE) in 2006, to ensure that all educators who work with gifted youth have core competencies in social and emotional areas of their makeup. The standards that follow in Table 1.1 offer a blueprint for such professional development that can be used along with this book.

The Organization of the Book

This book is organized to provide insights into the theory, research, and practice of provisions for gifted students in the socioaffective domain. It is meant to be a companion piece to the earlier NAGC text, *The Social and Emotional Development of Gifted Children: What Do We Know?*, published in 2002 that focused on what we know from research about the social and emotional needs of the gifted. This volume attempts to provide intervention approaches in response to those needs and suggest healthy responses to the problems and issues gifted students face in school and home settings.

The 12 chapters that comprise this book all provide insights about the social and emotional development of gifted learners and the interventions that can help promote mental health and stability across the lifespan. A brief summary of each follows.

The Moon chapter introduces all of the major theories currently available to guide the development of affective curriculum. She focuses on cognitive, affective, and conative theories that affect the development of gifted individuals in different ways at different stages of development. She chronicles the major ideas of these theories that affect both normal and gifted development and provides examples of how they could be or are used to teach affective skills both directly and indirectly in classroom settings. The theory of personal talent, developed by Moon, is explicated and applied as an exemplary framework for developing affective curriculum opportunities at elementary, middle, and high school levels.

The Olenchak chapter introduces a new model for thinking about the development of social and emotional competency called the *Bull's Eye*. Olenchak integrates the literature on brain research with more contemporary theories of psychology to demonstrate a research-based approach that may be taken in providing needed support to the gifted learner in optimizing

Table 1.1
Standards for Preparation of Gifted Education Teachers Focusing on Social-Emotional Needs of Students

Standard	Social-Emotional Knowledge and Skills
Standard 2: Development and Characteristics of Learners	K1: Cognitive and affective characteristics of individuals with gifts and talents, including those from diverse backgrounds, in intellectual, academic, creative, leadership, and arts domains.
Standard 3: Individual Learning Differences	K2: Academic and affective characteristics and learning needs of individuals with gifts and talents and disabilities.
Standard 5: Learning Environments and Social Interaction	K2: Influence of social and emotional development on interpersonal relationships and learning of individuals with gifts and talents.
	S1: Design learning opportunities for individuals with gifts and talents that promote self-awareness, positive peer relationships, intercultural experiences, and leadership.
	S2: Create learning environments for individuals with gifts and talents that promote self-awareness, self-efficacy, leadership, and lifelong learning.
	S3: Create safe learning environments for individuals with gifts and talents that encourage active participation in individual and group activities to enhance independence, interdependence, and positive peer relationships.
	S4: Create learning environments and intercultural experiences that allow individuals with gifts and talents to appreciate their own and others' language and cultural heritage.
	S5: Develop social interaction and coping skills in individuals with gifts and talents to address personal and social issues, including stereotyping and discrimination.
Standard 10: Collaboration	S1: Respond to concerns of families of individuals with gifts and talents.

Note. From National Association for Gifted Children and Council for Exceptional Children (2006, pp. 1–3, 5).

self. His review of the newer literature in neuroscience links the role of affect with the act of cognition, suggesting that emotion undergirds the capacity of cognitive functions to perform at optimal levels in complex tasks like decision making. The positive psychology movement has furthered studies of learned optimism, flow, and hope, all of which emphasize the positive affective traits of individuals in life situations that lead to perseverance and resilience in adversity. Using this literature base, Olenchak creates the Bull's Eye Model in four fluid stages, each influencing the other: natural affect, world contexts, meta-affect, and personal niche. The model loosely parallels the Gagné and Sternberg views of intelligence as mapped on personal and environmental collisions that affect how one thinks (as opposed to feels) about one's talent and its development. The final part of the chapter applies the model to what might be done in classrooms to stress affective development.

The Renzulli chapter introduces the Houndstooth Theory as a way of acknowledging the importance of the comingling of affective development with cognitive development. He focuses on six conative or co-cognitive factors—optimism, courage, sensitivity to human concerns, romance with a discipline, physical/mental energy, and vision or a sense of destiny—to make the case that gifted learners must be able to internalize these qualities in the development and expression of their talent areas. He also provides research-based approaches to such development through different typologies of program interventions that provide opportunities to learners to understand and apply skills and strategies in leadership and service venues. He concludes the chapter by stressing the importance of the background of affective development in areas of learning for the gifted to ultimately push forward the creative and productive expression in their lives.

In her chapter on affective curriculum, VanTassel-Baska emphasizes the range of interventions that teachers and other educators can provide gifted learners inside and outside of the classroom. She focuses specifically on the use of an emotional intelligence framework to create lesson plans that address the need to express emotions, channel them, and ultimately regulate them through the use of literature, movies, history, and the arts. She also suggests that affective curriculum should be integrated into cognitive areas in order to ensure that it is effective and used in classrooms. A list of topics for use in bibliotherapy also is provided that may guide practitioners in the choice of reading materials for students in need of connecting to protagonists who share their concerns and problems.

The Kwan and Hilson chapter focuses on racial minority groups and providing social and emotional guidance to these groups. The authors wisely focus on the similarities in counseling needs to majority groups in order to suggest a value-added model and approach. The authors introduce conceptual models useful for counseling non-White clients and apply them to two case studies of students from different minority groups as a way to help readers understand that social and emotional costs are borne by both underrepresented and overrepresented minority populations. Their chapter concludes with practical ideas to be considered in counseling racially diverse gifted students.

The Day-Vines, Patton, Quek, and Woods chapter targets African American adolescents as the population of interest for interventions that are culture-specific, yet also provides more generic ideas for social-emotional curriculum. Issues of teachers and counselors being attuned to cultural differences is one theme found throughout the chapter with practical suggestions for how to implement a counseling program that provides such support. The themes of resilience, self-efficacy, and developing leadership competencies also are played out in the chapter as psychological tools to use in the development of these students across the critical adolescent years.

The Peterson chapter is grounded in the author's experiences as a clinical counselor who has worked extensively with gifted secondary students. She advocates for a broad definition of who should be included in a counseling program for the gifted, going beyond high achievers and those from the majority culture. She suggests three approaches to an affective curriculum: a proactive one that deliberately advances the agenda of personal growth, a reactive one that responds to individual problems that interfere with learning, and an integrated one that is embedded in content-based activities. Peterson also discusses the importance of the collaboration between teachers and counselors in ensuring that the social and emotional needs of gifted learners are met. The professional bridges that are built between these two roles can spell the difference in the lives of many gifted students. She defines the role and responsibility of each professional and delineates ways they can work together to map out a strong program of intervention for gifted learners.

The VanTassel-Baska, Buckingham, and Baska chapter focuses on the role of the arts in developing social and emotional health. A review of the literature is included that stresses the therapeutic value of the arts in unleashing creative potential and calming the pain of social and emotional scars. Several examples of arts curricula are included for teachers to use in classrooms along with ideas for more in-depth work that could be done by arts professionals in the schools. Special emphasis is placed on the use of literature and the visual arts as mechanisms for involving students in affective activities. The chapter also addresses the role of educators in ensuring that the arts are effectively integrated into the core subject areas as the most effective strategy to ensure their inclusion in school curriculum.

The Hébert chapter targets the use of biography and autobiography as powerful tools to guide the social and emotional development of gifted children in school. He notes the value of these tools in establishing role models, helping with identity development, and reducing alienation in gifted students, especially during the adolescent years. He provides examples of books to be employed and the processes of discussion and questioning that should accompany the readings. Hébert's ideas are very compatible with the discussion model found in Chapter 11. The two chapters could be used together to build appropriate units of study.

The Peterson, Betts, and Bradley chapter discusses the importance of discussion groups as a mode of working on social and emotional issues with gifted children. The authors provide a variety of resources to help practitioners use discussion, a long list of content topics to discuss based on the needs and interests of these learners, and tips on the procedures for conducting effective discussion groups, especially with adolescents. The chapter details the importance of employing active listening with students, deliberate use of core questions, and employment of existing resources to conduct successful counseling groups.

The Cross, Frazier, and McKay chapter delineates ideas for the prevention of suicide and suicidal behavior in gifted youth. They focus on the warning signs and the preventive measures that school people and parents alike must take to ensure the safety of at-risk gifted children. They outline the nature of intervention strategies that may be applied to ease the pain of these young people and suggest that we are not vigilant enough in our attention to their social and emotional development.

The Brown chapter provides a model for professional development in gifted education that would allow school leaders to plan effectively for promoting the social and emotional development of gifted students at all stages of development. She argues for the importance of school leaders acknowledging this area of programming and holding teachers and counselors accountable for providing it. Her chapter suggests the use of both the new teacher education standards and the NAGC program standards as a basis for constructing a model professional development program in this area. Key questions and modes of delivery also are discussed.

The concluding chapter of the book pulls together the major themes noted across the chapters and examines new directions for addressing the social and emotional development of gifted learners in schools and outside of schools. It raises new issues and questions about how attention to the whole gifted child will be possible in the current climate of No Child Left Behind and suggests the need to consider alternative services outside of traditional schools to effect optimal support for the social and emotional needs of our best learners. Optimal social contexts for learning may include residential schools for the gifted, university programs, community-based programs like museum studies and research, and online opportunities that provide mentors to these learners. Counseling emphases will need to stress bibliotherapy in various forms and the use of discussion, preferably in groups, and provide empathy for the cultural background of the learner. Yet, even as these tasks are difficult to accomplish, the editors note that a collaborative spirit among educators, counselors, and parents can make them much easier to accomplish, and they reiterate their overall importance in the talent development process for our best learners.

Common Issues and Themes

What do each of these chapters have in common? They all suggest the absence of sufficient emphasis on the social and emotional development of gifted learners, perhaps in both school and home settings. Because newer brain research suggests that affect precedes cognition, not the other way around (see Damasio's [1999] work), concerns for stimulating and motivating gifted learners in these ways appears to be a paramount concern, yet is unmatched by actual interventions to do so.

Each chapter also stresses the use of deliberate approaches and strategies to address social and emotional concerns of the gifted in both direct and indirect ways. We have known for some time that these learners have special concerns not always shared by the general population of students in schools. These concerns often have been misdiagnosed or ignored in the larger scheme of delivering cognitive instruction. Yet, these concerns have been identified and targeted by the authors of this volume as significant for the total functioning of the gifted child. They include, but are not limited to: perfectionism, developing relationships, concern for others and the state of the world, procrastination, and feelings of inadequacy, called the *imposter syndrome* by some.

The chapters all call for more involvement of teachers in the role of providing nurturance for social and emotional development. Many of the interventions called for in the book ultimately will be delivered by teachers, if they are delivered at all. This suggests the need for a major emphasis on the professional preparation of teachers to provide such support and the complicit agreement of administrators that it is important enough for the time to be expended, even in a standards-based and assessment-driven environment.

Finally, all of the chapters suggest that the development of positive habits of mind and heart are integrative in nature and that an affective curriculum for gifted students cannot be delivered in the absence of thoughtful integration with other required classroom activities. Such an integration of curriculum emphases also suggests a big job for educators in order to effect positive growth in all of the cognitive and affective arenas that gifted students need to exhibit them.

Concluding Commentary

It is our hope that this book will provide new directions for educators in thinking about the affective development of gifted learners, that it will be a useful companion to the earlier NAGC publication on what we know about the social and emotional development of the gifted, and suggest that, based on what we already know, we can provide positive interventions that have proven to be effective. I sincerely believe that caring educators have the potential to make an important difference in the lives of many of our gifted children if they believe that their intervention means something. Our research and clinical practice literature clearly suggest that the interventions promulgated in this book *do* matter in the lives of gifted and talented individuals at all stages of development.

References

Damasio, A. R. (1999). *The feeling of what happens: Body and emotion in the making of consciousness*. New York: Harcourt Brace.

National Association for Gifted Children, & Council for Exceptional Children. (2006). *NAGC-CEC teacher knowledge & skill standards for gifted and talented education*. Retrieved May 29, 2008, from http://www.nagc.org/uploadedFiles/Information_and_Resources/NCATE_standards/final%20standards%20(2006).pdf

Neihart, M., Reis, S. M., Robinson, N. M., & Moon, S. M. (2002). *The social and emotional development of gifted children: What do we know?* Waco, TX: Prufrock Press.

Theories to Guide Affective Curriculum Development

Sidney M. Moon

Introduction

There are three broad categories of intrapersonal human functioning: cognitive, affective, and conative. The *cognitive* category includes the abilities assessed by intelligence and IQ tests, the areas we normally think of as being associated with thinking. These abilities are the primary focus of schooling. The *affective* category includes emotions and emotional development. For example, researchers interested in affect regulation investigate people's ability to understand, label, and manage their emotions. *Conation* is everything related to motivation. Conative researchers investigate things like goal setting, persistence, and student interests. Because all motivational processes involve emotions, many current theorists include both affective and conative processes under the general heading of "affective." In addition, interpersonal processes are considered to be affective by most scholars and practitioners. In keeping with current trends, this chapter takes a broad view of the affective landscape and includes theories that combine affective and conative processes. The chapter provides an overview of a wide variety of types of theories that can guide the development of curriculum to support the emotional, social/interpersonal, and/or motivational/conative development of high-ability youth.

There are two types of curriculum that can be used to promote affective development. The first type provides *direct instruction* of affective knowledge and skills. Examples of direct instruction include curricula explicitly developed to teach social skills such as active listening, "I messages," or conflict mediation. Curricula designed to teach independent study often provide direct instruction on affective skills such as identifying interests and prioritizing tasks. Many of the theories in this book could be useful in guiding the development of explicit affective curricula. For example, the theory of successful intelligence has led to curricula that teach practical thinking, including lessons on affective skills such risk taking, handling personal difficulties, setting priorities, and developing self-confidence (Sternberg & Grigorenko, 2000). Gifted students can benefit greatly from direct teaching of affective knowledge and skills. Both teachers and school counselors can provide direct instruction in affective skills. Jean Sunde Peterson's (1993, 1995) series of books on talking with teens provides an example of affective curriculum designed to be implemented by school counselors in group counseling settings. Chapters 5, 9, and 10 in this volume provide examples of affective curriculum that can be implemented by teachers in classroom settings.

The other type of affective curriculum is *indirect*, and more readily adapted to classroom environments. It involves activities like creating classroom climates that foster positive affective development and teacher modeling of affect regulation skills such as anger management or expressions of grief following loss. Indirect affective curricula often include experiential activities that require students to process emotions such as historical simulations, novel reading, or the creation and sharing of expressive works of art. This type of affective curriculum is more easily integrated into Pre-K–12 classrooms, particularly in subjects like the arts and humanities. This type of curriculum is discussed more fully by VanTassel-Baska, Buckingham, and Baska in Chapter 9 about the role of the arts in the socioemotional development of the gifted.

The theories presented in this chapter can be helpful in guiding the development of both types of curricula (direct and indirect) to foster positive affective development among high-ability youth. At the end of the chapter an extended example of the application of one of the theories—personal talent theory—is provided. Personal talent theory is a personal development metatheory that provides a framework for helping talented youth select and achieve challenging goals that fit their ability, interest, and value profiles. The personal talent theory example shows how the theory can be used to guide the development of both direct and indirect affective curricula in a coherent, comprehensive, and effective way.

Overview of Relevant Theories

The theories described here are illustrative, not exhaustive, and generally were developed to highlight normal developmental processes, rather than to guide interventions for gifted and talented students. They have been grouped into six broad categories: human development, emotional and social development, cognitive/social–cognitive, personal development, identity/career development, and moral development. Within each category, I provide examples of each type, give suggestions for using the theory to develop affective curricula, and discuss special considerations for applying the theory to gifted and talented students.

Broad Human Development Theories

The field of human development has developed many theories to describe normal developmental processes across the lifespan that can provide guidance on the most important issues to address at particular ages. It is important for educators of gifted students to be aware of stage theories of development because they suggest sequences of life tasks that human beings must master. For example, Erikson's (1963, 1972) theory proposes eight stages of psychosocial development over the lifespan: trust vs. mistrust (infancy), autonomy vs. shame/doubt (toddler years), initiative vs. guilt (preschool), industry vs. inferiority (elementary school), identity vs. role confusion (adolescence), intimacy vs. isolation (young adulthood), generativity vs. stagnation (middle age), and integrity vs. despair (retirement). This theory suggests that gifted programming during the elementary school years should provide challenges that help students learn that their efforts can make a difference in learning and problem solving and that high achievement requires hard work. In other words, Erikson's theory suggests that gifted children in the elementary school years need tasks and programs that challenge them and involve them in meaningful work. A good example of such a program is the Schoolwide Enrichment Model (Renzulli & Reis, 1997). This model is developmentally appropriate for gifted children at the elementary level because it encourages them to develop "learned industriousness" (Eisenberger, 1992) as they pursue self-selected projects with meaningful outcomes. However, it also is true that the timelines embedded in stage theories such as Erikson's may need to be accelerated for gifted students because gifted students may move more quickly through the proposed stages. Evidence that this is the case with respect to the stage of identity development is discussed later in this chapter in the section on theories of identity and career development. Many of the broad human development theories also need adjustment for gifted females and minorities because they were developed from observations of White male populations.

Maslow's (1970) theory of self-actualization is another broad human development theory that is quite relevant for gifted and talented students. Unlike the stage theories, this theory has no linkages to particular age ranges and is based on human needs that are present at all ages, rather than on developmental tasks. It is similar to Erikson's stage theory, however, in that it describes a hierarchy of needs, with each rung of the hierarchy depending on successful resolution of the rungs beneath it. The needs in Maslow's theory range from basic survival needs (physiological needs such as food, water, oxygen, and shelter), to needs relevant to self-actualization (the optimization of human potential, becoming all one is capable of becoming). In between are

needs for safety, love and belonging, and esteem. This seminal theory can be used as an overarching framework for affective needs assessment and the promotion of optimal personal
development. It is a useful diagnostic tool when working with
underachievers.

Ecological theories look at the effect of context on human
development and so are especially useful in constructing affective
curricula that address issues like how culture can impact student
choices or the ways in which family, peer, and school environments inhibit or facilitate talent development (Moen, Elder,
& Luscher, 1995). Many of these theories incorporate systems
theory (Bronfenbrenner, 1989; Whitchurch & Constantine,
1993). Systems theory is useful in constructing affective curricula that can help gifted and talented students to understand the
complexity of human relationships and the reciprocal nature of
causality in human systems. These theories can guide affective
curriculum that is intended to help remove sociocultural barriers to talent development. For example, a tailored curriculum
might be designed for low socioeconomic status (SES), urban
youth to teach them the ways in which their family, peer, and
community environments create barriers to aspiration development (Ambrose, 2003) or a special curriculum might be created
to help middle school girls move beyond social stereotyping and
become more androgynous (Arnold, Noble, & Subotnik, 1996;
Callahan & Reis, 1996; Noble, Subotnik, & Arnold, 1999;
Reis, 1998).

Emotional and Social Development Theories

Emotional Development

For a long time, psychologists ignored emotions. They studied behavior instead of internal processes or they studied cognition rather than affect. Recently, however, there has been a
strong upsurge of interest in the study of emotional development
and affect regulation (Cherniss & Goleman, 2001; Goleman,
1995; Mayer & Salovey, 1997; Salovey & Sluyter, 1997). This
interest has given rise to theories of emotional intelligence that
can guide the development of affective curricula designed to

increase the ability of gifted students to understand, express, and regulate emotions. For example, Mayer and Salovey (1997; Salovey, Mayer, & Caruso, 2002) propose a model of emotional intelligence that includes four hierarchical levels: (a) emotional perception and expression; (b) emotional facilitation of thought; (c) emotional understanding; and (d) emotional management. Their model provides a framework for both the assessment of emotional abilities and for the development of affective curricula designed to increase emotional expertise. Joyce VanTassel-Baska also discusses this model in Chapter 5 in relation to affective curriculum and instruction for gifted learners.

Social Development

Social intelligence has been investigated for a longer period of time, and more thoroughly, than emotional intelligence (Kelly & Moon, 1998). There is good empirical evidence that social intelligence is a multidimensional construct that is different from academic intelligence (Marlowe, 1986). Based largely on biological evidence, Gardner (1983, 1999) included interpersonal intelligence as one of the intelligences in his multiple intelligences model. Social psychology is an active field of investigation (Van Hasselt & Hersen, 1992). Theories of social development have emerged from the field of social psychology that may be applicable to affective curriculum for gifted and talented students. These theories include *attachment theory* (Bowlby, 1984), theories of the development of *prosocial behavior* (Eisenberg, 1982; Eisenberg, Carlo, Murphy, & Van Court, 1995), and theories about *interpersonal problem solving, friendship*, and *social competence* (Gross, 2000, 2004; Rubin & Rose-Krasnor, 1992; Selman, 1980; Selman & Schultz, 1990).

Matching Theory to Purpose

Affective curricula related to the social and emotional development of gifted and talented students can have different aims. The theories chosen to guide such affective curricula should be consistent with the aims of the curricula. For example, one possible purpose might be to identify students who have high levels of social and/or emotional intelligence so they can receive special programming designed to help them gain further expertise in the social and/or emotional domains or prepare for careers that require high levels of social-emotional expertise such as counseling, teaching, and leadership. Theories of social and emotional intelligence and/or intrapersonal problem solving provide good frameworks for affective curriculum in this type of talent development program. For example, some theorists have developed lists of social competencies that promote school success such as perspective taking, appreciation of diversity, communication, negotiation, empathy, and cooperation (Elias et al., 1997; Zins, Bloodworth, Weissberg, & Walberg, 2004). These competencies could be converted to behavioral checklists that might aid in identifying social talent.

A second possible purpose might be to help highly intelligent students who lack social and/or emotional intelligence develop sufficient social-emotional competence to be able to develop their academic talents, build strong friendships, and work effectively with others. This purpose is particularly appropriate for special populations of gifted students who are at risk for difficulties with social-emotional adjustment such as twice-exceptional students (Moon, Zentall, Grskovic, Hall, & Stormont, 2001; Reis, Neu, & McGuire, 1995), students with family problems (Peterson, 2001, 2002), and underachievers (Moon, 2004; Reis & McCoach, 2000). Attachment theory, theories of prosocial behavior, and interpersonal problem-solving theories might be used as frameworks for work on social competence with these students.

Affective curriculum development based on theories of social and emotional development already is taking place at a few academic centers in the United States. The Center for Social and Emotional Education (CSEE; see http://www.csee.net/climate) and the Collaborative for Academic, Social, and Emotional Learning (CASEL; see http://www.casel.org) are examples of interdisciplinary academic centers that have developed theory-driven affective curricula. The CASEL center uses a theory of social intelligence competencies that includes self-awareness, self-management, responsible decision making, social awareness, and relationship management to guide research-based curriculum development. However, this work is focused on general population students and on reversing behavior problems, rather than on identifying and developing high levels of social and emotional talent (Moon & Ray, 2006).

Cognitive and Social-Cognitive Theories

Cognitive science has produced theories that address specific, narrowly circumscribed aspects of affective development such as theories of volition and social information processing. Cognitive scientists define *volition* as an individual's ability to initiate and maintain intentions or goals. In the early part of the 20th century, Ach developed a comprehensive theory of volition that encompassed both the determinants of intentions and the cognitive processes that mediate the enactment of an intention after it has been formed (Kuhl & Beckman, 1985b). The theory includes phenomenological attributes of volition and cognitive mediators of volition such as selective attention, selective encoding, successive attention-adjustment, and determining feelings (Kuhl & Beckman, 1985a). In the same tradition, the action control theories attempt to specify which of several competing goals a person will actually implement in a given situation (i.e., which goal will become dominant and, therefore, drive goal-directed behavior; Kuhl, 1985, 1996; Kuhl & Kraska, 1989). Such theories are needed because people do not always behave in ways that are consistent with their values, attitudes, or intentions. Action control theory models the various mental processes that mediate self-regulatory functions and suggests that a number of internal processes can influence whether a particular gifted child achieves a particular goal. Some of these processes include self-regulation strategies and skills, perceptions of control, social pressures, and level of commitment to the goal. In this theory, self-regulation is broken down into six specific self-regulatory strategies that enable individuals to accomplish difficult goals in the face of competing priorities: active attentional selectivity, encoding control, emotional control, motivation control, environment control, and parsimony of information processing (Kuhl, 1985).

Action control theory provides a useful theoretical framework for analyzing the reasons that some gifted and talented students have difficulty persisting toward their goals and deferring gratification in order to achieve long-term objectives. Action control theory also might be a helpful theoretical framework for counseling gifted and talented adolescents who are having difficulty changing ingrained behavior patterns that are health-impairing, such as smoking or excessive drinking. Finally, action control theory provides a cognitive explanation for the performance decrements that can occur following exposure to uncontrollable failure and points the way to cognitive interventions that can help gifted and talented children overcome the often paralyzing effects of the failure experiences that can occur when they are first exposed to more challenging or competitive learning environments.

Social information processing theory focuses on the cognitive processes involved in thinking about and interpreting social situations and relationships (Crick & Dodge, 1996; Dodge, 1986). Social information processing theory has been used to explain both negative social interactions, such as aggressive or bullying behavior (Dodge, 1986), and positive social interactions, like those involved in building friendships (Crick & Dodge, 1996; Gross, 2004). The theory suggests that six steps can explain the behaviors that are enacted in social situations. The cognitive steps explain why two children can react completely differently to the same social situation. The first step is to encode both external and internal cues related to the situation. Then the individual interprets those cues, and selects a goal. To develop a response, the individual accesses his or her existing repertoire of possible responses, makes a response decision, and enacts the resulting behavior. These steps occur very rapidly in actual social interactions. Children with behavior problems often distort social cues, resulting in their interpretation of situations more negatively than is warranted. On the other hand, children with high levels of social skills are particularly adept at making accurate interpretations of social situations and have a broad repertoire of appropriate responses. Social cognitive theories may form the foundation of curricula designed to enhance children's social skills by encouraging perspective taking, directly teaching appropriate social interpretations and behaviors, and providing instruction in social problem-solving skills such as conflict mediation.

Cognitive scientists are interested primarily in internal processes that are mediated by cognition. Social–cognitive theorists are interested in similar phenomena but take a broader view of those phenomena, more like that of the ecosystemic theorists. Social–cognitive theorists believe that human behavior is best explained by reciprocal interactions among behavior, the environment, and the person. Social–cognitive theories use the term *self-regulation* for the processes that are called *volitional control* in action control theory, and they see self-regulatory processes as recursive in nature and heavily influenced by context (Pintrich & Schunk, 1996). The social–cognitive paradigm has produced a great deal of educational and psychological research on constructs like *self-concept* (Harter, 1999; Marsh, Chessor, Craven, & Roche, 1995; Mendaglio & Pyryt, 2003), *self-efficacy* (Bandura, 1997; Schunk, 1989, 1991), *goal setting* (Locke & Latham, 2002; Markus & Ruvolo, 1989), and *motivation* (Dai, Moon, & Feldhusen, 1998; Pintrich & Schunk, 1996; Wolters, 1998, 2003). These constructs are especially relevant to affective curricula that aim to help gifted and talented students develop personal talent (Moon, 2003b).

Personal Development

Personal development theories explain the factors that lead to optimal personal development. Some of the broad human development theories, such as Maslow's theory of *self-actualization*, also are personal development theories. However, this category also includes much narrower theories like Csikszentmihalyi's (1990, 1997) *flow* theory, which explains the conditions that lead to optimal experiences in everyday life and Deci and Ryan's (1985; Ryan & Deci, 2000) *self-determination theory*, which explains the role of intrinsic and extrinsic motivation in productive, autonomous behavior. Composite theories of the ability and personality factors that lead to success like

Goleman's (1995; Cherniss & Goleman, 2001) theory of *emotional intelligence* and Sternberg's (1996; Sternberg & Grigorenko, 2000) theory of *successful intelligence* also belong in this category because they explain why some individuals are more successful than others in achieving their goals. Similarly, broad theories of *resilience* (Bland, Sowa, & Callahan, 1994; Masten, 2001; Neihart, 2002) and more narrow theories about mediating personal characteristics that are associated with resilience such as *hope* (Snyder, 1994) and *optimism* (Carver & Scheier, 2002; Peterson, 2000; Scheier & Carver, 1992; Seligman, 1998) are classified here as theories of personal development.

The *stress and coping* literature also includes personal theories that can guide the development of affective curriculum and help explain the developmental trajectories of gifted and talented students (Lazarus, 1991; Sowa & May, 1997). Similarly, theories about positive constructs like *gratitude* (Emmons & Shelton, 2002) and *forgiveness* (McCullough & Witvliet, 2002) can help guide the creation of curricula that will help gifted students develop these characteristics. Work on the factors that lead to *resilience* can help with the creation of affective curricula that build resilience in high-ability youth, many of whom are not resilient at all, especially when faced with failure (Bland et al., 1994; Masten, 2001; Masten & Marie-Gabrielle, 2002; Neihart, 2002; Noble, 1996). An example of instructional strategies that build resilience can be found in the empirical work of Albert Ziegler and his colleagues (Ziegler & Heller, 1997, 2000b). These researchers have developed methods that help gifted females at the middle school level change the ways they think about success and failure in subjects like physics. These strategies include feedback that attributes their successes to ability and their failures to either lack of effort or poor strategy use. As middle school girls change the things they say to themselves when working on physics problems, they become more resilient, improve their performances, and develop more positive attitudes toward the subject matter.

Dabrowski's theory of positive disintegration is a theory of personal development that has received considerable attention in the gifted and talented literature because there are aspects of

the experience of gifted people that it seems to capture exceptionally well (Ackerman, 1997; Dabrowski, 1972; Dabrowski &
Piechowski, 1977; Mendaglio, 2008; Mendaglio & Pyryt, 2003;
Piechowski, 1997). Dabrowski's theory suggests that personality development occurs when the press of internal and environmental forces propels a person to grow through a paradigm
shifting mechanism that begins with disintegration of current
psychic structures and ends with a higher order reintegration.
Similar concepts of the way higher order change occurs are
found in systems theory (Whitchurch & Constantine, 1993).
Like many of the other theories reviewed here, Dabrowski's
theory is a stage theory. His stages of development are somewhat similar to those of the moral development theorists discussed later in this chapter because they progress from lower
stages where individuals are self-centered and conforming,
to higher stages where individuals are selfless, altruistic, and
autonomous. Dabrowski is unique, however, in believing that
growth occurs only through emotional suffering and that inner
anguish reflecting discrepancies between a person's real and
ideal self can be a sign of advanced development rather than
neurosis. Dabrowski's theory has been applied to the identification of gifted students with high levels of emotional intelligence
(Piechowski, 1997).

The field of gifted education itself has produced some theories that belong in the personal development category because
they specify the processes that facilitate high levels of talent
development. Some of these theories are fairly simple and defi-
nitional, like Renzulli's familiar three-ring model that suggests
that three factors must combine to produce high-level achievement (above-average ability, creativity, and task commitment;
Renzulli, 1978). Others, like Gagné's differentiated model of
giftedness and talent (DMGT; 2000), attempt to explain and
specify what Gagné calls the *complex choreography of talent development*. Most talent development models include affective components. In the three-ring model, both task commitment and
creativity involve affective skills. In addition, more recent elab-
orations of the three-ring model in a project called "Operation
Houndstooth" have specified additional affective factors that

influence talent development such as optimism, passion, and courage (Renzulli & Systma, 2001; see Chapter 4 of this volume). Gagné's DMGT model includes many affective components. For example, socioaffective abilities are considered one of several types of natural abilities that serve as building blocks for the development of talent. Several affective processes such as motivation (needs, interests, values) and volition (willpower, effort, persistence) are included in this model as intrapersonal catalysts that influence talent development. Finally, the DMGT model has an ecosystemic flavor because it recognizes that many types of environmental influences can enhance or inhibit the talent development process. Hence, the DMGT model combines several of the theoretical perspectives cited in this chapter and focuses them on the process of talent development. This model would be a good one to include in a direct instruction unit on talent development because it is focused on the elements that must come together to convert abilities into fully developed talents.

Other theories of this type include the developing expertise theory (Sternberg, 2000) and the Munich model of giftedness (Ziegler & Heller, 2000a). Like Gagné's model, these theories attempt to specify the factors that contribute to the development of expertise, high performance, or talent. Sternberg's theory is more cognitive than most, thus it does not have an explicit affective emphasis. However, motivation is central to his theory, and motivation involves the ability to understand and manage emotions. In the Munich model, affective factors are potentially involved in all four of the major components of the model: (a) talent factors (social competence, practical intelligence), (b) noncognitive personal characteristics (coping with stress), (c) environmental mediators (family and classroom climate), and (d) performance areas (social relationships).

Two additional personal development theories from our field that are more explicitly affective are the theory of *personal talent* (Moon, 2003b) and *wisdom theory* (Sternberg, 1990). These related theories provide frameworks for creating interventions that facilitate a broader range of outcomes than achievement, outcomes such as personal happiness and social justice. Personal talent theory is a metatheory that encompasses many of the previously discussed theories, especially those in the cognitive and social-cognitive category. Personal talent provides a framework for the development of direct and indirect educational interventions to help gifted and talented students improve their ability to select challenging goals that fit their interests, abilities, values, and contexts, and accomplish the goals they set for themselves (Moon, 2003a, 2003b). It focuses affective curriculum on personal problem finding (i.e., What am I good at? What do I want to accomplish in my life? What price am I willing to pay to achieve my goals?), as well as on personal problem solving (i.e., How can I achieve the goals I've set for myself? What do I do when my priorities conflict? What can I do when my plans are thwarted by a lack of environmental resources?).

Wisdom theories have similar goals to personal talent theory in that they attempt to specify the factors that assist individuals in solving problems in the complex, unstructured, and often predominately affective domain of life management (Baltes & Staudinger, 2000). However, wisdom theories add a valence toward the common good—wisdom is conceptualized as being able to provide helpful advice to others (Baltes & Staudinger, 2000) or as being able to balance individual interests with the common good (Sternberg, 1998). Hence, wisdom theories are particularly helpful in guiding affective curricula focused on social justice, service learning, and other efforts to improve society. They also overlap somewhat with the theories of moral development discussed later in this chapter.

Identity Development

Theories of identity development provide another source of ideas for theoretical frameworks to use in designing affective curricula, especially at the secondary level. These theories include stage theories, identity formation theories, and career development theories (Hébert & Kelly, 2006). It is very important to pay attention to diversity issues when using identity theories to guide affective curriculum. Indeed, specialized identity theories have been developed for specific subpopulations like females (Gilligan, 1982; Noble, 1996; Reis, 1998) and racially diverse students (Ford, Harris, & Schuerger, 1993; Plucker, 1996). Identity issues also are complex for gifted individuals who have an additional exceptionality, such as those students who are learning disabled (Baum, Owen, & Dixon, 1991).

In addition, theories of identity development in the general psychological literature may need adjustment for gifted and talented students. For example, the major task of adolescence in both Erickson's (1963, 1972) and Marcia's (1980) theories is identity development. Marcia's theory is more complex than Erickson's theory. He has found empirical evidence for four different identity statuses in adolescence, rather than the two Erickson proposed (Marcia, 1966). In addition to diffusion (lack of commitment) and successful identity development (commitment following a crisis period), Marcia added the stages of moratorium (seeking) and foreclosure (high commitment without self-reflection). Marcia suggested that only a small minority of high school students have begun to think seriously about their career and life goals. However, research in the field of gifted studies suggests that gifted middle school students are ready for career development work that normally is reserved for high school students (Kelly, 1992). This suggests that gifted and talented students can benefit from affective curricula focused on identity development much earlier than other students.

Some curriculum developers in the field of gifted education have promoted an emphasis on identity as an affective theme in all curricula developed for gifted students. For example, the Parallel Curriculum model (Tomlinson et al., 2002), stresses the curriculum of identity, which helps students build self-knowledge about their identity as a learner and assess the extent of fit between themselves and the discipline they are studying. Teaching methods that further identity development of students in this model include opportunities to shadow professionals in a field, simulations, role-plays, and independent study.

Moral Development

Teachers can play a significant role in the moral develop-ment of their students by the behaviors that they model on a daily basis and the climate they create in their classrooms. In addition, some academic domains require students to reflect on moral issues or make moral decisions. For example, much of the best world literature involves characters that face moral dilemmas, and many emergent areas of science pose new moral dilemmas for society. Some programs for high-ability students, such as the special high school for the gifted in the arts and sci-ences in Israel, include the development of social responsibility as part of their curriculum (Passow, 1994; Rachel & Zorman, 2003). Affective curriculum for gifted students can help high-ability students develop moral awareness and higher level moral reasoning.

Prominent theories of moral reasoning include those devel-oped by Kohlberg (1984) and Gilligan (1982). Kohlberg pro-posed a stage theory developed by studying how people resolve moral dilemmas. Kohlberg identified three levels of moral development, each of which includes two stages. In the low-est stage, Punishment Avoidance and Obedience, individu-als make decisions based only on what is best for themselves without any regard for the needs of others. In the highest stage, Universal Ethical Principles, individuals have a strong ethical compass and are guided by universal principles such as tolerance and human rights. In between, individuals are guided in their moral decision making primarily by pleasing others, societal customs and laws, or social contracts. Because the subjects in Kohlberg's studies were predominantly male, some of his critics have argued that his theory did not adequately address female moral development. For example, one critic has suggested that Kohlberg overemphasized fairness and justice, which tend to be more salient for males, and underemphasized compassion and caring, which tend to be more salient for females (Gilligan, 1982). Both Kohlberg and Gilligan saw moral development as primarily cognitive (i.e., as the ability to solve moral dilemmas through moral reasoning).

More recent theories emphasize the emotional aspects of moral development. For example, Eisenberg (1982; Eisenberg et al., 1995) has developed a stage theory of prosocial reasoning that reflects different levels of a person's ability to empathize with others. In her theory, children progress from the self-centered orientation of most preschoolers to the empathetic orientation and internalized values of helping other people possessed by many high school students. Eisenberg believes that academic curricula in subjects like social studies and language arts can help foster empathy and prosocial development, particularly if teachers design activities that emphasize perspective taking.

Application: Using the Theory of Personal Talent as a Guide for Affective Curriculum

The purpose of this section is to illustrate how theory can be used to guide affective curriculum by providing an extended example. The theory I've selected for this example is the theory of personal talent (Moon, 2001). Personal talent is an effective framework for affective curriculum development for high-ability students because of its emphasis on developing personal skills that facilitate both talent development and life satisfaction.

One of the first decisions to make in working with any theory is whether the approach to theory application will emphasize direct instruction or indirect, experiential activities. In the case of personal talent theory, indirect approaches would teach personal talent skills through teacher modeling, creation of adaptive classroom climates, and personal talent activities embedded in the regular curriculum. Direct approaches, on the other hand, would provide explicit instruction in personal talent theory, knowledge, skills, and dispositions through specific, structured, psychological curricula. Using the direct approach, units would be developed and taught on personal talent topics such as goal selection, time management, and decision making.

After the basic approach has been selected, goals of the curriculum for each developmental level can be developed. Based on the theory of personal talent, these goals would focus on developing personal talent knowledge, skills, and dispositions.

For example, an elementary-level curriculum that combines direct and indirect strategies for building personal talent might include the following goals:

1. developing awareness of personal interests and abilities through a variety of high-interest, warm-up activities in combination with formal and informal assessments of abilities, interests, and personality traits;
2. increasing problem-solving and decision-making abilities through sequenced experiences with both structured and unstructured problems;
3. providing a variety of challenging learning experiences coupled with instructor feedback associated with adaptive explanatory styles for both success and failure to build the dispositions associated with well-being and achievement;
4. creating a supportive classroom climate that encourages intrinsic motivation, self-expression, and positive peer relationships; and
5. involving all students in collaborative work on independent projects.

This curriculum would be very process-oriented, making it especially appropriate for the elementary school years when students need to learn good work habits. In elementary school, it's relatively easy to incorporate interdisciplinary instruction with a focus on learning processes such as independent learning. The curriculum uses indirect approaches for the development of all personal talent skills except self-awareness, where some direct strategies, like formal assessments of abilities and personality, are utilized.

At the middle school level, a combination of approaches and venues might be effective in developing personal talent. Indirect strategies could be incorporated into content-based classes and direct strategies could be offered through weekly or monthly group counseling sessions led by the school counselor. Some direct group counseling work is recommended at this age level to help students address achievement-affiliation conflicts (Clasen & Clasen, 1995) and develop effective strategies for dealing with antiachievement peer pressure (Cross, Coleman, & Terhaar-Yonkers, 1991; Steinberg, 1996). In addition, this is an ideal age to begin working on the identity and career development components of personal talent (Hébert & Kelly, 2006; Kelly, 1991). Goals for the indirect component of the middle school curriculum to develop personal talent might include the following:

1. develop resilience through the study of biographies of high achievers in each domain with a focus on how each individual overcame obstacles to achieve success;
2. build time management skills through facilitated independent projects in each domain;
3. provide sufficient challenges to induce failure experiences coupled with instructor feedback associated with adaptive explanatory styles (i.e., attributing success to ability and failure to lack of effort or poor strategy use); and
4. deliberately counter cultural and gender stereotypes in math, science, and humanities classes by using materials that do not support the stereotypes and providing students with opportunities to interact with professionals from all cultural backgrounds.

The direct component of a personal talent curriculum at the middle school level could include weekly or biweekly group counseling sessions with other talented youth focused on the following:

1. improving goal selection and attainment skills through guided practice in recursive cycles of setting, monitoring, and revising self-selected life goals with group debriefing sessions and group discussions of barriers and facilitators of goal attainment in their current lives and contexts;
2. developing intrapersonal qualities that research has shown facilitate goal attainment such as optimism and hope through direct teaching about the research findings supporting each construct, followed by individual practice of the desired qualities; and

3. developing career aspirations through individualized career interest assessments followed by group debriefing and interpretation sessions.

At the high school level, an elective course could be developed in personal psychology that provides direct instruction in personal talent knowledge (i.e., the research base underlying personal talent theory), and experiential activities to enable students to build personal talent skills by applying what they are learning from the research literature to their own lives and reflecting on their efforts in individual journals. Topics that might be covered in such a curriculum include: systems theory and its implications for human relationships in both personal and organizational environments; communication skills; relationship skills; personality characteristics and the implications of those characteristics for life and career choices; dispositions that are associated with positive outcomes like health and well-being; flow theory; decision-making theories; organizational psychology; and goal attainment theories.

Another approach that could be taken at the high school level is to adopt a comprehensive gifted program that includes components that facilitate the development of personal talent. A good model for this purpose is the Autonomous Learner Model (ALM; Betts, 1985; Betts & Kercher, 1999). This model facilitates collaborative, affective instruction of gifted and talented high school students by counselors and teachers. It incorporates direct instruction of personal talent skills in Dimensions One (orientation) and Two (individual development) and experiential opportunities to practice personal talent skills in Dimensions Three (enrichment), Four (seminars), and Five (in-depth study). The emphasis of the ALM on personal development and independent learning can complement the more typical, discipline-focused offerings at the high school level like honors and Advanced Placement classes. It encourages high-ability students to extend their independent learning and personal talent skills and become lifelong learners.

Conclusion

Affective curriculum is essential if gifted and talented students are to optimize their potential, relate well to others, express themselves fully, and make good life decisions. Many theories exist that can help guide the development of affective curriculum. Affective curriculum should be more than fragmented collections of affective activities. The theories overviewed here can help ensure that affective curriculum is comprehensive, integrated, and sound. As the extended example shows, theory can help school personnel to make decisions about what to include in affective curriculum for talented students at different developmental levels and about whether direct or indirect approaches will best accomplish the curricular goals.

References

Ackerman, C. M. (1997). Identifying gifted adolescents using personality characteristics: Dabrowski's overexcitabilities. *Roeper Review, 19*, 229–236.

Ambrose, D. (2003). Barriers to aspiration development and self-fulfillment: Interdisciplinary insights for talent discovery. *Gifted Child Quarterly, 47*, 282–294.

Arnold, K., Noble, K. D., & Subotnik, R. F. (1996). *Remarkable women: Perspectives on female talent development.* Cresskill, NJ: Hampton Press.

Baltes, P. B., & Staudinger, U. M. (2000). Wisdom: A metaheuristic (pragmatic) to orchestrate mind and virtue toward excellence. *American Psychologist, 55*, 122–136.

Bandura, A. (1997). *Self-efficacy: The exercise of control.* New York: W. H. Freeman.

Baum, S. M., Owen, S. V., & Dixon, J. (1991). *To be gifted and learning disabled: From identification to practical intervention strategies.* Mansfield Center, CT: Creative Learning Press.

Betts, G. T. (1985). *The Autonomous Learner Model for the Gifted and Talented.* Greeley, CO: ALPS.

Betts, G. T, & Kercher, J. (1999). *Autonomous learner model: Optimizing ability.* Greeley, CO: ALPS.

Bland, L. C., Sowa, C. J., & Callahan, C. M. (1994). An overview of resilience in gifted children. *Roeper Review, 17*, 77–80.

Bowlby, J. (1984). *Attachment and loss* (2nd ed.). New York: Basic Books.

Bronfenbrenner, U. (1989). Ecological systems theory. In R. Vasta (Ed.), *Annals of child development* (Vol. 6, pp. 189–250). Greenwich, CT: JAI.

Callahan, C. M., & Reis, S. M. (1996). Gifted girls, remarkable women. In K. Arnold, K. D. Noble, & R. F. Subotnik (Eds.), *Remarkable women: Perspectives on female talent development* (pp. 171–192). Cresskill, NY: Hampton Press.

Carver, C. S., & Scheier, M. F. (2002). Optimism. In C. R. Snyder & S. J. Lopez (Eds.), *Handbook of positive psychology* (pp. 231–243). Oxford, England: Oxford University Press.

Cherniss, C., & Goleman, D. (Eds.). (2001). *The emotionally intelligent workplace: How to select for, measure, and improve emotional intelligence in individuals, groups, and organizations.* San Francisco: Jossey Bass.

Clasen, D. R., & Clasen, R. E. (1995). Underachievement of highly able students and the peer society. *Gifted and Talented International, 10,* 67–76.

Crick, N. R., & Dodge, K. A. (1996). Social information processing mechanisms in reactive and proactive aggression. *Child Development, 67,* 993–1002.

Cross, T. L., Coleman, L. J., & Terhaar-Yonkers, M. (1991). The social cognition of gifted adolescents in schools: Managing the stigma of giftedness. *Journal for the Education of the Gifted, 15,* 44–55.

Csikszentmihalyi, M. (1990). *Flow: The psychology of optimal experience.* New York: Harper & Row.

Csikszentmihalyi, M. (1997). *Finding flow: The psychology of engagement in everyday life.* New York: Basic Books.

Dabrowski, K. (1972). *Psychoneurosis is not an illness.* London: Gryf.

Dabrowski, K., & Piechowski, M. M. (1977). *Theory of levels of emotional development.* Oceanside, NY: Dabor.

Dai, D. Y., Moon, S. M., & Feldhusen, J. F. (1998). Achievement motivation of gifted students: A social cognitive perspective. *Educational Psychologist, 33*(2/3), 45–63.

Deci, E. L., & Ryan, R. M. (1985). *Intrinsic motivation and self-determination in human behavior.* New York: Plenum Press.

Dodge, K. A. (1986). A social information processing model of social competence in children. In M. Perlmutter (Ed.), *Minnesota Symposium on Child Psychology: Vol. 18. Cognitive perspectives in children's social and behavioral development* (pp. 77–125). Hillsdale, NJ: Lawrence Erlbaum.

Eisenberg, N. (1982). The development of reasoning regarding prosocial behavior. In N. Eisenberg (Ed.), *The development of prosocial
behavior* (pp. 219–249). San Diego, CA: Academic Press.

Eisenberg, N., Carlo, G., Murphy, B., & Van Court, N. (1995).
Prosocial development in late adolescence: A longitudinal study.
Child Development, 66, 1179–1197.

Eisenberger, R. (1992). Learned industriousness. *Psychological Review,
99*, 248–267.

Elias, M. J., Zins, J. E., Weissberg, R. P., Frey, K. S., Greenberg, M. T.,
Haynes, N. M., et al. (1997). *Promoting social and emotional learning:
Guidelines for educators.* Alexandria, VA: Association for Supervision
and Curriculum Development.

Emmons, R. A., & Shelton, C. M. (2002). Gratitude and the sci-
ence of positive psychology. In C. R. Snyder & S. J. Lopez (Eds.),
Handbook of positive psychology (pp. 459–471). Oxford, England:
Oxford University Press.

Erikson, E. H. (1963). *Childhood and society* (2nd ed.). New York:
Norton.

Erikson, E. H. (1972). Eight ages of man. In C. S. Lavateli & F. Stendler
(Eds.), *Readings in child behavior and child development* (pp. 19–30). San
Diego, CA: Harcourt Brace Jovanovich.

Ford, D. Y., Harris, J., & Schuerger, J. M. (1993). Racial identity
development among gifted Black students: Counseling issues and
concerns. *Journal of Counseling and Development, 71*, 409–417.

Gagné, F. (2000). Understanding the complex choreography of talent
development. In K. A. Heller, F. J. Mönks, R. J. Sternberg, & R.
F. Subotnik (Eds.), *International handbook of giftedness and talent* (pp.
67–79). Amsterdam: Elsevier.

Gardner, H. (1983). *Frames of mind: The theory of multiple intelligences.*
New York: Basic Books.

Gardner, H. (1999). *Intelligence reframed: Multiple intelligences for the 21st
century.* New York: Basic Books.

Gilligan, C. F. (1982). *In a different voice.* Cambridge, MA: Harvard
University Press.

Goleman, D. (1995). *Emotional intelligence.* New York: Bantam.

Gross, M. U. M. (2000, May). *From "play partner" to "sure shelter:" How
do conceptions of friendship differ between average-ability, moderately gifted,
and highly gifted children?* Paper presented at the Fifth Biennial Henry
B. and Jocelyn Wallace National Research Symposium on Talent
Development, Iowa City, IA.

Gross, M. U. M. (2004). *Exceptionally gifted children.* London: Routledge-
Falmer.

Harter, S. (1999). *The construction of the self: A developmental perspective.* New York: Guilford.

Hébert, T. P., & Kelly, K. R. (2006). Identity and career development in gifted students. In F. A. Dixon & S. M. Moon (Eds.), *The handbook of secondary gifted education* (pp. 35–64). Waco, TX: Prufrock Press.

Kelly, K. R. (1991). A profile of the career development characteristics of young gifted adolescents: Examining gender and multicultural differences. *Roeper Review, 13,* 202–206.

Kelly, K. R. (1992). Career maturity of young, gifted adolescents. A replication study. *Journal for the Education of the Gifted, 16,* 36–45.

Kelly, K. R., & Moon, S. M. (1998). Personal and social talents. *Phi Delta Kappan, 79,* 743–746.

Kohlberg, L. (1984). *The psychology of moral development: The nature and validity of moral stages.* San Francisco: Harper & Row.

Kuhl, J. (1985). Volitional mediators of cognition-behavior consistency: Self-regulatory processes and action versus state orientation. In J. Kuhl & J. Beckman (Eds.), *Action control: From cognition to behaviors* (pp. 101–128). New York: Springer Verlag.

Kuhl, J. (1996). Who controls whom when "I control myself." *Psychological Inquiry, 7,* 61–68.

Kuhl, J., & Beckman, J. (1985a). Historical perspectives in the study of action control. In J. Kuhl & J. Beckman (Eds.), *Action control: From cognition to behavior* (pp. 89–128). New York: Springer-Verlag.

Kuhl, J., & Beckman, J. (1985b). Introduction and overview. In J. Kuhl & J. Beckman (Eds.), *Action control: From cognition to behavior* (pp. 1–8). New York: Springer-Verlag.

Kuhl, J., & Kraska, K. (1989). Self-regulation and metamotivation: Computational mechanisms, development, and assessment. In R. Kanfer, P. L. Ackerman, & R. Cudeck (Eds.), *Abilities, motivation, and methodology: The Minnesota symposium on individual differences* (pp. 343–374). Hillsdale, NJ: Lawrence Erlbaum.

Lazarus, R. (1991). Cognition and motivation. *American Psychologist, 46,* 352–367.

Locke, E. A., & Latham, G. P. (2002). Building a practically useful theory of goal setting and task motivation. *American Psychologist, 57,* 705–717.

Marcia, J. E. (1966). Development and validations of ego-identity status. *Journal of Personality and Social Psychology, 5,* 551–558.

Marcia, J. E. (1980). Identity in adolescence. In J. Adelson (Ed.), *Handbook of adolescent psychology* (pp. 159–187). New York: Wiley.

Markus, H., & Ruvolo, A. P. (1989). Possible selves: Personalized representations of goals. In L. A. Pervin (Ed.), *Goal concepts in personality and social psychology* (pp. 211–241). Hillsdale, NJ: Lawrence Erlbaum.

Marlowe, H. A. (1986). Social intelligence: Evidence for multidimensionality and construct independence. *Journal of Educational Psychology, 78*, 52–58.

Marsh, H. W., Chessor, D., Craven, R., & Roche, L. (1995). The effects of gifted and talented programs on academic self-concept: The big fish strikes again. *American Educational Research Journal, 32*, 285–319.

Maslow, A. H. (1970). *Motivation and personality*. New York: Harper and Row.

Masten, A. S. (2001). Ordinary magic: Resilience processes in development. *American Psychologist, 56*, 227–238.

Masten, A. S., & Marie-Gabrielle, J. (2002). Resilience in development. In C. R. Synder (Ed.), *Handbook of positive psychology* (pp. 74–88). London: Oxford University Press.

Mayer, J. D., & Salovey, P. (1997). What is emotional intelligence? In P. Salovey & D. Sluyter (Eds.), *Emotional development and emotional intelligence: Implications for educators* (pp. 3–31). New York: Basic Books.

McCullough, M. E., & Witvliet, C. V. (2002). The psychology of forgiveness. In C. R. Snyder & S. J. Lopez (Eds.), *Handbook of positive psychology* (pp. 446–458). Oxford, England: Oxford University Press.

Mendaglio, S. (2008). *Dabrowski's theory of positive disintegration*. Scottsdale, AZ: Great Potential Press.

Mendaglio, S., & Pyryt, M. (2003). Self-concept and giftedness: A multi-theoretical perspective. *Gifted and Talented International, 18*(2), 76–82.

Moen, P., Elder, G. H., & Luscher, K. (Eds.). (1995). *Examining lives in context*. Washington, DC: American Psychological Association.

Moon, S. M. (2001, May). *Personal talent: What is it and how can we study it?* Paper presented at the Fifth Biennial Henry B. and Jocelyn Wallace National Research Symposium on Talent Development, Iowa City, IA.

Moon, S. M. (2003a). Developing personal talent. In F. J. Mönks & H. Wagner (Eds.), *Development of human potential: Investment into our future. Proceedings of the 8th Conference of the European Council for High Ability (ECHA). Rhodes, October 9–13, 2002* (pp. 11–21). Bad Honnef, Germany: K. H. Bock.

Moon, S. M. (2003b). Personal talent. *High Ability Studies, 14*, 5–21.

Moon, S. M. (Ed.). (2004). *Social/emotional issues, underachievement, and counseling of gifted and talented students.* Thousand Oaks, CA: Corwin Press.

Moon, S. M., & Ray, K. (2006). Personal and social talent development. In F. A. Dixon & S. M. Moon (Eds.), *The handbook of secondary gifted education* (pp. 249–280). Waco, TX: Prufrock Press.

Moon, S. M., Zentall, S. S., Grskovic, J. A., Hall, A., & Stormont, M. (2001). Emotional and social characteristics of boys with AD/HD and/or giftedness: A comparative case study. *Journal for the Education of the Gifted, 24*, 207–247.

Neihart, M. (2002). Risk and resilience in gifted children: A conceptual framework. In M. Neihart, S. M. Reis, N. M. Robinson, & S. M. Moon (Eds.), *The social and emotional development of gifted children: What do we know?* (pp. 113–122). Waco, TX: Prufrock Press.

Noble, K. D. (1996). Resilience, resistance, and responsibility: Resolving the dilemma of the gifted woman. In K. D. Arnold, K. D. Noble, & R. F. Subotnik (Eds.), *Remarkable women: Perspectives on female talent development* (pp. 413–426). Cresskill, NJ: Hampton Press.

Noble, K. D., Subotnik, R. F., & Arnold, K. D. (1999). To thine own self be true: A model of female talent development. *Gifted Child Quarterly, 43*, 140–149.

Passow, A. H. (1994). Israel's residential high school for gifted in the arts and science. *Gifted and Talented International, 9*(2), 54–57.

Peterson, C. (2000). The future of optimism. *American Psychologist, 55*, 44–55.

Peterson, J. S. (1993). *Talk with teens about self and stress: 50 guided discussions for school and counseling groups.* Minneapolis, MN: Free Spirit.

Peterson, J. S. (1995). *Talk with teens about feelings, family, relationships, and the future: 50 guided discussions for school and counseling groups.* Minneapolis, MN: Free Spirit.

Peterson, J. S. (2001). Gifted and at risk: Four longitudinal case studies of post-high school development. *Roeper Review, 24*, 31–39.

Peterson, J. S. (2002). A longitudinal study of post-high school development in gifted individuals at risk for poor educational outcomes. *Journal of Secondary Gifted Education, 14*, 6–18.

Piechowski, M. M. (1997). Emotional giftedness: The measure of intrapersonal intelligence. In N. Colangelo & G. A. Davis (Eds.), *Handbook of gifted education* (pp. 366–381). Boston: Allyn & Bacon.

Pintrich, P. R., & Schunk, D. H. (1996). *Motivation in education: Theory, research, and applications.* Englewood Cliffs, NJ: Prentice Hall.

Plucker, J. A. (1996). Gifted Asian-American students: Identification, curricular, and counseling concerns. *Journal for the Education of the Gifted, 19*, 314–343.

Rachel, S., & Zorman, R. (2003). Gifted students as path breakers: The Israeli experience. *Gifted and Talented International, 18*(1), 36–43.

Reis, S. M. (1998). *Work left undone: Choices and compromises of talented females.* Mansfield Center, CT: Creative Learning Press.

Reis, S. M., & McCoach, D. B. (2000). The underachievement of gifted students: What do we know and where do we go? *Gifted Child Quarterly, 44*, 152–170.

Reis, S. M., Neu, T. W., & McGuire, J. M. (1995). *Talents in two places: Case studies of high ability students with learning disabilities who have achieved.* Storrs: National Research Center on the Gifted and Talented, University of Connecticut.

Renzulli, J. S. (1978). What makes giftedness? Re-examining a definition. *Phi Delta Kappan, 60*, 180–184, 261.

Renzulli, J. S., & Reis, S. M. (1997). *The Schoolwide Enrichment Model: A how-to guide to educational excellence.* Mansfield Center, CT: Creative Learning Press.

Renzulli, J. S., & Systma, R. (2001, November). *Operation houndstooth: Refining concepts and examining perceptions.* Paper presented at the National Association for Gifted Children annual convention, Cincinnati, OH.

Rubin, K. H., & Rose-Krasnor, L. (1992). Interpersonal problem solving and social competence in children. In V. B. Van Hasselt & M. Hersen (Eds.), *Handbook of social development: A lifespan perspective* (pp. 283–323). New York: Plenum.

Ryan, R. M., & Deci, E. L. (2000). Intrinsic and extrinsic motivations: Classic definitions and new directions. *Contemporary Educational Psychology, 25*, 54–67.

Salovey, P., Mayer, J. D., & Caruso, D. R. (2002). The positive psychology of emotional intelligence. In C. R. Synder & S. J. Lopez (Eds.), *Handbook of positive psychology* (pp. 159–171). Oxford, England: Oxford University Press.

Salovey, P., & Sluyter, D. J. (1997). *Emotional development and emotional intelligence: Educational implications.* New York: Basic Books.

Scheier, M. F., & Carver, C. S. (1992). Effects of optimism on psychological and physical well-being: Theoretical overview and empirical update. *Cognitive therapy and research, 16*, 201–228.

Schunk, D. H. (1989). Self-efficacy and achievement behaviors. *Educational Psychology Review, 1*, 173–208.

Schunk, D. H. (1991). Self-efficacy and academic motivation. *Educational Psychologist, 26*, 207–231.

Seligman, M. E. P. (1998). *Learned optimism.* New York: Pocket Books.

Selman, R. L. (1980). *The growth of interpersonal understanding.* San Diego, CA: Academic Press.

Selman, R. L., & Schultz, L. H. (1990). *Making a friend in youth.* Chicago: University of Chicago Press.

Snyder, C. R. (1994). *The psychology of hope.* New York: Free Press.

Sowa, C. J., & May, K. M. (1997). Expanding Lazarus and Folkman's paradigm to the social and emotional adjustment of gifted children. *Gifted Child Quarterly, 41*(2), 36–43.

Steinberg, L. (1996). *Beyond the classroom.* New York: Simon & Schuster.

Sternberg, R. J. (Ed.). (1990). *Wisdom: Its nature, origins, and development.* Cambridge, England: Cambridge University Press.

Sternberg, R. J. (1996). *Successful intelligence.* New York: Simon & Schuster.

Sternberg, R. J. (1998). A balance theory of wisdom. *Review of General Psychology, 2*, 247–365.

Sternberg, R. J. (2000). Giftedness as developing expertise. In K. A. Heller, F. J. Mönks, R. J. Sternberg, & R. F. Subotnik (Eds.), *International handbook of giftedness and talent* (pp. 55–66). Amsterdam: Elsevier.

Sternberg, R. J., & Grigorenko, E. (2000). *Teaching for successful intelligence.* Arlington Heights, IL: Skylight Professional Development.

Tomlinson, C. A., Kaplan, S. N., Renzulli, J. S., Purcell, J., Leppien, J., & Burns, D. E. (2002). *The parallel curriculum: A design to develop high potential and challenge high ability learners.* Thousand Oaks, CA: Corwin Press.

Van Hasselt, V. B., & Hersen, M. (Eds.). (1992). *Handbook of social development.* New York: Plenum.

Whitchurch, G. G., & Constantine, L. L. (1993). Systems theory. In P. G. Boss, W. J. Doherty, R. LaRossa, W. R. Schumm, & S. K. Steinmetz (Eds.), *Sourcebook of family theories and methods: A contextual approach* (pp. 325–355). New York: Plenum.

Wolters, C. A. (1998). Self-regulated learning and college students' regulation of motivation. *Journal of Educational Psychology, 90*, 224–235.

Wolters, C. A. (2003). Regulation of motivation: Evaluating an underemphasized aspect of self-regulated learning. *Educational Psychologist, 38*, 189–205.

Ziegler, A., & Heller, K. A. (1997). Attribution retraining for self-related cognitions among women. *Gifted and Talented International, 12*(1), 36–41.

Ziegler, A., & Heller, K. A. (2000a). Conceptions of giftedness from a meta-theoretical perspective. In K. A. Heller, F. J. Mönks, R. J. Sternberg, & R. F. Subotnik (Eds.), *International handbook of giftedness and talent* (pp. 3–22). Amsterdam: Elsevier.

Ziegler, A., & Heller, K. A. (2000b). Effects of an attribution retraining with female students gifted in physics. *Journal for the Education of the Gifted, 23*, 217–243.

Zins, J. E., Bloodworth, M. E., Weissberg, R. P., & Walberg, H. J. (2004). The scientific base linking social and emotional learning to school success. In J. E. Zins, R. P. Weissberg, M. C. Want, & H. J. Walberg (Eds.), *Building academic success on social and emotional learning: What does the research say?* (pp. 3–22). New York: Teachers College Press.

Creating a Life: Orchestrating a Symphony of Self, a Work Always in Progress

F. Richard Olenchak

. . . raising [children] is about taking their marvelous strength— I call it "seeing into the soul,"—amplifying it, nurturing it, helping [them] to lead [their lives] around it, to buffer against [their] weaknesses and the storms of life. Raising children, I realized, is vastly more than fixing what is wrong with them. It is about identifying and nurturing their strongest qualities, what they own and are best at, and helping them find niches in which they can best live out these strengths . . .

Martin E. P. Seligman, Psychologist/Researcher
(Seligman & Csikszentmihalyi, 2000, p. 6)

Educational attention to affective development through specific curriculum and instruction has been akin to *A Tale of Two Cities.* The best of times has found affective curriculum to be the theme of discussions and professional development seminars, while the worst of times has found affective curriculum to be avoided altogether or even the brunt of jokes. In general, affective programming has been viewed by school professionals and parents alike to lack rigor and utility in preparing students for adult life and has thus led to its exclusion from school curricular efforts (Zins, Bloodworth, Weissberg, & Walberg, 2004). Among gifted program educators, this exclusionist view appears to have thwarted even those with intense interest in affective development from pursuing it to greater depth in terms of both research and practice (VanTassel-Baska & Stambaugh, 2006).

And, even if educators were of the mind to increase attention to teaching and learning in the affective realm, it is unlikely to take place against a backdrop composed of numerous state-based legislative initiatives designed for educational accountability, as well as the federal No Child Left Behind Act. Although several empirical studies have examined the impact of test-driven and other accountability policies on teaching practices in the United States, the emphases of these studies largely have not focused specifically on how students' affective development is influenced. However, certainly one can infer that outcomes from policies of this ilk, such as increased drop-out rates (McNeil, Coppola, Radigan, & Vasquez-Heileg, 2008), increased rates of students enrolling in GED programs to avoid high school graduation tests (Amrein & Berliner, 2002), and increased incidents of both educator and student cheating (Nichols & Berliner, 2005), do have damaging repercussions on student affective development.

One study of a Massachusetts testing program that analyzed student's drawings of themselves, although not comprehensive in nature, concluded that test anxiety and emotional stress yielded reduced student motivation and greater generalized angst (Wheelock, Bebell, & Haney, 2000). Although not conducted in the United States, two comprehensive examinations of the impact of policy on the affective aspects of education among secondary school classroom teachers and their pupils in the United Kingdom, France, and Denmark concluded that:

> . . . both projects suggested that teachers were concerned that externally imposed educational change had not only increased their workload but also created a growing tension between the requirements of government and the needs of their pupils. A perceived demand for a delivery of "performance," for both themselves and their pupils, had created a policy focus that emphasized the managerially "effective," in the interests of account-

ability, while ignoring teachers' deeply rooted commitment to the affective aspects of teaching and learning.
(McNess, Broadfoot, & Osburn, 2003, p. 243)

Based on these European research studies, as well as the
implications extracted from the more generalized inquiry in
the United States, it seems efficacious at least to hypothesize
that American educators feel a similar tension between govern-
mental mandates and students' needs. The persistent demands
for accountability, which are almost always unidimension-
ally measured using standardized tests that contain no affective components, probably serve as the real culprits behind the
exclusion of affective education from most classrooms in the
United States.

However, emotions are at the helm of thinking to the
extent that cognition is activated by emotional stimuli, and
thinking, problem solving, and decision making are improved
by positive emotions (Damasio, 1994, 1999; Isen, 2004; Zins et
al., 2004). Feelings about ourselves, others, events, and things
serve as important triggers for firing cognitive activity; it is
one's feelings that in fact launch thinking and improve facility for handling problems. As a result, school programs that
enhance students' emotional development are likely to provide
concurrent enhancement of students' thinking. Affective learning engenders cognitive learning (Walberg, Zins, & Weissberg,
2004). Goleman (1993, 1998) contended that people who are
emotionally underdeveloped or who are otherwise affectively
upset are incapable of recalling information accurately, attending to tasks, learning material, drawing logical conclusions, or
making effective decisions.

Research Linking Affect With Cognition

Although educators apparently dismiss the importance of
the cognitive-affective relationship for school performance—
even in gifted programs—extant research tells us differently.
Study after study has probed varying aspects of the critical role
affective development plays in overall human performance.

Even the need to like one's teacher has been shown to have a significant impact on student motivation and achievement (Davis & Lease, 2007).

Landmark research in neuroscience highlights connections between affective and cognitive dimensions of the brain with emotions to the extent that it has "the potential to revolutionize our understanding of the role of affect in education" (Immordino-Yang & Damasio, 2007, p. 3). In particular, neurobiological evidence suggests that the aspects of cognition that are most heavily courted in schools—learning, attention, memory, decision making, and social functioning—are both profoundly affected by and subsumed within the processes of emotion. Moreover, evidence from studies of brain-damaged patients suggests the hypothesis that emotion-related processes are required for skills and knowledge to be transferred from the structured school environment to real-world decision making because they provide an "emotional rudder" (Immordino-Yang & Damasio, 2007, p. 7) to guide judgment and action.

Aside from studies in the neurological sciences, it increasingly is clear from studies of educational practice that learning and academic performance are very much dependent on attention to the affect. In a large study that used several sophisticated quantitative analyses and involved more than 7,000 students in 212 elementary schools in the Netherlands, a significant relationship was found between cognitive, academic outcomes and affective, emotional outcomes (Knuver & Brandsma, 1993). Using these data, the researchers concluded that for pupils to function academically at a level approaching optimal performance, they first had to be functioning affectively conducive for optimal academic performance to transpire. Students in the study needed to feel reasonably at peace with themselves and their surroundings prior to academic engagement.

Numerous research studies that have examined various aspects of the relationship between academic performance and affective development individually and collectively underscore the importance of emotions to success—academic and otherwise. An exhaustive meta-analytic study conducted by Lyubomirsky and her colleagues (2005) revealed that success in personal pursuits does not yield happiness, but that actually the converse is more true: that happiness—or positive affect— produces success. Although this examination probed evidence from 225 empirical studies, most of those addressed generalized happiness and success without regard to age or circumstances of the subjects in each study. Still, it makes logical sense that positive affect is positive affect regardless of the age or situation of the people displaying happy feelings; as a result, this meta-analysis has powerful implications for schools and educators. It is fair to conclude that students with positive affect are likely to experience success in school, while those who hold negative feelings are less likely to succeed. Although this conclusion's generalizability certainly would be amended by the effects of the intervening variable of overall potential, when one con-templates populations of gifted and talented or otherwise high-potential pupils, this intervening variable would largely become a nonissue.

Reinforcing the importance of affect to cognitive develop-ment are two groups of studies: (1) those examining the rela-tionship of affect and cognition among persons confronted with a variety of physical or environmental challenges; and (2) those probing cognitive and affective development among young children. These collectively have reinforced the notion that affective development probably is a prerequisite to one's overall cognitive development.

In the first group, a pioneering study found that young, deaf children had well-developed feelings about self-derived fantasies that served to intrude on and interfere with cogni-tive functioning to the degree that, until the affective concerns were addressed, cognitive development was truncated (Sarlin & Altshuler, 1978). In a review of literature pertaining to the three levels of affective-cognitive interaction (neurophysiological-biochemical, motor-expressive, and experiential) and subse-quent applications to occupational therapy with children and adults, Dickerson (1993) concluded that affect occurs indepen-dently at the experiential level and, as such, mediates cognition to the degree that she recommended occupational therapists treat affective development explicitly as a prerequisite for all cognitive interventions with clients. And, in an examination of health care and social services utilization among 1,134 elderly persons with mental disorders, Roelands and his colleagues (2003) concluded that the affective dimension, specifically depressive mood, had significantly predicted their subjects' use of health and social services, while cognition had relatively no predictive value. This suggests that affect plays a critical role in important features of life such as decision making, even when cognitive abilities may be compromised by the presence of mental disabilities.

In the second group—those studies focusing on affective and cognitive development in young children—the theoretical and later practical works of Lacan (1973, 1977), building on those of Gagné (1965), suggest that human beings' very existence is from the onset driven by an innate desire revolving around the quest for a secure identity that is defined by one's affect. Years later, young children were found to recall information about events more positively or more negatively depending less on their thinking about the events and more on their feelings about those same events, meaning that affectivity has a noteworthy role in governing cognition at an early age (Belsky, Spritz, & Crnic, 1996). Finally, Flavell, Flavell, and Green (2001) reported on two studies that assessed the development of children's under-standing that thoughts and feelings are closely interlinked and concluded that cognition follows affective development; emo-tions and feelings are experienced as foundations for thought—that thinking is assembled based on one's emotions.

Human beings naturally seek a place of well-being in their lives. Amidst situations and environments that threaten one's personal sense of security and contentment, people invariably work to create at least some semblance of the idealized envi-ronment they connote with a personally defined impression of peace. Adults' "comfort food," children's "blankies," and families' "memory walls" of old photos are individually and collectively emblematic of the fact people are inclined to craft atmospheres reflective of the qualities they equate with safety, support, love, caring, and tranquility. The literature examining the linkage between the cognitive and affective dimensions of the brain suggest that environments prompting positive affectivity tend to engender cognitive activity, while those prompting negative feelings likely discourage thinking.

Positive Psychology and Hope

As has already been discussed, there is ample reason to believe that one's emotions have an influence on one's thinking and in turn have an impact on one's overall adjustment and ultimate success (Lyubomirsky et al., 2005). The body of literature underlying this perspective has generated efforts toward nurturing positivism in people, known as positive psychology. Extending to the construct of hope, there is an attendant collection of research focusing attention not only on the fact that positive psychology can be developed but on systems for doing so. Certainly, cognate constructs such as motivation present their own bodies of research that serve to inform the notion of positive affectivity and methods for its cultivation, but the emphasis here is on scholarly studies about how positive affect ultimately comes to bear on students' overall development, particularly among gifted and talented individuals.

Positive Psychology's Roots

Positive psychology, the study of optimal human functioning, is an attempt to respond to the systematic bias inherent in psychology's historical emphasis on mental illness rather than on mental wellness. Some humanistic psychologists developed theories along these lines but without solid empirical support. The pioneering research of a new generation of psychologists has led to a renewed interest in this approach, providing a firm scientific foundation for the study of human happiness and optimal function, thus adding a positive side to the discipline of psychology that has been predominately aimed at reparations of mental problems.

Early theories of positive psychology were constructed by several leading humanistic psychologists, most notably Maslow, Rogers, and Fromm. Maslow (1962), using his basic needs hierarchy as a foundation, postulated that human beings can assemble contentment in life by learning from their "peak experiences." Meanwhile, basing his theoretical perspective on phenomenology in which the individual's observations and assessments of life events form the nucleus of either psychological adjustment or maladjustment, Rogers (1961) postulated that the "good life" ultimately is framed by each person's developing an optimistic outlook about experiences. Finally, Fromm (1941) contributed his analyses of social and political occurrences, including his interpretations of the Talmud, to form his theory rooted in humankind's difficulty in handling freedom to the extent that failure to do so inhibits full development of each individual. Individually and collectively these theorists helped to set the stage for later research addressing the developmental aspects of positive psychology—that it is nurturable and can be managed by individuals (Seligman, 1990).

Learned Optimism, Flow, and Hope

Research by a number of psychologists has documented diverse benefits of optimism and concomitant drawbacks of pessimism. Optimism, conceptualized and assessed in a variety of ways as positive affectivity, has been linked to upbeat mood and good morale; to perseverance and effective problem solving; to academic, athletic, military, occupational, and political success; to popularity; to good health; and even to long life and freedom from trauma. Pessimism, in contrast, foreshadows depression, passivity, failure, social estrangement, morbidity, and mortality. These lines of research are surprisingly uniform to the extent that positive psychology has been reinforced significantly as a discipline (Gillham, 2000).

Seligman (1990, 2004) and his view of "learned optimism," Csikszentmihalyi (1990; Nakamura & Csikszentmihalyi, 2002) and his theory of "flow," and Snyder (1994, 2001) and his construction of "hope" represent some of the contemporary positive psychology theorists whose perspectives are undergirded by research. Each of these translations of positive psychology offers potentially important contributions for formulating guiding principles in the affective domain in terms of optimizing gifted-ness and talent educationally. There are several studies provid-ing empirical support for these most recent theories of positive psychology.

Studies Supporting Seligman's Theory

Shatté and his colleagues (1999) concluded that learning to be optimistic is at the core of young people's ability to address challenges confidently and develop resilience when one does not perform particularly well. Another study examined positive affect's impact on longevity of 180 Catholic nuns and concluded that positive affect during early life has a strong association with longevity (Danner, Snowdon, & Friesen, 2001). Those two studies taken together certainly give rise to the notion that when young people can be taught to be optimistic, they not only will have more productive, satisfying lives, but their lives will be longer. Bolstering the impact of these studies is a review of Seligman's Penn Resiliency Program in which children and adolescents are explicitly taught to develop their abilities to be optimistic; the results revealed that the participants appeared to handle life stressors to the extent that it was felt the direct instruction of skills in positive affectivity may well "prevent symptoms of depression and anxiety" (Gillham & Reivich, 2004, p. 146). Seligman himself concluded from the research that had been conducted about positive psychology that hap-piness could in fact be taught explicitly. In so doing, teachers equip their protégés with the skills and behaviors most neces-sary for finding personally meaningful, fulfilling roles within the context of the larger world by systematically accentuating their greatest attributes while coping with, yet de-emphasizing their shortcomings (Seligman, 2004).

Studies Supporting Csikszentmihalyi's Theory

The theory of flow was found to be a contributing factor to student engagement among 526 high school students when their interests, enjoyment, and concentration served as barometers for classroom activities and instructional strategies (Shernoff, Csikszentmihalyi, Schneider, & Shernoff, 2003). In essence, flow—a mental state in which one is fully immersed in what he or she is doing, characterized by a feeling of energized focus, full involvement, and success in the process of the activity—is best conceptualized as a collection of responses to stimuli when those stimuli accurately reflect one's personal interests and needs. In another study that examined flow by using diary analyses and experience sampling, the researchers concluded that adolescents repeatedly experienced more positive affect when they were engaged in self-reported altruistic activities and that such activities were likely to yield improved coping ability for life challenges, such as rigorous cognitive tasks involved in problem solving (Csikszentmihalyi, Patton, & Lucas, 1997). Flow in reading was examined in specific academic areas. Where readers across a variety of academic age groups had either selected the literature themselves or had an interest in assigned reading, flow was likely to develop (McQuillan & Conde, 1996). Similarly, a longitudinal study of talented students in math, science, art, and music concluded that flow was operationalized when the students felt above-average spontaneous interest (i.e., excitement, openness, and involvement), while also reporting above-average goal-directed interest (i.e., that their task was important to their goals). As a collective, the research undergirding Csikszentmihalyi's theory helps clarify positive affect as a multifaceted state of being that is at least partially reliant on one's environment and what it offers.

Studies Supporting Snyder's Theory

Viewed as a subset of positive psychology, hope theory has been studied at least as often as flow and learned optimism. Among the empirical evidence is an examination of hope traits and their effects on grades and on athletic success among collegiate sportspersons where it was concluded that hope significantly predicted both academic and athletic outcomes beyond variance related to abilities and affectivity (Curry, Snyder, Cook, Ruby, & Rehm, 1997). In a 6-year longitudinal study, the degree of hopefulness among college students served as a significant predictor of academic performance, those with more hope outdistancing the academic records of those with less hope (Snyder, Shorey, et al., 2002). In a collection of studies, Snyder (2001), Snyder and Lopez (2002), and Snyder, McDermott, Cook, and Rapoff (2002) reported that, based on results from samples of more than 2,000 students ages 7–16, hope as measured by the Children's Hope Scale (Snyder, 1994) serves as a predictor of academic performance. Given that the Children's Hope Scale and the Hope Scale that predated it have been repeatedly shown to correlate significantly with trait variables associated with positive psychology, it is rational to infer that intentional efforts to teach children how to be hopeful ultimately would yield not only greater school success but greater happiness for life in general.

Positive Psychology and Its Implications for Giftedness and Talent Development

Developing excellence, let alone nurturing positive psychological adjustment in young people, at least occasionally appears to be impossible in American schools. The average student reports being bored about one third of the time he or she is in school, while students enrolled in honors and other advanced and/or accelerated school programs report being bored just more than half the time (Larson, 2000). Considering that we go to school for at least one fifth of our lives, this is not good news.

Regardless of ability level, it seems that youth in our society rarely have the opportunity to take initiative, and their education largely encourages passive adaptation to external rules instead of extending opportunities for them to explore pathways toward personal fulfillment. Such pathways certainly encompass extracurricular activities found in sports, the arts, and civic organizations as providing opportunities for concentrated, self-directed effort applied over time. Students are at a disadvantage regardless of their innate abilities, but based on Larson's (2000) research, there is ample reason to believe that regardless of the domain of ability, the greater the potential a young person has, the more likely it is that she or he will end up developing psychological attributes that deviate from those advocated in the positive psychology literature. When human beings spend substantial amounts of their time in environments that either barely or never kindle motivation due to variables such as disinterest and disconnection, it is probable that their energies will be expended in mastering coping strategies instead of being dedicated to mastering techniques associated with optimizing self-development. Although having a repertoire of coping skills certainly is part of the foundation for building contentment later in life, when those skills dominate one's learning, it seems inevitable that one will emerge as mostly underdeveloped in terms of one's strengths.

Skills relied upon for coping with experiences that one values as mundane are composed predominately of basic, perhaps even remedial or compensatory, techniques and have little to do with expanding one's facility for paving routes toward personal growth. For example, what if a world-class athlete such as Tiger Woods had expended much of his psychological energy creating ways to cope with personally boring situations that did not align very well with his interests and talents? Would his talents in golf have emerged to today's extent? Although the answer of course is conjectural, it makes rational sense that his abilities may not have developed to the sophisticated degree they have and perhaps may not have developed *at all*. Particularly given that Tiger Woods' childhood was literally gauged around what his father had assessed early on as an innate gift for golfing (Strege, 1997), would it be possible to "make up" for developmental time lost had Tiger's childhood been largely preoccupied by activities that deviated from his strengths and abilities? Again we cannot be sure, although we can make some connections to psychological literature that may support an answer.

When highly capable individuals devote significant time and energy toward simply surviving situations that are personally understimulating, they are likely to develop behavioral patterns that lack the necessary psychological tension as to evoke deep, positive emotions that become important not only for overall emotional development but for handling stressors effectively (Folkman & Moskowitz, 2000). The ability to respond to stimuli that are both positive and negative is critical for everyone, yet for the purposes of nurturing one's sense of self and, in turn, finding and developing one's talent, being able to handle stress is pivotal. Consequently, for persons with gifted potential where the likelihood for existential and environmental stress is great (Silverman, 2002), it is fundamental that they spend as much time and energy as possible on tasks and areas that are personally rewarding.

Accordingly, with respect to Tiger Woods, it would be unlikely that he would have had sufficient exposure to a wide range of both positive and negative stimuli *associated with* and *important to* his particular talent had the route toward his talent development and "finding himself" begun much later in life. In other words, the task of finding oneself and, as a result, realizing and then actualizing one's strengths obviously is componential—that even prodigies, whose extreme abilities are apparent earlier and more frequently than typical among even other similarly talented persons, develop along a continuum. Hence, the sooner that continuum begins, the more likely it is that one's talents will have maximal opportunities to mature through practice. In contrast, if time that could be allocated to practice and to talent development is largely wasted by merely muddling through understimulating activities, the talent may very well not ever mature as much as it could have. And, while this statement is extrapolative to all talent domains from a body of literature about physical talent development (e.g., Helsen, Hodges, Van Winckel, & Stakes, 2000; Patrick et al., 1999; Smith & Smoll, 1997; Williams & Reilly, 2000), once again logic seems to dictate that practice time does, in fact, matter even in the face of extreme talent.

Beyond the domains of physical talent, a variety of studies and theories have probed talent development's relationship to positive psychology. Among them, Larson (2000) extolled the importance of developing initiative as a critical aspect of talent formation and concluded that the primary forum for nurturing initiative takes place when young people are involved in "structured voluntary activities, such as sports, arts, and participation in organizations" (p. 170). Examining a wide range of literature related to the role of initiative in developing talent, Larson crystallized the literature thusly:

> Each activity would have enough structure so that youths are challenged, but also enough flexibility so that, as youths gain experience, they assume responsibility for the direction of the activity. As a result, participants progressively learn to internalize an operating language for sustaining their own motivation and directing and monitoring their actions over time, a language that is generative and that carries over, helping them to create order, meaning, and direction when they encounter ill-structured choices in other parts of their lives. (p. 181)

Larson's words generate a perspective of talent as a subset of one's overall sense of self—a subset of one's overall life. When coupling Larson's conclusions with the aforementioned research about talented athletes, a clear sense emerges that environmental influences are of fairly high importance to finding and nurturing one's talent.

Further, another body of work provides additional foundations for considering the critical role of one's talent with regard to the larger world and its values and demands. Barab and Plucker (2002) argued that gifted ability is part of the individual-environment transaction that can be enhanced or diminished by circumstances in one's life. Hodges and Clifton (2004), using a review of literature in the adult workplace as a foundation, commended the value of helping individuals find and then work in areas emphasizing their strengths as the optimal means for concurrently promoting both individual and workplace productivity at the highest levels. And, Beltman and Volet (2007) used longitudinal qualitative analyses to conclude that sustained motivation: (1) appears to be complexly linked to both individuals as well as to contexts; (2) is dependent on each person's facility for continual assessment of both contextual and personal circumstances; and (3) is constantly adjusting in reaction to what the individual appraises as either constraining or facilitating aspects present in personal life and in talent contexts.

Literature suggests (across many domains of talent, numerous contexts from work to school, and wide age ranges) that talent development among persons who have capacity for performance at the highest levels of quality, such as that associated with productivity among gifted and talented individuals, is at least partially dependent on one's psychosocial state of being. Persons who can manifest a strong sense of personal and contextual well-being, even in the face of adversity, tend to be able to persevere, refine their strengths, and ultimately achieve outcomes that are appropriately reflective of their abilities joined with their efforts. Without a psychosocial foundation that not only is resilient to obstacles but also is secured further in that it is regenerative thanks to a patent understanding of one's inner self, exceptional ability alone along with superior ability conjoined with optimizing contexts are probably insufficient for development of talent among persons capable of gifted and talented behaviors. How can educators, parents, and others who genuinely care about optimizing student talent facilitate gifted students' growth and development? How can schools and homes enhance the opportunities for gifted young people to develop their individual sense of identity?

The Bull's Eye Model for Affective Development: Orchestrating One's Optimal Self

It is clear from the literature relating to personal security and adjustment that humans continually engage in a quest for affective integration to find ways to flourish, and talent development is reliant on the success of that journey. Three segments of extant literature demand action: (1) supporting theories and research that link cognition with affect (e.g., Flavell et al., 2001; Immordino-Yang & Damasio, 2007); (2) bodies of evidence examining hope and positive psychology generally (e.g., Seligman, 2002; Snyder & Lopez, 2002); and (3) positive psychology with respect to giftedness and talent development (e.g., Barab & Plucker, 2002; Larson, 2000). For individuals to reach their place of personal contentment, several components in which one's talents and abilities are maximized and in which adjustment and contentment prevail must be addressed along each individual's pathway. Furthermore, the previously noted inquiry undertaken by Folkman and Moskowitz (2000) provides the backdrop for an important affective developmental concern: that gifted and talented individuals require frequent exposure to opportunities in which they can practice behaviors in response to high-level stimuli or else they will lack strength of positive emotionality required for effectively handling life's stressors.

Using this broad literature foundation, a model that coalesces the various aspects of positive psychology, hope, and giftedness would provide a mechanism for addressing the affective development of persons of high ability, just as models exist for addressing this population's cognitive development. The model that emerges, the Bull's Eye Model for Affective Development (see Figure 3.1), proposed as a reflection of existing literature, is composed of four fluid stages of development, each influencing the next: Natural Affect, World Contexts, Meta-Affect, and Personal Niche. Each of these stages is discussed below.

Natural Affect

> Nature, we are starting to realize, is every bit as important as nurture. Genetic influences, brain chemistry, and neurological development contribute strongly to who we are as children and what we become as adults. For example, tendencies to excessive worrying or timidity, leadership qualities, risk taking, obedience to authority, all appear to have a constitutional aspect.
>
> Stanley Turecki, psychiatrist/author
> (1985, p. 21)

One's personality inevitably has an important impact on emotionality; how one reacts to environmental stimuli, processes and extrapolates those reactions into feelings, expresses those feelings, and then stores them as referents for the future all are shaded by personality. The affective dimension of one's

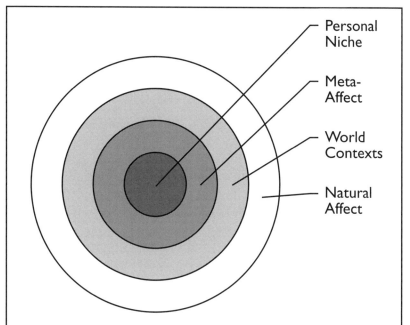

Figure 3.1. Bull's Eye Model for Affective Development.

Note. **Natural Affect** includes personality, native social proclivity, natural emotional attributes, innate abilities for handling affective information, genetic predispositions, and modifiers imposed by giftedness. **World Contexts** includes home and family influences, peer pressures, school and work expectations and mores, affective norms of society, views of others about giftedness, and "big world" circumstances. **Meta-Affect** includes affective self-examination, social and emotional regulation, impact of giftedness, and adjusting natural affect with world contexts for self-adjustment and coping. **Personal Niche** includes affective integration (innate with world with meta) to find ways for one's social and emotional sense to flourish.

personality, native social proclivity, natural emotional attributes, innate abilities for handling affective information, temperament, and genetic predispositions are embraced in Natural Affect. Further, comprehensive literature reviews, such as that provided in *The Social and Emotional Development of Gifted Children: What Do We Know?* (Neihart, Reis, Robinson, & Moon, 2002), point to a wide variety of mediating effects that giftedness imposes on personality. However, a comprehensive examination of personality research is not the point here, but there are a few studies worth noting.

Bierhoff, Klein, and Kramp (1991) explored the existence of an altruistic personality type among persons who intervened to assist victims of a traffic accident and concluded that there seemed to be a collection of empathic feelings inborn as part of one's personality that predisposed the first aiders to help the accident victims. Hence, at least insofar as one type of personality is concerned, affective dimensions are aligned closely with personality type.

Examining the relationship between personality and affect from a differing perspective, Berry and her colleagues (2000) investigated the relationship of affect and personality in determining the nature and quality of friendships among a group of 131 young adult dyads. The researchers concluded that personality features of affect such as extraversion, neuroticism, agreeableness, and openness predicted the degree of friendship quality. In fact, it was stated that while personality remains mostly stable, variations in affect are predictors of the quality of people's friendships.

It seems that each of us does have some "original factory equipment" that serves as a platform on which we are able to construct our identities in both the cognitive and affective domains. Cognitively one's mental horsepower clearly has an impact on one's thinking potential and how it can be developed; similarly, one's personality provides a parallel set of potentialities for developing one's affective abilities. In day-to-day life, the cognitive dimension of individual differences is more easily understood: each individual has an internal set of attributes, interests, and proclivities that can be developed to some degree of sophistication.

To illuminate this point, let us reference Tiger Woods once more by considering his golf talent in contrast to that of the Saturday afternoon sand-trap duffer. Tiger Woods' success is emblematic of his having applied his cognition to analyze each golf hole and by coupling those analyses with his physical attributes, he consistently has been able to produce excellent outcomes. The Saturday duffer lacks one or more of those ingredients for golf success: cognitive or physical.

Now think of the affective domain and personality. Tiger Woods, who is known for customarily presenting a mature and controlled personality, occasionally and humanly demonstrates behavior that seems to deviate from what onlookers see as his persona. As evinced by few but nonetheless occasional reports of Tiger presenting emotions that seem to not reflect his personality, such as the 2002 British Open "when he snapped at a photographer on the *first* hole of the *first* day of the tournament" (Czaban, 2002, p. 1). Meanwhile, our Saturday duffer may very well, depending on the affective potential in his personality, respond differently to the very same stimuli that caused Tiger Woods to react affectively as he did. And, incidentally, Tiger's overall performance at the end of that particular British Open placed him barely in the top 30. Was he feeling affectively "out of sorts" from the beginning of the tournament as revealed by behavior not in keeping with his typical personality? Do external stimuli play a part in finding one's affective self?

World Contexts

> The route through childhood is shaped by many forces, and it differs for each of us. Our biological inheritance, the temperament with which we are born, the care we receive, our family relationships, the place where we grow up, the schools we attend, the culture in which we participate, and the historical period in which we live—all these affect the paths we take through childhood and condition the remainder of our lives.
>
> Robert H. Wozniak, Psychologist/Researcher
> (Ginsberg, 1996, p. 44)

Regardless of whatever nature provides us from the onset in terms of personality and temperament, one's life context serves to shape our natural affect. Even if there were no research literature whatsoever, logic alone begins to underscore the reality that the circumstances of one's life—time, place, and conditions—impact one's overall development. Situational components such as home and family influences, peer pressures, school and work expectations and mores, the affective norms of society, and "big world" conditions individually and collectively influence affective development. Moreover, the way in which gifted individuals adjust to the manner in which significant others, as well as how the larger world, view giftedness has an impact on psychosocial development.

Once again, however, the developmental phenomenon seems simpler to grasp when considered first in the cognitive realm. For example, were one superior at strategic thinking and lived in World War II Britain, it is probable that the strategic thinking gift would be nurtured and encouraged to a greater extent, or at least nurtured for application in differing contexts, than it might be during a time of peace. However, again relying on logic, it makes sense to believe that the same sort of contextual influences may well play out in the affective realm, as well.

Although there has been a great deal of inquiry about the effects of environment on intellectual development (e.g., Sternberg & Grigorenko, 1997), literature of similar quality about the effects of environment on affective development tends to focus on psychological disturbance. Steinberg and Avenevoli (2000), in a thorough examination of the research bases regarding the contexts of behavioral problems, concluded simply that negative environmental situations yield behaviorally negative outcomes and that affective development is shaped by environmental dynamics including location, home life, and timing. To corroborate those conclusions, one only needs to reflect on the apparent rise in youth and teen violence during the last few decades to wonder about the relationship between negative, psychopathological events in academic settings and the complexities for young people growing up in the fast-paced, technology-oriented, goal-driven culture prevalent in Westernized societies today. Still, one also must speculate that if individuals of relatively sound mental health can in some way find scaffolding sufficient to emphasize the positive aspects of their lives, while de-emphasizing the negative, might destructive emotional development be thwarted?

Like much of cognitive development, affective maturation generally is never-ending; as an octogenarian may very well acquire new knowledge and translate it into his or her daily repertoire of thought, similarly awareness and integration of new feelings about self and others likely takes place throughout one's lifespan—that affect matures at least as much as cognition does. As a result, world events, location, personal experiences, and the like mediate the way in which affect develops over time, and of course, that mediating process is individualized for each us dependent on the vagaries of our lives as we mature.

By way of illustration, I conducted a series of interviews with Vivian, a highly accomplished woman who had broken a number of barriers to become a physician. Having previously experienced the sudden death of her 94-year-old husband, she often discussed her own affective development during the years between her husband's death and her own at age 104. This excerpt from a series of interviews took place when Vivian was age 100.

> You know that when R. J. [her husband] was alive, I went through each day happily thinking of how wonderful life was for us. Even when we had been married but a few years, already had three children, and were trying to complete medical training, I would think about the elation I felt in my life and how my cheerful feelings influenced everything I did. But it was not until after his death that I began to recognize some new feelings and to put them to use in my life. One of these is the feeling of sadness which most folks would discount as an emotion to be avoided, but I have embraced sadness as a way to ponder not only my years with R. J. but also the days ahead. Understanding my sadness makes my happiness that much more precious. I am honestly capable of greater happiness today than I have ever been because I so well understand what it means to feel sadness. I can even feel other's sadness and happiness more clearly than I ever could before because I am intimate with both sets of feelings.

Vivian's words illustrate an individual whose affect has matured in that she described two dichotomized emotions and how she has utilized her experiences with those emotions to frame a personal awareness of and sensitivity for her own feelings. Perhaps more indicative of sophisticated affective development is her reference to empathy and how it has been refined because she has internalized her own feelings. As with each of us, affective development is susceptible to the events that come our way, and those events naturally are determined by many variables, not the least of which are place, time, and the persons involved.

Meta-Affect

> *A little kingdom I possess,*
> *Where thoughts and feelings dwell;*
> *And very hard the task I find*
> *Of governing it well.*
>   Louisa May Alcott, excerpt from "My Kingdom"
>   (1875, p. 37)

Although the term *meta-affect* may seem contrived, there is little doubt from Vivian's example that as people mature psychosocially, they begin to consider more frequently how they feel about their own feelings and then translate those assessments into refinement of their overall repertoire of affective skills. Many psychologists refer to a similar process by using the term *adjustment*, yet meta-affect seems to be more accurately descriptive and inclusive of the complex process that takes place when individuals spend time examining their feelings and then using those self-inquiries to regulate and refine their own emotions. This introspective assessment, while involving thinking, is conducted not so much cognitively as the term *analytically* connotes; rather, it occurs *affectively* with individuals purposefully making an effort to probe their feelings about their own affective traits by relying predominantly on their emotions to do so.

First described by mathematical researchers DeBellis and Goldin (1997), meta-affect has been proposed as an important variable in considering the nature of students' affective domain when they are involved with mathematics curriculum and instruction. Based on a decade of research in mathematics education, the construct of meta-affect has been further explained by one of its originators as:

> An idea that has assumed a central role in our thinking is *meta-affect*, referring to: 1. affect about affect; 2. affect about and within cognition that may again be about affect; and/or 3. monitoring of affect both through cognition and affect. Our hypothesis is that meta-affect is *the most important aspect of affect.* (Goldin, 2004, p. 113)

Given that when one assesses one's feelings the cognitive domain inevitably is involved, meta-affect might be thought of as a state in which the individual takes stock of emotionality using affective skills first and then turning to those in the cognitive sphere. This represents an almost flip-flop of how humans ordinarily move through life where thinking functions take place first and feeling functions second.

One way to examine the phenomenon of meta-affect is to look at the work of a Swiss psychiatrist who began examining the intricacies of meta-affective behaviors in the 1980s. Using clinical studies of schizophrenia as the foundation for his exploration of the linkage between cognition and affect with regard to what he called *affect logic*—what amounts to a synonym for meta-affect—Ciompi (1982, 1988, 1991, 1999) concluded that feeling and thinking, while dissimilar, are inexorably related and must, of essence, be considered as a single unit regardless of the activity in which one is engaged. In other words, cognition cannot and will not take place effectively if affect is disregarded, and affect cannot and will not function well if cognition is overlooked. He further concluded that one's psyche develops and matures over time as the result of assimilations and accommodations with reality. Ciompi's assumptions were supported by psychiatric findings regarding the role of the limbic and hypothalamic system for the regulation of emotion, on neuronal plasticity, and on the phenomenon of state-dependent learning and memory (Ciompi, 1991). This essentially means that cognition and affect are segments of one unitary psyche that is a complex system for feeling, thinking, and behaving.

Among the various functions of the psyche is the storing of previous experiences that provide the basis for further cognition and communication. The affective aspect of the psyche endows individuals with specific qualitative values—such as motivation—connects cognitive elements, contributes to their storage and application according to context, and appears to help in differentiating cognitive systems at higher levels of abstraction (Ciompi, 1991). In a later work and with additional research upon which to base his conclusions, Ciompi (1999) posited that affect forms one of the significant platforms on which all of cognition is based.

Given Ciompi's landmark research, contemplate how any typical individual might interact with an environment that fails to provide adequate stimulation in either the cognitive or affective domains. Too much cognitive attention that ignores affect might be described by the person as "taxing" or "difficult," while too much affective attention that neglects cognition could be dismissed as "fluffy" or "soft." Now imagine a gifted individual (who by definition is capable of much faster and deeper thinking and feelings) who is confronted with a classroom that fails to account for cognitive and affective development in an appropriate fashion. Suddenly, what has been all too frequently categorized in gifted research literature as understimulating academic situations may, in fact, just as easily be categorized as understimulating affective situations!

Meta-affect is a critical psychosocial stage of development in which each person begins to improve executive function in a manner that is not simply cognitive but also affective in nature. During meta-affect, persons are likely first to create and later to revise definitions for a range of schema based on emotions that are generated through life experiences. Although it is believed that some emotions and their regulation are innate, most are derived through schematic development as we encounter life experiences (Ciompi, 1988). Consequently, life experiences not only provide the opportunity for each of us to use our emotions, those encounters with reality actually help us to *define* our emotions through the act of examining our own affective traits using feelings as the primary tool, with thinking being a secondary tool upon which we can rely.

Developing schema for emotions appears to be completely reliant on the meta-affective process, so exposure to a wide variety of experiences that prompt a broad range of feelings to emerge is as requisite to promoting full development of each individual as is exposure to numerous academic stimuli. In other words, learning to manipulate and apply academic subject matter is no more or less important than learning to manipulate and apply affective schema (Wimmer & Ciompi, 1996).

Personal Niche

> People speak of finding one's niche in the world. Society, as we have seen, is one vast conspiracy for carving one into the kind of statue it likes, and then placing it in the most convenient niche it has.
>
> Randolph S. Bourne, literary critic/social reformer
> (1913, p. 212)

The optimal goal of each individual, as well as that of the society in which one finds oneself, is to assemble a set of circumstances where one can feel a sense of belonging, yet at the same time exercise some degree of independence. Certainly, this sense of belonging is governed to a large extent by affect, but cognition also is important here; in fact, it would be fair to conclude that the stages in the Bull's Eye Model, although to some degree fluid and flexible depending on the individual and situations, increasingly integrate affect with cognition as one matures from natural affect through world contexts and meta-affect and into the optimal place of personal niche. Moreover, it makes rational sense to presume that the greatest likelihood for fluidity among stages occurs across world contexts, meta-affect, and personal niche as one grapples with messages delivered by one's location and era (world contexts), refinements of one's emotions by developing sophisticated schema (meta-affect), and enters a place of contentment and adjustment affectively and cognitively (personal niche). Yet, each of those developmental stages remains highly reliant on one's native affective abilities as contained in natural affect.

Although the term *personal niche* may be somewhat novel, the concept is not. In fact, theorists and researchers in psychology and psychiatry have wrestled with this notion for some time. Perhaps the first conception of personal niche was explored through research in psychiatry by focusing on an ecological dimension of psychotherapy, or the "fit" between each individual's capabilities and one's environment (Willi, 1999; Willi, Toygar-Zurmühle, & Frei, 1996). In this line of research, it is believed that each mentally healthy person constantly engages in a campaign to promote psychic well-being by shaping, arranging, and rearranging, and to the greatest extent possible, controlling the influence of ingredients (e.g., other people, environments, and stimuli) on one's life. Here, feelings are every bit as critical as thoughts: cognition and affect must work as coequals in a mechanism for streamlining what amounts to a never-ending task for each individual to erect a "nest" in which one feels at peace.

Assembling the various aspects of one's life essentially would equate to a situation or a series of situations in which one could comfortably balance independence with dependence, relaxation with work, participation with deferment, and thoughts with feelings; there would be congruence insofar as one had attained the "fit" alluded to in Willi's (1996) original research, or the notion of having achieved a level of personally defined contentment that was conceptually synthesized nearly a decade later in several chapters of *Recent Advances in Psychology and Aging, Volume 15* (Costa & Siegler, 2004). Those chapters describe a number of related studies and theories associated with gerontology and how people mature happily (Charles & Carstensen, 2004; Diener, Scollon, & Lucas, 2004; Trzesniewski, Robins, Roberts, & Caspi, 2004), all of which underscore the Bull's Eye Model's perspective of optimal psychosocial development being fluid and occurring over time.

The implication from extant literature is that healthy individuals gradually over their lifespan are able to pull together many aspects of their lives to construct what amounts to a position in the world that provides them with security both affectively and cognitively. However, referencing Vivian's realizations about her feelings related to her husband's death yet again, it seems correct to view this place—this personal niche—as ephemeral, one that must continually undergo examination using both meta-affect and world contexts, cast against the backdrop of one's individual affective abilities and predispositions in natural affect. This flexibility across stages of the Bull's Eye Model allows for one's emotions to be shaped as a means for addressing day-to-day, even momentary changes in the environment, and the personal niche stage being attained again only after one's repertoire of feelings has been revised according to inputs derived from world contexts and meta-affect.

Pragmatism: What Does This Matter to Gifted and Talented People and Talent Development?

Using the foundation of research in positive psychology, hope, and flow, then examining their interactions with psychosocial research relating to giftedness, talent, and talent development, a stage process has been proposed above in the Bull's Eye Model for Affective Development. Additionally, each stage of the process has clear linkages to theoretical, as well as empirical, research in psychology and psychiatry, disciplines that are particularly significant to any consideration of affective development. Still, the connection with giftedness and talent development has been addressed only fleetingly; therefore, that relationship will be clarified.

Schools and Classrooms for Affective Development

In view of the fact that the Bull's Eye Model contains three stages where environmental influences can serve to enhance or to deter emotional development—world contexts, meta-affect, and personal niche—these three stages should be considered categorically as the units for analysis and intervention in whole schools and classrooms alike. Comprehensive programming for affective development obviously entails similarly comprehensive analysis and intervention throughout all three stages. The stages of the model are intended as general guidelines and not as a recipe. Although the process of the Bull's Eye Model is likely to be more or less the same for each individual, we must constantly be reminded that affective development is not a process that can be formulaic; individual differences and personal circumstances require correspondingly custom-made treatment. Hence, while educators may provide certain interventions aimed at all students, responses to those stimuli inevitably will vary from student to student.

Classrooms that place a high value on the development of feelings through debriefing sessions where personal opinions not only are welcome but also encouraged and expected as part of learning promote affective growth. Infusing each learning sequence with reflection opportunities is of essence for triggering emotions, yet doing so randomly would prove to be counterproductive to the goal of showing students how to pursue emotional development integrated as part of learning. Showing students how to integrate considerations for emotions with academic tasks provides a model for them to use in later life when it is hoped they will integrate psychosocial perspectives with daily life events.

When solving mathematics problems, classrooms should engage in discussions about how those skills not only are useful in the world outside of school but how people feel when they work with familiar mathematical processes; analyses might focus on the struggle with new and unknown mathematical processes versus the relative comfort one feels with the well-known. When examining a particular language or literature concept, schools should seek ways for purposefully stimulating reflection about the importance that differing segments of society place on the concept being learned and how those societal distinctions make students feel. While pursuing science or social studies material, instructors should use controversies to cause students to debate and dialogue about the issues at hand, encouraging them to express their perspectives, as well as to support them, while closing with analyses of how the simulations caused students to feel.

Classrooms and schools that genuinely seek to nurture students' gifts and talents optimally embed affective development in curriculum and instruction regardless of the content discipline. Students who investigate world contexts related to the subject matter, who are provided time to contemplate their own feelings through meta-affect, and who are exposed to self-evolved people who are at least transiently living in their personal niche are practicing the foundations for comprehensive affective development. So long as those experiences are intentionally associated to the greatest extent possible with individual interests and motivations and are as self-fulfilling and personalized as possible in terms of delivery and response formats, high-ability students are likely to practice these process skills again.

Posing important content-related questions that evoke emotions and prompt the discussion of feelings is crucial for opening schools and classrooms to the degree of affective stimulation necessary for addressing world contexts, stimulating meta-affect, and pointing out the goal of personal niche. Even with the most gifted student, it is unlikely that feelings will be examined, analyzed, and evaluated unless the habit for doing so is established, and by providing an affective ambiance through content-based inquiry that demands the expression of feelings, classrooms rightfully can place affective engagement on an equal plane with the cognitive. Moreover, educators and mentors, who model their own affective stages of development and demonstrate them through expression of feelings, provide useful modeling of affective development. Certainly teaching gifted and talented learners about the Bull's Eye Model itself affords a strategic method for engendering its application.

Affective Development at Home

As with educators and mentors, parents and families must customarily engage in discussion of feelings and not simply in releasing them. Adding discussion and debriefing periods when the gifted and talented child or other family members experience a range of feelings as they interact with their environments can only stimulate development of habitual affective referencing. Young people, gifted or otherwise, are likely to contemplate world contexts only if they are routinely provoked to do so, but this is best accomplished through discussions that involve as many family members as possible, the message being that it is of value. Meta-affect is best stimulated when there is intentional time for each family member to consider personal feelings framed by a variety of situational events inside and outside the home; private reflection followed by discussion is advantageous for acquainting high-ability students with the utility of the process of pondering one's own emotions—pondering consisting of both cognitive and affective effort, the individual thinking and feeling about his or her emotions.

Conclusion

Framing gifted education and talent development with specific emphasis on the development of personal affect is imperative for optimizing cognitive growth and ultimately for inspiring productivity of the astute, novel type of which high-ability persons are capable. As we have seen, the literature is replete with theory and research demonstrating the necessity for attention to affective development for everyone, although the Bull's Eye Model has explicit application to high-ability people who, because of their tendency for asynchronous development, are the ones most likely to integrate cognitive and affective domains with early frequency and intensity (Silverman, 2002).

Given the special cognitive and affective needs indissolubly associated with individuals who have significant potential, precise attention to emotions is essential to their optimal maturation, and use of a theory- and research-based system such as the Bull's Eye Model makes logical sense. Ideally, educators and families gradually will adopt and adapt the affective growth process depicted in this model so that research of its efficacy as a framework for considering and stimulating methodical maturation of emotions can be undertaken.

At age 103, a year prior to her death, Vivian crystallized the need for systemic affective development among gifted and talented students:

> If I could have, about the only thing I would have transformed about my life is that I would have devoted greater time and effort to my feelings: feelings about rainy days, feelings about my brothers and sisters, feelings about medical school and my work and church. I would have mused over them and played with them in my mind, and I would have been better prepared for my life and all its laughter and its tears.

References

Alcott, L. M. (1875). My kingdom. In C. W. Wendte & H. S. Perkins (Eds.), *The sunny side: A book of religious songs for the Sunday school and the home* (p. 37). New York: William A. Pond.

Amrein, A. L., & Berliner, D. C. (2002). *An analysis of some unintended and negative consequences of high-stakes testing.* East Lansing, MI: The Great Lakes Center for Education Research and Practice. Retrieved April 23, 2008, from http://greatlakescenter.org/pdf/H-S%20Analysis%20final.pdf

Barab, S. A., & Plucker, J. A. (2002). Smart people or smart contexts? Cognition, ability, and talent development in an age of situated approaches to knowing and learning. *Educational Psychologist, 37,* 165–182.

Belsky, J., Spritz, B., & Crnic, K. (1996). Infant attachment security and affective-cognitive information processing at age 3. *Psychological Science 7,* 111–114.

Beltman, S., & Volet, S. (2007). Exploring the complex and dynamic nature of sustained motivation. *European Psychologist, 12,* 314–323.

Berry, D. S., Willingham, J. K., & Thayer, C. A. (2000). Affect and personality as predictors of conflict and closeness in young adults' friendships. *Journal of Research in Personality, 34,* 84–107.

Bierhoff, H. W., Klein, R., & Kramp, P. (1991). Evidence for the altruistic personality from data on accident research. *Journal of Personality, 59,* 263–280.

Bourne, R. S. (1913). *Youth and life.* Boston: Houghton Mifflin.

Charles, S. T., & Carstensen, L. L. (2004). A life span view of emotional functioning in adulthood and old age. In P. T. Costa & I. C. Siegler (Eds.), *Recent advances in psychology and aging* (Vol. 15, pp. 133–162). Amsterdam: Elsevier.

Ciompi, L. (1982). *Affektlogik [Affect Logic]*. Stuttgart, Germany: Klett-Cotta.

Ciompi, L. (1988). *Psyche and schizophrenia: The bond between affect and logic.* Cambridge, MA: Harvard University Press.

Ciompi, L. (1991). Affects as central organising and integrating factors: A new psychosocial/biological model of the psyche. *British Journal of Psychiatry, 159,* 97–105.

Ciompi, L. (1999). *Die emotionalen grundlagen des denkens [The emotional bases of thinking]*. Göttingen, Germany: Vandenhoeck & Ruprecht.

Costa, P. T., & Siegler, I. C. (Eds.). (2004). *Recent advances in psychology and aging* (Vol. 15). Amsterdam: Elsevier.

Csikszentmihalyi, M. (1990). *Flow: The psychology of optimal experience.* New York: Harper and Row.

Csikszentmihalyi, M., Patton, J. D., & Lucas, M. (1997). Le bonheur, l'experience optimale et les valeurs spirituelles: Une etude empirique aupres d'adolescents. *Revue Québécoise de Psychologie, 18,* 167–190.

Curry, L. A., Snyder, C. R., Cook, D. L., Ruby, B. C., & Rehm, M. (1997). Role of hope in academic and sport achievement. *Journal of Personality and Social Psychology, 73,* 1257–1267.

Czaban, S. (2002, July 24). Tiger's tantrum. *OnMilwaukee.com.* Retrieved March 15, 2008, from http://www.onmilwaukee.com/sports/articles/tigertantrum.html

Damasio, A. R. (1994). *Descartes' error: Emotion, reason, and the human brain.* New York: Grosset/Putnam.

Damasio, A. R. (1999). *The feeling of what happens: Body and emotion in the making of consciousness.* New York: Harcourt Brace.

Danner, D. D., Snowdon, D. A., & Friesen, W. V. (2001). Positive emotions in early life and longevity: Findings from the nun study. *Journal of Personality and Social Psychology, 80,* 804–813.

Davis, H. A., & Lease, A. M. (2007). Perceived organizational structure for teacher liking: The role of peers' perceptions of teacher liking in teacher–student relationship quality, motivation, and achievement. *Social Psychology of Education, 10,* 403–427.

DeBellis, V. A., & Goldin, G. A. (1997). The affective domain in mathematical problem solving. In E. Pehkonen (Ed.), *Proceedings of the Psychology of Math Education 21* (Vol. 2, pp. 209–216). Lahti, Finland: Lahti Research and Training Institute.

Dickerson, A. E. (1993). The relationship between affect and cognition. *Occupational Therapy in Mental Health, 12*, 47–59.

Diener, E., Scollon, C. N., & Lucas, R. E. (2004). The evolving concept of subjective well-being: The multifaceted nature of happiness. In P. T. Costa & I. C. Siegler (Eds.), *Recent advances in psychology and aging* (Vol. 15, pp. 187–220). Amsterdam: Elsevier.

Flavell, J. H., Flavell, E. R., & Green, F. L. (2001). Development of children's understanding of connections between thinking and feeling. *Psychological Science, 12*, 430–432.

Folkman, S., & Moskowitz, J. T. (2000). Stress, positive emotion, and coping. *Current Directions in Psychological Science, 9*, 115–118.

Fromm, E. (1941). *Escape from freedom.* New York: Farrar & Rinehart.

Gagné, R. (1965). *The conditions of learning.* New York: Holt, Rinehart and Winston.

Gillham, J. E. (2000). *The science of optimism and hope: Research essays in honor of Martin E. P. Seligman.* Radnor, PA: Templeton Foundation Press.

Gillham, J. E., & Reivich, K. (2004). Cultivating optimism in childhood and adolescence. *The Annals of the American Academy of Political and Social Science, 591,* 146–163.

Ginsberg, S. (1996). *Family wisdom: The 2,000 most important things ever said about parenting, children, and family life.* New York: Columbia University Press.

Goldin, G. A. (2004). Characteristics of affect as a system of representation. In M. Johnsen-Hoines & A. B. Fuglestad (Eds.), *Proceedings of the Psychology of Math Education, 28*(1), 109–114.

Goleman, D. (1993). *Emotional intelligence: Why it can matter more than IQ.* New York: Bantam Books.

Goleman, D. (1998). *Working with emotional intelligence.* New York: Bantam Books.

Helsen, W. F., Hodges, N. J., Van Winckel, J., & Stakes, J. L. (2000). The roles of talent, physical precocity, and practice in the development of soccer expertise. *Journal of Sports Sciences, 18*, 727–736.

Hodges, T. D., & Clifton, D. O. (2004). Strengths-based development in practice. In P. A. Linley & S. Joseph (Eds.), *Positive psychology in practice.* Hoboken, NJ: John Wiley

Immordino-Yang, M. H., & Damasio, A. (2007). We feel, therefore we learn: The relevance of affective and social neuroscience to education. *Mind, Brain, and Education, 1,* 3–10.

Isen, A. M. (2004). Some perspectives on positive feelings and emotions: Positive affect facilitates thinking and problem solving. In A. S. R. Manstead, N. Frijda, & A. Fischer (Eds.), *Feelings and emotions: The Amsterdam Symposium* (pp. 263–281). Cambridge, UK: Cambridge University Press.

Knuver, A. W. M., & Brandsma, H. P. (1993). Cognitive and affective outcomes in school effectiveness research. *School Effectiveness and School Improvement, 4*, 189–204.

Lacan, J. (1973). *Le séminaire de Jacques Lacan. Livre XI. Les quatre concepts fondamentaux de la psychanalyse.* Paris: Editions du Seuil.

Lacan, J. (1977). *Ecrits: A selection.* London: Tavistock.

Larson, R. W. (2000). Toward a psychology of positive youth development. *American Psychologist, 55*, 170–183.

Lyubomirsky, S., King, L., & Diener, E. (2005). The benefits of frequent positive affect: Does happiness lead to success? *Psychological Bulletin, 131*, 803–855.

Maslow, A. H. (1962). *Toward a psychology of being.* Princeton, NJ: VanNostrand.

McNeil, L. M., Coppola, E., Radigan, J., & Vasquez-Heileg, J. (2008). Avoidable losses: High-stakes accountability and the dropout crisis. *Education Policy Analysis Archives, 16*(3). Retrieved April 23, 2008, from http://epaa.asu.edu/epaa/v16n3

McNess, E., Broadfoot, P., & Osborn, M. (2003). Is the effective compromising the affective? *British Educational Research Journal, 29*, 243–257.

McQuillan, J., & Conde, G. (1996). The conditions of flow in reading: Two studies of optimal experience. *Reading Psychology, 17*, 109–135.

Nakamura, J., & Csikszentmihalyi, M. (2002). The concept of flow. In C. R. Snyder & S. J. Lopez (Eds.), *Handbook of positive psychology* (pp. 89–105). London: Oxford University Press.

Neihart, M., Reis, S. M., Robinson, N. M., & Moon, S. M. (2002). *The social and emotional development of gifted children: What do we know?* Waco, TX: Prufrock Press.

Nichols, S. L., & Berliner, D. C. (2005). *The inevitable corruption of indicators and educators through high-stakes testing.* East Lansing, MI: The Great Lakes Center for Education Research and Practice. Retrieved April 23, 2008, from http://www.greatlakescenter. org/g_l_new_doc/EPSL-0503-101-EPRU.pdf

Patrick, H., Ryan, A. M., Alfeld-Liro, C., Fredricks, J. A., Hruda, L. Z., & Eccles, J. S. (1999). Adolescents' commitment to developing talent: The role of peers in continuing motivation in sports and the arts. *Journal of Youth and Adolescence, 28,* 741–763.

Roelands, M., VanOyen, H., Depoorter, A. M., Baro, F., & VanOost, P. (2003). Are cognitive impairment and depressive mood associated with increased service utilisation in community-dwelling elderly people? *Health & Social Care in the Community, 11,* 1–9.

Rogers, C. (1961). *On becoming a person: A therapist's view of psychotherapy.* London: Constable.

Sarlin, M. B., & Altshuler, K. Z. (1978). On the inter-relationship of cognition and affect: Fantasies of deaf children. *Child Psychiatry and Human Development, 9,* 95–103.

Seligman, M. E. P. (1990). *Learned optimism.* New York: Knopf.

Seligman, M. E. P. (2002). Positive psychology, positive prevention, and positive therapy. In C. R. Snyder & S. J. Lopez (Eds.), *Handbook of positive psychology* (pp. 3–12). London: Oxford University Press.

Seligman, M. E. P. (2004). Can happiness be taught? *Daedalus, 133*(2), 80–87.

Seligman, M. E. P., & Csikszentmihalyi, M. (2000). Positive psychology: An introduction. *American Psychologist, 55,* 5–14.

Shatté, A. J., Reivich, K., Gillham, J. E., & Seligman, M. E. P. (1999). Learned optimism in children. In C. R. Snyder (Ed.), *Coping: The psychology of what works* (pp. 165–181). New York: Oxford University Press.

Shernoff, D. J., Csikszentmihalyi, M., Schneider, B., & Shernoff, E. S. (2003). Student engagement in high school classrooms from the perspective of flow theory. *School Psychology Quarterly, 18,* 158–176.

Silverman, L. K. (2002). Asynchronous development. In M. Neihart, S. M. Reis, N. M. Robinson, & S. M. Moon (Eds.), *The social and emotional development of gifted children: What do we know?* (pp. 31–40). Waco, TX: Prufrock Press.

Smith, R. E., & Smoll, F. L. (1997). Coaching the coaches: Youth sports as a scientific and applied behavioral setting. *Current Directions in Psychological Science, 6,* 16–21.

Snyder, C. R. (1994). *The psychology of hope: You can get there from here.* New York: Free Press.

Snyder, C. R. (Ed.). (2001). *Coping with stress: Effective people and processes.* New York: Oxford University Press.

Snyder, C. R., & Lopez, S. J. (Eds.). (2002). *Handbook of positive psychology.* London: Oxford University Press.

Snyder, C. R, McDermott, D., Cook, W., & Rapoff, M. (2002). *Hope for the journey: Helping children through the good times and the bad.* Clinton Corners, NY: Percheron.

Snyder, C. R., Shorey, H. S., Cheavens, J., Pulvers, K. M., Adams, V. H., & Wiklund, C. (2002). Hope and academic success in college. *Journal of Educational Psychology, 94,* 820–826.

Steinberg, L., & Avenevoli, S. (2000). The role of context in the development of psychopathology: A conceptual framework and some speculative propositions. *Child Development, 71,* 66–74.

Sternberg, R. J., & Grigorenko, E. (Eds). (1997). *Intelligence, heredity, and environment.* New York: Cambridge University Press.

Strege, J. (1997). *Tiger: A biography of Tiger Woods.* New York: Broadway Books.

Trzesniewski, K. H., Robins, R. W., Roberts, B. W., & Caspi, A. (2004). Personality and self-esteem development across the life span. In P. T. Costa & I. C. Siegler (Eds.), *Recent advances in psychology and aging* (Vol. 15, pp. 163–185). Amsterdam: Elsevier.

Turecki, S. (1985). *The difficult child.* New York: Bantam Books.

VanTassel-Baska, J., & Stambaugh, T. (2006). *Comprehensive curriculum for gifted learners* (3rd ed.). Needham Heights, MA: Allyn & Bacon.

Walberg, H. J., Zins, J. E., & Weissberg, R. P. (2004). Recommendations and conclusions: Implications for practice, training, research, and policy. In J. E. Zins, R. P. Weissberg, M. C. Wang, & H. J. Walberg (Eds.), *Building academic success in social and emotional learning: What does the research say?* (pp. 209–218). New York: Teachers College Press.

Wheelock, A., Bebell, D. J., & Haney, W. (2000, November 2). What can student drawings tell us about high-stakes testing in Massachusetts? *Teachers College Record.* Retrieved April 23, 2008, from http://www.tcrecord. org/content.asp?contentid=10634

Willi, J. (1999). *Ecological psychotherapy: Developing by shaping the personal niche.* Seattle, WA: Hogrefe & Huber.

Willi, J., Toygar-Zurmühle, A., & Frei, R. (1999). Die erfassung der persönlichen nische als grundlage der supportiven psychotherapie [The acquisition of the personal niche as basis of the supportive psychotherapy]. *Der Nervenartz, 70,* 847–854.

Williams, A. M., & Reilly, T. (2000). Talent identification and development in soccer. *Journal of Sports Sciences, 18,* 657–667.

Wimmer, M., & Ciompi, L. (1996). Evolutionary aspects of affective-cognitive interactions in the light of Ciompi's concept of "affect-logic." *Evolution and Cognition, 6*(2), 37–58.

Zins, J. E., Bloodworth, M. R., Weissberg, R. P., & Walberg, H. J. (2004). The scientific base linking social and emotional learning to school success. In J. E. Zins, R. P. Weissberg, M. C. Wang, & H. J. Walberg (Eds.), *Building academic success on social and emotional learning: What does the research say?* (pp. 3–22). New York: Teachers College Press.

Operation Houndstooth:
A Positive Perspective on
Developing Social Intelligence[1]

Joseph S. Renzulli

A good head and a good heart are always a formidable combination.

Nelson Mandela

Each time someone stands up for an ideal, or acts to improve the lot of others, or strikes out against injustice, he or she sends forth a tiny ripple of hope.

Robert F. Kennedy

When 11-year-old Aubyn heard about how many children in foster care programs are forced to carry their belongings in garbage bags because they cannot afford suitcases, she was shocked and saddened. "I thought they must feel like garbage themselves," she said. So, Aubyn founded Suitcases for Kids, dedicating herself to ensuring that every child in foster care would have a bag of his or her own.

1   The work reported in this article was supported under the Jacob K. Javits Act Program as administered by the Office of Educational Research and Improvement, U.S. Department of Education (Grant No. R-206R-00001), but the opinions expressed are those of the author. The author gratefully acknowledges contributions to this work by Rachel E. Sytsma and Kristin B. Berman. Portions of this chapter were previously published in "Operation Houndstooth Intervention Theory: Social Capital in Today's Schools," by J. S. Renzulli, J. L. Koehler, and E. A. Fogarty, 2006, *Gifted Child Today*, *29*(1), 15–24.

She asked 4-H groups and Boy and Girl Scout troops to help her, as well as members of her own church. She published notices in several church bulletins; put up posters at libraries, grocery stores, and community buildings; and she spoke to numerous Sunday School classes. The project spread like wildfire and at the end of the second year, Suitcases for Kids was active in all 50 states and Canada and was being introduced into the Soviet Union. Aubyn remained chairperson, overseeing the nationwide coordination of collections by churches, schools, 4-H clubs, Boy and Girl Scouts, department stores, airlines, YMCA's and YMHA's, Jaycees, and travel agents. Aubyn's personal collection of suitcases tallied nearly 17,000.

"I thought it was horrible that the children had nothing to carry their things in as they moved so many times. I wanted to make them feel special by giving them something of their own to keep. I tried to put myself in their place and think how I would feel," said Aubyn.

Background

Examining social and emotional issues can take many forms, ranging from dealing with maladaptive behaviors faced by gifted children to a positive psychology approach, which focuses on providing young people with the opportunities, resources, and encouragement to support matters that touch their social consciousness. I believe that all people have a "social intelligence," and I further believe that one of the challenges of our field is to devote resources to the development of this form of intelligence just as we have for so long focused on cognitive development.

The brief story of Aubyn is but one of numerous examples I have collected over the years to illustrate how a focus on student interests and the need to take positive action can help fulfill affective needs in young people who want to make positive differences in their community and sometimes even in the world. Too much of our focus on education in general, and even in gifted programs, has been on cognitive development; and while I am not criticizing this focus, we clearly need to give some balance to what I sometimes call *intelligences outside the normal curve*.

In the early 1970s, I began work on a conception of gift-edness that challenged the traditional view of this concept as mainly a function of high scores on intelligence tests. This work was greeted by a less than enthusiastic reception from the gifted establishment of the time including rejections of my writing by all of the main journals in the field of gifted education. My convictions about a broadened view of human potential caused me to seek an audience elsewhere, and in 1978 the *Phi Delta Kappan* published my article entitled, "What Makes Giftedness? Re-examining a Definition" (Renzulli, 1978). In the ensuing years scholars, practitioners, and policy makers began to gain a more flexible attitude toward the meaning of this complex phe-nomenon called giftedness, and the 1978 *Kappan* article is now the most widely cited publication in the field. I mention this fortunate turn of events mainly to call attention to the always expectant hope that people can change their minds about a long cherished belief, and to acknowledge the courage of Robert Cole, the then *Kappan* editor, who was willing to take a chance on what was at the time a decidedly unpopular point of view.

In what is now popularly known as the three-ring concep-tion of giftedness (above average but not necessarily superior ability, creativity, and task commitment), I embedded the three rings in a houndstooth background that represents the inter-actions between personality and environment (see Figure 4.1). These factors aid in the development of the three clusters of traits that represent gifted behaviors. What I recognized but did not emphasize at the time was that a scientific examination of a more focused set of background components is necessary in order for us to understand more fully the sources of gifted behav-iors and more importantly, the ways in which people transform their gifted assets into constructive action (*Note*: I prefer to use the word *gifted* as an adjective rather than a noun). Why did Aubyn devote her time and energy to a socially responsible project that would improve the lives of children in foster care? And, can a better understanding of people who use their gifts in socially constructive ways help us create conditions that expand the number of people who contribute to the growth of social, as well as economic, capital? Can our education system produce

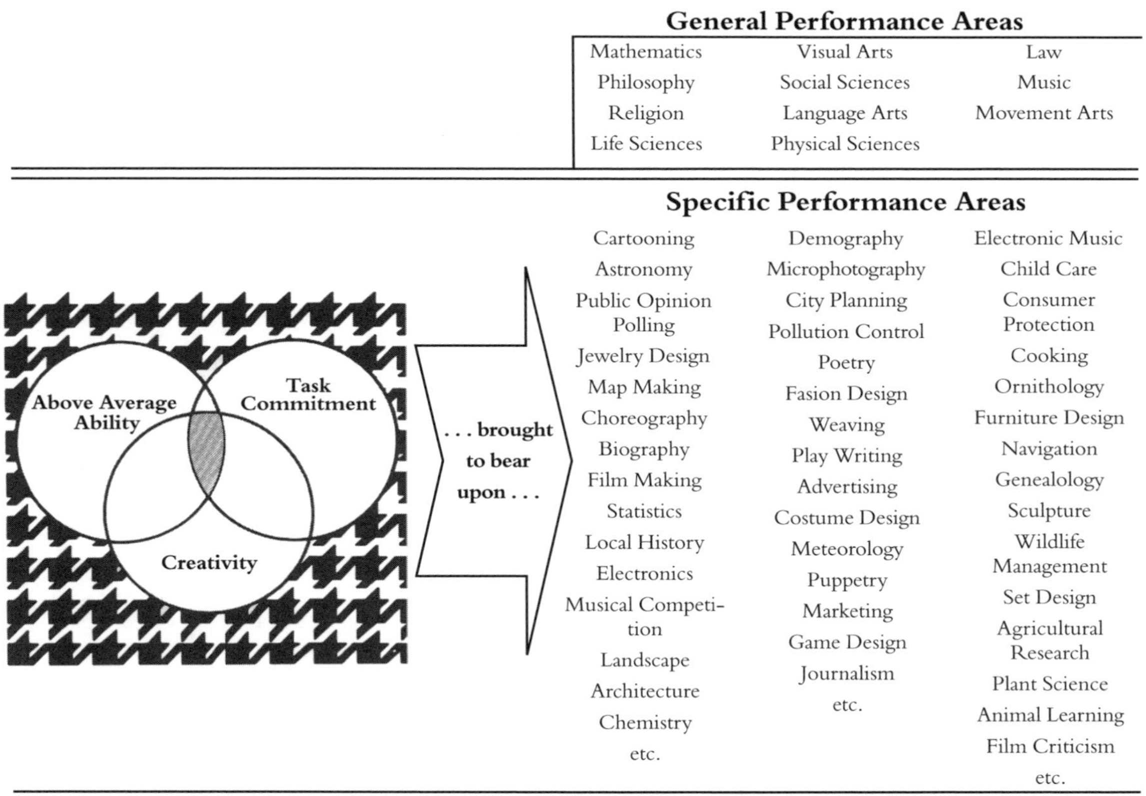

Figure 4.1. Operation Houndstooth Intervention Theory.

future corporate leaders who are as sensitive to aesthetic and environmental concerns as they are to the corporate bottom line? Can we influence the ethics and morality of future industrial and political leaders so that they place gross national happiness on an equal or higher scale of values than gross national product? These are some of the questions we are attempting to address in an ongoing series of research studies that examine the relationship between co-cognitive personal characteristics and the role that these characteristics play in the development of social capital.

What Is Social Capital and Why Is It Important?

Financial and intellectual capital are the well-known forces that drive the economy and result in generating highly valued material assets, wealth production, and professional advancement—all important goals in a capitalistic economic system. Social capital, on the other hand, is a set of intangible assets that address the collective needs and problems of other individuals and our communities at large. Although social capital cannot be defined as precisely as corporate earnings or gross domestic product, LaBonte (1999) eloquently defined it as

> something going on "out there" in people's day-to-day relationships that is an important determinant to the quality of their lives, if not society's healthy functioning. It is the "gluey stuff" that binds individuals to groups, groups to organizations, citizens to societies. (p. 431)

This kind of capital generally enhances community life and the network of obligations we have to one another. Investments in social capital benefit society as a whole because they help to create the values, norms, networks, and social trust that facilitate coordination and cooperation geared toward the greater public good.

Striking evidence indicates a marked decline in American social capital over the latter half of the century just ending. National surveys show declines over the last few decades in voter turnout and political participation, and membership in service clubs, church-related groups, parent-teacher associations, unions, and fraternal groups. For example, membership in the League of Women Voters has decreased by 42% since 1969 and an even greater decrease (59%) has been recorded for the Federation of Women's Clubs. Similar reductions are found in volunteerism to organizations such as the Red Cross and Boy Scouts, and to service and fraternal groups such as the Jaycees, the Elks, the Lions, and the Masons (Putnam, 1995). These declines in civic and social participation have been paralleled by an increasing tendency for young people to focus on narrow professional success and individual economic gain.

What is perhaps most striking when examining the commentary of leading scholars about the relationship between economic and social capital is that investments in *both* types of national assets can result in greater prosperity and improved physical and mental health, as well as a society that honors freedom, happiness, justice, civic participation, and the dignity of a diverse population. Putnam (1993, 1995) pointed out that the aggregation of social capital has contributed to economic development. He found that widespread participation in group activities, social trust, and cooperation created conditions for both good government and prosperity. Putnam traced the roots of investments in social capital to medieval times and concluded that communities did not become civil because they were rich, but rather became rich because they were civil. "Researchers in such fields as education, urban poverty, unemployment, the control of crime and drug abuse, and even health have discovered that successful outcomes are more likely in civically engaged communities" (Putnam, 1995, p. 66). Other researchers have concluded that social capital is simultaneously a cause and an effect leading to positive outcomes such as economic development, good government, reduced crime, greater participation in civic activities, and cooperation among diverse members of a community (Portes, 1998).

Researchers who have studied social capital have examined it mainly in terms of its impact on communities at large, but they also point out that it is created largely by the actions of individuals. They also have reported that leadership is a necessary condition for the creation of social capital. Although numerous studies and a great deal of commentary about leadership have been discussed in the gifted education literature, no one has yet examined the relationship between the characteristics of gifted leaders and their motivation to use their gifts for the production of social capital.

Gifted Education and Social Capital

Research on the characteristics of gifted individuals has addressed the following question: What causes some people to use their intellectual, motivational, and creative assets in ways that lead to outstanding manifestations of creative productivity, while others with similar or perhaps even more considerable assets fail to achieve high levels of accomplishment? Perhaps an even more important question so far as the production of social capital is concerned is: What causes some people to mobilize their interpersonal, political, ethical, and moral realms of being in such ways that they place human concerns and the common good above materialism, ego enhancement, and self-indulgence? How can we understand the science of human strengths that brings about the remarkable contributions of people like Nelson Mandela, Rachel Carson, Mother Theresa, and others who have focused their talents on bringing about changes that are directed toward making the lives of all people better?

The folk wisdom, research literature, and biographical and anecdotal accounts about creativity and giftedness are nothing short of mind boggling; and yet, we are still unable to answer these fundamental questions about persons who have devoted their lives to improving the human condition. Several writers (Gagné, 1985; Gardner, 1983; Mönks, 1991; Renzulli, 1978; Sternberg & Davidson, 1986; Tannenbaum, 1986) have speculated about the necessary ingredients for giftedness and creative productivity. These theories have called attention to important components and conditions for high-level accomplishment, but they fail to explain how the confluence of desirable traits results in commitments for making the lives of all people more personally rewarding, environmentally safe, peaceful, and politically free. Concern for a psychology that focuses on these positive human concerns is especially important because it will help give direction to the educational and environmental experiences we might be able to provide for the potentially gifted and talented young people who will shape both the values and the actions of the new century.

That certain ingredients are necessary for creative productivity is not debatable; however, the specific traits, the extent to which they exist, and the ways they interact with one another will continue to be the basis for future theorizing, research, and controversy. We need to learn more about all aspects of trait theory, but I also believe that new research must begin to focus on that elusive "thing" that remains after everything explainable has been explained. This "thing" is the true mystery of our common interest in human potential, but it also might hold the key to both explaining and nurturing that kind of genius that has been applied to the betterment of mankind.

Operation Houndstooth

One of the more fortunate new directions in the social sciences in recent years has been the development of the positive psychology movement. Championed by Martin E. P. Seligman (Seligman, 1991; Seligman & Csikszentmihalyi, 2000; Seligman, Reivich, Jaycox, & Gillham, 1995), this movement focuses on enhancing what is good in addition to fixing maladaptive behavior. The goal of positive psychology is to create a science of human strengths that will help us to understand and learn how to foster socially constructive virtues in young people. Although all of society's institutions need to be involved in helping to shape positive values and virtues, schools play an especially important part today because of changes in family structures and because people of all ages now spend more than a fifth of their lives in some kind of schooling. In a research study dealing with developing excellence in young people, Larson (2000) found that average students report being bored about one third of the time. He speculated that participation in civic and socially engaging activities might hold the key to overcoming some of the disengagement and disaffection that is rampant among American youth. Larson argued that components of positive development such as initiative, creativity, leadership, altruism, and civic engagement can result from early and continuous opportunities to participate in experiences that promote characteristics associated with the production of social capital.

The positive psychology movement, coupled with my continuing fascination about the scientific components that give rise to socially constructive giftedness, has resulted in an examination of personal attributes that form the framework of Operation Houndstooth. A comprehensive review of the literature and a series of Delphi technique classification studies led to the development of an organizational plan for studying the 6 components and 13 subcomponents presented in Figure 4.2. These components are briefly defined as follows:

- **Optimism**: Optimism includes cognitive, emotional, and motivational components and reflects the belief that the future holds good outcomes. Optimism may be thought of as the mood or attitude associated with an expectation about a future one regards as socially desirable, to his or her advantage, or to the advantage of others.
- **Courage**: Deriving from the Latin word for "heart," courage is the ability to face difficulty or danger while overcoming physical, psychological, and/or moral fears. Integrity and strength of character are typical manifestations of courage, and they represent the most salient marks of creative persons.
- **Romance With a Topic/Discipline**: When an individual is passionate about a topic or discipline, a true romance, characterized by powerful emotions and desires, evolves. The passion or love characteristic of this romance often becomes an image for the future in young people and serves as a primary ingredient for eminence.
- **Sensitivity to Human Concerns**: This trait is described as the ability to comprehend another's affective world and to accurately and sensitively communicate understanding

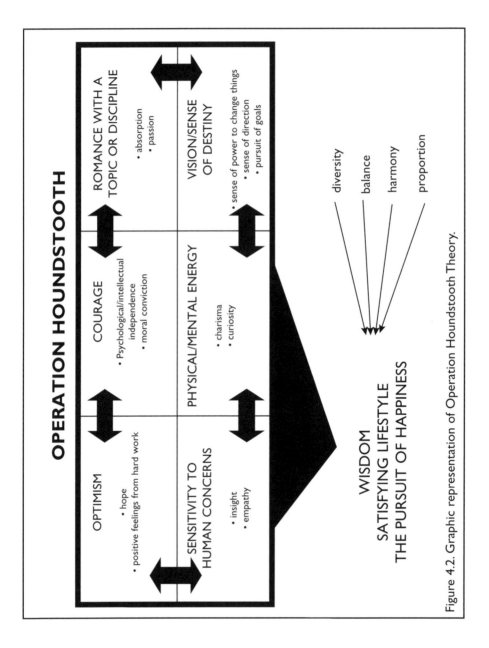

Figure 4.2. Graphic representation of Operation Houndstooth Theory.

through action. Altruism and empathy, aspects of which are evident throughout human development, characterize sensitivity to human concerns.

- **Physical/Mental Energy**: All people have this trait in varying degrees, but the amount of energy an individual is willing and able to invest toward the achievement of a goal is a crucial issue in high levels of accomplishment. In the case of eminent individuals, this energy investment level is a major contributor to task commitment. Charisma and curiosity are frequent correlates or manifestations of high physical and mental energy.

- **Vision/Sense of Destiny**: Complex and difficult to define, vision or a sense of destiny best may be described by a variety of intercorrelated concepts such as internal locus of control, motivation, volition, and self-efficacy. When an individual has a vision or sense of destiny about future activity, events, and involvement, that image serves to stimulate planning and to direct behavior; the image becomes an incentive for present behavior.

The goals of Operation Houndstooth are twofold. First, we have examined the scientific research that has been conducted on the components described above. The two-directional arrows in Figure 4.2 are intended to point out the many interactions that take place between and among these six components. I will refer to these components as co-cognitive factors because they interact with and enhance the cognitive traits that we ordinarily associate with success in school and the overall development of human abilities. The literature reviews and empirical research that resulted in the identification of these components can be found by visiting the framework's Web site (http://www.gifted.uconn.edu/oht/houndst.html). The first phase of our research includes clarifying definitions and identifying, adapting, and constructing assessment procedures that have extended our understanding of the components, especially in young people.

A major assumption underlying this project is that all of the components defined in our background research are subject to modification. Thus, the second phase consists of a series of experimental studies to determine how various school-related interventions can promote the types of behavior defined within the respective components. These interventions draw upon existing and newly developed techniques that can be used within various school and extracurricular contexts.

This article examines practical applications of our research by describing exemplars of the work of young people who have displayed these traits and the opportunities, resources, and encouragement that led to participation in experiences that promote the kinds of positive human concerns that are the raw material of increased social capital. It is important to point out that we are in the early stages of trying to understand very complex concepts that contribute to the development of socially responsible behaviors. Definitive answers to questions about promoting larger amounts of social capital as a national goal may be years away, but it is my hope that this article will motivate other investigators to sense the importance of this challenge and pursue studies that will contribute to our understanding of this complex concept. It also is my hope that school personnel will begin to think about steps that they can take now to make changes in the ways we promote in young people some of the virtues discussed below. Earlier is better! Howard Gardner has commented on the importance of early experiences in acquiring enduring habits of mind: "Research shows that when children are young they develop what you might call intuitive theories. It's like powerful engravings on your brain. Teachers don't realize how powerful they are, but early theories don't disappear, they stay on the ground" (as quoted in Kogan, 2000, p. 66). Wouldn't it be nice if we began engravings that will lead to societal improvements rather than the status, materialism, and self-indulgence that is so prevalent in the lifestyles of many of our young people?

How Can Schools Develop Houndstooth Components?

Although political controversy frequently has surrounded the role that schools should play in dealing with noncognitive abilities, character development and the moral, ethical, and

affective growth of young people have been a major concern
of educators since ancient times. The Houndstooth components certainly have implications for these noncognitive characteristics; however, the focus of this initiative, and the reason
I refer to them as co-cognitive factors, is that they support the
growth of cognitive attributes such as academic achievement,
research skills, creativity, and problem-solving skills. They also
have important implications for the development of high levels of motivation, interpersonal skills, and organizational and
management skills. Before discussing how to create learning
environments that nurture Houndstooth characteristics, there
are a few cautions we should acknowledge about things we
know don't work when it comes to instilling in young people the kinds of co-cognitive traits we have focused on in our
research. Direct teaching about these more complex capacities through prescriptive lessons simply doesn't work—you
can't teach or preach vision or sense of destiny. And, although
structured simulations of so-called "real-life" experiences and
group process training activities may familiarize students with
noncognitive traits, these approaches have not been highly successful in internalizing complex beliefs, behaviors, and commitments to action-oriented involvement. Long histories of
religious training and attempts over the centuries by govern-
ments to indoctrinate the young into one belief or another have
generally yielded minimal results. A recent *Phi Delta Kappan*
article (Glanzer, 2001) described communist moral education
programs as "tragic failures," and warned American educators
to be cautious about promoting lists of virtues, slogans, or aph-
orisms that serve political agendas. Just as attempts to legislate
morality or to brainwash people into believing or acting in certain ways have failed to produce lasting effects, so also will we
fail if we attempt to "teach" optimism or sensitivity to human
concerns through direct instruction. We also should avoid
requiring students to participate in programs and projects that
someone thinks will promote the more complex characteristics
and behaviors identified in Operation Houndstooth. Required
community service or forcing uncommitted young people to
participate in projects based on someone else's values or altruis-

tic goals often results in minimal and sometimes even reluctant compliance with yet another prescribed activity.

How then can we go about promoting the capacities represented in this expanded conception of giftedness? The answer lies in providing young people with a systematic approach to: (1) examining their individual abilities, interests, and learning styles; (2) exploring areas of potential involvement based on existing or developing interests; (3) providing them with the opportunities, resources, and encouragement for firsthand investigative or creative experiences within their chosen areas of interest; and (4) becoming involved oneself so that students can see positive traits being modeled by adults. All learning and personal growth resulting from these experiences, both cognitive and co-cognitive, take place within the context of work that students carry out with the primary purpose of having an impact on one or more intended audiences.

Examining Abilities, Interests, and Learning Styles

The best examples of positive behaviors identified in the Houndstooth research have resulted from students who have a good picture of their strengths. Although academic strengths usually are obvious and well-known by both students and teachers, information about interests, learning styles, thinking styles, and preferences for various modes of expression may require some guided exploration. Through a vehicle called the Total Talent Portfolio (TTP; Purcell & Renzulli, 1998) we have helped students gain insights into both general and specific areas of interest, the types of learning environments and adult and/or peer interactions they prefer in various learning situations, and their preferred modes of thinking and expression. Students achieve autonomy and ownership of the TTP by assuming major responsibility for the selection of items to be included, maintaining and regularly updating the portfolio, and setting personal goals by making decisions about items in the portfolio upon which they might like to elaborate. Although teachers should serve as guides in the portfolio review process, the ultimate goal is to create autonomy in students by turning control for the management of the portfolio over to them. The major purposes of the TTP are:

1. To **collect** several different types of information that portrays a student's strength areas and to regularly update this information.

2. To **classify** this information into the general categories of abilities, interests, learning styles, and related markers of successful learning such as organizational skills, content area preferences, personal and social skills, preferences for creative productivity, and commitments to beliefs, causes, and values.

3. To periodically **review and analyze** the information in order to make purposeful decisions about regular curricular enrichment opportunities and participation in special projects and extracurricular activities.

The portfolio also can be used for communicating with parents and for assisting students in the exploration of electives, extracurricular options, and career choices. The unique feature of the TTP is its focus on strengths and high-end learning behaviors. A tradition exists in education that has caused us to use student records mainly for spotting deficiencies. Our adherence to the medical (i.e., diagnostic-prescriptive) model has almost always been pointed in a negative direction: "Find out what's wrong with them and fix them up!" Strength assessment emphasizes the most positive aspects of each student's learning behaviors. Documentation should be carried out by inserting in the portfolio any and all information that calls attention to strong interests, preferred styles of learning, and high levels of motivation, creativity, and leadership, as well as the academic strengths that can be used as stepping stones to more advanced learning experiences. The theme of the Total Talent Portfolio might best be summarized in the form of two questions: What are the very *best* things we know and can record about a student? What are the very best things we can *do* to capitalize on this information?

Exploring Areas of Potential Involvement

Houndstooth capacities develop when students become passionately involved in an area of personal choice. The best way to promote such involvement is to expose young people to dynamic experiences within their general area(s) of interest. Speakers who deliver powerful messages about important topics are one way of stimulating active involvement in a particular area. A key feature of presentations designed to promote student involvement is the passion and commitment of the speakers. Our experience has shown that the more dynamic the presentation, the greater the likelihood of triggering follow-up action on the parts of one or more students.

A powerful presentation to middle school students by the young leader of Free the Children, an advocacy group that addresses child labor issues around the world, resulted in a multiyear commitment on the part of a student in Connecticut to work on this problem. She helped form several school chapters of the organization, raised money for the emancipation of children sold into servitude because of parental debt, and traveled to Pakistan to lobby officials about the use of child labor in the rug making industry.

A presentation by a local scientist about the hazardous effects of acid rain resulted in a yearlong collection and analysis of precipitation specimens by a group of elementary school students. Interviews with environmental department officials, examinations of reports by fish and wildlife agencies, and advanced training in chemical analysis procedures provided the background for a very professional final report that contributed data to a Northeast regional environmental impact study. The study eventually resulted in the enactment of regulations on power plant emissions.

Another way to stimulate intensive involvement is by visits to places where research or creative activity of a consequential nature is taking place. Once again, understanding students' interests and learning styles also helps to economize resources that are used to stimulate interests and problem-focusing activities. Thus, for example, a group of high school students who expressed a strong interest in athletics and recreation visited a newly constructed recreation center in their city. They were given opportunities to talk with their city's recreation director and to visit and photograph other recreation facilities. Under the guidance of a teacher who shared their interest, they also took field trips to neighboring communities, examined many books and articles about community recreation, and sent away for brochures and catalogues distributed by the manufacturers of recreation equipment. They compared differences between and among communities in their region, discussed various ways in which recreational facilities in their city could be improved, and subsequently developed a very sophisticated proposal for a citywide bicycle path system. After a great deal of advocacy through a public information campaign, an analysis of costs and potential benefits to their city and political action directed toward the recreation department and city council, their proposal was approved and funds were allocated to build bicycle paths in high traffic sections of the city.

Participation in lively discussions about controversial issues, events, books, and media presentations is another way to stimulate intensive follow-up on the parts of individuals and small groups. A lively classroom discussion and debate about nuclear energy motivated a group of middle school students in Richland, WA, a city that grew up around the development of the nuclear industry, to study the 1986 Chernobyl disaster in the Soviet Union. After extensive background research, the students contacted a group of students in the Ukrainian city of Slavutych, which was created following the Chernobyl reactor meltdown. Using almost daily e-mails and frequent videoconferences, the students explored common concerns, exchanged ideas for research projects and essay topics, traded photos, and conducted interviews about attitudes and influences of nuclear facilities in their respective cities. Research focused on environmental impact, employment and economic issues, and the deep and profound influences that living in nuclear communities have on the daily lives of young people and adults. After 18 months of intense involvement in this work, the students jointly published a hardcover book of their essays presented in both English and Ukrainian. The book, entitled *Nuclear Legacy: Students of Two Atomic Cities,* includes many color photographs plus historical photos of their respective cities.

Experiences that may trigger the types of student involvement described above also can take place outside of school, so it is important for students to know that the school, and especially any special programs or independent study options, are inviting places where they can "take" their interests to get the help they need. Orientation about opportunities for the types of involvement described above, a referral process that will connect students with teachers or community mentors who have interest and expertise in various areas of student curiosity or potential involvement, and guidelines for teachers and mentors are important considerations for producing the kinds of intense participation described above. Presentations of student work at assemblies and through newsletters and displays are good ways to awaken other students to the opportunities that they might like to pursue. Public relations information also is a good way to inform parents and the general public about high-level student achievement that is different from the present-day obsession with test scores.

The projects described above are profound illustrations of the behaviors we have been attempting to study and develop in Operation Houndstooth. Interviews with these students (as well as numerous others who engaged in similar endeavors) consistently showed remarkable degrees of optimism, a sense of power to change things, and a romance (sometimes bordering on passion) with the work they were doing. Students talked about their work with "stars in their eyes," frequently recounting clever and creative ways in which they overcame obstacles. Although they did not speak of themselves as being courageous, their actions in tackling difficult problems and the physical and mental energy they expended clearly attested to their willingness to challenge existing practices and to address issues above and beyond typical curricular topics. In all cases, an underlying theme was "we changed things . . . we made something happen." And, it was not uncommon for students to report that their involvement in these types of projects influenced the things they wanted to study in college and pursue in their careers. This finding is consistent with biographical accounts of how the lives of persons committed to social action were frequently influenced by early experiences. Perhaps the most important outcome was the sheer enjoyment students experienced from this type of learning. Many pointed out the contrast between these ventures and the increasing pressure they are under to do well on objective tests. "Why can't all school be like this?" was a typical comment when asked to compare the regular school curriculum with their investigative or creative projects.

The work that these students did also illustrates a number of programmatic and pedagogical issues underlying the development of Houndstooth characteristics. Although all students might have benefited in varying degrees from the experiences made available to the groups and individuals described above, the high degree of follow-up and the commitment to work over long periods of time undoubtedly resulted from the fact that the supplementary opportunities and resources were made available to groups or individuals that expressed strong interests in particular topics. And, because there are no right answers to the problems posed in this type of learning, teachers took on a very different role and relationship with students. They became the proverbial guide-on-the-side rather than the disseminator of information. They helped students develop plans of operation, identify and secure resources, learn the investigative skills necessary for addressing their work, and develop procedures for identifying and approaching target audiences. In the group projects, teachers helped students appreciate divisions of labor and the importance of mutual cooperation and respect. One teacher commented " . . . this is what I always thought teaching was about" and another teacher said that working with students in this type of situation was better "training" about how to be a good teacher than the hundreds of hours of in-service training through which he had sat.

The Role of Gifted and General Education
in Leadership Training

The history and culture of mankind can be charted to a large extent by the creative contributions of the world's most gifted and talented men and women. Advocates for special services for the gifted regularly invoke the names of persons such as Thomas Edison, Marie Curie, Jonas Salk, Isadora Duncan, and Albert Einstein as a rationale for providing supplementary resources to improve the educational experiences of potentially gifted young people. If we assume that it has, indeed, been these people who have created the science, culture, and wisdom of centuries past, then it also is safe to assume that persons who are the stewards and nurturers of today's potentially able young people can have a profound effect on shaping the values and directions toward which our society's future contributors of remarkable accomplishments devote their energies. Such stewardship is an awesome responsibility, and yet it has some intriguing overtones, because the names of persons who will be added to the lists of Edisons and Einsteins are in our homes and classrooms today. It also is important to point out that this stewardship does not rest solely with teachers who are directly responsible for gifted programs. Aubyn did, in fact, do her work as part of a special program for the gifted, but many other instances of creative productivity and problem solving by young people are guided by teachers in general education programs. In spite of our best efforts to identify students for special programs, predicting who will be our most gifted contributors is still a very inexact science. What is even more significant, so far as our work on Operation Houndstooth is concerned, is that by expanding our conception of giftedness beyond traditional high scoring test-takers and good lesson-learners, we will find as rich a source of high-potential young people in broad and diverse populations of nonselected students as we find in students traditionally selected for gifted programs. Houndstooth factors are independent of the traditional normal curve approach to identifying gifted potentials. Said another way, does anybody really care about the test scores or grade point average of people like Aubyn, Mother Theresa, or Martin Luther King, Jr.?

Houndstooth Intervention Theory

Our examination of the co-cognitive factors that influence the development of abilities, creativity, and task commitment parallels a great deal of theory and research that has looked at other noncognitive concerns such as social and emotional development, the development of self-concept and self-efficacy, character development, and the development of attitudes and values. Untold numbers of studies have examined the effects of various programmatic approaches that influence these types of development among persons who have experienced a range of adjustment problems and within the contexts of promoting positive, beneficial adjustment in healthy individuals and groups. Such approaches include a wide range of therapies, individual and group counseling techniques, social and psychological experimental treatments, and a broad array of educational interventions. Because the focus of Operation Houndstooth draws upon the theory and direction established in the emerging field of positive psychology, and because our own interest is the constructive development of gifted behaviors rather than healing maladaptive conditions, the research reviewed in this chapter generally focuses on school-related opportunities and alternatives for the development of positive changes in the generally healthy population of young people.

It is difficult to organize a categorical inventory of the large amount of information available on noncognitive approaches to positive development because several recommended approaches range across what might form the parameters of discrete categories. We have, nevertheless, attempted to examine recommended practices and related research with an eye toward the most common characteristics of particular approaches. Based on literature reviews, we have divided these approaches into six areas, ranging from what research indicates as the least powerful to the most powerful approaches for making strong attitudinal and behavioral changes in students (Vess & Halbur, 2003).

Because one of our major concerns is the *internalization* of behaviors that eventually leads to the development of both a value system and the capacity to act upon positive characteristics, we have tended to view each category with an eye toward awareness versus a more deeply ingrained manifestation of certain values and behaviors. A graphic representation of Houndstooth Intervention Theory is presented in Figure 4.3.

Before reviewing the six approaches included in the Houndstooth Intervention Theory, it is important to point out that each approach may contribute in varying degrees to positive growth.

The Rally-Round-the-Flag Approach

This approach, sometimes referred to by others as "the cheerleading method," involves visual displays (posters, banners, bulletin boards) featuring certain values, slogans, or examples of virtuous or desired behaviors. Also included are verbal slogans delivered over the school's public address system or presented orally in classrooms and at assemblies. The rationale for this approach to promoting values, virtues, morality, and character development is that a steady regimen of affirmations and positive messages result in desirable beliefs, attitudes, and behaviors in young people.

In Tarkington School in Wheeling, IL, lists of behavioral and academic expectations are posted throughout the school (Murphy, 1998). These moral codes are known to students as "Tarkington Tiger Traits." The traits exemplify desirable characteristics of citizenship.

The Gold Star Approach

This approach is not unlike the ways in which we traditionally have rewarded students for good academic work. The approach makes use of techniques such as providing positive reinforcement through merit badges, placement on "citizen-of-the-week" lists, extolling good behavior at award assemblies or other events, and even having students earn points, gold stars,

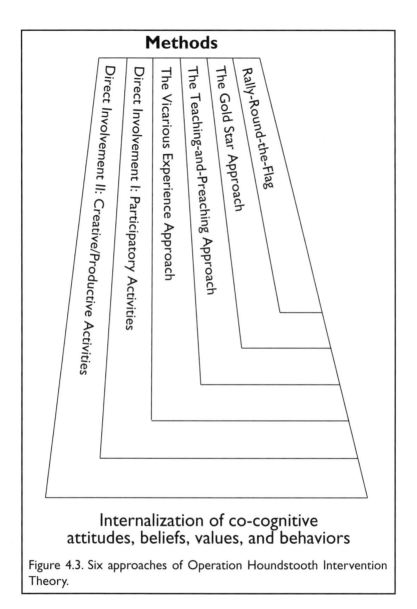

Methods

Direct Involvement II: Creative/Productive Activities

Direct Involvement I: Participatory Activities

The Vicarious Experience Approach

The Teaching-and-Preaching Approach

The Gold Star Approach

Rally-Round-the-Flag

Internalization of co-cognitive
attitudes, beliefs, values, and behaviors

Figure 4.3. Six approaches of Operation Houndstooth Intervention
Theory.

or other tokens that can be exchanged for prizes or privileges. Based on classic behaviorism, the rationale underlying this approach is that positive reinforcement for desirable behaviors will increase the frequency of these behaviors. Although providing positive feedback for desirable behaviors may produce greater awareness about the issues under consideration, and even more desired behaviors in situations in which rewards may be earned, the importance of students' actions so far as internal beliefs and values are concerned may be of secondary consequence when compared to the award being offered for good behavior.

One prevalent program that utilizes the gold star approach is Girl Scouts of America. The four program goals of the Girl Scouts are to develop self-potential, to relate to others, to develop values, and to contribute to society. Scouts are rewarded with pins, badges, patches, and awards in return for demonstrating desirable behaviors. More information about the Girl Scouts of America can be obtained at http://www.girlscouts.org/program. Research regarding the effectiveness of Girl Scouts is varied. Some studies claim that the program helps to enable moral development, while other studies question the efficacy of the program (Dubas & Snider, 1993; Smalt, 1997).

The Teaching-and-Preaching Approach

The direct teaching of noncognitive material is probably the most frequently used method to promote attitudes and behaviors related to character and value development. This approach resembles the kinds of training commonly used over the centuries in religious instruction and in situations in which allegiance to particular ideologies is the goal of persons responsible for the curriculum. The direct teaching approach spans a broad range of techniques ranging from recitation and drills about desirable beliefs and behaviors that require students to repeat back slogans or answer in prescribed ways ("What is meant by honesty?"), to dialogue, discussions, and debate about character- or value-laden issues. The direct teaching approach might include discussions based on fiction, films, and videos, or examinations of personal characteristics or decision points by noteworthy persons portrayed in biographies, autobiographies, or other nonfiction genres.

One example of a teaching and preaching program is Character Counts, which uses six pillars of character: trustworthiness, respect, responsibility, fairness, caring, and citizenship. The program was developed by the Josephson Institute and more information can be found at its Web site: http://www. charactercounts.org/defsix.htm. Through lessons, students learn of historical figures who have exemplified each of these pillars of character. For example, when learning about citizenship, they will study Dorothea Dix who pioneered better conditions for the mentally ill; and when learning about trustworthiness, they will study Pat Tillman, who sacrificed millions of dollars when he left the NFL to join the U.S. Army after the attacks on America in September of 2001[2]. Through learning about these heroes and heroines (the program has an outline of 48 specific heroes and heroines), they will see examples of people who have embodied the six pillars of character. Ideally, the students then will want to emulate the behaviors of these people. Programs such as Character Counts arguably are the most common types of teaching-and-preaching programs used in America today.

The Vicarious Experience Approach

This approach often is used as an extension of direct teaching; however, it uses techniques that place students in situations in which they are expected to experience a particular personal or emotional reaction to situations in which a specified non-cognitive goal is being pursued. Role-playing, dramatization, and simulations of significant or critical incidents are examples of the vicarious experience approach. The rationale underlying this approach is that deep and enduring effects on attitudes, values, or character must be experienced at a more active and participatory level than merely learning about them through general awareness or direct teaching approaches. For example, Nucci (1987) stated higher levels of moral reasoning can be fostered through the use of dilemma discussions in classrooms.

The Markkula Center for Applied Ethics, an organization based at Santa Clara University in California, provides a character education program entitled Character-Based Literacy. In this program, students study plays, poems, and novels. These

---

2   Sadly, Pat Tillman was killed in action in Iraq.

literary devices initially are used to teach reading and writing. Then students critically discuss the characters in the literature, often trying to place themselves in the situation or environment of the character in order to reflect on and internalize values such as integrity, self-control, and respect. Units include responsibility, self-direction, self-control, respect, integrity, moderation, and justice. This approach is very similar to its precursor, the teaching-and-preaching approach, but it seeks to more highly internalize the values it teaches by asking students to take on the role of the character (Markkula Center for Applied Ethics, 2003).

Direct Involvement–I

Many people believe that the best way to internalize non-cognitive characteristics is to provide young people with experiences in which they come into direct contact with situations and events where affective behaviors are taking place. Commonly referred to as *service learning*, it includes community service, internships that deal with provisions for helping others or remediating injurious events, and participation in events where social or political action is being formulated or taking place.

According to the U. S. Bureau of Labor Statistics (2007), 26.6% of teenage females and 22.5% of teenage males engaged in some type of volunteer activity, which may be attributed to an increased emphasis on volunteerism in schools. Many schools require their students to volunteer at local organizations. Volunteering exposes students to situations and experiences that they may not have been exposed to previously and thus raises their awareness about local, national, and global issues. Although promoting this exposure moves students in a positive direction, it may not help them internalize the co-cognitive factors if it is a forced requirement rather than an involvement based on a personalized commitment on the part of students.

Direct Involvement–II

This type of direct involvement consists of situations in which young people take an active leadership role to bring about some kind of positive social, educational, environmental, or political change—especially change that promotes justice, peace, or more harmonious relations between individuals and groups. In most instances, the fact that a young person has made a personal commitment to pursue a change-oriented course of action means that certain positive attitudes or values already are present, but putting the values or character traits into action helps to solidify and deepen the commitment to particular beliefs. The rationale for this type of involvement is that a deep internalization of positive attitudes and attendant behaviors has a more enduring influence on developing wisdom, a satisfying lifestyle, and a lifelong value system than quick-fix behavioral changes that may result from experiences that do not culminate in personally fulfilling activities based on action-oriented involvement.

In 2000, Stacy Hillman read in a magazine that police dogs were in need of bulletproof and stab-proof vests (ICGate Inc., 2004). Stacy, then 10 years old, decided that she could help by raising money. She began by approaching the local police chief to tell him her plan. She placed a picture of her with a police dog on collection bottles and put them in vet's offices and pet stores to collect donations. Today, Stacy is the president of the charity Pennies to Protect Police Dogs. Stacy's story serves as a good example of the second direct involvement approach because she took an active leadership role to bring about change.

Adding It All Up

The internalization of co-cognitive attitudes, beliefs, values, and behaviors cannot be achieved through any one of these interventions alone. Schools should adopt several approaches. If our goal is to move more students toward initiating action and promoting social capital, then our schools need to provide them with more opportunities to achieve higher levels of social engagement.

The progression of individuals through the levels of the Houndstooth interventions mirrors the progression through Kohlberg's (1978) stages of moral development. At any stage, one can understand all stages up to their current level of involvement, but can only be influenced by their current stage of moral development. As a basis for moral development, rules are placed upon young people both in societies and schools, such as in the rally-round-the-flag approach, gold star approach, and teaching-and-preaching approach. These methods are effective for students in the preconventional stage in Kohlberg's theory. The vicarious experience approach, as well as direct involvement I, are more appropriate methods for use with students who have reached the conventional level. It is during this stage that students gain an understanding of their place in society according to societal norms. Reaching the level of postconventional thought allows students to examine societal rules in order to establish their own moral relativism. Prior to this stage, students are unable to take a critical view of ethical principles and simply accept the standards with which they are presented. The direct involvement II intervention is most effective for students at the postconventional level because it enables them to evaluate and resolve societal deficits.

Kohlberg (1978) reported that only 20% of the adult population will reach the postconventional stage of thinking. Progression through the stages is not guaranteed. Progression necessitates continued exposure to advanced stages of moral reasoning. Schools have the potential to promote internalization of the co-cognitive factors needed to progress toward postconventional thought through a myriad of experiences at all levels of the Houndstooth Intervention Theory. Social capital only can be enhanced by members of society who have achieved this level.

Conclusion

The goal of Operation Houndstooth is to instill in students the six co-cognitive factors mentioned previously: optimism, courage, romance with a topic/discipline, sensitivity to human concerns, physical/mental energy, and vision/sense of destiny. These are traits that many gifted students already exhibit and may adopt quickly. Each level of the Houndstooth Intervention Theory leads students closer and closer to the constructive development of gifted behaviors and the internalization of the co-cognitive factors. Students like Stacy and Aubyn have become creative producers at the highest level of the Houndstooth Intervention Theory by internalizing a combination of the six co-cognitive traits. By employing this intervention, schools will encourage a new generation of students to use their gifts in socially constructive ways and seek ways to improve the lives of others rather than merely using their talents for economic gain, self-indulgence, and the exercise of power without a commitment to contribute to the improvement of life and resources on the planet.

Are the Goals of Operation Houndstooth Realistic?

There have been times in the history of civilization when the zeitgeist has resulted in elevating a society's values toward concerns that emphasize the production of social capital. The focus on democracy in Ancient Greece, the ascendancy of the arts during the Renaissance, and the elevation of man as a logical and rational thinker during the Reformation are examples of times when entire cultures and societies brought new ways of thinking to bear on issues that enriched the lives of people. And, even in our own country, there were times when our culture placed a higher value on a sense of community and the dedication of individual and group efforts toward improvement of the greater good. In 1830, Alexis de Tocqueville, the French philosopher and celebrated commentator on our emerging democracy, wrote about the need and desire for civil associations of all kinds on the parts of Americans who, he observed, worked together with their fellow citizens toward common goals. "Americans of all ages, all conditions, and all dispositions constantly form associations . . . ," he noted. "Nothing in my opinion is more deserving of our attention than the intellectual and moral associations of America" (de Tocqueville, 1945, p. 109). de Tocqueville went so far as to say that the key to making democracy work in America was the propensity of our ancestors to form all kinds of civic associations—to view the building of community as important as personal success and prosperity. If, as studies have shown, self-interest has replaced some of the values that created a more socially conscious early America, and if the negative trends of young people's overindulgences and disassociations are growing, then we must ask if there is a role that schools can play in gently influencing future citizens and, especially future leaders, toward a value system that assumes greater responsibility for the production of social capital.

Look around—everything is going faster. The average soundbite by persons running for President of the United States is less than 30 seconds. We've traded in-depth stories in *The New York Times* and *Atlantic Magazine* for the six o'clock news and *USA Today,* and we've replaced reading a good biography with a quick trip through *People* magazine. Fed Ex, cell phones, e-mail, round-the-clock stock trading, and drive-thru breakfasts are the way many people run their lives. And, we also have sped up other things that should be important reflections of the *quality* of life. Recent studies have shown that we spend less than 31 minutes a day caring for our children and 7 minutes caring for our pets. Each day adult college graduates spend 16 minutes or less per day reading nonwork-related material, and young married couples spend an average of 4 minutes a day engaged in anything that in polite company we might call romantic encounters! Our fast-paced world and scientific technology have created the mechanisms of production and consumerism that define the present American way of life, but they also have created a mindset that sees the world as an endless resource for consumption. Nowhere is this mindset more evident than in the lifestyles of young people. And, who can blame them when they are subjected to an educational system that focuses mostly on skills that will give them a competitive advantage in the marketplace and a commercial media establishment that barrages young people with constant messages about consumption and material gain?

Is it beyond our vision as educators to imagine a role for schools that can influence the future leaders of the new century in ways that would help them acquire values that result in the production of social capital, as well as material consumption and economic gain? The general goal of this work is to infuse into the overall process of schooling experiences related to the Houndstooth components that will contribute to the development of wisdom and a satisfying lifestyle. It would be naïve to think that a redirection of educational goals can take place without a commitment at all levels to examine the purposes of education in a democracy. It also is naïve to think that experiences directed toward the production of social capital can, or are even intended to, replace our present-day focus on material productivity and intellectual capital. Rather, this work seeks to enhance the development of wisdom and a satisfying lifestyle that are paralleled by concerns for diversity, balance, harmony, and proportion in all of the choices and decisions that young people make in the process of growing up. What people think and decide to do drives some of society's best ideas and achievements. If we want leaders who will promote ideas and achievements that take into consideration the components we have identified in Operation Houndstooth, then giftedness in the new century will have to be redefined in ways that take these co-cognitive components into account. And, the strategies that are used to develop giftedness in young people will need to give as much attention to the co-cognitive conditions of development as we presently give to cognitive development.

Although there is no silver bullet or institutional fix for infusing these components into the curriculum or creating a greater awareness about the need to produce more social capital, there are things that lend feasibility to this endeavor. First, the entire positive psychology movement is growing in popularity and promises to enhance research endeavors of the type we are pursuing. Second, already completed research in psychology, sociology, and anthropology clearly indicate that these co-cognitive traits can be assessed (at varying levels of precision) and that the environment in general, and schooling in particular, can nurture and influence the components we have identified in Operation Houndstooth. Third, economists have pointed out the benefits of a reciprocal relationship between material and social capital, and many social, political, spiritual, and educational commentators have indicated that nurturing these traits must become an imperative.

We are only in the early stages on this path toward once again attempting to expand the definition of giftedness. We believe that an expanded definition will not only help us understand the unique contributions of persons who have used their talents to make the world a better place, it also will help us to extend supplementary opportunities and services to potentially able young people who have been overlooked because of the overemphasis of cognitive traits in the identification of giftedness. Each area of inquiry brings us closer to understanding the complexity of the concepts, identifying promising practices and assessment techniques that are being used in present and future scientific studies, and bringing this message forward to interested educators. Although the whole notion of changing the big picture seems awesome and overwhelming, the words of Margaret Mead remind us that it can be done: "Never doubt that a small group of thoughtful, committed citizens can change the world . . . indeed, it is the only thing that ever does."

References

de Tocqueville, A. (1945). *Democracy in America* (Vol. 2). New York: Alfred A. Knopf.

Dubas, J. S., & Snider, B. A. (1993). The role of community-based youth groups in enhancing learning and achievement through nonformal education. In R. M. Lerner (Ed.), *Early adolescence: Perspectives on research, policy, and intervention*. Hillsdale, NJ: Lawrence Erlbaum.

Gagné, F. (1985). Giftedness and talent: Reexamining a reexamination of the definitions. *Gifted Child Quarterly, 29*, 103–112.

Gardner, H. (1983). *Frames of mind: The theory of multiple intelligences.* New York: Basic Books.

Glanzer, P. L. (2001). Exit interviews: Learning about character education from post-Soviet educators. *Phi Delta Kappan, 82,* 691–693.

ICGate Inc. (2004). *Pennies to protect police dogs.* Retrieved March 10, 2004, from http://www.penniestoprotectpolicedogs.org/en-us

Kogan, M. (2000). Teaching truth, beauty, and goodness. [An interview with Howard Gardner]. *Monitor on Psychology, 31*(12), 66–67.

Kohlberg, L. (1978). The cognitive-developmental approach to moral education. In P. Scharf (Ed.), *Readings in moral education* (pp. 36–51). Minneapolis, MN: Winston Press.

LaBonte, R. (1999). Social capital and community development: Practitioner emptor. *Australian and New Zealand Journal of Public Health, 23,* 430–433.

Larson, R. W. (2000). Toward a psychology of positive youth development. *American Psychologist, 15,* 170–183.

Markkula Center for Applied Ethics. (2003). *Character based literacy program.* Retrieved March 2, 2004, from http://www.scu.edu/ethics/publications/cblp

Mönks, F. J. (1991). Kann wissenschaftliche argumentation auf aktulität verzichten? [Are scientific arguments dispensable in the discussion on identification of the gifted?] *Zeitschrift für Entwicklungspsychologie und Pädagogische Psychologie, 23,* 232–240.

Murphy, M. M. (1998). *Character education in America's blue ribbon schools.* Lancaster, PA: Technomic Publishing Company.

Nucci, L. (1987). Synthesis of research on moral development. *Educational Leadership, 44*(5), 86–92.

Portes, A. (1998). Social capital: Its origins and applications in modern sociology. *Annual Review of Sociology, 24,* 1–24.

Purcell, J. H., & Renzulli, J. S. (1998). *Total talent portfolio: A systematic plan to identify and nurture gifts and talents.* Mansfield Center, CT: Creative Learning Press.

Putnam, R. (1993). *Making democracy work: Civic traditions in modern Italy.* Princeton: Princeton University Press.

Putnam, R. (1995). Bowling alone: America's declining social capital. *Journal of Democracy, 6,* 65–78.

Renzulli, J. S. (1978). What makes giftedness? Re-examining a definition. *Phi Delta Kappan, 60,* 180–184.

Seligman, M. E. P. (1991). *Learned optimism.* New York: Knopf.

Seligman, M. E. P., & Csikszentmihalyi, M. (2000). Positive psychology. *American Psychologist, 55,* 5–14.

Seligman, M. E. P., Reivich, K., Jaycox, L., & Gillham, J. (1995). *The optimistic child*. New York: Houghton Mifflin.

Smalt, R. H. (1997). *The influence of Girl Scouting as a character-building organization on the moral development of young Girl Scouts.* Unpublished doctoral dissertation, Fordham University, New York.

Sternberg, R. J., & Davidson, J. E. (1986). *Conceptions of giftedness*. New York: Cambridge University Press.

Tannenbaum, A. J. (1986). Giftedness: A psychosocial approach. In R. J. Sternberg & J. E. Davidson (Eds.), *Conceptions of giftedness* (pp. 21–52). New York: Cambridge University Press.

U.S. Bureau of Labor Statistics. (2007). *Volunteering in the United States, 2007.* Retrieved June 11, 2008, from http://www.bls.gov/news. release/volun.nr0.htm

Vess, K. A., & Halbur, D. A. (2003). *Character education: What counselor educators need to know.* Greensboro, NC: ERIC Clearinghouse and Student Services. (ERIC Document Reproduction Service No. ED475389)

CHAPTER 5

Affective Curriculum and Instruction for Gifted Learners

Joyce VanTassel-Baska

Affective curriculum is a topic more honored in the breach than in the observance. Several reasons may account for this neglect. One might be that educators of the gifted have shied away from creating programs that are viewed as "soft," and affective curriculum carries that label because of the difficulty associated with assessing learning. Another reason might be that limited resources tend to drive out an emphasis on areas that are considered marginal. Or, biases against the sense of need in this area by educators also could impact the paucity of development.

So, why is it so important to include an emphasis on affective curriculum for gifted learners? We have several valid reasons for doing so:

1. Feelings drive thinking—The work of Damasio (1994, 1999) and other neurological researchers suggest that thought is triggered by the stimulus of emotion. We feel, which in turn, encourages cognitive brain activity. If these studies are correct, then focusing on a student's emotional state should be an important motivational tool for enhancing learning. Goleman (1993) has suggested that people cannot remember, attend, learn, or make clear decisions when they are emotionally upset.

2. Research in gifted education past and present suggests that attention needs to be paid to the social and emotional side of gifted learners because they are vulnerable in many aspects on this dimension of development. Since Terman (1925) and Hollingworth (1926), we have known that the picture of the puny, myopic "egghead" as the embodiment of giftedness is a myth, and that gifted children are more likely to be healthy, attractive, active youngsters with above-average emotional stability, personalities, and social competence (Colangelo & Davis, 1991; Noble, Robinson, & Gunderson, 1993; Oram, Cornell, & Rutemiller, 1995). Yet, we also know that expectations for performance from these children without taking into account the emotional and social dimensions of their lives exacts a cost in social relationships, as well as the development of a healthy self-concept (Robinson, 2001). Such students may be under stress due to career indecision or internal struggles that serve to isolate them (Plucker & Levy, 2001).

3. Research on motivation and will also suggest that conative characteristics appear to be underlying supports to the talent development process (Piechowski, 1998). Why is it that so many great contributions to society have been made by people who were not groomed for top-level performance for their period of time and field of study (Gruber, 1976)? Charlotte Brontë, for example, was a female writer who had to assume a male identity to be published, was motherless from the age of 5, lived in near poverty as the daughter of a church cleric, and lacked formal education and opportunities, yet managed to be a cornerstone of Victorian literature (VanTassel-Baska, 1995).

Finally, it is fair to note that there is a problematic mix of characteristics in many gifted learners that inhibits a smooth cognitive development pathway. Their often uneven development creates a sense of being out of sync with others and the world around them (Neihart, 2001; Silverman, 1993). The

American poet Frank O'Hara captures this feeling well in his poem, *Autobiographia Literaria*:

> When I was a child
> I played by myself in a
> corner of the schoolyard
> all alone.
>
> I hated dolls and I
> hated games, animals were
> not friendly and birds
> flew away.
>
> If anyone was looking
> for me I hid behind a
> tree and cried out "I am
> an orphan."
>
> And here I am, the
> center of all beauty!
> writing these poems!
> Imagine!

Their own rapid learning rate coupled with complex thought processes also contributes to these students' experiencing disequilibrium in many social contexts. Preference for complexity in thinking also can exacerbate social relationships in untold ways, causing a sense of being stigmatized (Coleman & Cross, 2001). Although gifted students may prefer individual responsibility, often they are not ready to assume the risks and pitfalls associated with negotiating a real-world situation.

Other characteristics associated with their emotional makeup also can be troublesome. Sensitivity can lead to problems of being hypercritical of self and others (Schuler, 2001). Questioning of authority can lead to problems in adult relationships, especially teachers and parents. Often the feedback mechanism in the lives of gifted children causes an interpretation of these differences as being inadequate and not living up to expectations which in turn can contribute to low self-concept, underachievement, and depression (Penzel, 2000).

Affective Components in a Gifted Program

Program developers need to consider several issues in developing an affective program for gifted learners. First of all, such a program must be deliberate and planned, not put in place in response to problems but rather proactively forged to prevent their occurrence. Secondly, it must be developed with an eye to developmental changes, acknowledging that needs will change as students mature but that some aspects of the plan need to continue from early childhood through adolescence. Finally, program development in the affective realm needs to consider the connections to cognitive development as well and serve as an appropriate catalyst for enhancing student productivity through the types of strategies employed.

The areas of an affective program for gifted learners ideally would contain the following components: self-assessment, philosophy of life, bibliotherapy, a talent development plan, and an emotional intelligence curriculum emphasis.

Self-Assessment

A key to strong social-emotional development is understanding how one fits in respect to predisposition, temperament, and ability. Helping students understand their abilities in light of their personalities, aptitudes, and interests is a critical component of any effective social-emotional emphasis in a gifted program. Consequently, giving a battery of relevant tests and interpreting test results in achievement, ability, aptitude, and vocational interests would seem prudent. Not all gifted people can become anything they want to be, based on predispositions, values, and personality (Achter, Lubinski, Benbow, & Eftekhari-Sanjani, 1999). Thus, helping them understand optimal matches early is a special need.

Philosophy of Life

Helping students discern their true values and beliefs, especially in the preteen years, can ward off problems during adolescence with excessive experimentation. Students need to start addressing the large questions of: How do I define "meaning" for myself? What do I believe and value? What are my life themes? Such questions then can lead to creating reflective journals where ideals are readily shared in a number of written and graphic forms.

Bibliotherapy

Much has been written about the use of bibliotherapy for gifted learners. Yet, continued use of both targeted literature and biography to help students understand themselves through characters and role models can be a useful tool at any age. Halsted's (2002) work is an exceptionally effective tool to promote affective insight into problems. Halsted has organized affective themes and assigned them to grade-level considerations and particular texts that she has arranged for easy use by readers.

Her grade 6–8 themes, for example, include: achievement, aloneness, arrogance, creativity, differentness, drive to understand, identity, intensity, introversion, moral concerns, perfectionism, relationship with others, sensitivity, and using ability.

Issue-based current fiction that has gifted children as protagonists also can be effective as a tool for discussions. Three examples in this category include:

- Tartt, Donna. *The Little Friend*. This novel has as its protagonist a 10-year-old gifted girl named Harriet who feels alienated from people in her world. The book explains the process by which she comes to understand the value of society as she searches for an explanation of her younger brother's death.
- Lamb, Wally. *She's Been Undone*. This novel chronicles the life of a 13-year-old who faces central issues of identity in the context of overcoming trauma. Told with authentic-

ity and humor, the reader identifies with the young girl's struggle to "get a grip" on life.

- Sebold, Alice. *The Lovely Bones*. This novel takes the perspective of a murdered young girl and the ways that a violent act affects the dynamics of family and friends left behind, taking a twist on the familiar dream of "looking down from heaven after you've died to see how sorry everyone will be." The novel transcends kitsch and offers a poignant portrait of hope and redemption.

These three novels all allow gifted students to see themselves in the fiction and to discuss affective issues of development at a safe distance.

Talent Development Plan

One way to ensure metacognitive control over the development of social-emotional areas of a student's life is to encourage the development of his own personal talent plan (Moon, 2003). Students need to develop their goals at each year of development, monitor progress across a year, and assess outcomes at the end of a year. Keeping a journal might be a part of recording worthwhile crystallizing experiences that occur during the year and linking them to a goal of the plan. Many schools for the gifted require student portfolios to demonstrate cognitive growth; these plans could exemplify affective growth across the same span of time as well. Goals could be affective, cognitive, and/or aesthetic with clear implementation strategies and resources to be outlined. A one-year plan example in the affective area for a 10-year-old boy might be:

1. *Goal:* To develop relationships with same-age peers
2. *Strategies:*
   a. Invite 1 or 2 boys over to my house to do an activity
   b. Get together with the boys on a weekly basis to discuss ideas
   c. Submit a project together for a school assignment
   d. Spend time together on activities of common interest

3. *Assessment of Progress:*
   a. Submitted project
   b. Journal of experiences

Emotional Intelligence

Although much rhetoric about emotional intelligence has not progressed to the level of sustained research, the work of Salovey and Mayer (Mayer & Salovey, 1997; Salovey, Bedell, Detweiler, & Mayer, 2000; Salovey & Mayer, 1990) has. Their continued work to develop a theoretical framework for understanding emotional intelligence and a test to assess it provide an important avenue for gifted curriculum developers to proceed with curriculum emphases at each relevant stage of development for K–12 learners in school. Mayer and Salovey (1997) define emotional intelligence as "the ability to perceive emotions, to access and generate emotions so as to assist thought, to understand emotions and emotional knowledge, and to reflectively regulate emotions so as to promote emotional and intellectual growth" (p. 5). This type of emphasis on emotional intelligence feeds into our concerns about gifted learners' development in this area and uses a metacognitive orientation to enhance student growth. Because it is defined well within a framework, approaches to assessment can be developed readily, and the overall structure supports existing gifted programs well, dispelling some of the more common criticisms leveled against including such an emphasis in a gifted program.

The following section of this chapter outlines each aspect of the emotional intelligence framework and includes a prototypical lesson that may be used as a model for translating framework ideas into discrete classroom use. It is presented for use in secondary classrooms, beginning at grade 6, but could be used throughout high school. It may be considered one manifestation of the prevention curriculum for gifted learners to be implemented by both counselors and teachers.

The Emotional Intelligence Framework:
Perception, Appraisal, and Expression of Emotion
    In a classroom setting, gifted students would be able to:

- Identify emotion in one's physical and psychological states. *Recognition of emotions such as anger.*
- Identify emotions in other people and objects. *How other people respond to us—what emotions we evoke (fear, dislike).*
- Express emotions accurately and to express needs related to those feelings. *Owning one's emotions to the extent of being able to depict them: "I am angry because . . ." "I feel stupid when I don't know an answer and need to be affirmed."*
- Discriminate between accurate and inaccurate, or honest and dishonest, expressions of feelings. *How to read social cues such as paying a compliment to someone authentically or recognizing sycophants (false flatterer).*

Sample Lesson 1 provides a lesson that educators can incorporate as a model for using the ideas in the perception, appraisal, and expression of emotion section of the framework.

Sample Lesson 1: Study of Emotion
Goal: To study emotion in self and others.
Outcome: Students will be able to analyze, evaluate, and express emotions in various forms.
Activities:

1. Analyze feelings based on your response to selected art, music, and poetry.
2. Express an emotion that frequently affects you in an artistic form of choice.
3. Evaluate a scene from a Shakespeare play for its emotional content, watch a film, or create a role-play scenario. What emotions are displayed? How authentic are they?
4. Use a real-world scenario to analyze your own and others' emotions.
5. Analyze your emotional response to stimuli.
6. Use any art form to express your emotions.

> 7. View your emotions as if you were looking down on yourself and make judgments about how you feel.
>
> **Assessment**: Prepare a written response that documents emotional understanding of a predetermined scenario. Provide *your* emotional response, as well as your understanding of others' emotions based on their perspectives represented in the scenario.

The Emotional Intelligence Framework:
Emotional Facilitation of Thinking

In a classroom setting, gifted students would be able to:

- Redirect and prioritize one's thinking based on the feelings associated with objects, events, and other people. *We come to like particular people who share values. These feelings produce a desire to spend more time together. We come up with projects to do in the company of these people. We form study groups, think tanks, and scholarly communities, which we see as priorities in our work schedule.*
- Generate or emulate vivid emotions to facilitate judgments and memories concerning feelings. *Call up emotions to cognitively reflect on them.*
- Capitalize on mood swings to take multiple points of view; ability to integrate these mood-induced perspectives. *Use emotional understanding of different selves.*
- Use emotional states to facilitate problem solving and creativity. *For example, feeling sad might lead you to write poetry. Feeling happy might cause you to work on a hard problem.*

Sample Lesson 2 provides a lesson that educators can incorporate as a model for using the ideas in the emotional facilitation of thinking section of the framework.

> *Sample Lesson 2: Channeling Emotion to Promote Thinking*
> **Goal**: To apply emotional understanding to cognitive tasks.
> **Outcome**: Students will be able to use emotional understanding to advance cognition.

Activities:

1. Use your understanding of emotional issues surrounding selected current events to craft an appropriate solution (e.g., understanding the emotions behind terrorism or the varied emotional reactions of people to the presidential candidates in the U.S.).
2. Analyze the emotional content of a given speech and its potential impact on an audience (e.g., judging the power of emotion, such as the impact of the Gettysburg Address on soldiers, families, and people in the local area).
3. Use your own given emotional state or memory of it to create a product of interest.

Assessment: Prepare a journal entry describing how you were able to employ emotion to enhance thinking.

The Emotional Intelligence Framework: Understanding and Analyzing Emotional Information; Employing Emotional Knowledge

In a classroom setting, gifted students would be able to:

- Understand how different emotions are related. *How does shame lead to anger?*
- Perceive the causes and consequences of feelings. *Unpleasant experiences with peers may lead to sadness, which leads to lowered achievement patterns.*
- Interpret complex feelings, such as emotional blends and contradictory feeling states. *A friend moves away. I am happy for her but sad for myself.*
- Understand and predict likely transitions between emotions. *Anticipating a joyful event produces positive feelings; the aftermath brings letdown or sadness.*

Sample Lesson 3 provides a lesson that educators can incorporate as a model for using the ideas in this section of the framework concentrating on understanding and analyzing emotional intelligence and employing emotional knowledge.

Sample Lesson 3: Developing and Applying Emotional Knowledge
Goal: To develop and apply emotional knowledge
Outcome: Students will be able to analyze and evaluate emotional content.
Activities:

1. Read selected books with a gifted protagonist who experiences emotional problems. (*Use bibliotherapy to describe the emotional state of characters.*)
2. Discuss the emotions displayed, their antecedents and consequences, and the ambiguity of individual emotional states.
3. Create a dialogue between two characters who are angry with one another over a misunderstanding. Show how their emotions change as they discuss their perspective. (*Use creative writing to demonstrate emotional knowledge.*)

Assessment: Assess the dialogue using a rubric that focuses on:

a. the ability to interpret feelings,
b. the ability to show feeling transitions, and
c. the ability to demonstrate contradictions in feelings.

The Emotional Intelligence Framework: Regulation of Emotion

In a classroom setting, gifted students would be able to:

- Be open to feelings both pleasant and unpleasant. *Openness to experience (risk-taking behavior) is essential for creativity.*
- Monitor and reflect on emotions.
- Engage, prolong, or detach from an emotional state, depending upon its judged informativeness or utility. *Use emotion to perform important tasks or subdue emotions to prevent their interfering with other tasks.*
- Manage emotions in oneself or others. *Learn to control emotion, given the situation, checking anger or moderating sadness.*

Sample Lesson 4 provides a lesson that educators can use to help students learn the regulation of their emotions.

Sample Lesson 4: Regulation of Emotions

Goal: To regulate emotion in self and others

Outcome: Students will be able to apply judgment to the use of emotional knowledge.

Activities:

1. Use selected moral dilemmas as a basis for judging emotional reactions. *How does emotion work and how can we control it?*
2. Discuss the dilemmas, noting different emotional perspectives that prevail in the scenario and in yourself.
3. Write an essay on the role of emotion in dealing with real-life problems and dilemmas.

Assessment: Have students engage in three-person role-plays where two people are in conflict and the third is a mediator. After 10 minutes, rotate roles. Engage in peer, self, and teacher assessment of the efficacy shown in emotional regulation. (Conflict resolution is partially about regulating emotions).

Writing About Emotions

Newer research suggests that writing and talking about emotional trauma can minimize its detrimental effects. Pennebaker (1997) has shown that disclosing emotional trauma in writing has numerous beneficial effects. These can be achieved by writing just once to a few times over several weeks, and writing can be anonymous. Benefits include fewer health center visits and improved grades among college students, enhanced immune system functioning, and in some cases fewer self-reports of physical symptoms, distress, and depression. These findings have been replicated many times and with diverse populations. Outward linguistic expression appears to facilitate the coping process, whereas internally ruminating over a negative event makes things worse (Salovey et al., 2000). Thus the lesson designs are structured to encourage written and oral communication about emotional issues.

Reflective Regulation

One of the most advanced skills in the reflective regulation of emotions is the ability to ameliorate negative emotions and promote pleasant ones. A further component of reflective regulation is the ability to understand emotions without exaggerating or minimizing their importance (Mayer & Salovey, 1997). Truly satisfying experiences consist of *doing*, not just *having*. What fills life with happiness is the process of accomplishment, not simply having accomplishments. Control over consciousness is not simply a cognitive skill. At least as much as intelligence, it requires the commitment of emotions and will (Csikszentmihalyi, 1991).

Affective Strategies for Working With Gifted Learners

Teacher and Parent Strategies for Promoting Affective Development

Several strategies can be employed by relevant adults to enhance such affective development. A few of these are inferred from the major program components delineated, such as being a discussion leader for a bibliotherapy session or serving as a facilitator of talent development planning. However, it also is crucial that teachers and parents assume more overt stances in promoting this type of development. If teachers know students well in respect to personality, interests, and needs, then they can better help promote self-understanding, acceptance, and teach coping skills most relevant for life events (Cross, 2000; Olenchak, 1999).

Using Sanctions and Rewards

One strategy that can help students take safe risks in the environment is to reward students for displaying openness to sanctioning "closed" behavior. Both teachers and parents can be proactive about requiring students to be flexible in their thinking, and communicating with others about ideas that may not be fully formed. Encouraging open communication about ideas and pressing for fluency in expression all contribute to reducing perfectionist behaviors.

Swiatek (1998) suggested the use of the proactive strategy of various grouping approaches to promote emotional well-being and acceptance, again encouraging social coping mechanisms that include communication.

Using the Arts

The arts become a wonderful tool to promote affective development, both in the appreciation and the performance areas. They provide students the opportunity for key expression of feelings, so necessary to maintaining mental health. They also are provokers of emotional response, encouraging the openness to experience that marks the talent development process. Finally, the arts lead to affective awareness and then sophisticated reflection on major issues and problems in the world, creating both a buffer and a reality check for gifted students. Chapter 9 provides specific ideas for applying the arts to enhance social-emotional development.

Use of Problem-Based Learning

Another key strategy for use with gifted learners is problem-based learning. A strategy originally used to create empathy in the professional world between doctor and patient and between teacher and administrator, it makes students both think and feel about real-world situations that require an acknowledgment of the undercurrents of emotion that drive real-world decision making.

Teachers and parents also may wish to include an emphasis on moral and ethical dilemmas that frame real-world decision making. Similar to problem-based learning, dilemmas force students to invest in an issue and grapple with its essence. Problem-based or dilemma-based learning emphasizes taking a perspective as a stakeholder in a problem, thereby engaging students' motivational level and providing a challenging venue for their understanding of emotion in themselves and others.

Development of Counseling Skills

Peterson (2003) has suggested that specific counseling skills might be useful to teachers in working with gifted students on social-emotional concerns. These include a major emphasis on effective listening, validating feelings, summarizing what the student is saying, and being nonjudgmental. These skills also would be useful to parents in many ways to engage their child in meaningful dialogue about school and related situations.

Tailoring Affective Curriculum and Instruction for Low-Income and Minority Students

The use of constructivist approaches in curriculum encourages safe risk-taking, discussion in small collaborative groups, and group research, all of which address the research-based needs of low-income and minority populations for tailored curriculum. Additional special features of the curriculum that especially match learning characteristics and research on these populations are the following:

- use of creative expressive activities including open-ended ones,
- use of concept mapping and metacognition strategies,
- use of multicultural materials and strategies, and
- use of inquiry approaches.

Learner Characteristics of Low-Income and Minority Students

Low-income students who are not members of minority groups tend to exhibit similar characteristics to those who are members in several respects. Both groups may appear socially marginalized in school settings due to their socioeconomic backgrounds in respect to clothing, mannerisms, and circle of friends. Often these students have difficulty penetrating the inner circle of popularity or even the circle of "nerds" because their behaviors are not really aligned with either group. Rather, it is more likely that they become independent in their mode of operation and thereby limited in opportunities for learning from productive social interactions. By the same token, their mode of learning tends to be pragmatic, focused on what is necessary to get by, and "close to the ground" in respect to the day-to-day existence their circumstances compel them to lead. This pragmatic outlook thus encourages their preference for concreteness in learning, for practical applications of knowledge in their world, and for examples that both come from and hearken back to that world.

For these students, the world of the arts is more freeing, both psychologically from their deprived circumstances but also in modes of expression that defy verbal explanation. The arts provide a perceptively different way of knowing and moving within the world (Eisner, 1985), and students from different cultural backgrounds may respond more to the integration of cognitive and affective elements inherent to the arts because of the integration of cognition and affect within their own culture (Ford & Harris, 1999). In the arts, these students can choose to revel in just "being" or address cognitive and academic needs in conjunction with artistic endeavors. Use of the visual arts, dance, music, and theater all have their special pull for these students because they can serve as an emotional and aesthetic outlet, as well as offer cognitive challenge in a noncore area of the curriculum.

Because fluid intelligence is the prominent ability of these students, they gravitate well to real-world thinking and problem-solving situations, especially those that are highly open-ended and require the use of fluency and flexibility in attempting solutions. Many also like to verbalize their thinking and use this technique to develop elaborative skills orally. Transference of this process to written form is much more difficult and often takes many more years of practice to develop proficiency.

These students have all learned disappointment early, whether in their single-parent family constellation or the denial of material possessions taken for granted by other students, or by the impoverished nature of their lives, lived without the richness of learning resources such as private lessons, special summer programs and camps, and other opportunities afforded those of greater means. Such early learning from adverse circumstances propels these students to want to make their world better, for which metacognitive skills are essential. Thus these students can be deeply influenced by self-help algorithms that focus on ways to achieve upward mobility. The skills of planning, monitoring, and assessing one's progress are central to such growth, as is serious reflection upon one's goals and strategies to accomplish them.

In such lives, the role of individuals who take a special interest is central to keeping their dream of a better life alive. Sometimes it is a family member, but many times it also is an educator who sees a spark and encourages its ignition. Low-income students disproportionately need these individuals to teach them informally what they need to know to be successful, thus serving as role models extraordinaire. Although mentors can be a wonderful resource to such students, the likelihood of mentor matches for all of the promising low-income students who need them appears limited. Therefore, the educational community needs to find other means for encouraging and nurturing such students on an informal basis.

Many times these students have skill gaps in learning, especially in core areas of the curriculum. A targeted tutorial, using good diagnostic-prescriptive approaches, can go a long way in improving such students' performance. If the tutor also is an older student of similar background or an adult of the same gender and ethnicity, the informal message is even more strongly communicated.

If the foregoing discussion provides a psychological profile of low-income students, it also provides a blueprint to the central learning characteristics they possess, which typically include the following:

- openness to experience,
- nonconformity and independence in thinking,
- creativity and fluency in their thinking,
- preference for oral expression,
- tendency to blend feelings with thoughts,

- responsiveness to multiple modes of learning as displayed in the arts,
- preference for hands-on applications,
- preference for real-world connections, and
- responsiveness to individual learning patterns.

A curriculum that is responsive to such learners will need to possess enough flexibility to address these characterological needs to a great extent.

Conclusion

Honoring the affective development of the gifted is integral to a comprehensive, balanced curriculum view. Students need to understand their own exceptionality, their intensity and sensitivity of feelings, and their need for coping strategies to help them deal with their own perfectionism and vulnerability. Gifted students also can benefit from teachers and parents who are sensitive to their needs and can respond to their psychological profiles. For low-income and minority students, using affective curriculum and instructional techniques are crucial to advanced development in all other areas.

References

Achter, J. A., Lubinski, D., Benbow, C. P., & Eftekhari-Sanjani, H. (1999). Assessing vocational preferences among gifted adolescents adds incremental validity to abilities: A discriminant analysis of educational outcomes over a 10-year interval. *Journal of Educational Psychology, 91,* 777–786.

Colangelo, N., & Davis, G. A. (Eds.). (1991). *Handbook of gifted education*. Needham Heights, MA: Allyn & Bacon.

Coleman, L. J., & Cross, T. L. (2001). *Being gifted in school: An introduction to development, guidance, and teaching*. Waco, TX: Prufrock Press.

Cross, T. L. (2000). *On the social and emotional lives of gifted children*. Waco, TX: Prufrock Press.

Csikszentmihalyi, M. (1991). *Flow: The psychology of optimal experience*. New York: HarperCollins.

Damasio, A. R. (1994). *Descartes' error: Emotion, reason and the human brain*. New York: Grosset/Putnam.

Damasio, A. R. (1999). *The feeling of what happens: Body and emotion in the making of consciousness*. New York: Harcourt Brace.

Eisner, E. (1985). Aesthetic modes of knowing. In E. Eisner (Ed.), *Learning and teaching the ways of knowing: Eighty-fourth yearbook of the National Society for the Study of Education* (pp. 23–26). Chicago: The University of Chicago Press.

Ford, D. Y., & Harris, J. J., III. (1999). *Multicultural gifted education*. New York: Teachers College Press.

Goleman, D. (1993). *Emotional intelligence: Why it can matter more than IQ*. New York: Bantam Books.

Gruber, H. (1976). *Darwin on man*. London: Wildwood House.

Halsted, J. (2002). *Some of my best friends are books: Guiding gifted readers from pre-school to high school* (2nd ed.). Scottsdale, AZ: Great Potential Press.

Hollingworth, L. S. (1926). *Gifted children: Their nature and nurture*. New York: Macmillan.

Mayer, J. D., & Salovey, P. (1997). What is emotional intelligence? In P. Salovey & D. Sluyter (Eds.), *Emotional development and emotional intelligence: Implications for educators* (pp. 3–31). New York: Basic Books.

Moon, S. M. (2003). Personal talent. *High Ability Studies, 14*, 5–21.

Neihart, M. (2001). Risk and resilience in gifted children: A conceptual framework. In M. Neihart, S. M. Reis, N. M. Robinson, & S. M. Moon (Eds.), *The social and emotional development of gifted children: What do we know?* (pp. 113–122). Waco, TX: Prufrock Press.

Noble, K. D., Robinson, N. M., & Gunderson, S. A. (1993). All rivers lead to the sea: A follow-up study of gifted young adults. *Roeper Review, 15*, 124–130.

Olenchak, F. R. (1999). Affective development of gifted students with nontraditional talents. *Roeper Review, 21*, 293–297.

Oram, G., Cornell, D., & Rutemiller, L. (1995). Relations between academic aptitude and psychosocial adjustment in gifted program students. *Gifted Child Quarterly, 39*, 236–244.

Pennebaker, J. W. (1997). Writing about emotional experiences as a therapeutic process. *Psychological Science, 8*, 162–166.

Penzel, F. (2000). *Obsessive-compulsive disorders: A complete guide to getting and staying well*. New York: Oxford.

Peterson, J. S. (2003). An argument for proactive attention to affective concerns of gifted adolescents. *Journal of Secondary Gifted Education, 14*, 62–71.

Piechowski, M. M. (1998). The self victorious: Personal strengths, chance, and co-incidence. *Roeper Review, 20*, 191–198.

Plucker, J. A., & Levy, J. J. (2001). The downside of being talented. *American Psychologist, 56*, 75–76.

Robinson, N. M. (2001). Introduction. In M. Neihart, S. M. Reis, N. M. Robinson, & S. M. Moon (Eds.), *The social and emotional development of gifted children: What do we know?* (pp. xi–xxiv). Waco, TX: Prufrock Press.

Salovey, P., Bedell, B. T., Detweiler, J. B., & Mayer, J. D. (2000). *Current directions in emotional intelligence research.* In M. Lewis & J. M. Haviland-Jones (Eds.), *Handbook of emotions* (2nd ed., pp. 504–520). New York: Guilford Press.

Salovey, P., & Mayer, J. D. (1990). Emotional intelligence. *Imagination, Cognition, and Personality, 9*, 185–211.

Schuler, P. A. (2001). Perfectionism and the gifted adolescent. *Journal of Secondary Gifted Education, 11*, 183–196.

Silverman, L. K. (1993). A developmental model for counseling the gifted. In L. K. Silverman (Ed.), *Counseling the gifted and talented* (pp. 51–78). Denver: Love.

Swiatek, M. A. (1998). Helping gifted adolescents cope with social stigma. *Gifted Child Today, 21*(1), 42–46.

Terman, L. M. (1925). *Genetic studies of genius: Vol. 1. Mental and physical traits of a thousand gifted children.* Stanford, CA: Stanford University Press.

VanTassel-Baska, J. (1995). The talent development process in women writers: A study of Charlotte Brontë and Virginia Woolf. In R. Subotnik, K. Arnold, & K. Noble (Eds.), *Remarkable women* (pp. 295–316). New York: Hampton.

Counseling Gifted Students From Non-White Racial Groups: Conceptual Perspectives and Practical Suggestions

Kwong-Liem Karl Kwan and Wayne J. Hilson, Jr.

Being gifted and talented often is associated with a presumed sense of positive self-esteem. Many parents take pride in their children being labeled as gifted and talented, as can be seen in such bumper stickers as: "Proud parent of a gifted child," or "My child is an honor student at . . . school." Teachers and the school system, likewise, feel honored when their students achieve an honor-roll status. Clasen (1992) reported that high-ability minority middle and high school students often identified their teachers and parents/family as forces for their academic achievement. The National Research Council's Committee on Minority Representation in Special Education reported that the achievement or behavior of students in gifted and talented, as well as special education, programs is determined by the interaction of the child, the teacher, and the classroom; the internal child characteristics, including biology, family, and community experiences, also play a clear role (Donovan & Cross, 2002, p. 3).

Donovan and Cross (2002) recognized the crucial roles contextual factors play in sustaining the development of the gifted and talented from racially diverse groups. Some of these contextual factors operate inside the classroom, such as diversity of student body, cognitive and behavioral development of peers, and quality of teacher-student interaction. Other factors operate outside the classroom, such as socioeconomic status and family context (Donovan & Cross, 2002).

The pride and honor for being gifted and talented, however, are not achieved without social and emotional cost. Gollnick and Chinn (2002) noted that gifted and talented students often suffer isolation from mainstream society, rejection by peers due to jealousy, and seek peers who may provide a feeling of acceptance, as well as intellectual and emotional stimulation. As such, giftedness is more than a product of the student's intellectual predisposition and academic status. Giftedness also connotes a psychological reaction to achievement expectations projected by parents, teachers, and society, as well as to the social acceptance or rejection messages in the peer culture. When academic excellence is not valued or overvalued in the peer culture, the fear of social ostracism and the need to feel a sense of belonging may set up an achievement-affiliation conflict for the gifted and talented and may account for the underachievement of highly able students (Clasen & Clasen, 1995).

Among gifted students from racial and ethnic minority groups, the achievement-affiliation conflict further can be exacerbated by racial identity conflict. For example, African American gifted students, who are statistically underrepresented in the gifted population, may be alienated by their Black peers for aspiring to "White values" through academic achievement. Asian American gifted students, who are statistically overrepresented in the gifted population, may strive to achieve to fulfill the model minority myth ascribed to Asian Americans. As such, a contextual approach is necessary when conceptualizing the identity development and stress experienced by gifted students, as well as providing competent guidance and counseling to gifted students.

This chapter will focus on the social and emotional needs of gifted students who are members of non-White racial groups in the U.S. First, the authors will review conceptual models we believe are useful tools for educators who work with this population. Second, we will analyze two cases to illustrate how the conceptual models can be applied. The two cases were purposefully chosen to highlight the social and emotional cost experienced by students who are underrepresented (e.g., African American) and overrepresented (e.g., Asian American) in the gifted population. Although these two cases are not intended to be generalized to all African American and Asian American gifted students, the experiences reported are commonly encountered in the authors' academic advising and consultation practice. In the last section, the authors will propose some practical conceptual anchors to be considered when advising and counseling racially diverse gifted students.

Achievement-Affiliation Conflict

Many studies have shown that one of the costs of being gifted is social acceptance and friendship. More than half of the African American girls in Ford's (1994/1995) study, for example, indicated that they were teased by their peers for high achievement and one third were accused of "acting White." Not one of the high-achieving African Americans in Brown and Steinberg's (1990) study was willing to be considered part of the "brain crowd." In peer culture where academic achievement is not valued, the fear of social ostracism and the developmental need for acceptance and belonging has been considered a reason for underachievement among high-ability students, regardless of grade levels, racial and ethnic groups, and schools (Clasen & Clasen, 1995).

The desire for academic achievement and the need for peer acceptance set up an achievement-affiliation conflict that many gifted students have to confront. Based on preference for or prioritization of achievement and affiliation needs, Clasen and Clasen (1995) delineated five types of student responses to reconcile the conflict. *Denial of ability*, which involves self-rejection and loss of identity, is a common response when students choose affiliation over achievement needs. *Submersion in ability*, which may have long-term negative impact on socialization development, is resorted to when students choose achievement over affiliation needs. *Ambivalence* is experienced when students vacillate between the needs to achieve and to belong, and between feeling proud of, yet also embarrassed about, their ability and achievement. *Alienation*, though not a common response, may be manifested in students (psychologically) dropping out of school when they reject both achievement and affiliation needs and give up resolving the conflict. *Resolution* is characterized by students who seek to maintain a balance between achievement and affiliation needs; these students usually are autonomous, possess high self-esteem, and strive to establish friendship circles through participating in school activities.

Racial Salience

In a multicultural environment where there is a differential representation of members from visible racial ethnic groups (VREG; Helms, 1995; e.g., an Asian American student in a predominantly White school), salient physical characteristics, notably skin color, predispose non–White people to experiences of racism, perceived "differences," and identity conflicts (Helms & Cook, 1999; Kwan, 2005; Smith, 1991). In cross-racial contact situations, racial salience (e.g., being Black or Asian) elicits perceived ethnic and cultural differences, which leads to differential acceptance or rejection, depending on the (positive or negative) nature of race-related stereotypes their peers harbor (Kwan, 2005). At both intrapersonal and interpersonal levels, racial identity conflicts are experienced when individuals cannot relate to their own racial membership group as a positive identity reference group (Smith, 1991).

Despite the vast sociocultural (e.g., U.S.-born vs. foreign-born) and psychocultural (e.g., identifying with White majority group vs. own ethnic group as reference group) diversity, members of a particular VREG often are ascribed a collective demographic identity (e.g., Asian and Pacific-Islander Americans) based on salient physical characteristics (e.g., skin color). During cross-racial contacts, these visible characteristics may provoke ethnicity-specific images (e.g., cultural practices such as speaking with an accent, food preference) and nonethnicity-related stereotypes (e.g., inferred traits such as "Asians are good at science") that are used as attributional, emotional, and attitudinal referents to categorize and treat VREG members (Kwan, 2005). In other words, certain interpersonal behaviors might not occur or might be different in the absence of such salient physical characteristics. Therefore, Smith (1991) noted that "[m]embers of minority groups often struggle to cope with multiple realities, meaning differing minority and majority group interpretations of what it means to be a member of each group" (p. 183).

In predominantly White environments, non-White people often denigrate the racial aspect of their identity in an attempt to minimize perceived difference and to gain social acceptance (Helms, 1995; Sue & Sue, 2007). However, their racial salience and the ascribed stereotypes will always expose them to perceived interracial and interpersonal differences (Kwan, 2005). As such, non-White individuals' attempts to identify with their White peers are not always reciprocated. For example, for an African American student, being Black elicits race-related images and stereotypes that people in the environment use in varying degrees during cross-racial contacts. A Black student who considers him- or herself White would not be seen as White, and his or her psychological identification with being White would probably be differentially accepted or rejected by White peers.

The manner and extent that "sociorace" and "psychorace" (Helms & Cook, 1999) are integrated is a developmental task non-White children in predominantly White environments have to confront. According to Helms and Cook, sociorace refers to racial group membership externally ascribed based on visible characteristics, while psychorace refers to racial group affiliation and identity as subjectively construed. In racially and culturally diverse environments, such as the U.S. school system, it is crucial to delineate and differentiate sociorace and psychorace because an individual's externally ascribed racial group membership does not always correspond to one's subjective ethnic identification. Multicultural psychologists have concurred that positive identification with one's own racial and ethnic group is necessary for psychological health as well as for protection against societal racism and alienation by racial in-group members (Helms, 1995; Smith, 1991).

Racial Identity Development

As summarized by Kwan (2001), racial identity models (Helms, 1995; Sue & Sue, 2007) describe a process in which non-White racial and ethnic people vary in their capacity to (a) confront and abandon an idealized relationship with the White majority group, (b) regard their racial and ethnic membership group as a positive identity reference group, and (c) develop a sense of self that is anchored on, yet autonomous of, race and ethnicity. A number of identity stages (Sue & Sue, 2007) or statuses (Helms, 1995) have been delineated to describe the attitudinal experiences, emotional conflicts, coping mechanisms, and behavioral consequences associated with the developmental journey.

Conformity/pre-encounter is the least mature status in racial identity development. In light of the sociopolitical privilege and power ascribed to the White dominant group and the historical racism that persists, non-White people in conformity/pre-encounter status often idealize White values, aspire to White standards of merit, and regard other non-White groups, including their own membership group, as inferior. They are oblivious to the sociopolitical history of minority groups and to the existence of racism. They tend to be color-blind and deny and repress information that heightens awareness of the racial aspect of their identity.

Dissonance/encounter marks the next status in racial identity development. As much as a non-White person denigrates his or her own racial group and prefers (and pretends) to be "White," his or her racial salience, notably skin color, predisposes him or her to differential acceptance and rejection by peers from his or her racial group and the White group. For example, he or she may be accused of being a "sell-out" by people from his or her own racial group, and he or she may have experiences that would not have happened if he or she were White during their interactions with White people. These encounters induce catalytic dissonance experiences that propel the non-White individual to confront and come to terms with the implications of race on his or her identity, which may be accompanied by shame, anxiety, ambivalence, and confusion.

Progression to the resistance or immersion/emersion racial identity status usually is facilitated by certain intense and personally meaningful racial catalysts, such as exposure to experiences that enhance pride of and affiliation to one's racial group, or repeated encounters with White racism. Juxtaposed to conformity/pre-encounter, immersion/emersion is marked by idealization of one's racial group and denigration of the White group. Individuals are hypervigilant toward racial stimuli, and their identity configures around race, which often is the lens through which social and personal events or occurrences are interpreted. Individuals tend to engage in dichotomous thinking, unable and unwilling to evaluate events objectively beyond racial lines. In addition, they often make decisions and participate in activities to combat racism and promote social justice for one's racial group.

Internalization/integrative awareness represents a mature racial identity status characterized by a healthy commitment to one's racial group and the ability to view White people as individuals without preconceived bias. Beyond showing positive commitment to one's racial group, the person also has the capacity to empathize and collaborate with other oppressed racial minorities. The non-White person is able to exercise flexibility, analytic thinking, and complexity when exploring racial issues.

Racial Identity Conflict

Among the gifted and talented from visible racial and ethnic groups (e.g., African Americans, Asian Americans, and Mexican Americans), the achievement-affiliation conflict intertwines with racial identity conflicts. These conflicts are compounded when race-related stereotypes are ascribed to intelligence and academic ability. Asian Americans, for example, have been found to be statistically overrepresented among the gifted and talented (Donovan & Cross, 2002; Ford, 1998). Coupled with the "model minority" image as portrayed by the media, the expectation to conform to the gifted and achievement stereotypes creates undue stress for many Asian American students. On the other hand, African Americans have been statistically underrepresented among the gifted and talented, while overrepresented among students in special education programs (Donovan & Cross, 2002). Biographical (Suskind, 1998) and research (Clasen & Clasen, 1995) reports have shown that high-achieving African Americans often were accused of being a "sell-out" by their African American peers. For both racial groups, there is a social and psychological cost whether academic excellence is considered a "norm" or "sell-out" by peers from the same racial group, because conformity to and deviation from ascribed racial stereotypes may lead to potential alienation from their peers. Consequently, along with the stress that comes from competition or social alienation, achieving students also experience self-alienation that stems from affiliation–rejection conflict by racial in-group peers. The social and emotional development and stressors of non-White gifted and talented students, therefore, cannot be understood independently from their racial identity development.

The Case of Cedric Jennings (Suskind, 1998)

[The school principal] Washington steps forward, "I will be reading names of students who got straight A's in the second marking period. I'd like each one to come forward to collect his [or her] $100 cash prize and a special shirt from WPGC. We're all . . . very, very proud of them."

Washington takes a list from his breast pocket and begins reading names. He calls four sophomore girls who quietly slip, one by one, onto the gym floor. Then he calls a sophomore boy. Trying his best to vanish, the boy sits stone still in the bleachers, until a teacher spots him, and yells, "You can't hide from me!" and drags him front and center. A chorus of "NEEERD!" rains down from every corner of the room.

At the start, the assemblies were a success. The gymnasium was full, and honor students seemed happy to attend, flushed out by the cash. But after a few such gatherings, the jeering started. It was thunderous. "Nerd!" "Geek!" "Egghead!" And the harshest, "Whitey!" Crew members, sensing a hearts-and-minds struggle, stomped on the bleachers and howled. No longer simply names on the Wall of Honor, the "Whiteys" now had faces. The honor students were hazed for months afterwards. With each assembly, fewer show up . . .

Pride. Cedric's 4.02 grade point average virtually ties him for first in the junior class . . . Pride in such accomplishment is acceptable behavior for sterling students at high schools across the land, but at Ballou and other urban schools like it, something else is at work. Educators have even coined a phrase for it. They call it the crab/bucket syndrome: when one crab tries to climb from the bucket, the others pull it back down. The forces dragging students toward failure—especially those who have crawled farthest up the side—flow through every corner of the school. Inside the bucket, there is little chance of escape. (Suskind, 1998, pp. 3–4)

In the book *A Hope in the Unseen*, Suskind (1998) documented the journey of an African American boy, Cedric Jennings, from the poverty-stricken Ballou school in Washington, DC to Ivy-League Brown University. Cedric Jennings was an honor student in a predominantly African American school where academic achievement was not a popular norm. As a high achiever with an academic ambition to attend an Ivy League university, Cedric Jennings became an obvious social outcast who had to confront peer isolation, hostility, and fear. These experiences are not uncommon among the gifted and talented. Yet, when academic success also is associated with White values (i.e., being a "nerd" also means being a "Whitey") and viewed as a "sellout" (especially among African American students; Fordham & Ogbu, 1986) while living among members of one's own racial group, peer rejection sets off a potential racial identity crisis.

Statistics consistently have shown the low incidence of African American and Hispanic students in gifted and talented programs and the high incidence of these two groups in special education classes (Donovan & Cross, 2002; Ford, 1998). Despite the inadequacy of the assessment and classification systems (Donovan & Cross, 2002), these statistics often associate African Americans and Hispanic students with negative achievement stereotypes. When children internalize the negative stereotypes directed at their own racial group, they often engage in a psychological process to denigrate that, to dissociate from group membership and affiliation (e.g., becoming "color-blind"), and to aspire to the (White) group that represents privilege and power. This psychological dynamic of internalized racism is characteristic of non–White people in the conformity/pre-encounter racial identity status (Helms, 1995; Sue & Sue, 2007).

Something to Push Against

Cedric Jennings was torn between two unyielding "masters," aspiring to standards of success often established from a traditionally White worldview while maintaining some semblance of affiliation with his own Black identity. Gifted students whose racial group is not so stereotyped may harbor feelings of shame and denigration that reflect internalized racism against their own racial group. Along with peer rejection and alienation due to his intellectual prowess, these experiences may likely fuel the emergence of the conformity/pre-encounter racial identity status (i.e., devaluing of one's own racial group while idealizing the White standards of merit; Helms, 1995). As a coping mechanism, gifted students such as those Cedric represents often choose to adopt a "do-it-myself" mentality as they believe this as the only way to compete with students from the "harder" schools. Although some may have little interaction with White people, these students figure that the White world is superior to the stark contrast they face on a daily basis. Even though students in conformity/pre-encounter status may not necessarily harbor an anti-Black attitude, they are constantly "pushing against" internalizing the negative Black stereotypes they have been exposed to (Vandiver, 2001).

Challenges to Self

Students in conformity/pre-encounter status often feel ecstatic when offered the opportunity to attend what they consider to be a traditional American school, such as a magnet school or a summer enrichment program for gifted students at a predominantly White university, where they could study with other "smart" and "well-behaved" students (Suskind, 1998). They attribute such achievement to their intellectual capabilities rather than the belief that their giftedness may be externally ascribed. Yet, when transitioning to a new learning environment where achievement norms and academic aspiration of racial minority peers are different, the giftedness of these students is challenged. In fact, it is not uncommon for these students to question if they are good enough to be accepted or recruited.

As Suskind (1998) has documented, Cedric Jennings was accepted by a summer enrichment program for high achievers at the Massachusetts Institute of Technology, where he took classes with other racial and ethnic gifted students from around the country. The anxiety that stemmed from potential threats to one's gifted identity may manifest in a number of ways. First, they may feign apathy to marginalize their longing to be accepted so as to cope with the possibility of failure. Second, they may develop a sense of hatred against other African American and Hispanic applicants from better schools. How gifted African American students express their conformity/pre-encounter status also is likely influenced by socioeconomic status. Students from higher socioeconomic backgrounds who are exposed to educational experiences and expectations more aligned with "White standards" will likely approach academic and interpersonal challenges differently from those who attended less than exemplary educational institutions. Depending on the racial composition of their immediate environment, some of these students may choose to actively distance themselves from other African Americans. Some may focus solely on pursuing what they perceive as successful in the White world. Some may seek to reconceptualize race as a less salient, nonfactor. Based on the our years of counseling experience with this student group, the majority of gifted adolescents in middle school and high school rarely progress to latter racial identity statuses. This may account for the ambivalent relationships African American students afford to one another, to discussions of race issues, and to White peers, which collectively contribute to a sense of disengagement from their peer and academic environment (Ogbu, 2003).

The Case of Mrs. Chen

Asian Americans have a disproportionately high representation in the gifted population (Ford, 1998). Despite their bimodal distributions in levels of education and income in the U.S. population, Asian Americans often are collectively perceived as the "model minority"—a racial stereotype that all Asian Americans are successful, achieving, and have "made it" in U.S. society. Many Asian immigrant parents consider academic achievement as a means for attaining social mobility and family honor. As such, many Asian Americans experience intense pressure from both outside and within the family to excel to fit in the gifted stereotype and to fulfill parental expectations.

Yet, such pressure to excel has been conjectured by many to be related to the increasing incidence of mental health problems, especially those experienced among Asian American youths. According to the National Asian American Pacific Islander Mental Health Association (NAAPIMHA; http://www.naapimha.org/issues), Asian and Pacific-Islander American females have the highest suicide rate among females between 15 and 24 years of age. Native Hawaiian youths have a significantly higher rate of suicide attempts than other adolescents in Hawaii. Among girls in 5th through 12th grade, 30% of Asian Americans reported depressive symptoms as compared to 22% of non-Hispanic White students, 17% of African American students, and 27% of Hispanic American students. There are many negative psychological effects of the model minority myth, which has been challenged by Asian American scholars in psychology and education (e.g., Lee, 1996; Sue & Sue, 2007). The social and emotional cost, as well as the long-term developmental impact associated with being gifted is vividly captured in the following verbatim report by Mrs. Chen, a second-generation Chinese American woman in her mid-30s who sought counseling.

> My husband and I fight a lot. We disagree on many things. What really ticks me off recently is that he wants our son to be placed in gifted classes. He said our son needs to catch up with other Asian kids . . . My brother once received an academic award. Dad scolded at me and said "You should also be getting it!" . . . I grew up being labeled as gifted. I was always and only seen as a gifted kid. That's it, and I hated it! I don't want my son to be called gifted. I just want him to be a normal and happy kid, and I want him to know who he is . . .

Mrs. Chen initially sought counseling for marital conflict, which centered primarily on spousal disagreement in child-rearing practices. Her presenting concern quickly focused on her resentment toward her husband's plan to place their child in the school's gifted program. Upon further exploration, Mrs. Chen revealed that her strong reaction reflected her rebellion against the gifted identity she was ascribed and expected to fulfill while she was growing up.

The presenting concern was *marital conflict* due to disagreement on child-rearing practice in relation to crafting the child's educational path. On a deeper level, the struggle to rebel against childhood gifted identity underlies adult relationship conflicts. Many Asian American parents experience social pressure within the Asian American community to fit their children into a racial norm. Such pressure is projected as expectations for children to aspire to, sometimes regardless of the children's intellectual capability. In other words, being gifted or striving to be gifted reflects the child's *internalization of parental stress to cope with social pressure and gain "face" for family.*

Mrs. Chen's case illustrates a number of other counseling issues. The stress associated with being gifted has a pervasive, developmental impact from childhood, through adolescence, and into adulthood. The pressure to fulfill filial expectations, sibling rivalry, and the lack of self-differentiation all are stressors the gifted and talented have to confront. When giftedness is stereotyped across racial lines, Asian Americans also have to cope with the pressure to conform to racial norms.

Giftedness sets up potential sibling rivalry when parents compare children's academic achievements. Gifted students, therefore, may have to *confront social alienation at school, as well as competition at home*. Such competition for academic excellence may turn into competition for parents' attention and affection, which may persist into adult sibling relationships. Filial conflict was experienced when students struggle between meeting parents' achievement expectations and their own developmental needs. Such pressure may lead to resentment, depression (anger turned inward), and rebellious behaviors (anger externally projected).

Racial identity conflict could be triggered when Asian Americans conform to or rebel against the giftedness stereotype often ascribed to Asian Americans. Parents (Mr. Chen in this case) may expect their children to be gifted because Asian Americans "are supposed to be gifted." Others (Mrs. Chen in this case) may distance themselves from the Asian identity to cope with the pressure to be gifted. Incongruity between the parents' racial identity statuses may complicate children's understanding of the enmeshed relationship between race and giftedness, and cause confusion for children's racial identity development. Loss of sense of self may result when children are so preoccupied with investing in their gifted identity that they cannot identify and differentiate other aspects of who they are.

Developing Gifted Programs for the Racially Diverse: What Do We Do?

Intellectual capability stereotyped along racial lines predisposes non-White gifted and talented students to an accompanying sense of racial alienation that compounds the common achievement-affiliation conflicts. From a developmental perspective, earlier and more immature racial identity statuses (i.e., conformity/pre-encounter, dissonance/encounter, and immersion/emersion) are likely to be predominant among middle school and high school students. Students in the conformity/pre-encounter status tend to have negative attitudes toward one's own racial group. When alienated by racial peers, they may further denigrate their own racial group and risk subsequent rejection by multiple racial groups, or they may resort to academic apathy in exchange for acceptance and affiliation.

While resolving the conflicts between the needs for academic achievement and peer acceptance, non-White gifted students also have to socially and psychologically struggle with claiming their own racial group as a positive identity reference group. The cases of Cedric Jennings and Mrs. Chen have shown that these conflicts can be experienced by racial groups that are underrepresented (e.g., African Americans) and overrepresented (e.g., Asian Americans) in the gifted population. How non-White gifted students resolve the achievement-affiliation conflict, therefore, cannot be separated from their racial identity development. This is the conceptual anchor by which the following recommendations are offered when developing programs for non-White gifted students.

First, school personnel, including principals, teachers, and school counselors, need to demonstrate cultural competence, especially in the application of racial identity models (Helms, 1995; Sue & Sue, 2007) to understand the academic, emotional, and interpersonal coping associated with various statuses. Knowledge of the application of racial and cultural models allows (mal)adaptive behaviors to be conceptualized in the proper context so that prevention or intervention strategies can be planned accordingly. Knowledge and awareness of race-based biases and stereotypes is another critical dimension of cultural competence.

When a sample of teachers in Southern California was asked to list and rate stereotypic traits of Asian, African American, and White students, Chang and Demyan (2007) found that teachers held certain stereotypes that were significantly differentiated along racial lines. In particular, Asians were perceived as the most industrious, intelligent, and gentle; African American students were perceived as the most athletic and rhythmic; and White students, the most selfish and materialistic. Chang and Demyan noted that most of the distinguishing stereotypic traits associated with Asians were positive, which is consistent with the "model minority" image ascribed to this racial group. Counseling personnel need to examine and check if one's racial stereotype colors one's academic expectations or decisions, and be aware of the potential stress non-White gifted students experience when they attempt to conform to or rebel against ascribed racial stereotypes.

Second, knowing that the common achievement-affiliation conflict is compounded by racial identity conflict, it is important that a counseling system be in place in the school. The counseling unit can serve a prevention role through reaching out to these students. Support groups are useful outlets for students to disclose and normalize the conflicts and struggles they may experience. In the helping process, it is important to develop empathic skills to facilitate students to admit that being gifted does not make one immune to psychological and interpersonal difficulties. In particular, school counselors can listen to concerns of acceptance/rejection (e.g., by classmates, racial peers, parents) and subsequent feelings of alienation, and explore strategies (either adaptive or maladaptive) students have developed to cope.

Using the achievement-affiliation conflict model, school counselors can provide psychoeducation and design self-exploration exercises to help students articulate their experiences. While listening to students' self-disclosure, school counselors can use the racial identity model to assess how students feel about being a member of a non-White racial group, and whether ethnic identification is related to rejection by ethnic peers who do not espouse similar academic achievement value. Because students in the earlier (pre-encounter, encounter) statuses of the model tend to denigrate their own racial group membership and feel anxious and resistant discussing race, reflection skills are necessary to enable students to understand and articulate how their fears of rejection by student peers and racial peers contribute to feelings of ambivalence and confusion about who they are.

Third, it is important to include parents in the counseling and support system. As a minority student affairs administrator, the second author used to work for many years with many gifted and talented African American students recruited to a world-class engineering program at a predominantly White university. We found it important to speak with parents of these gifted students, and allow the parents to speak candidly about their worries and concerns. Rather than feeling excited about their children's opportunity, these parents' primary source of trepidation centered upon nonacademic issues, particularly regarding establishing positive, interpersonal relationships within the predominantly White environment. The majority of these parents recounted many past incidents before college when their academically astute children were teased or ostracized by both their peers and families, and these negative experiences were common among families from various socioeconomic strata, as well as from both urban and suburban neighborhoods. Because of such experiences, it is good practice to maintain contacts with parents whose children are identified as gifted, and provide psychoeducation, especially on the social and emotional adjustment and costs associated with giftedness.

Finally, beyond focusing on here-and-now intellectual development, gifted and talented educators should take into consideration the immediate and pervasive impact of placement in gifted programs on students' racial identity development. In particular, what students gain intellectually needs to be evaluated against the social and emotional cost, especially when students are not able to embrace their racial group as their identity reference group. As giftedness often is drawn along racial lines, gifted curriculum may include psychoeducational and self-development materials that help students disentangle the enmeshed relationship between race and giftedness.

Conclusion

Programs or counseling sessions that facilitate healthy perception of and affiliation to one's own racial group are critical. Given that racial salience predisposes non-White individuals to differential acceptance and rejection by members from other racial groups, it is important to help students understand how positive identification with one's own racial group is necessary to protect oneself from societal racism and ostracism by one's racial and ethnic peers.

References

Brown, B. B., & Steinberg, L. (1990, March). Skirting the brain-nerd connection: How bright students save face among peers. *Education Digest, 15*(4), 57–60.

Chang, D. F., & Demyan, A. (2007). Teachers' stereotypes of Asian, Black, and White students. *School Psychology Quarterly, 22,* 91–114.

Clasen, D. R. (1992). Changing peer stereotypes of high-achieving adolescents. *NASSP Bulletin, 76,* 95–102.

Clasen, D. R., & Clasen, R. E. (1995). Underachievement of highly able students and the peer society. *Gifted and Talented International, 10,* 67–76.

Donovan, M. S., & Cross, C. T. (Eds.). (2002). *Minority students in gifted and special education.* Washington, DC: National Academies Press.

Ford, D. Y. (1994/1995, Winter). Underachievement among gifted and non-gifted Black females: A study of perceptions. *Journal of Secondary Gifted Education, 6,* 165–175.

Ford, D. Y. (1998). The underrepresentation of minority students in gifted education: Problems and promises in recruitment and retention. *Journal of Special Education, 32,* 4–14.

Fordham, S., & Ogbu, J. U. (1986). Black students' school success: Coping with the burden of "acting White." *Urban Review, 18,* 176–206.

Gollnick, D. M., & Chinn, P. C. (2002). *Multicultural education in a pluralistic society* (6th ed.). Upper Saddle River, NJ: Prentice Hall.

Helms, J. E. (1995). An update of Helms' "White and people of color racial identity models." In J. Ponterotto, M. Casas, L. Suzuki, & C. Alexander (Eds.), *Handbook of multicultural counseling* (pp. 181–198). Newbury Park, CA: Sage.

Helms, J. E., & Cook, D. (1999). *Using race and culture in counseling and psychotherapy*. Boston: Allyn & Bacon.

Kwan, K.-L. K. (Guest Ed.). (2001). Counseling racially diverse clients. *Journal of Mental Health Counseling, 23*(3).

Kwan, K.-L. K. (2005). Racial salience: Conceptual dimensions and implications for racial identity development. In R. Carter (Ed.), *Handbook of racial-cultural psychology* (pp. 115–131). New York: John Wiley.

Lee, S. J. (1996). *Unraveling the "model minority" stereotype: Listening to Asian American youth*. New York: Teachers College Press.

Ogbu, J. (2003). *Black American students in an affluent suburb: A study of academic disengagement*. Mahwah, NJ: Lawrence Erlbaum.

Smith, E. J. (1991). Ethnic identity development: Toward the development of a theory within the context of majority/minority status. *Journal of Counseling and Development, 70,* 181–188.

Sue, D. W., & Sue, D. (2007). *Counseling the culturally diverse: Theory and practice* (5th ed.). New York: Wiley.

Suskind, R. (1998). *A hope in the unseen: An American odyssey from the inner city to the Ivy League*. New York: Broadway Books.

Vandiver, B. J. (2001). Psychological nigrescence revisited: Introduction and overview. *Journal of Multicultural Counseling and Development, 29,* 165–173.

Addressing Social-Emotional and Curricular Needs of Gifted African American Adolescents

Norma L. Day-Vines, James M. Patton,
Chwee G. Quek, & Susannah Wood

African Americans remain conspicuously absent from today's cohort of gifted and talented students (Milner & Ford, 2007). Although they represent 17.2% of the public school population, they comprise a meager 3.5% of the total gifted population (National Center for Education Statistics, 2007). At times the rate of underrepresentation has hovered between 50% and 70% (Ford & Grantham, 2003). Several causal factors have been attributed to the lack of students in these programs. As an example, biased attitudes and assumptions about African American children; failure to recognize culturally mediated attributes that constitute giftedness; narrowly constructed assessment procedures; lack of multicultural competence among school personnel; and student and family concerns about the social isolation that may result from enrollment in gifted programs have been cited as salient factors that contribute to the limited participation of African American students in gifted program initiatives (Ford & Grantham, 2003; Ford, Harris, Tyson, & Trotman, 2002; Milner & Ford, 2007).

Once matriculating in gifted programs, it is important for African American students to have curricular experiences that address their affective needs for security, belonging, trust, competency, and mastery in order to profit from the learning experience. In this chapter we provide an overview of socioemotional and curricular needs of gifted African American adolescents. The chapter begins with a definition and rationale for promoting cultural competence among educators and continues with a discussion of factors that impact the socioemotional functioning of these learners. These factors include issues related to African American cultural values, field dependent versus field independent learning styles, underachievement, stereotype threat, teacher expectations, overexcitabilities, racial identity functioning, and fictive kinship networks. The chapter continues with a set of curricular and instructional strategies that address the socioemotional needs of gifted and talented African American adolescents, and closes with practical strategies for using gifted education as a vehicle with which to bridge the gap between the curricular and socioemotional needs of gifted and talented African American adolescents.

Cultural Competence

Cultural competence refers to a set of congruent attitudes, practices, policies, and structures that come together among individuals or within a system or agency to enable professionals to work more effectively with members of culturally distinct groups in a manner that values and respects the culture and worldview of those groups (Hanley, 1999). Patton and Day-Vines (2003) have outlined a compelling rationale that supports the development of cultural competence among school personnel.

Rationale Supporting Cultural Competence

Demographic Factors

The demographic composition of the student population relative to the teaching force supports the need for cultural competence training. According to data issued by the National Center for Education Statistics (Strizek, Pittsonberger, Riordan, Lyter, & Orlofsky, 2006), 60.3% of students in K–12 schools are Caucasian, while 16.8% are African American. At the same time, Caucasians constitute 83.1% of the teaching force while

African Americans comprise 7.9% of all teachers. Sadly, only 1.2% of all teachers are African American men (Education Trust, 2003). These figures represent significant disproportionality within the teaching profession and reflect an extreme lack of cultural synchronization, especially given the fact that significant student academic gains have been shown when African American teachers and students were paired by race (Dee, 2004). More disturbingly, African American teachers are woefully underrepresented among the teachers of the gifted. The profession can ill afford to wait until such time as more teachers of color join the ranks. It is incumbent upon all teachers to develop the requisite cultural awareness, knowledge, skills, and dispositions in order to work effectively with African American adolescents.

Cultural Discontinuity

The student's culture of origin frequently remains unsynchronized with the culture of the school. Inattention to these differences can result in cultural schisms between dominant and subordinate groups (i.e., students and teachers) that can impede academic and socioemotional progress among African American adolescents (Ford, Howard, Harris, & Tyson, 2000; Gay, 2000).

Achievement Levels of African American Students

A considerable amount of documentation identifies the underperformance of African American students relative to certain Asian American groups and their Caucasian counterparts. According to the Education Trust (2003), 61% of African American students performed at below basic levels on an eighth-grade measure of math attainment, in comparison to 21% of Caucasian students. Similarly, 7% of African American students have earned proficient and advanced scores on this same instrument, compared with 36% of Caucasian students.

Structural Inequality

Other forms of attribution have been offered in the literature. Some experts have identified structural inequities as an explanation for the achievement gap between African American and Caucasian students. For instance, math and science classes with a larger percentage of minority students often are taught by less qualified and experienced teachers, which can adversely affect learning outcomes for students (Education Trust, 2003). Further, teachers in high-poverty schools spend less time developing reasoning skills (Education Trust, 2003). Published reports indicate that 25.7% of African American students in comparison to 34.1% and 42.1% of White and Asian students enroll in college preparatory curricula (Education Trust, 2003).

Ecological Realities

Several scholars have attributed the underperformance of African American students to: (a) the tendency for them to live in depressed urban areas that lack certified and experienced teachers, (b) the prevalence of dilapidated facilities, (c) inadequate resources for education, (d) limited student access to accelerated courses, and (e) parents who may not understand the demands and expectations of mainstream educational institutions (Gay, 2000). Additional reasons offered include ineffective connections between school communities, as well as the presence of teachers who may not understand how to deliver culturally responsive educational services (Holcomb-McCoy, 1998). Curiously, many middle-class African American students suffer from poor academic achievement as well (Ogbu, 2003). Later in this chapter we explore underachievement in more detail.

Preservice Preparation

Last, the preservice education and preparation of school personnel does not routinely equip them with the cultural knowledge, skills, and dispositions to work effectively with diverse student populations. A 1997 study noted that accreditation reviews of schools of education conducted by the National Council for the Accreditation of Teacher Education (NCATE) found that only 56% of the institutions surveyed addressed cultural diversity *adequately* in the professional education curriculum (Goodwin, 1997). Finally, educators have an ethical responsibility to meet the needs of diverse student populations irrespective of race, ethnicity, culture, gender, sexual orientation, or social class (Patton, 2000). Given this context of need, a conceptual framework for addressing culturally competent educators of African American adolescents exists, as discussed in the next section.

Conceptual Framework for Developing Cultural Competence

Pedersen's Model of Cultural Competence

Awareness Competencies

In 1994, Pedersen developed a three-part model of cultural competence to promote cultural understanding. This model of cultural competence adheres to established developmental tenets while encompassing three distinct stages—awareness, knowledge, and skills. During the awareness stage, it is proposed that individuals acknowledge, explore, and examine their own attitudes, biases and assumptions and consider how these factors may influence the delivery of culturally responsive educational services. Simply stated, they engage in a form of critical self-examination referred to as *cultural therapy* by Spindler and Spindler (1994).

Greenwald, McGhee, and Schwartz (1998) have distinguished between implicit and explicit attitudes. Implicit attitudes are reinforced over time, and people may not even be aware of them. An explicit attitude, on the other hand, is the result of conscious thought, and is overtly expressed. According to Wilson, Lindsay, and Schooler (2000), it is possible for people to have dual attitudes. For instance, a teacher may have a positive explicit attitude and be supportive of alternative identification models that address the issue of underrepresentation of minority students in gifted programs. At the same time, this teacher's implicit attitude may be such that African American children in gifted programs are less able and unlikely to cope. Often, it may be the negative implicit attitude that will guide judgment and action (Wilson et al., 2000). Therefore, it is important for teachers of the gifted to be aware of and confront their dual attitudes, or address the unconscious neglect of African American children that could lead to them opting out of gifted programs or remaining academically disengaged (Ford et al., 2000; Milner & Ford, 2007).

Other competencies in Pedersen's (1994) awareness stage include an understanding of how sociopolitical forces shape a child's social, psychological, emotional, and educational experience. In the previous section of this chapter we outlined some awareness factors related to the underrepresentation of African American adolescents in gifted education programs, as well as addressed sociopolitical factors that support a rationale for cultural competence training.

Knowledge and Skills Competencies

The second stage of Pedersen's (1994) model addresses knowledge competencies. These competencies challenge educators to acquire factual information about a particular ethnic minority group such as their cultural values and orientations, their historical experiences with oppression, issues related to nomenclature, instructional and behavioral strategies, social and educational experiences, as well as mechanisms of support available within their indigenous communities. In an effort to achieve stage three or skills competencies, educators should build upon and translate cultural awareness and knowledge competencies into culturally responsive skills that enable them to engage more effectively with African American children. More specifically, culturally responsive teachers incorporate students' familiar cultural contexts into their curricular and instructional experiences (Patton & Day-Vines, 2003).

The ability to recognize and integrate children's cultural funds of knowledge into their curricular and instructional experiences makes logical sense, especially given that from a developmental perspective, individuals normally incorporate new learning into their existing schemas (Gay, 2000). As an example, when a young child first learns to recognize cows he or she may mistakenly identify a cow as a dog. It is through the child's initial understanding of dogs as animals that they can begin to integrate cows into the family of animals. Similarly, students from culturally distinct groups require opportunities to use their culture as resources and springboards for the acquisition of new learning.

In the next section of this chapter we present a definition of socioemotional functioning as often manifested in African American adolescents and outline some cultural and race specific issues that influence the curricular and institutional experiences of African American adolescents.

Socioemotional Functioning

Factors Impacting Socioemotional Functioning of Gifted African American Adolescents

The term *socioemotional functioning* has not been well defined in the literature or in practice. In this chapter we define socioemotional functioning as the developmental awareness of the student's interaction with both peers and adults and the emotions that these interactions engender. Because of their heightened intellectual abilities, gifted and talented students often are more attuned to environmental stimuli than their peers. This natural sensitivity often gives rise to an affective reaction to stimuli such as social injustice and inequality. Teachers can best assist gifted African American students by acknowledging their culturally mediated thoughts and reactions to situations; normalizing students' reactions; recognizing the turmoil that such situations often produce for students; helping students obtain some coping strategies; and finally understanding one's own (i.e. teacher's) reactions. In fact, an emerging body of research documents an empirical relationship between perceived racial discrimination, coping styles, and psychological well-being among African American adolescents (Scott & House, 2005; Sellars, Copeland-Linder, Martin, & Lewis, 2006).

Previously we stated that culturally competent instruction required a basic understanding of a learner's cultural values and orientation. Effective and culturally competent teachers integrate their understanding of a child's "culture" into their repertoire of curricular and instructional strategies. In this section of the chapter we provide research that sheds light on distinct cultural values, related style implications, and examples of applying those insights to teachers' curriculum and instruction. Additionally we address the nexus of stereotypes, teacher expectations, overexcitability, racial identity functioning and peer influences on the socioemotional development of African American adolescents. In the final section of this chapter we discuss curricular and instructional strategies that teachers can use to incorporate this understanding into their repertoire of instructional strategies.

African American Cultural Values

In this section we compare and contrast mainstream American cultural values and orientations with African American cultural values and orientations. As a caveat, we acknowledge that many of the "values" associated with traditionally oriented African Americans represent "modal characteristics" that apply to many though certainly not all of those referenced. Factors such as social class, education, dominant cultural assimilation, ethnic identification, and affiliation likely will influence the manifestation of these cultural attributes (Gay, 2000).

Given this scenario, mainstream American cultural values and African American cultural values often are at odds. For example, a dominant American cultural orientation or worldview often promotes individualism, competition, material accumulation, religion as distinct from other parts of culture, and mastery over nature (Patton & Day-Vines, 2003). In marked contrast, in a classic study Boykin (1983) described the nine dimensions through which many African Americans perceive the world as spirituality, harmony with nature, movement, verve, affect, communalism, expressive individualism, orality, and social time perspective. Adolescents' learning styles often correspond to their cultural preferences and orientations (Tucker, 1999). Teachers who are culturally competent can translate what is known about African American adolescents' culture into effective curricular and instructional strategies. Moreover, they create learning environments that integrate students' cultural preferences. As an example, consistent with the cultural preference for communalism, social relationships are highly prized among African Americans and failure to connect personally with many African American students may contribute to academic disengagement (Day-Vines, 2000). Culturally competent teachers translate this knowledge about social relationships into effective curricular and instructional strategies, and focus on developing a relationship with a child before any teaching occurs, as they generally understand certain culturally derived behaviors that govern learning, namely warmth, nurturing, and hospitable classroom environments (Day-Vines, 2000).

Field Dependence as a Culturally Mediated Learning Style

Frequently, students' cultural orientations influence their learning styles and preferences. As an example, much has been written about field dependence and field independence as it pertains to African American adolescents. Students with field independent learning styles are more likely to impose structure and organization upon discrete tasks or information (Franks & Dolan, 1982). Accordingly, the onus is on the student to make sense of the material and organize it in reference to previously presented information in a way that makes sense. However, many African American students are typically field-dependent and field sensitive, which means these students organize and conceptualize information based on external cues. That is, they may rely on other people's opinions and viewpoints and integrate presented information in a social context (Daniels, 2002). Classrooms that rely on field independence as a predominant mode of instruction fail to give information in a manner that is readily accessible to African American students. Recognition of students' culturally mediated cognitive structures represents an essential component for maximizing educational outcomes, particularly when teachers can develop compatible instructional strategies (Gay, 2000).

Multiple Sensory Stimulation

Many traditionally oriented African American students have a propensity toward verve, or an intense sensory stimulation (Gay, 2000). These students, especially those with gifts and talents, prefer and respond better to instructional strategies that rely on visual stimuli, tactile and kinesthetic learning, as well as personal reinforcement. Additionally, many African American students respond favorably to learning that integrates movement, rhythm, and music. Similarly, teachers who employ engaging, energetic, and performance-oriented teaching approaches are more likely to sustain the attention and interest of African American youngsters. Such teaching approaches cohere with the oratorical and communication styles that generally govern social interactions within the African American church and community. Adopting culturally compatible instructional strategies holds considerable promise for fostering academic achievement among gifted and talented African American adolescents.

Group Orientation

Cooperative learning refers to educational situations in which students work in small groups to accomplish academic tasks (Tucker, 1999). African American students often respond well to this particular instructional medium because it relies on shared responsibility and cooperation, factors that are familiar within African American cultural contexts. In this sense, a group orientation takes precedence over an individual and competitive oriented focus, which can be perceived by many students as threatening and intimidating. When teachers consider the culturally mediated cognitive, affective, and behavioral manner in which students acquire new information they can begin to structure culturally congruent learning experiences that enhance academic performance.

Stereotype Threat

Steele and Aronson's (1995) classic study attributes the underachievement of many African Americans at least in part to a phenomenon they label *stereotype threat*. Essentially, their research has concluded that African Americans internalize negative assumptions about their intellectual functioning, which in turn impedes academic progress. In a study of Caucasian and African American undergraduates who were administered portions of the Graduate Record Exam (GRE), African American students who were required to report race scored less well than their Caucasian counterparts. In marked contrast, African American students who were not required to report race scored equally as well as Caucasian students. In a related study, when test administrators informed African Americans that their intellectual skills were being assessed by responding to the English section of the GRE, they routinely scored below Caucasian students. Connecting performance on the GRE with intelligence served as a "threat" to the stereotype of lesser intelligence often associated with African Americans. However, African Americans who were told the GRE simply measured a problem-solving task typically scored about the same as Whites. These findings led Steele and Aronson to conclude that stereotypes attributed to people in stigmatized groups such as African Americans can have adverse effects on academic performance. Gifted African American adolescents are particularly susceptible to the negative assumptions others maintain about their abilities (Patton & Townsend, 1997).

The above discussion underscores how African American student perceptions, that they cannot compete on par with their Caucasian counterparts, can possibly undermine performance and pose serious socioemotional and instructional challenges, resulting in fear, anxiety, and diminished self-efficacy levels. This phenomenon often continues beyond middle and high school. Culturally competent educators can address this issue with students by seeking opportunities to encourage students, maintaining high expectations for students, and ensuring that other professionals engage students in ways that promote social and cognitive competence.

Teacher Expectations/Perceptions

In her groundbreaking work, Ladson-Billings (1994) elaborated on the aspects of the classroom that make it a safe and nurturing place within which African American students can learn and grow. She noted that successful teachers of these students exude warmth and respect the personhood of the students by demonstrating simple kindness through praise, listening, smiling, and showing respect for other students. To reiterate this point, the cultural orientation of African American students often relies on an affinity toward social interactions. Moreover, many African American students historically have experienced educational institutions as oppressive forces that negatively impact educational outcomes (Patton & Day-Vines, 2003). Healthy socioemotional functioning rests upon a child's ability to feel a sense of connectedness, support, and security. Classroom climates that lack this dynamic seriously undermine a child's ability to profit from the learning experience.

The research of Neal, McCray, Webb-Johnson, and Bridgest (2003) has concluded that teachers' perceptions and expectations affect their interactions with students and the academic and social-emotional outcomes of those children. If those expectations are based on a deficit paradigm in which teachers expect less of certain students because they do not share a common background, race, culture, or social class as the teacher, then those expectations will influence the teacher's interactions toward those children and possibly hamper the youngsters' socioemotional well-being and academic performance. Teachers often may misinterpret those students' aggression, underachievement, and behaviors that may be characteristic of potentiality for special education programs when in fact, students behave in accordance with their culturally derived behaviors such as dress, speech patterns, or other nonverbal behaviors (Neal et al., 2003).

In the case of gifted and talented students, teachers also may slip into different expectations or inequitable treatment based on the behaviors common to the gifted child. Divergent thinking and asking questions often are greeted by teachers with irritation and annoyance and typically are less tolerated in females than in males (Lovecky, 1993). The behaviors of gifted students such as nonconformity and the questioning of authority often may seem threatening to adults who may either try to break the child's spirit or ignore the child altogether and, in so doing, diminish the child's socioemotional well-being (Ford et al., 2000). Thus, gifted African American students have, to some teachers, two strikes against them if they appear inquisitive and study in-depth on topics so that their learning surpasses their teachers, and behave and learn in ways that are culturally mediated, such as field dependent learning styles. For many of these students, the classroom may not be a safe or nurturing environment in which to explore their gifts and talents. As we discuss in the next section, an adolescent who may be characterized as being overly excitable may perceive the classroom environment as one that diminishes her or his socioemotional well-being.

Overexcitabilities

It has been found that students with overexcitabilities have a heightened awareness and greater capacity to respond to stimuli (Silverman, 1993). First conceptualized by the Polish psychiatrist Dabrowski (1964), the idea of overexcitability, translated from the Polish as "superstimulatability," carried positive connotations as those individuals who demonstrated this phenomenon had an abundance of physical, sensual, creative, intellectual, and emotional energy (Silverman, 1993). Overexcitabilities (OEs) are seen as different ways an individual experiences the world and have been believed to be an indicator of giftedness (O'Connor, 2002) However, manifestations of some of these overexcitabilities have been viewed as pathological or at the very least, not considered "normal" or socially acceptable. It is beyond the scope of this chapter to discuss in detail the different overexcitabilities; however, a brief discussion of three (intellectual, imaginational, and psychomotor) seems appropriate as they may influence perceptions of gifted African American students.

Psychomotor Overexcitabilities. Piechowski and Colangelo (1984) described psychomotor OE as love of movement for movement's sake or a heightened excitability of the neuromuscular system. Students with psychomotor OE may be perceived as impulsive, restless, or hyperactive. Manifestations of this OE may challenge educators' perceptions and planning.

Psychomotor OEs allow gifted students to maintain focus on a project or task for a long period of time and produce in great quantities if the projects provide mental stimulation and align with the students' gifts and talents. These students can exhaust adults who may require more sleep and who have difficulty providing for the need for novelty and stimulus that these students require (Silverman, 1993).

Intellectual Overexcitabilities. An intellectual OE results in students developing a passion for learning and the capacity for sustained concentration and curiosity. Students who display intellectual OEs can become impatient with those who do not process concepts and ideas as fast as they do and may tend to blurt out their thoughts and interrupt others in their excitement over an idea (Lind, 2001). These children ask questions and probe for answers (Silverman, 1993). Furthermore, attention to class material and sitting for long periods of time can be difficult for these children but precisely the behaviors required and commended in the schools. While question-asking often is marked as a sign of student engagement, students who ask too many questions may be perceived as annoying, needy, showing off, or lacking in social skills.

Imaginational Overexcitabilities. Imaginational OEs may prompt students to draw and write stories instead of doing seat work as they build and explore their own private words or fantastical landscapes in an effort to head off boredom they may be experiencing in class (Lind, 2001).

Dual Diagnosis and Twice-Exceptionality

Within the fields of psychology and education, there has been a great deal of discussion about dual and misdiagnosis in the case of gifted students who display some of these behaviors. Impulsive actions, increased bodily movement, and rapid speech coupled with apparent boredom or lack of attention and doodling in class can be seen by educators as characteristics of ADD or ADHD (Mika, 2006).

There has been a great degree of confusion in distinguishing ADD/ADHD from common gifted characteristics indicating the need for appropriate diagnosis, as well as research (Hartnett, Nelson, & Rinn, 2004). However, gifted children often are inaccurately diagnosed with ADHD and receive medical treatment although they may respond equally well if not better to modifying the educational environment to better fit their gifted needs (Goerss, Amend, Webb, Webb, & Beljan, 2006; Webb et al., 2005).

Culturally competent teachers will want to ascertain the accuracy of their perceptions and assumptions about their students' behaviors, as well as explore possible alternative explanations for behavior. If gifted African American students also have challenges to learning such as a learning disability, this can create additional challenges to identity development and academic performance. Gifted students who have a learning disability may evidence problems with sequential skills, rote memorization, spelling, phonetics, difficulty with legible handwriting, and may describe or evidence an inability to persevere in the pursuit of goals (Reis & Colbert, 2004; Silverman, 1989). These students also may experience and report anxiety, frustration with the inability to articulate their knowledge in a useful manner, lack of self-confidence, and the avoidance of competition of certain tasks in which failure may occur (Reis & Colbert, 2004; Vespi & Yewchuk, 1992). Educators should be alert to these students' anger based on the conflicting beliefs in both their inability to reach their own goals and their beliefs that they are failures if they cannot reach their goals (Silverman, 1989; Vespi & Yewchuk, 1992).

Given the disproportionate numbers of African American students placed in special education (Adkison-Bradley, Johnson, Rawls, & Plunkett, 2006; Losen & Orfield, 2002), diligence is needed before making recommendations that might negatively impact a student's educational prospects. Educators may wish to become more familiar with issues concerning dual and misdiagnosis and twice-exceptionality. As with any decision making regarding student placement or further testing and evaluation, the student's thoughts, behavior, functionality, environment, context, and personal and medical history all should be explored (Mika, 2006; Goerss et al., 2006). Furthermore, an understanding of the identity functioning of African Americans would be invaluable.

Identity Functioning
and Gifted African American Students

Identity Development as a Correlate of Socioemotional Functioning

Identity development is an important correlate of human functioning without which individuals experience psychological distress and a sense of personal worthlessness. African Americans typically must negotiate multiple competing identity structures simultaneously. For instance, DuBois (1903/1999) addressed the concept of a bifurcated cultural identity construct of African Americans when he noted, "One ever feels his twoness,—an American, a Negro; two souls, two thoughts, two unreconciled strivings; two warring ideals in one dark body, whose dogged strength alone keeps it from being torn asunder" (p. 45).

Analogously, in breakthrough conceptual and empirical research, Boykin and Toms (1985) articulated a "triple quandary" model indicating that healthy cultural identity functioning rests upon successful, simultaneous negotiation of three separate, complex, and competing identities. Boykin and Toms maintained that African Americans are socialized in three distinct ways: as members of (a) mainstream American culture, (b) minority culture, and (c) African American culture. The mainstream American identity involves the adoption of certain dominant American cultural values such as competition and individualism, as well as attitudes that result more from assimilation into American culture as opposed to their minority existence. The second identity structure includes socialization of the individual as a minority that includes the inevitable exposure to varying forms of racism and discrimination (Tatum, 1997). The third identity structure recognizes the tapestry of African and African American heritage. It has been found that gifted African American students have the added burden of integrating these identity structures with their gifted status (Townsend & Patton, 1995). An integral part of identity development is racial identity development.

Racial Identity Theory

As stated above, identity refers to the psychological orientation of the self toward a particular reference group. One's psychological orientation or identity can be catalogued along a number of different dimensions including occupation, religion, and sex roles, as well as racial identity (Erikson, 1955). Racial identity is a specific identity domain that pertains to one's sense of affiliation or disassociation with others who possess the same racial heritage (Helms, 1993). Racial identity addresses an individual's reference group orientation or attitudes toward a particular social group as opposed to personal identification, which refers more to a universal set of personality variables such as self-esteem. Racial identity theories help school personnel consider the vast heterogeneity of individuals and avoid the tendency to view people from a particular racial group as monolithic entities. That is, although people may share a common racial heritage, they may have very distinct perceptions and attitudes about people of their own or others' racial designation. As we discuss later in this chapter, given the theoretical and empirical relationship between healthy racial identity functioning, academic achievement, and psychological well-being, and the fact that aside from families, schools serve as primary socializing agents, teachers have a compelling rationale for identifying culturally responsive curricular and instructional strategies to optimize the racial identity state of gifted African American students (Ford, 2001; Grantham & Ford, 2003; Harper, 2007; Sellars et al., 2006).

Cross's Racial Identity Model. Early in the development of racial identity theories, Cross (1991) articulated four distinct statuses of racial identity that explain the vast heterogeneity or within group differences that characterize African Americans. They are as follows: (a) pre-encounter, (b) encounter, (c) immersion-emersion, and (d) internalization. In this paradigm, individuals transition from orientations in which race has limited significance in their lives to self-prescribed conceptualizations of blackness that esteem African American worldviews, as well as other cultural orientations. Each stage in this model has important implications that teachers can employ to facilitate student self-understanding and subsequently enhance counseling outcomes for gifted African American students

Pre-encounter status. During the pre-encounter status, individuals often endorse Eurocentric notions of blackness. More recent advances in the measurement of racial identity functioning has resulted in a more differentiated set of statuses (Vandiver, Cross, Worrell, & Fhagen-Smith, 2002). As an example, individuals operating in the pre-encounter status can assume a more differentiated profile that encompasses assimilationist or an anti-Black perspective. Pre-encounter adolescents with an assimilationist posture have low-salience attitudes and often assign limited relevance to their racial identity while granting higher priority to their status as human beings, students, athletes, religious group members, or other distinctive statuses that de-emphasize race. Some pre-encounter adolescents who harbor anti-Black attitudes minimize contact with and maintain stereotyped attitudes toward other African Americans. Vandiver (2001) has attributed this behavior to miseducation and racial self-hatred. Consistent with Fordham's (1988) early analysis, pre-encounter adolescents frequently adopt a "raceless persona" and risk accusations by their peers of selling out. Students with a preponderance of pre-encounter attitudes may prefer or request to work with a White teacher and may express reluctance toward an African American teacher. Gifted African American adolescents may be particularly susceptible to pre-encounter identity attitudes because of the attendant feelings of isolation and alienation that can result from being one of few African Americans in classes for the gifted and some negative reactions engendered by some of their African American peers (Ford, 2001). We explore this phenomenon further later in the chapter. Appropriate instructional strategies would help pre-encounter adolescents with anti-Black attitudes gain more self-acceptance and accordingly function more effectively socioemotionally (Grantham & Ford, 2003; Parham & Helms, 1981).

Encounter status. The pre-encounter phase draws to a close once the individual experiences a catalytic or jolting event that causes her or him to challenge pre-encounter attitudes and transition into the encounter status. Catalytic events include, but are not limited to, racial slights and indignities such as being told he or she cannot compete on par with his or her Caucasian peers. Positive experiences such as exposure to a new aspect of African or African American culture also can facilitate movement into the encounter status. Encounter individuals often experience cognitive dissonance as a result of vacillating between two identity states—the previous identity and the emerging identity—and consequently, often pledge to begin an active search for their identity (Ford, 2001; Grantham & Ford, 2003; Vandiver, Fhagen-Smith, Cokely, Cross, & Worrell; 2001; White & Parham, 1990). Students in this stage might express a preference for working with an African American teacher. Teachers working with encounter students would probably want to explore the thoughts and circumstances that contributed to movement into this stage (Vandiver, 2001).

Immersion-emersion status. During stage three, immersion-emersion, individuals generally bask in their newfound Black identity, subscribe to externally driven dictates of what constitutes blackness, and engage in "ostentatious displays" of racial pride. Such displays may include adherence to Black norms of speech, garb, and social activity, although the individual would probably not internalize this behavior. Adolescents functioning in the immersion-emersion stage can exhibit anti-White attitudes where they direct overt hostility toward Whites or they may exhibit intense Black involvement such that they idealize everything that is Black (Vandiver, 2001). Students operating in this stage may have a strong preference for an African American teacher and may even reject or demonstrate hostility toward a White teacher. These intense displays of emotion may include rage at Whites for having promulgated stereotypic notions of blackness, a personal sense of shame and guilt for having previously denied Black racial identity, and feelings of overwhelming pride that result from new levels of awareness and consciousness. Given their heightened sense of perceptiveness and keen sensitivity to perceived injustices, gifted African American students operating in the immersion–emersion stage may exhibit high levels of emotional intensity in response to perceived injustices (Grantham & Ford, 2003). During the latter phase of this stage, emersion individuals emerge from this identity state with less idealistic and more objective views of blackness. Given the emotional intensity of the immersion–emersion individual, a teacher would need to demonstrate considerable compassion and understanding and might need to interpret the student's behavior more as a reaction against the system of racism and oppression rather than viewing his or her behavior as a personal attack. Teaching objectives for students in this stage may include an exploration of their vast range of emotions and behaviors reflective of this stage of racial identity development.

Internalization status. During stage four, internalization, African Americans generally demonstrate a greater sense of personal comfort and do not feel the overwhelming anger and hostility characteristic of the immersion–emersion stage. Given their more inclusive worldview, adolescents at this stage generally prescribe for themselves acceptable notions of blackness and have a healthy appreciation toward members of their own racial group, as well as acceptance of the racial identity development of those with other racial backgrounds. During internalization, the teacher's race becomes less of an issue (Parham & Helms, 1981).

Grantham and Ford (2003) asserted that for gifted students in particular, racial identity functioning must be valued and nurtured because it represents an important correlate of socioemotional well-being. In fact, there exists a theoretical and empirical relationship between racial identity and emotional well-being such that healthy psychological functioning is associated with higher levels of racial identity functioning (Seaton, Scottham, & Sellars, 2006; Sellars et al., 2006; Yasui, Dorham, & Dishion, 2003).

Ideally, teachers should be able to recognize certain behavioral attributes of students functioning at various racial identity statuses. Accurate conceptualization of student behavior may prevent teachers from making negative attributions about students. Further, teachers can develop assignments that permit students to address socioemotional issues related to self-awareness and self-exploration while simultaneously addressing curricular objectives. Later in this chapter we outline some additional strategies.

Fictive Kinship Networks

In a classic study, Fordham (1988) conducted a qualitative study of high-achieving African American students and concluded that students felt compelled to make a mutually exclusive choice between social acceptance among the peer group and academic success. More specifically, the peer group, which she termed *fictive kinship networks*, dissuaded successful students from maintaining an academic focus. Fictive kinship networks can exert negative peer pressure on academically oriented students by using social isolation, ostracism, and making accusations that scholastic achievement is tantamount to "acting White." Incidentally, the notion of acting White includes behaviors such as speaking standard English; adopting hobbies or extracurricular activities that attract few African American students (i.e., orchestra, swimming, forensic teams, and the like); having friendships outside the African American peer group; and listening to music that has a White orientation (Day-Vines, Patton, & Baytops, 2003). Sadly, some achievement-oriented students may regard academic success as an act of betrayal to the peer group and consequently opt for underachievement (Suarez-Orozco & Suarez-Orozco, 1995). In Fordham's study academically successful students adopted a "raceless persona" by assimilating into mainstream American society and thereby distancing themselves socially and psychologically from their African American peers. Culturally competent teachers help students recognize the feasibility of functioning successfully among the fictive kinship networks and the American cultural mainstream simultaneously.

Townsend and Patton (1995) conducted a qualitative analysis of the experiences of gifted African American high school students who failed to demonstrate that gifted African American students adopted a raceless persona. In fact, they found that, as a

result of the use of cultural "code switching" and other socioemotional strategies, gifted African American students could
maintain and even integrate their three often distinct cultural
identities. In this study of "three warring souls" their findings
indicated that the gifted African American students felt compelled to negotiate simultaneously three specific identity structures: (a) mainstream American culture, (b) African American
culture, and (c) gifted culture. Teachers who recognize the
"three warring souls" dilemma that students confront related
to identity and peer pressure can provide a measure of warmth,
support, and nurturing that can promote socioemotional well-
being and help students successfully negotiate identity related
conflict, thus helping to prevent underachievement.

Underachievement

This chapter has discussed the social, personal, and academic issues experienced by and frequently found challenging
to gifted African American students. Significant factors such
as the lack of appropriate identification, the training of culturally competent educators, the need for a fit between instructional style and learning needs, the awareness of and respect
for African American cultural values, recognition of the extent
to which racial identity functioning shapes psychological well-
being, and the provision of an integrative multicultural curriculum have been addressed in this chapter. It is the lack of these
factors that can contribute to the underachievement of gifted
African American students.

Although there is no consensus on one operational definition of underachievement, in general, underachievement
refers to the discrepancy between ability and performance over
a substantial period of time (Reis & McCoach, 2000). Varying
school districts quantify the concept of underachievement using
different criteria such as grade point average, standardized tests,
achievement tests, checklists, and a reliance on teachers' sub-
jectivity about student performance that makes identifying students who are underachieving challenging. When determining
if a student is underachieving, multiple issues should be considered including the following: the duration of time (persistent,

temporary, or situational); the subject; and the source of the underachievement (Ford & Thomas, 1997). Although a detailed discussion of underachievement lies beyond the scope of this chapter, we provide some contextual factors that can contribute to the underachievement of gifted African American students.

Possible Causes of Underachievement. Ford and Thomas (1997) suggested peer pressure, low self-esteem, poor student-teacher relationships, poor test performance, and low teacher expectations as critical influences on underachievement. In their review of literature Reis and McCoach (2002) listed the following as possible environmental and individual causes that singularly or in combination can lead to underachievement: underchallenging classroom placements or curricula; peer pressure; loneliness and isolation; family dynamics; internalizing issues such as depression, anxiety, and perfectionism; externalizing issues such as rebellion, irritability, nonconformity, and anger; unrecognized learning disabilities; having nontraditional gifts; challenges to self-regulation; unhealthy coping strategies; and social immaturity.

Cultural Mismatch. African American gifted underachievers in Ford's (1995) study reported that they had fewer affirmative student-teacher relationships, little time to understand content, less supportive classroom climates, limited levels of motivation, and feelings of disinterest in school that was tied to a lack of multicultural education (Ford & Thomas, 1997). Ford's findings support Irvine's (1990) theory of cultural mismatch proposing that when the four situations of learning contexts, curriculum and instruction, student-teacher relationships, and teacher expectations are culturally incongruent, underachievement and dropping out can result (Ford et al., 2000). This chapter has addressed many of these particular situations and various intertwining factors.

We have outlined several issues that have the potential to undermine healthy socioemotional development among African American adolescents. We proffer that culturally competent teachers of the gifted can use their existing repertoire of teaching strategies to meet the social-emotional needs of their students if they begin to look at their curriculum using an *affective* lens. We recommend that teachers remain cognizant of the contextual dimensions of race, ethnicity, and culture so that they may better support African American adolescents, and, by so doing, demonstrate a measure of cultural competence. In the final section of this chapter we further identify some instructional strategies teachers can use to address the socioemotional and curricular needs of African American students. We begin by addressing critical thinking strategies.

Increasing the Cultural Relevance of Instructional Strategies

Critical Thinking Models

Critical thinking models represent an appropriate vehicle for stimulating and promoting socioemotional adjustment and well-being among African American adolescents and by extension all students. We recognize that the vast majority of gifted African American students will matriculate within integrated classroom settings. Although the strategies we recommend in this section pertain to all students, we describe their particular relevance to African American adolescents.

Instructional Recommendations

According to Resnick (1987), many effective programs for improving thinking skills have something in common—they rely on a social setting and social interaction for teaching and practice. Teachers can design lessons that engage students in problem-solving activities. These groups can occur in dyads, triads, or small groups. As discussed in an earlier section of this chapter, cooperative learning has been identified as an appropriate instructional strategy for African American youngsters because it accommodates the socioemotional preference for field dependent learning.

In a culturally diverse gifted class, the teacher would have to coordinate student grouping arrangements. For instance, as much as possible, teachers should ensure that the composition of the groups reflects the cultural heterogeneity of the class. Such an approach will enhance students' ability to gain multiple perspectives about various issues and topics, thus promoting interracial and intercultural understanding and empathy.

Initially, the teacher would establish a set of ground rules in an effort to structure safe group interactions among students. These ground rules may address issues such as confidentiality, especially because sharing personal thoughts and feelings outside of a family context often is negatively sanctioned in African American culture (Day-Vines et al., 2003). Establishing respect for divergent thoughts and opinions as a ground rule gives students permission to talk openly without fear of reprisals. Teachers also may stipulate that each student will contribute in meaningful ways to the group process. This last guideline avoids individuals participating as spectators or voyeurs and promotes an atmosphere that facilitates trust and open communication. Finally, each student should be permitted to share as much or as little as he or she chooses so that he or she is not volunteering information that may be personally intrusive.

During the group process, the teacher could choose materials, problems, and issues that promote interracial and intercultural understanding and empathy. Each student could be required to think aloud. This model of instruction that makes thinking *visible* is what Collins, Brown, and Newman (1989) refer to as *cognitive apprenticeship*. In cases where students may lack readiness for such activities, the teacher could model the process. As a best practice the teacher may preassess students in an effort to diagnose the students' strengths, aspirations, and potential obstacles. This information can be used to monitor the student's progress and to design appropriate activities and assessments. For instance, with a group of newly admitted gifted students, a teacher might ask each student to respond individually to each of the following questions:

- Why I am in the gifted program?
- What do I hope the program can do for me?
- What do I hope to achieve in the program?
- What would I have to do to attain my goals?

- What are some possible problems I may face in the program?
- What perceptions do people have of me as a student who is gifted?

The answers to these questions need not be elaborate. However, the information should be referred to regularly as teachers find ways to help students overcome obstacles, encourage those who lack confidence and have limited self-efficacy levels and develop students' promise and potential. As teachers seek to do this, they should engage in a form of cultural self-assessment—what additional cultural knowledge and competencies are needed for them to be effective teachers?

Gifted African American adolescents are likely to respond to these prompts in ways that parallel the responses of White students. For instance, African American students may express their pride, joy, ambivalence, and aspirations related to matriculation in the gifted program. At the same time, they may express some culture-specific concerns such as the stereotype threat. Given what is commonly understood about the stereotype threat and the cultural preference for field dependent learning among many African American students, instructional strategies such as the one described above can positively impact socioemotional functioning by bolstering self-efficacy levels and enhancing classroom climates, as well as increasing opportunities for academic engagement and success. Similarly, African American students may allude to issues related to racial identity development and their particular sense of identification or disidentification with other African American students. Additively, this particular exercise helps African American students recognize both their similarities and differences with their gifted counterparts and promotes shared cultural understanding and respect among the gifted peer group.

Thinking aloud then should be followed by having students share their *feelings* about what and how others *think* about the issues. At this stage, teacher sensitivity is critical as students with differing viewpoints could look to the teacher for "resolution." In dealing with the issue of different perspectives arising from varied cultural experiences and racial identities, it is important that both majority and minority students are affirmed, and at the same time, accept seemingly contradictory views and practices without making value judgments. For instance, a White student may have difficulty comprehending why an African American student relies heavily on the African American peer group for validation, despite a certain amount of ostracism from the same race peer group. The rules established governing group discourse specifies that students must respect varying viewpoints as no less legitimate. Although Caucasian students may not have had identical experiences, they probably can identify with the affective experience of their African American peers. It is through this shared affective process that students may achieve mutuality, adopt new modes of problem-solving mechanisms, and develop connections within the gifted peer group. Validation of students' sense of cultural identity will enhance their self-concept, which will in turn preempt the problem of underachievement (Grantham & Ford, 2003). The goal is to make everyone in the class feel that his or her cultural identity, culture, and ways of thinking, feeling, and functioning are different, not superior or inferior to that of another student.

A follow-up activity to the student's reflection could be an orientation activity wherein a small group could get students to introduce themselves, using the set of guiding questions that follow: How do I see myself? Why? How do I think others see me? What could be the reasons for their perception of me in this way? What do others think about me? How can the differences be reconciled? Once a month, a scenario based on issues similar to those raised by students can be posted on the class bulletin board and students can be invited to respond to the scenario. It is important to allow students channels to exchange views and verbalize their feelings as learning represents a social activity.

Bloom's Taxonomy

Bloom's taxonomy represents another critical thinking model that can address both curricular issues and the socioemotional development of gifted students simultaneously. Bloom's Revised taxonomy (Anderson & Krathwohl, 2001) has expanded the types of skills associated with each level of reasoning: knowledge, comprehension, application, analysis, evaluation, and synthesis. Gifted education students are far more likely to employ the three highest reasoning levels and would benefit from activities such as determining points of view, and exploring bias, values, or intent underlying presented material. According to Bloom's taxonomy, appropriate tasks involve having students take curriculum content and consider what is fact and what is opinion; analyze assumptions underlying opinions; examine author motives; and use evidence to evaluate what is more important, moral, better, logical, valid, or appropriate. These strategies help students explore controversial issues that are likely to arise from bias, stereotypes, and limited worldviews. Controversy provides an excellent opportunity for students (guided by teachers, if necessary) to think through moral issues. How does one make an informed judgment? What is a fair judgment? How does one remain open to new evidence that might weaken one's stance?

As an example, a lesson based on Rosa Guy's (1993) *The Ups and Downs of Carl Davis III,* addresses dilemmas related to racism, prejudice, perceptions, fear, and pride in one's heritage. In a series of letters addressed to his father 3 months after Carl, an African American adolescent male, has been sent to live with his grandmother in South Carolina, Carl describes his experiences as he attempts to teach others about his heritage. Teachers could generate discussion questions that address conflicts Carl encountered with his teacher and peers. For instance, why was Reggie ashamed? Why did he dislike Carl? How had Carl contributed to this misunderstanding? In his letters, Carl had mentioned the Johnsons from Sweden. How were Carl's problems similar to those of the Johnsons? Suggest a plan of action the school can adopt to promote better understanding among students of different backgrounds and cultures.

Teachers may not always have the latitude within which to introduce new materials, particularly given the standardized nature of many state curricula. Teachers may, however, use Bloom's model to allow students to critique, analyze, and interrogate conventional constructions of knowledge, thereby responding to the fact that many African American students remain disengaged because they do not perceive school curricula as culturally relevant (Delpit, 1995). In a government course, for example, students may discuss the applicability of the U.S. Constitution to diverse groups during the 19th century. For instance, teachers might ask students to look at what groups experienced exclusion or inclusion according to the constitution and how that has changed today. Such discussions require comprehension of the subject matter before students can venture off into their own interpretations and evaluations of phenomena.

Paul's Reasoning Model

Another model that lends itself to nurturing the affect of critical thinkers is Paul's reasoning model (Paul & Elder, 2001). Not only does the model provide the traits, elements, and standards of critical thinking, it also provides an important link integrating cognition and the affect. This model is most consistent with the socioemotional and cultural needs of African American adolescents given the previously discussed general cultural orientations of African Americans. It clearly stipulates both the affective and intellectual traits required in a critical and fair-minded thinker. Through frequent practice and application guided by the rigorous standards of thought, one can become self-directed, self-disciplined, self-monitored, and self-corrective. Hence, developing critical thinking among African American adolescents also can help to provide insight and depth of thought related to certain socioemotional and cultural issues such as fictive kinship networks, the stereotype threat, and racial identity functioning. In the context of nurturing the social-emotional growth of students, teachers should apply critical thinking and reasoning skills and judgment in areas where there might be a tendency toward egocentric or sociocentric bias.

There are eight elements of reasoning and the teacher can start with any of these elements in discussing a piece of writing. The eight elements and their standards are as follows:
- point of view;
- goal or purpose;

- question or problem;
- facts and data experience;
- ideas, concepts, laws, theories, and principles;
- assumptions;
- implications or consequences; and
- inferences or conclusions.

The following intellectual standards also are recommended to check the quality of one's thinking (Paul & Elder, 2002):
- Clarity: Could you elaborate on what you mean with an example?
- Accuracy: How could we check the correctness of the facts?
- Precision: Could you give some specific details?
- Relevance: How does that help readers better understand the issue/problem?
- Depth: Are you dealing with the complexities of the problem?
- Breadth: Have you considered alternative points of view?
- Logic: Does your conclusion follow from the evidence at hand?
- Significance: Is this the most important question we should be dealing with?
- Fairness: Have I represented views that contradict my own?

Cultivation of Students' Dispositions. Not every element has to be touched on in a lesson. Resnick (1987) also encouraged teachers to cultivate students' *dispositions* to use their thinking skills widely and frequently. More frequent applications would sharpen students' thinking and reasoning abilities, as well as their socioemotional development. Resnick asserted that there is a social dimension to this. A student has to have the moral courage to disagree with someone in authority (e.g., the teacher or the top student) if he feels he is able to support his line of argument. The student may have to be persistent enough to find evidence to support his stance and have the strength to stand by his work if it is being questioned and challenged by other critical thinkers or have the willingness to admit error.

Table 7.1
Web References and Resources
for Multicultural Education

http://members.aol.com/mcsing29
http://falcon.jmu.edu/~ramseyil/multipub.htm
http://www.4children.org/news/9-97mlit.htm
http://www.mindspring.com/~mlmcc/kidsbooks.htm
http://www.soe.usfca.edu/institutes/childlit
http://www.miscositas.com
http://www.icdlbooks.com

Likewise, the student has to have the humility to acknowledge the better quality of other people's ideas and arguments if the evidence points to such a conclusion and a desire to keep learning and searching for the truth. As previously stated, teachers can engage students in higher cognitive processes and meet their socioemotional needs as long as teachers bring these needs into their consciousness.

What teachers teach is as important as *how* teachers teach. A common challenge faced by teachers of African American gifted adolescents is the dearth of appropriate multicultural curriculum materials for different grade levels. Again, we cannot wait for these materials to be developed and do little about multicultural and international education. We believe that teachers can use existing resources and adapt them to address the diverse needs of students. Table 7.1 provides some appropriate Internet resources to help you do this.

In the context of teaching for better cultural understanding, teachers can design curricular activities to assess students' biases and stereotypes. In a language arts lesson, students could be asked to write a short story with at least two main characters from different racial groups, one of which must be the student's own. The theme of the story could be any one of the following: courage, kindness, compassion, persistence, respect, exploitation, cruelty, alienation, or discrimination. The students' stories can be a powerful indicator of their implicit attitudes to others who are different from them (i.e., by race, gender, SES).

The teacher should note the areas that needed work, and for subsequent lessons, choose materials that lend themselves to discussion of biases and stereotypes, and focus mainly, but not exclusively, on the cultures that are most misunderstood and misperceived. After the unit(s) has been completed, the teacher could conduct a postassessment, asking students whether their views have changed and why or why not. The teacher could provide another assignment that will tap into students' implicit attitudes toward differences among people. For example, in a grammar lesson, the teacher could get students to list the bare facts in the text. Next, students could be asked to add the adjectives, adverbs, phrases, and clauses to describe how these facts are treated in the story. Then ask them: What are the implications of these additional descriptors on the author's portrayal of a character or depiction of an event?

In a culturally diverse class, teachers should promote the reading of biographies and autobiographies of people of different races. For African American adolescents who might have been socialized into a culture of inferiority, encouraging them to read about people who have overcome adversity may serve as a critical source of empowerment (Day-Vines, Moore-Thomas, & Hines, 2005). Similarly, students from the dominant culture can use multicultural literature to examine their own socially conditioned assumptions. Relatedly, *The Pact* (Davis, Jenkins, & Hunt, 2002) is a biography of three high school friends from Newark, NJ, who, despite the exigencies associated with urban living, pledge to become medical doctors after attending a college recruitment seminar for minority students interested in premed programs. Protagonists within the literature do not necessarily have to be of the same race as the student. The book could be about a female pioneer struggling for recognition in a male-dominated field; a newly arrived immigrant finding himself in his new country; or a freedom fighter championing the cause of the oppressed.

A common misperception is that culturally homogeneous classes do not need culturally responsive education or that it is not as easy to discuss points of view of other cultures because these are not represented in the class. The environment should provide abundant natural opportunities to highlight multi-cultural and affective issues. As an example, all students are exposed to the media. One could provide opportunities to dis-cuss stereotypes perpetuated by the media and the motivation for them. Teachers should encourage students to use critical thinking skills to deconstruct advertisements, get at underly-ing assumptions, and consider what evidence to seek and use to "correct'" these stereotypes. News, movies, songs, art—all of these mediums can be used to get students to examine different perspectives, underlying assumptions, and consequences.

Another culturally relevant instructional strategy related to critical thinking involves getting students interested in what is happening to age peers elsewhere, in other parts of the country, and other parts of the world. Teachers can harness technology to overcome the expanse of geography. For instance, they can identify partner schools that are willing to establish e-pal pro-grams for students. Through e-mail and Web pages, students can see and vicariously experience the life of people different from themselves. As students learn more about their e-pals, we hope they would be able to empathize and at the same time appreciate what they themselves have and enjoy. As students learn empathy, they hopefully will be motivated to do some-thing to improve the state of the world.

It is not difficult for teachers to look for ways to bring stu-dents to the social action level of Banks' (1997) model of multi-cultural education, where students examine social issues, make decisions, and take action to improve the situation. Teachers can look for service-learning possibilities (Billig, 2000) as extensions of the curriculum, or alert students to areas of need that they have the means to address. For example, teachers could conduct a toy collection to send to needy children in strife-torn countries. (To decide on appropriate toys would require students to learn more about the children who will be receiving the toys!)

Summary and Conclusion

This chapter has suggested that addressing the socioemotional needs of gifted African American adolescents requires culturally competent and responsive educators. It further has discussed selected culturally mediated factors that have been advanced as being relevant to the socioemotional needs of gifted African American adolescents. Given these contextual variables, we have offered a host of culturally mediated strategies that should respond to the contextual issues and guide educators as they journey down the path of cultural competence. Hopefully, the research, ideas, and suggestions made in this chapter can be used with adolescents from other culturally distinct groups as well.

Although this is usually not an easy, quick, and problem-free trip, not to begin this journey could be even more disastrous. This challenge, while educational in nature, also requires an ethical, social, cultural, and political response. Indeed, the future of this nation and the valuable resources of gifted African American adolescents are dependent on the successful completion of this cultural competence journey on the part of us all.

References

Anderson, L. W., & Krathwohl (Eds.). (2001). *A taxonomy for learning, teaching, and assessing: A revision of Bloom's taxonomy of educational objectives*. New York: Longman.

Adkison-Bradley, C., Johnson, P. D., Rawls, G., & Plunkett, D. (2006, September 5). Overrepresentation of African American males in special education programs: Implications and advocacy strategies for school counselors. *Journal of School Counseling, 4*(16). Retrieved May 14, 2008, from http://www.jsc.montana.edu/articles/v4n16.pdf

Banks, J. (1997). *Multicultural education: Goals and dimensions*. Retrieved March 19, 2004, from http://depts.washington.edu/centerme/view.htm

Billig, S. (2000). The effects of service learning. *School Administrator, 57,* 14–18.

Boykin, A. W. (1983). The academic performance of Afro-American children. In J. Spence (Ed.), *Achievement and achievement motives* (pp. 321–371). San Francisco: Freeman.

Boykin, A., & Toms, F. (1985). Black child socialization: A conceptual framework. In H. McAdoo & J. McAdoo (Eds.), *Black children: Social, educational, and parental environments* (pp. 33–51). Beverly Hills: Sage.

Collins, A., Brown, J. S., & Newman, S. E. (1989). Cognitive apprenticeship: Teaching the craft of reading, writing and mathematics. In L. B. Resnick (Ed.), *Knowing, learning and instruction: Essays in honor of Robert Glaser* (pp. 453–494). Hillsdale, NJ: Lawrence Erlbaum.

Cross, W. (1991). *Shades of Black: Diversity in African-American identity.* Philadelphia: Temple University Press.

Dabrowski, K. (1964). *Positive disintegration.* Boston: Little, Brown.

Daniels, V. I. (2002). Maximizing the learning potential of African American learners with gifts and talents. In F. E. Obiakor & B. A. Ford (Eds.), *Creating successful learning environments for African American learners with exceptionalities* (pp. 95–105). Thousand Oaks, CA: Corwin Press.

Davis, S., Jenkins, G., & Hunt, R. (2002). *The pact: Three young men make a promise and fulfill a dream.* New York: Penguin Putnam.

Day-Vines, N. L. (2000). Ethics, power and privilege: Salient issues in the development of multicultural competencies for special education teachers serving African American children with disabilities. *Teacher Education and Special Education, 23,* 3–18.

Day-Vines, N. L., Moore-Thomas, C., & Hines, E. (2005). Processing culturally relevant bibliotherapeutic selections with African American adolescents. *Counseling Interviewer, 38*(1), 13–18.

Day-Vines, N. L., Patton, J. M., & Baytops, J. L. (2003). Culturally responsive counseling of African American adolescents: Responding to the impact of race, culture and middle class status. *Professional School Counseling, 7,* 40–51.

Dee, T. S. (2004). Teachers, race, and student achievement in a randomized experiment. *The Review of Economics and Statistics, 86,* 195–210.

Delpit, L. (1995). *Other people's children: Cultural conflicts in the classroom.* New York: New Press.

DuBois, W. E. B. (1903/1999). *The souls of Black folk.* New York: New American Library.

Education Trust. (2003). *Achievement in America.* Retrieved July 14, 2004, from http://www2.edtrust.org/EdTrust/achievement+in+america. htm

Erikson, E. (1955). *Identity: Youth and crisis.* New York: Norton.

Ford, D. Y. (1995). *A study of achievement and underachievement among gifted, potentially gifted, and regular education Black students.* Storrs: National Research Center on the Gifted and Talented, University of Connecticut.

Ford, D. Y. (2001). Racial identity among gifted African American students. In M. Neihart, S. M. Reis, N. M. Robinson, & S. M.

Moon (Eds.), *The social and emotional development of gifted children: What do we know?* (pp. 155–163). Waco, TX: Prufrock.

Ford, D. Y., & Grantham, T. C. (2003). Providing access for culturally diverse gifted students: From deficit to dynamic thinking. *Theory Into Practice, 42,* 217–226.

Ford, D., Harris, J. J., Tyson, C., & Trotman, M. (2002). Beyond deficit thinking: Providing access for gifted African American students. *Roeper Review, 24,* 52–59.

Ford, D., Howard, T. C., Harris, J. J., & Tyson, C. A. (2000). Creating culturally responsive classrooms for gifted African American students. *Journal for the Education of the Gifted, 23,* 397–427.

Ford, D. Y., & Thomas, A. (1997). *Underachievement among gifted minority students: Problems and promises.* Reston, VA: ERIC Clearinghouse on Disabilities and Gifted Education. (ERIC Document Reproduction Service No. ED409660)

Fordham, S. (1988). Racelessness as a factor in Black students' school success: Pragmatic strategy or pyrrhic victory? *Harvard Educational Review, 58,* 54–84.

Franks, B., & Dolan, (1982). Affective characteristics of gifted children: Educational implications. *Gifted Child Quarterly, 26,* 172–178.

Gay, G. (2000). *Culturally responsive teaching: Theory, research, & practice.* New York: Teachers College Press.

Goerss, J., Amend, E., Webb, J. T., Webb, N., & Beljan, P. (2006). Comments on Mika's critique of Hartnett, Nelson, and Rinn's article "Gifted or ADHD? The possibilities of misdiagnosis." *Roeper Review, 28,* 249–251.

Goodwin, A. L. (1997). Historical and contemporary perspectives on multicultural teacher education: Past lessons, new direction. In J. E. Kings, E. R. Hollins, & W. C. Haymond (Eds.), *Preparing teachers for cultural diversity* (pp. 5–22). New York: Teachers College Press.

Grantham, T. C., & Ford, D. Y. (2003). Beyond self-concept and self-esteem: Racial identity and gifted African American students. *High School Journal, 87,* 18–29.

Greenwald, A. G., McGhee, D. E., & Schwartz, J. L. K. (1998). Measuring individual differences in implicit cognition: The implicit association test. *Journal of Personality and Social Psychology, 74,* 1464–1480.

Guy, R. (1993). *The ups and downs of Carl Davis III.* Madison, WI: Demco Media.

Hanley, J. (1999). Beyond the tip of the iceberg: Five stages toward cultural competence. *Today's Youth: The Community Circle of Caring Journal, 3*(2), 9–12.

Harper, B. E. (2007). The relationship between Black racial identity and academic achievement in urban settings. *Theory Into Practice, 46*, 230–238.

Hartnett, D. N., Nelson, J. M., & Rinn, A. N. (2004). Gifted or ADHD? The possibilities of misdiagnosis. *Roeper Review, 26*, 73–76.

Helms, J. (1993) The measurement of Black racial identity attitudes. In J. Helms (Ed.), *Black and White racial identity: Theory, research, and practice* (pp. 33–47). Westport, CT: Greenwood Press.

Holcomb-McCoy, C. (1998). *School counselor preparation in urban settings*. Reston, VA: ERIC Clearinghouse on Disabilities and Gifted Education. (ERIC Document Reproduction Service No. ED418343)

Irvine, J. J. (1990). *Black students and school failure*. Westport, CT: Greenwood.

Ladson-Billings, G. (1994). *The dreamkeepers: Successful teachers of African American children*. San Francisco: Jossey Bass.

Lind, S. (2001). Overexcitability and the gifted. *The SENG Newsletter, 1*(1), 3–6.

Losen, D. J., & Orfield, G. (2002). Introduction. In D. Losen & G. Orfield (Eds.), *Racial inequality in special education* (pp. xv–xxxvii) Boston: Harvard Education Publishing Group.

Lovecky, D. V. (1993). The quest for meaning: Counseling issues with gifted children and adolescents. In L. K. Silverman (Ed.), *Counseling the gifted and talented* (pp. 29–50). Denver, CO: Love.

Mika, E. (2006). Research commentary point-counterpoint: Diagnosis of giftedness and ADHD. *Roeper Review, 28*, 237–242.

Milner, R. H., & Ford, D. Y. (2007). Cultural considerations in the underrepresentation of culturally diverse elementary students in gifted education. *Roeper Review, 29,* 166–173.

National Center for Education Statistics. (2007). *Digest of education statistics*. Retrieved May 15, 2008, from http://nces.ed.gov/programs/digest/d07

Neal, L. I., McCray, A. D., Webb-Johnson, G., & Bridgest, S. (2003). The effects of African American movement style on teachers' perceptions and reactions. *Journal of Special Education, 37,* 49–57.

O'Connor, K. J. (2002). The application of Dabrowski's theory to the gifted. In M. Neihart, S. M. Reis, N. M. Robinson, & S. M. Moon (Eds.), *The social and emotional development of gifted children: What do we know?* (pp. 51–60). Waco, TX: Prufrock Press, Inc.

Ogbu, J. U. (2003). *Black American students in an affluent suburb: A study of academic disengagement*. Mahwah, NJ: Lawrence Erlbaum.

Parham, T., & Helms, J. (1981). The influence of Black students' racial identity attitudes on preferences for counselor's race. *Journal of Counseling Psychology, 28,* 250–257.

Patton, J. M. (2000). *On point: On the nexus of race, disability, and overrepresentation: What do we know? Where do we go?* Tempe, AZ: National Institute for Urban School Improvement.

Patton, J. M., & Day-Vines, N. L. (2003). *A curriculum and pedagogy for cultural competence: Strategies to guide the training of special and general education teachers.* Richmond, VA: Department of Education.

Patton, J. M., & Townsend, B. L. (1997). Creating inclusive environments for African American children and youth with gifts and talents. *Roeper Review, 20,* 13–17.

Paul, R., & Elder, L. (2001). *Critical thinking: Tools for taking charge of your learning and your life.* Upper Saddle River, NJ: Prentice Hall.

Paul, R., & Elder, L. (2002). *Critical thinking: Tools for taking charge of your professional and personal life.* Upper Saddle River, NJ: Prentice Hall.

Pedersen, P. (1994). *A handbook for developing multicultural awareness* (2nd ed.). Alexandria, VA: American Counseling Association.

Piechowski, M., & Colangelo, N. (1984). Developmental potential of the gifted. *Gifted Child Quarterly, 28,* 80–88.

Reis, S. M., & Colbert, R. (2004). Counseling needs of academically talented students with learning disabilities. *Professional School Counseling, 8,* 156–167.

Reis, S. M., & McCoach, D. B. (2000). The underachievement of gifted students: What do we know and where do we go? *Gifted Child Quarterly, 44,* 152–170.

Reis, S. M., & McCoach, D. B. (2002). Underachievement in gifted students. In M. Neihart, S. M. Reis, N. M. Robinson, & S. M. Moon (Eds.). *The social and emotional development of gifted children: What do we know?* (pp. 81–92). Waco, TX: Prufrock Press, Inc.

Resnick, L. B. (1987). *Education and learning to think.* Washington, DC: National Academies Press.

Scott, L. D., & House, L. E. (2005). Relationship of distress and perceived control to coping with perceived racial discrimination among Black youth. *Journal of Black Psychology, 31,* 254–272.

Seaton, E. K., Scottham, K. M., & Sellars, R. M. (2006). The status model of racial identity development in African American adolescents: Evidence of structure, trajectories, and well-being. *Child Development, 77,* 1416–1426.

Sellars, R. M., Copeland-Linder, N., Martin, P. P., & Lewis, R. L. (2006). Racial identity matters: The relationship between racial discrimination and psychological functioning in African American adolescents. *Journal of Research on Adolescence, 16*, 187–216.

Silverman, L. K. (1989). Invisible gifts, invisible handicaps. *Roeper Review, 12*, 37–42.

Silverman, L. K. (1993). The gifted individual. In L. K. Silverman (Ed.), *Counseling the gifted and talented* (pp. 1–28). Denver, CO: Love.

Spindler, G., & Spindler, L. (1994*). Pathways to cultural awareness: Cultural therapy with teachers and students.* Thousand Oaks, CA: Sage.

Steele, C. M., & Aronson, J. (1995). Stereotype threat and the intellectual test performance of African Americans. *Journal of Personality and Social Psychology, 69*, 797–811.

Strizek, G. A., Pittsonberger, J. L., Riordan, K. E., Lyter, D. M., & Orlofsky, G. F. (2006). *Characteristics of schools, districts, teachers, principals, and school libraries in the United States: 2003–04 schools and staffing survey (NCES 2006-313 Revised).* Washington, DC: U.S. Government Printing Office.

Suarez-Orozco, C., & Suarez-Orozco, M. M. (1995). *Transformation: Immigration, family life, and achievement motivation among Latino adolescents.* Stanford, CA: Stanford University Press.

Tatum, B. (1997). *"Why are all the Black kids sitting together in the cafeteria?" and other conversations about race.* New York: Basic Books.

Townsend, B. L., & Patton, J. M. (1995). *Three "warring souls" of African American high school students.* (ERIC Document Reproduction Service No. ED400250)

Tucker, C. M. (1999). *African American children: A self-empowerment approach to modifying behavior problems and preventing academic failure.* Boston: Allyn & Bacon.

Vandiver, B. J. (2001). Psychological nigrescence revisited: Introduction and overview. *Journal of Multicultural Counseling and Development, 29*, 165–173.

Vandiver, B. J., Cross, W. E., Worrell, F. C., & Fhagen-Smith, P. E. (2002). Validating the Cross Racial Identity Scale. *Journal of Counseling Psychology, 49*, 71–85.

Vandiver, B. J., Fhagen-Smith, P. E., Cokely, K. O, Cross, W. E., & Worrell, F. (2001). Cross's nigrescence model: From theory to scale to theory. *Journal of Multicultural Counseling and Development, 29*, 174–200.

Vespi, L., & Yewchuk, C. (1992). A phenomenological study of the social/emotional characteristics of gifted learning disabled children. *Journal for the Education of the Gifted, 16*, 55–72.

Webb, J. T., Amend, E. R., Webb, N. E., Goerss, J., Beljan, P., & Olenchak, F. R. (2005). *Misdiagnosis and dual diagnosis of gifted children and adults: ADHD, bipolar, OCD, Asperger's, depression, and other disorders.* Scottsdale, AZ: Great Potential Press.

White, J., & Parham, T. (1990). *The psychology of Blacks: An African-American perspective* (2nd. ed.). Upper Saddle River, NJ: Prentice Hall.

Wilson, T. D., Lindsay, S., & Schooler, T. Y. (2000). A model of dual attitudes. *Psychological Review, 107,* 101–126.

Yasui, M., Dorham, C. L., & Dishion, T. J. (2004). Ethnic identity and adjustment: A validity analysis for European American and African American adolescents. *Journal of Adolescent Research, 19,* 807–825.

Focusing on Where They Are:
A Clinical Perspective

Jean Sunde Peterson

My perspective on an affective curriculum in education for gifted students is colored by my clinical experiences as a counselor, including those as a counselor of gifted children, adolescents, and adults. During my last 5 years as a teacher in K–12 education, I directed a complex program for gifted high school students, which included an emphasis on affective concerns (Peterson, 1990). Ten discussion groups per week, geared almost entirely to social and emotional development and involving 115 students per year, taught me a great deal about nonacademic concerns of highly able students. The program actively sought out gifted underachievers, who became approximately 30% of total participants and were articulate contributors in the groups as well.

Later, I facilitated several similar groups for diverse gifted middle school students, counseled gifted children and adolescents and their families in a clinic geared to giftedness, and also worked with medical students and others with high ability in private practice. The individuals I met while doing ethnographic research on perceptions of giftedness in nonmainstream cultures educated me further. I also sometimes encountered gifted individuals as a counselor in two substance-abuse treatment centers, in an alternative school for expelled high school students, and as a substance-use evaluator in a K–12 school district. Currently I prepare counselors for work in K–12 schools and advise and supervise many highly capable graduate students. These varied clinical experiences with gifted individuals inform this chapter.

A Panoramic Lens

A clinical perspective is important when contemplating the content and format of an affective curriculum. Without it, perceptions about what should be included may be narrow and inappropriate. Creators of such curricula need to have a broad range of students in mind, including those who do not fit common stereotypes and who may not even be identified for programs for gifted students. The "multiple criteria" long espoused for identifying gifted children (Baldwin, 1994) may be only cosmetic in some school districts, with a standardized test score being the only measure considered seriously (Shore, Cornell, Robinson, & Ward, 1991). If that is true, there probably are many gifted children who, because they are not motivated or able to demonstrate their strengths at the crucial time when screening occurs, are not identified.

Problems related to identification, discussed for decades in the literature (e.g., Frasier, 1997), have implications for the creation of an affective curriculum. For example, scores on a standardized group-administered assessment often are examined during initial screening for eligibility for special programs; yet many children with high ability may not perform well on these tests or may not perform well consistently. There likely are many false negatives (i.e., scores too low to qualify for special programs) when large-group ability assessments are used for screening, because a number of factors can affect performance (Cohen & Swerdlik, 1999). In fact, during the years in which I annually studied the files of 500–600 incoming high school students in order to identify gifted underachievers, I saw that many had test scores that varied considerably from year to year. Some had been identified as gifted in third grade, but had been dropped from the program in eighth, when their scores and grades fell. Some had opted out of the program in middle school because the program was not a good fit for them, or they saw participation as involving social risk. If samples for studies examining giftedness are from programs for which identification and participation require high scores on standardized assessments, high academic performance, and a good fit with a program, research findings may apply only to students who are able and willing to demonstrate their abilities in the classroom and on tests and to be involved in a program geared to such students. Therefore, circumstances potentially affecting school and test performance might not only affect identification, participation in programs, and research samples, but also affect research conclusions and educators' assumptions about affective concerns of gifted students.

Whose affective concerns might not be considered? Bright children who come from chaotic and high-stress homes or are experiencing family crises may have behavior problems, be unable to concentrate in the classroom, suffer from depression, and not be identified for gifted programs (Peterson, 1997). They may not be aware of, or not be able to take advantage of, enrichment options (Peterson, 1998b). Those whose insecure identities contribute to lack of focus (Peterson, 2001b), who are bullied or otherwise uncomfortable at school (Peterson & Ray, 2006a), or who have physical (Taub, 2006) or emotional disabilities (Johnson, Karnes, & Carr, 1997) also are among those who may be missed. In addition, gifted students from nonmainstream groups, whose value orientation may not match the individual, competitive, conspicuous achievement orientation of their dominant-culture teachers, may not be identified at all. They may have low English proficiency, and their culture may not promote "showing what you know." They may be intellectually nimble, multitalented, and impressively bilingual, but not demonstrate the behaviors teachers look for when identifying students for further assessment—verbal assertiveness, social ease, contribution to class discussion, and behaviors that affirm and support the teacher (Peterson, 1997, 1999a). A broad-based affective curriculum can affirm high ability in all of the students discussed here and connect them meaningfully with intellectual peers, including with high achievers.

It should be noted here that programs that conscientiously look beyond the screening test often rely on classroom teachers to refer children for further testing. However, those teachers may not be informed about program philosophy or program type. If they identify students who need support for social and emotional concerns even more than they need academic enrichment, they may identify some whose needs will not be adequately met by "more-and-faster" programs geared largely to high academic achievement. This chapter will argue that a sound affective curriculum can meet needs of the students discussed above, as well as of those who fit the high-achieving stereotype.

Affective Concerns in a Broadly Considered Population

All of the preceding is meant to underscore, from a clinical perspective, that giftedness should not be considered narrowly when contemplating how to address the social and emotional concerns of high-ability students. An expansive view is no less appropriate when creating academic curricula for these diverse, complex, and highly idiosyncratic individuals. Regardless of program philosophy or view of giftedness, however, the following discussion about affective curriculum is pertinent.

In fact, it is important to consider that *all* gifted children, including those who are from high-functioning families and who are excelling in school (or from *not*-so-well functioning families who are excelling in school), have social and emotional concerns related to life circumstances and "normal development." The students I became acquainted with in the high school and middle school discussion groups were generally in the top 3–5% nationally in terms of intellect and potential to achieve academically. Yet, both high achievers and underachievers in those groups seemed to appreciate the opportunity to talk discreetly about general and specific developmental concerns. Many indicated that they believed they were perceived as being simply academic performers (or nonperformers), rather than as complex human beings struggling to survive the frustrations, disappointments, angers, doubts, sadness, and general emotional lability of adolescence. Many commented that it was helpful to hear that others were experiencing similar emotions and circumstances (Peterson, 1990, 2008).

Three Approaches to an Affective Curriculum

There are proactive, reactive, and integrative ways to address concerns related to social and emotional development in gifted children and adolescents. All can be geared to current concerns—where students *are,* including simply "growing up." These approaches can be summarized as follows:

- *proactive*—offering psychoeducational activities to facilitate personal growth and provide support during developmental transitions,
- *reactive*—responding to concerns that interfere with learning and effective social functioning and negatively affect emotional health, and
- *integrative*—including attention to affective dimensions in gifted education instruction and activities.

Proactive Affective Curricula: Content Options

Proactive affective curricula, intended to promote social and emotional health and enhance personal growth, can be created and delivered in several ways, including through both small- and large-group work. School counselors alone can provide such psychoeducational content and activities, especially when they are aware of characteristics and concerns related to giftedness. However, classroom teachers and gifted education teachers, preferably trained in workshops focusing on affective concerns of gifted students, also can do that. In addition, gifted education teachers and/or classroom teachers can work collaboratively *with* school counselors to create a proactive, developmentally oriented dimension in education for gifted students.

The following discussion applies mostly to students in grades 4–12, although younger gifted children also can benefit from a developmentally appropriate psychoeducational curriculum, a focus on developing expressive language, and interaction with intellectual peers around social and emotional development. It is important, of course, not to assume that the level of social and emotional development matches the level of cognitive development—or that it should. For instance, young children with extraordinary intellectual ability may not be ready to self-reflect or engage in discussion involving abstract concepts—but may, quite appropriately, engage in discussion about concrete events and observations of their world, offering extraordinary insights. They also can benefit from opportunities to express their feelings in a safe, nonjudgmental environment. Small-motor skills may not be developed enough for complex, time-constrained activities involving writing or drawing. Similarly, primary-level children may "play parallel" and interact with only the group facilitator, rather than with the group, just as others their age do. With these caveats in mind, however, educators can be confident that young children can benefit, just as older gifted children can, from affective curriculum. But what is appropriate for a proactive affective curriculum?

Development

A prevention-oriented curriculum might include semi-structured small-group or whole-classroom discussion, assigned readings, or discussion in response to media presentations. The focus is on the developmental realities of the present, but it may periodically shift to planning for the future as well. However, *prevention* here means giving adequate attention to current social and emotional development in the interest of avoiding difficulties in the future. For adolescents, for example, focusing on challenges related to developing identity, career direction, autonomy, and mature relationships can help them to accomplish those developmental tasks in a supportive environment. For younger children, a focus on early career awareness and on peer relationships can be incorporated into a curriculum geared to enhancing general self-awareness and helping students learn to articulate feelings and needs, develop interpersonal skills, and build a sense of confidence by increasing social and emotional competence.

For either whole-classroom (in the case of homogeneously grouped high-ability students) or small-group sessions, discussing general information about development and the implications of giftedness for social and emotional development is useful. Gifted students are developing in ways that are fairly universal, and they certainly are not exempt from difficulties related to developmental challenges. It is important to keep in mind that some gifted students may receive little information about "normal development," and adults and peers may indeed not see them as "normal" at all (Cross, Coleman, & Stewart, 1993), given their cognitive precocity. Their and others' preoccupation with academic and talent achievement may preclude conversation even about physical changes. For some, few opportunities to socialize with age peers, who are likely to be experiencing physical, social, and emotional changes similar to their own, also may limit information about development. Therefore, dialogue that has little or no reference to giftedness is important and appropriate in an affective curriculum. It should be recognized, however, that discussing development with intellectual peers makes the experience inherently geared to giftedness.

Offering some perspectives on developmental challenges also is appropriate. For instance, early school years may involve separation anxiety, a poor fit with a teacher, a sense of differentness among peers, being bullied, and having to share a significant adult with peers in a classroom. Debilitating perfectionism can be apparent even at this school level (Adderholdt-Elliott, 1987; Kottman & Ashby, 2000). Middle school years, with departmentalized instruction, may involve the loss of the kind of identity one has with the teacher in a self-contained classroom; difficulty navigating a larger social world; adjustments to more academic and social competition; self-consciousness about physical development; concerns about sexuality, sexual orientation, and social expectations about gender-appropriate behavior; a wide array of bullying behaviors; new peer pressures; depression; concerns about family; and even doubts about ability. Underachievement also may become established (Peterson & Colangelo, 1996). These concerns are not unusual during high school as well. However, there may be more anxiety about the future, including "paralysis" from expectations and fears about social and financial aspects of post-high-school education. Gifted adolescents also may experience difficulties with the increasingly competitive school environment, have issues related to earlier abuse or other trauma, and have tension related to the ongoing process of differentiating from parents. Relationship difficulties; substance use/abuse; tense, perfectionistic high achievement; or underachievement also may become significant problems during high school. Gifted students are not exempt from any of these concerns or from difficulties related to stressful family transitions occurring during the school years.

However, adults can offer hope and optimism as they communicate with gifted students. Intelligence is a factor of resilience (Higgins, 1994). Cognitive ability in itself can help to resolve personal difficulties. In that regard, one message can be that problems often are "figured out over time." Everyone has personal strengths which, perhaps with assistance, can be applied to current problems. Developmental challenges can contribute to stress, but people usually, eventually, complete developmental transitions. In addition, people usually develop increasingly more integrative perspectives over time (Adams, 1991). It also is likely that there will be increasingly more intellectual and interest peers available at each successive level of education. In the present, however, adults can reassuringly normalize developmental experiences and communicate that strange feelings and anxieties probably "make sense," under the circumstances.

Giftedness

Certainly how scholars have presented giftedness can become psychoeducational content as well. The following are examples of discussion starters for small and large groups at the middle and high school levels:
*   Giftedness may be associated with cognitive and emotional sensitivity to self and others (Mendaglio, 2003) and sensitivity to change, including during family and normal developmental transitions and at times of loss and grief (cf. Lovecky, 1992; Peterson, 2007; Piechowski, 1999).
*   Intelligence is related to resilience (Higgins, 1994), but also can contribute to a poor fit in the school milieu (Plucker

& Levy, 2001; Rimm, Rimm-Kaufman, & Rimm, 1999; Webb, Meckstroth, & Tolan, 1982).

- Gifted individuals may need to give themselves permission to take appropriate risks—socially (e.g., approaching someone with a request or assertively setting a personal boundary), academically (e.g., taking calculus), and emotionally (e.g., entering into a relationship) (Peterson, 2008; Schuler, 2001).
- Perfectionists might have difficulty beginning, ending, and enjoying academic projects—or enjoying doing anything that will be evaluated. Perfectionists may be highly critical of themselves and others and be difficult to be around (Greenspon, 2000; Schuler, 2001).
- It may be difficult to be launched into adulthood from a high-functioning home with loving parents (Peterson, 1999b).
- Gifted females from protected environments may not be prepared for the social and sexual aggressivity that may characterize university social life (Peterson & Ray, 2006b).
- Gifted students, like anyone else, want to be known—and to be known as more than just an achiever or underachiever (Peterson, 2008).
- It is not socially smart to brag about one's grade point average or SAT scores. Arrogance usually is ineffective for building social networks and actually may reflect lack of interpersonal intelligence (cf. Gardner, 1985).
- In their families, gifted students may play roles that are uncomfortable and unwanted (Peterson, 1998a; see Peterson, 2008, for a discussion guide).
- Many gifted students probably do not fit the stereotypes associated with giftedness (see Peterson, 2008, for a discussion guide).
- Being feisty, especially when dealing with difficult circumstances, may reflect strengths that help gifted students to be successful as adults (Peterson, 2001a).
- Overcommitment and overinvolvement in activities and work can be highly stressful (Peterson, Duncan, & Canady, 2008).

- Having a good fit among personality, interests, and a career *context* is important (Kerr & Sodano, 2003).

At the elementary level, the following statements might be used to generate conversation:

- Some gifted kids have a hard time finding friends who have similar interests.
- Sometimes kids have a way of learning that matches their teachers' way of teaching. Sometimes their styles don't have a good match (Peterson, 2008).
- Some gifted kids are bullied, and some are bullies (Peterson & Ray, 2006b).
- It's hard for teachers to give attention to every child equally.
- Some gifted kids think they have to be perfect (Adderholdt-Elliott, 1987).
- Some gifted kids worry a lot (Peterson, 2008).
- Kids in fifth grade often wonder what middle school will be like.
- It's interesting to think about having a job someday.

Young children also can benefit from playing board games together, especially games that have interpersonal, psychoeducational dimensions. Landing on a certain color or shape, for instance, may require a response to a card, drawn from a pile (e.g., "Give the person on your left a compliment" or "I used to worry about ___, but now I worry about ___" or "The nicest time I ever spent with my family was . . . ").

Group Work

It is important to recognize that small- or large-group formats that are somewhat open-ended allow mutual, reciprocal learning, in contrast to adult-controlled content presented didactically. Trust is more easily established in a small group, of course, and facilitators who are comfortable with the dynamic nature of groups can help students to give voice to affective concerns. Such expression may help someone to keep a psychiatric disorder at bay—or keep anger and rage from being expressed in dangerous ways. The discovery of commonalities in small-group discussions may enhance learning and social ease at school. An affective curriculum in the form of group work can meet students where they are, without judgmentally prodding them to be different.

It should be noted that if information about sexual abuse, substance abuse, eating disorders, or dating violence, for instance, is presented and discussed in groups or classrooms, it is not likely that students will reveal traumatic experiences there. They are more likely to seek out the facilitator privately to discuss their concerns. Gifted education or other teachers can then, after offering support and validation (e.g., "I'm so sorry to hear that you experienced that") and after indicating openness to listening, can then suggest that they go together to a school counselor, who has professional training for making referrals or following through with individual counseling in response to identified needs (e.g., "I'm certainly open to listening. Yes, let's talk. Maybe we'll decide that it would be best to talk with your counselor, too, because she or he has more expertise than I do about how to be helpful. But let's talk.").

Particularly with group work, it is essential that prevention strategies be formalized as curriculum. When group leaders cannot explain what groups do, parents, teachers, and administrators may be justifiably uneasy. If conducting a series of small-group sessions, the facilitator can say to parents and educators, for example, "We've been focusing on stress for 4 weeks—recognizing it, dissecting it, and talking about coping strategies." When a series of psychoeducational lessons is scheduled for a homogeneously gifted classroom (e.g., Peterson, 2008), the same is true. Parents not only have a right to be informed about school curriculum, but usually also about what kinds of counseling services their children are involved in. Therefore it is imperative that a rationale for small- or large-group affective curricular components be available in print—and explained orally when necessary. Chapter 11 provides a more detailed explanation of small-group approaches and curricula.

Career Development

Career development currently is a significant focus in the proactive, prevention dimensions of school counseling. From kindergarten through high school, counselors are trained to promote self-awareness, social skills, and knowledge of career options, all of which help to prepare children and adolescents for the workplace. Gifted students need guidance here as well, and they probably need it earlier than other students (Hébert & Kelly, 2006). For example, even though some may believe, based on their own and others' expectations, that they need to decide on a career path early, the emphasis on career development for gifted students might actually be *not* on deciding, but rather on becoming more aware of personal *needs* as related to potential career contexts (e.g., variety, closure at the end of the day, contact with people, order, a calm environment, an urban setting, predictability, or selling something). Experiencing a full day of career-shadowing during high school can be developmentally valuable, because students might be able to experience both mundane and dramatic aspects of the work, both physical and emotional stressors related to that context, and a sense of their own fit with the types of personalities found in the field. Through shadowing, a stellar math or science student might discover that classroom teaching is actually a better fit than engineering, in terms of work environment, or that working in medical research is a better fit than practicing medicine.

Reactive Services: When There Are Problems

Reactive measures respond to concerns that interfere with learning, effective social functioning, and emotional health. Often referred to clinically as *interventions*, these measures, such as individual and small-group counseling for specific issues, are usually the domain of school counselors, mental health counselors, family therapists, psychologists, or psychiatrists. However, semistructured psychoeducational small-group discussion in schools (probably therapeutic, but not intended to be therapy) allows gifted education teachers to monitor the social and emotional health of gifted students informally, alerting school counselors if someone seems distressed and probably discussing that observation with the student privately. Teachers in programs that include attention to affective concerns are in a good position to note changes in behavior, isolation or withdrawal, a flat (emotionless, disengaged, withdrawn) affect, suicidal ideation, or problems with eating and can alert a school counselor.

In school-based groups, just talking about various types of issues (e.g., underachievement; perfectionism; shyness; cross-cultural communication; socialization; friendship and relationship issues; parental or other family illness or death; and family transitions such as separation, divorce, blended families, relocation, or parental unemployment) often can be enough to prevent crises. However, there clearly are situations that should be referred to the school counselor, who might in turn make a referral to an agency counselor or psychologist. School counselors are trained to do individual and small-group work in a variety of areas, but should make outside references for students with symptoms of diagnosable mental disorders, because large counselor-to-student ratios typically constrain school counselors from devoting the time necessary for long-term counseling of individuals. In addition, even though most of their coursework matches that of mental health counselors, and even though some may have had additional training related to working with diagnosed disorders, their training typically focuses more on comprehensive programming involving individuals, small groups, and classrooms; consultation with school personnel and parents; advocacy; and data-based decision making. Proactively and reactively, they help students to be comfortable and productive and create programs that contribute to a school environment conducive to learning. School counselors also are trained to address school-related developmental issues of children and their families and be a referral hub when services are needed outside of the school.

When Referral Is Appropriate

When gifted students have experienced trauma (e.g., verbal, emotional, sexual, or other abuse; witnessing violence; being involved in a serious accident) or are distressed by family transitions (e.g., divorce, remarriage, severe illness or accident, relocation, parental unemployment, parental incarceration, death of someone close), it is appropriate for educators and school counselors to encourage parents to seek help from professionals trained and experienced in working with children and adolescents. When gifted individuals appear to be abusing substances, such interventions also are in order. Similarly, when gifted students show early or well-developed symptoms of mental disorders (e.g., anorexia or bulimia, obsessive-compulsive disorder, depression, anxiety, schizophrenia), it is important that treatment (e.g., counseling/therapy, hospitalization) be sought. The school counselor can help to facilitate that.

Based on informal observation, my own research, and student input during the small groups I facilitated, many gifted students are reluctant to seek out school counselors, teachers, and parents for help, convinced that they should "figure it out" by themselves. In one retrospective study of the adolescent experience of 18 gifted individuals who were gay (Peterson & Rischar, 2000), even though 72% reported being suicidal at some point during their school years, none told a teacher, and only 31% told a parent of their despair. For 39%, no one, including best friends, knew about their sexual orientation during the school years. In a study of bullying among gifted students (Peterson & Ray, 2006b), school and other counselors ranked fifth and eighth, respectively, among those told. "No one" ranked fourth. It appears that gifted education personnel need to be prepared to pay attention to social and emotional concerns of their students. It is too late when one commits suicide or shoots a classmate, parent, or teacher. Situations sometimes are difficult to rectify when distressed students self-medicate with illegal substances. Some gifted adolescents do drop out of school (Seeley, 2004). Some gifted children stay home from school because school does not feel safe (Peterson & Ray, 2006a).

Offering Information

Offering books and other materials related to a topic of concern also is an appropriate response to students in distress. School counselors typically are inundated with catalogs of psychoeducational materials and can offer suggestions for books about a wide range of topics. Students can check these out and then discuss their responses individually with the teacher, counselor (especially if the concern is serious), or an organized group of peers with similar issues, if such a group has been assembled (and is facilitated by a counselor, if the issues are heavy).

Integrative Affective Curriculum: An Extra Dimension in Programming

Integrative dimensions of an affective curriculum can be one domain of the work of gifted education teachers, although school counselors may be involved as well. Integration means giving attention to affective dimensions during regular, typical gifted education activities and experiences, which might intentionally include time for play, socializing, self-reflection, and peer feedback (Peterson, 2003). Certainly all group projects, field trips, and small-group work on projects in the classroom are inherently social and therefore provide opportunities to pay attention to social and emotional development. Even Advanced Placement courses can intentionally incorporate social discourse and attention to the affective into the classroom. English teachers can encourage self-reflection when discussing or assigning papers about literature. Family science, social science, art, music, and health teachers can do the same at various school levels. Even science classes can include at least brief questions and comments about feelings experienced during challenging activities.

Reflecting on Academic and Other Experiences

Utilizing a technique that will be explained later in this chapter, classroom and gifted education teachers can process any of the experiences just mentioned—whenever there is opportunity to do so:

- "How did that feel when you were giving your strong opinions?"
- "How was it to work together in your group today?"
- "How was the process of *preparing for* the exam?"
- "What was different about your group today?"

- "How well do you think you would fit into the environment we observed today at the engineering firm?"
- "Let's just sit back for a moment and consider the atmosphere here."
- "We're being quite intense today. How does that feel to you?"

Students then can gain skills in articulating feelings and concerns, recognizing that these skills potentially can help them in relationships in the future. A coach preparing teams for science, math, debate, or creativity competitions; a gifted education teacher coaching students for a writing competition; or a coach of a gifted musician or athlete can ask similar questions, encouraging self-reflection, helping students to cope with stress, and allowing them to be in the moment, instead of preoccupied with an exam, an upcoming competition, a performance, a group product, or the distant future.

Speakers

In addition, especially at the middle and high school levels, community psychologists, mental health counselors, physicians, social workers, and nurses can present afterschool lectures about social and emotional concerns of school-age individuals, societal trends, and community support systems. These presentations can be informative about the larger world and helpful to individual students as well. Besides advanced academic content related to law, urban planning, economics, and futuristic visions of medicine, for example, topics such as adolescent depression, teenage pregnancy, sexuality, addiction, eating disorders, perfectionism, relationship aggression and violence, and coping with stress are appropriate for gifted teens. Classroom teachers in related subject areas can be encouraged to publicize the presentations to *all* students and give extra credit for attendance, thereby broadening the impact of the gifted program and combating perceptions of elitism as well (Peterson, 1993). It is possible that gifted students do not have as much access to, or room for, courses related to marriage and family relationships and consumer economics, for instance, as do less able students.

Presenters can address these areas as well in this type of affective curriculum.

Panels

To relieve anxiety about entering unfamiliar territory, panels of gifted sixth graders can discuss the transition from elementary school to middle school, and panels of gifted first-year high school students can do the same for gifted eighth graders. Panels of first-year college students home for the holidays can tell gifted high school students about adjusting to new academic and social environments, managing time and money, being homesick, living with roommates, finding people to eat with, maintaining good physical and emotional health, communicating with professors, being tested less frequently than in high school, being more responsible for their own learning, and finding meaningful nonacademic activities (Peterson, 2000b). Panels of successful, productive adults who were adolescent underachievers, have learning disabilities, or had difficulty with authority can give hope to gifted students who are discouraged, lack motivation, or are sabotaging their own progress (Peterson, 2003). A panel of adults who have made career changes can convey that one does not have to have "perfect" career direction at a young age, and that later changes are possible. In fact, such a panel may help to prevent early foreclosure (commitment without questioning and exploring possible choices; cf. Marcia, 1980). Many gifted high school graduates change college academic majors more than once (Peterson, 2000a).

Parent Support

School counselors and gifted education teachers can even offer parent support groups for the purpose of enhancing the social and emotional lives of gifted students. The counselors might teach basic listening skills to gifted students as part of the affective curriculum and to their parents in the support groups. Both counselors and teachers can provide parents with information related to the social and emotional development of gifted children and adolescents. Problem solving and strategizing for enhanced family communication also can be the focus of these groups.

The Human Side of Giftedness

The message communicated in these formal and informal settings is clear. Gifted students are more than just performers with potential to "make people proud." Like anyone else, they have social and emotional concerns and need to gain non-academic skills to help them live their lives effectively in the present and after their formal education ceases. Even under-achievement then becomes something other than failure, catastrophe, or pathology. Instead, it is viewed respectfully in the context of social and emotional development in the present.

Focusing on Where They Are, Not Where We Think They Should Be

The three approaches to addressing social and emotional concerns of gifted students differ significantly, but all focus largely on *now*—the present. Regardless of circumstances or concerns, it is important to meet gifted school-age individuals where they are, to hear their current perspectives on themselves, and to recognize that, like every growing child and adolescent (and adults as well), they are observing, feeling, wondering, doubting—and continually developing. The clinical perspective being presented here emphasizes the present, where gifted students experience the complexity and, to a great extent, the universality of human development.

If there is little time or encouragement to consider complex feelings and contemplate physical, social, and emotional development, gifted youth may feel like, and assume they are seen as, "robots," as one gifted eighth grader noted in a small-group discussion I facilitated. For a variety of reasons, many may actually miss out on basic social information that helps to facilitate successful movement through various developmental stages. One such circumstance might be when difficult family circumstances move even young gifted children into positions of adult-like responsibility—or simply into confusion and anxiety. Even in the best of circumstances, some may not be encouraged to just play, thereby potentially missing out on an important developmental component of childhood (Elkind, 1981).

In addition, high expectations may fuel constant evaluation by self and others and consequent high stress, even at a young age. Not being able to talk about complex developmental transitions with peers may exacerbate an already well-entrenched sense of differentness as a gifted person. Considering hormonal changes and sexual development, the complexities of relationships, the challenge of determining a career path when "you can do anything," the confusion of random thoughts and even the thought of parenting someday can overwhelm sensitive gifted youth who have hypersensitive antennae and a tendency to ruminate anxiously (Peterson, 1998a). Advanced Placement classes, competitive extracurricular activities, and packed daily schedules are not necessarily conducive to assisting these students with physical, social, and emotional developmental challenges (Peterson, Duncan, & Canady, 2008).

A clinical perspective assumes that school-age gifted individuals struggle with such concerns, at least now and then. As educators and counselors offer activities and other help during stressful times, basic counseling tenets can be useful regardless of whether an approach is proactive, reactive, or integrative, including:

- nonjudgment,
- focusing on strengths,
- respecting and fostering autonomy,
- active listening,
- open-ended questioning,
- avoiding teacher/facilitator self-disclosure,
- respecting privacy, and
- processing.

Becoming a counselor usually involves 2 full years of study, and expertise involves complex skills and dispositions. However, even rudimentary skills can be helpful to noncounselors. The postures listed above encourage receptivity to where gifted youth *are*, not just where they have been or are going. Each of these aspects is explained further in the following sections.

Nonjudgment

Among several basic counseling tenets is the idea that counselors should be nonjudgmental (Ivey & Ivey, 2003). In both proactive (e.g., psychoeducational group work) and reactive (e.g., group or individual counseling/therapy) work, counselors can assume a respectful one-down posture, with the client teaching the counselor about his or her life, feelings, and perspectives. After all, the client is the expert there.

If participating in counseling voluntarily, clients probably come because they want to live more effectively, and counselors work collaboratively with them toward that end. If counseling (reactive) is mandated, and clients are not receptive to it, it is the counselor's responsibility to understand, respectfully, what might seem to be resistant behaviors (Ivey & Ivey, 2003), recognizing that these might be adaptive, functional, and understandable. Certainly, counseling may seem threatening or frightening. The counselor, not the client, is charged with making appropriate adjustments in order to meet the client where he or she is in order to do the work of counseling.

Regardless of client attitudes and responses, a counselor enters a client's world nonjudgmentally and respectfully, including recognizing the values and beliefs that are part of that world. The counselor listens carefully, gives feedback, and helps the client make sense of confusing emotions and behaviors. Faithful to the American Counseling Association (ACA) *Code of Ethics and Standards of Practice* (ACA, 2005), counselors do not impose their values on clients. Collaboratively created homework assignments may help the client to gain insights and move toward appropriate goals between sessions.

In parallel fashion, it is important for parents and educators to remember the tenet of nonjudgment when interacting with gifted children and adolescents. Too often, well-meaning adults are preoccupied with how the student should be different (e.g., more motivated), or behave differently (e.g., better), or be more or less of something (e.g., organized, perfectionistic), or be somewhere else (e.g., in the future). The student, in turn, is not encouraged to be in the present—and to pay attention to it. A nonjudgmental counselor is open to learning about the student's *current* world, without being voyeuristic. It means listening to the student's perspectives, without rushing in to fix or steer or advise (Nichols, 1995). It means validating feelings as important and legitimate. It means not saying, "Yes, but wouldn't it be better if you . . ." Nonjudgment allows proactive programming to stay positive and hopeful, without moving inappropriately into pushing for change. Adolescents, in particular, often complain about not being heard. Listening nonjudgmentally helps to keep communication channels open (Ivey & Ivey, 2003; Nichols, 1995).

Significant adults in a gifted student's life may be highly invested in the student's success. Parents, teachers, coaches, and mentors may live through the student's success, with that success possibly more important to them than to the student. They may speak continually and exclusively about grades and grade point averages, requirements for the next education level, quality of academic and other performance, or long-term plans. A weak boundary between adult and student may mean that neither recognizes that they are separate entities, with unique aspirations, personalities, interests, and needs.

Gifted students may feel judged and burdened by their own and others' expectations. Some members of the groups I facilitated felt valued only for performance and were preoccupied with fears about less-than-perfect grades, which they believed meant failure and unworthiness. I was astonished that gifted seventh graders in groups I led in a university town spent the first two group sessions agonizing mostly over their grade points. Clearly, their academic performance was basic to their identity, and I needed to enter that high-stakes world nonjudgmentally. Interestingly, as a result of activities that focused on affective concerns, they relaxed, expanded their range of conversation topics, and frowned less often. The groups focused proactively on healthy development, including providing helpful information and encouraging them to talk about their perspectives on giftedness as well. Along the way, they seemed more and more able to put competitive academic performance into perspective, to make connections with each other, and be more open about imperfections and developmental struggles. The groups therefore appeared to serve as an intervention for improving social skills and emotional health as well.

Such proactive affective curriculum, in the form of small groups at middle and high school levels, provides a chance for students not to feel judged and not to judge themselves. Without fail, students in the groups I facilitated referred to them as "an oasis" or a welcome break in the midst of an intense life. They could just *be*. In the groups they did not feel they had to be better, or do something better, or direct their attention continually toward the future. They were not evaluated. That freedom helped them to step back and discuss their development with peers within the so-important school context. Underachievers could feel affirmed for their intelligence simply by being part of the discussion, regardless of whether they could or wanted to do better at that complex time in their life. High achievers seemed to appreciate feeling affirmed for just being. Group curricula focused on where they were *at that time*. Learning to express emotions and nonacademic concerns, as well as learning to set boundaries assertively with others, gave them skills that might help them with normal developmental challenges. These skills also might help them to be successful in the workplace, avoid roommate conflicts in college, and communicate effectively in marriage.

In integrative affective curriculum as well, such as when school counselors and gifted education teachers collaborate and cofacilitate whole-classroom lessons, nonjudgment should prevail. Otherwise, these classroom experiences offer nothing different from the usual. Delivery of affective curricula should be fundamentally different from the evaluative, competitive academic culture of schools. Affective curricula should meet students where they are, be nonjudgmentally open to their world, be developmentally relevant and appropriate, and affirm strengths.

Focusing on Strengths

Counseling generally focuses on strengths, not on pathology, while helping clients to help themselves (cf. Ivey &

Ivey, 2003). Currently, positive psychology (Seligman & Csikszentmihalyi, 2000), a developing field, also focuses on human assets. Similarly, the resilience literature (e.g., Masten & Coatsworth, 1998) discusses protective factors that help children cope with troubling situations. The solution-focused approach (DeShazer, 1985), continuing to gain in popularity, moves quickly and intentionally from a focus on a problem to a focus on solutions, illuminating clients' personal resources, helping them visualize positive change, and helping them change their language from problem language to solution language (e.g., "What were you doing differently when it wasn't a problem?" "What would your life be like if this weren't a problem?") in order to break ineffective patterns and move forward. Listening carefully, counselors wait until they can credibly identify strengths and resources and then help clients put them to use (e.g., "You seem to be strong, managing well in a difficult situation." "You've used your intelligence to make sense of it." "You know how to get adults to pay attention." "You read people well." "You're taking care of yourself."). Rather than saying, "You shouldn't be discouraged (or depressed, anxious) when you have so many strengths" (i.e., invalidating a feeling), references to being resilient, wisely seeking out a counselor, being able to engage others, being a good listener, "making sense," or knowing when to ask for help can be credible and helpful comments.

In proactive program components, credible references to personal and emotional strengths by adults affirms self-critical gifted students. Peers, too, in semistructured group discussions, can give helpful feedback about strengths they perceive in others. In reactive work by school counselors and other helping professionals, strengths also can be a focus, with the goal of empowerment for problem solving and change. In integrative work with gifted students, the same is possible. Even in whole-classroom lessons and when coaching competitive academic teams, acknowledging and affirming strengths (instead of focusing only on "what can you do better"), without moving into a hollow, strident, cheerleading mode, can change an atmosphere of tense and critical perfectionism into a collaborative, supportive environment.

Respecting and Fostering Autonomy

Focusing *credibly* on strengths may help to foster beliefs in self-efficacy (Bandura, 1994) and to develop self-sufficiency instead of dependence. The ACA (2005) ethical code, in fact, admonishes counselors to avoid fostering dependency. Counselors therefore are trained not to "rescue" clients and not to assume responsibility for "fixing" them, because these postures can preclude important exploration of troubling feelings. In the counseling relationship, a counselor therefore plans to be needed less and less as the client improves. The counselor avoids implying that the client must always look outside of the self for guidance.

Ethically, counselors also are admonished to respect and protect clients' autonomy—unless, for example, the latter are in danger or are a danger to self or others. Kitchener (1984), in fact, placed autonomy at the top of a list of five *prima facie* valid principles offering guidance in ethical decision making. Autonomy means being able to make choices, and, as much as possible, even young clients should have choices appropriate to their developmental level and cognitive ability.

Similarly, in proactive program components, gifted students should have choices—to make reasoned judgments, to learn from their mistakes, to accept the "humanity" in their own and others' errors in judgment, and to pay attention to their needs and preferences when making choices. Proactive small-group discussion offers a safe, nonjudgmental venue for discussing decisions, errors, and choices. In reactive aspects of affective education, trained professionals undoubtedly will keep the primary ethical concern of client autonomy in mind as well. In integrative programming, educators and counselors can work together to respect and protect gifted students' autonomy in regard to choices, while offering guidance through information and experiences that foster a sense of competence. For parents and educators, knowing when to push and when to step back requires a fine-line distinction. Gifted students may make undesirable and dangerous choices, of course, like others their age. However, common wisdom contends that making choices within a supportive environment promotes healthy development (Baumrind, 1991).

Active Listening

Active listening is basic to affective education and is helpful in all interpersonal communication, regardless of school level. It especially is important when a child or adolescent needs to be heard by an adult. In that case, the interaction is not conversation—not equal and not meant to meet mutual needs. The adult and child are not peers. The adult has special responsibility. However, students, too, can learn to be effective, active listeners for their peers.

Hard Work

Active, intentional listening is hard work, and a listener's emotional triggers must be identified and harnessed if listening is to be employed effectively in building relationships (Nichols, 1995). A few of the listening skills that usually are included, in some form, in counselor preparation (e.g., Evans, Hearn, Uhlemann, & Ivey [1998] follow.

The listener concentrates on feelings that are expressed verbally and nonverbally and reflects and validates them when appropriate (e.g., "I can hear that you were really scared." "That sounds pretty disappointing." "You've had a very rough 3 weeks. It makes sense that you feel shaky."). Feelings often are more important than content—feelings of rage being more important than the details of an altercation with a peer, for example. Listening for feelings and meanings and *not* interrupting with questions and comments helps the speaker feel heard. Active listening also means checking whether understanding is accurate (e.g., "Let me see if I've got this right. . ."). It means paraphrasing along the way and summarizing at the end of a conversation (e.g., "So, after you went home, you were able to get some perspective." "You've decided you don't want to return."). Active listening also means not *controlling* the conversation with questions. Reflecting and validating with statements (e.g., "That sounds difficult.") instead of questions (e.g., Did you ask him what he wanted?") indicates that what the student is saying is important (Ivey & Ivey, 2003).

Responding to Unsettling Information

It is important for anyone receiving unsettling and even horrific information to stay poised. The listener can say something like "Wow—I'm so sorry to hear that," and then remind the student (limits to confidentiality should have been presented at the outset of groups, for instance) that it may be advisable to enlist the help of the counselor. However, it is important to "settle in" and actively listen initially. There is no need to give advice or immediately resolve something troubling. In fact, there might not be an identifiable problem to solve. Listening is the most important function, because those who reveal personal information not only have *chosen* the listener(s) carefully, but also may be testing whether an experience can in fact be told to anyone. A listener's "falling apart" after hearing a horrendous story sends the message that awful experiences are indeed too terrible to speak about. Poise and outward calm in a listener may be crucial to a student's well-being in a school (Peterson, 2008) and to openness to further assistance.

The same listening skills are recommended when a student reveals homosexuality. The study of gifted college-age individuals who were gay (Peterson & Rischar, 2000) found that 50% percent had wondered seriously about sexual orientation before leaving elementary school. Most did not "come out" to family or peers during their school years. However, many withdrew in distress, most feared for their personal safety, and, as mentioned earlier, most experienced severe depression. Some reported "hyperachievement" as compensation for perceived shame. Increasing public discourse about sexual orientation may mean that gifted education teachers are elected to hear revelations, because they may be the most trusted adults in school for gifted students. Given that there are probably at least a similar percentage of homosexual individuals among the gifted as in the general population, affective curriculum can at least acknowledge that students may be wondering about sexual orientation. Active listening when the subject of homosexuality comes up may be crucial to some students' survival, in addition to their reporting any harassment or bullying. Almost all of the subjects of the study just described said they believed that they were the only person with sexual-orientation concerns at school, wished that they had had access to rational dialogue about sexual orientation, and regretted that helpful information had not been available. An increasing number of pertinent materials are indeed available (e.g., Huegel, 2003), and counselors and gifted education teachers might place them on bookshelves at eye level or on a table, indicating openness to discussion and to lending the books.

Open-Ended Questioning

Open-ended questioning (Ivey & Ivey, 2003) is another skill that can be developed with practice. Closed questions (e.g., beginning with Do/Did, Have/Has, Was/Were, or Is/Are) can be answered with *yes* or *no* and usually do not generate extended exchanges, even though they are sometimes appropriate and useful. Closed questions actually can shut down a conversation. Questioners who assume inordinate responsibility, especially with a reticent student, sometimes find themselves stuck in a closed-questions mode. In contrast, open-ended questions are facilitative, providing opportunity for students to elaborate, clarify, inform, express, and be complex. Questions or prompts beginning with *how, what kind, what, tell me about, help me understand*, or *give me some examples*, for example, are likely to result in complex responses, which in turn can generate additional open-ended questions or reflections.

Avoiding Teacher/Facilitator Self-Disclosure

Teacher/facilitator/counselor/parent self-disclosure may at times be helpful to a student (Barrett & Berman, 2001). However, self-disclosure should always be judicious, culturally appropriate, and determined to be in the student's best interest. Helpers also should recognize that their adult authority may make their similar experience or choice seem like the only viable option for the student (Murphy & Dillon, 2003). In fact, I emphasize to my counselors-in-training that self-disclosure is not essential in a helping relationship. Good counseling, as well as good group facilitation and individual consultation, can occur without any self-disclosure by the counselor, other than perhaps making periodic observations with "I" statements (e.g., "I noticed a few minutes ago that you girls got quiet when he said that."). Those statements might be followed by "What did you feel (or think) when he said it?" The emphasis stays on the student—and on the present moment.

The student, not the adult, is ideally the focus of adult-student dialogue. Whenever an adult facilitator injects personal information in an interaction (e.g., "I remember when I . . . " or "When I was your age . . . "), attention immediately moves to the facilitator—and away from the child or adolescent. Active listening, with thorough concentration on the speaker, helps to prevent this. In general, adults must be careful not to be a needy adult, someone whose own needs take precedence over those of the student. Needing continually to insert one's own experiences into the discussion may reflect an inability to focus on the needs of students.

Respecting Privacy

School counselors are trained to respect the privacy of those they work with, whether that be teachers, students, principals, or parents. Gifted education teachers who conduct psycho-educational lessons are wise when they similarly do not comment elsewhere about information offered by students during group discussion (and also ask permission from, or respectfully inform, the student when making a referral). Sharing personal information about students without their permission, including with parents, puts trust at risk, and trust is essential in helping relationships. Unfortunately, based on my experience in schools, both a high degree of individual or family risk and the young age of students are associated with educators' disrespect of privacy rights.

According to the ACA (2005) ethical code, confidentiality is a right of the client and is expected in the counseling relationship. However, it is the counselor, not the client, who promises confidentiality; a client is free to share session information anywhere. Therefore, confidentiality cannot be guaranteed in a group, because more people are involved than just a counselor and one client. Group facilitators typically emphasize the desirability of confidentiality to group members at the outset, while also generating a group dynamic that promotes it. The usual caveats to confidentiality guidelines are related to abuse or neglect, imminent danger to a client, or a client's being a danger to self or others. These also are emphasized at the *outset* of counseling relationships and therapeutic groups, with clear reference to mandatory reporting (e.g., "I will keep whatever you say private unless I believe you might hurt yourself or someone else or if I suspect abuse or neglect. In that case, I'm required to protect you or that person, including seeking help."). Lay group facilitators also can apply these guidelines as they work with groups (Peterson, 2008). Initially cofacilitating groups with a school counselor, if possible, is a good way to learn about ethical behavior when first establishing an affective curriculum. Ideally, collaboratively, the counselor can model the guidelines presented in this section and help the lay-facilitator to develop appropriate skills, while the latter provides information pertinent to the implications of giftedness for social and emotional development.

Processing

"Processing the process," an important counseling skill (Murphy & Dillon, 2003), refers to stepping back from the content of a discussion or experience and posing process questions such as these, appropriate at the end of a meeting:
- "How do you feel about our discussion today?"
- "What was it like to talk about getting along with siblings today?"
- "What were some of your feelings when you were imagining a career?"

- "How did you feel when_____ told us about his scary experience?"

In a benign and meaningful way, processing (i.e., used as a verb) moments or whole sessions provides a chance to articulate feelings, an important skill that can be complimented. If students can step out of a situation, monitor their responses, and talk about them, they may be able to do that in the midst of relational conflict in the future. Processing a significant moment in a group also may help a high-stress child or adolescent feel heard and validated. When implementing an affective curriculum, process is more important that product, the latter being specific, quantifiable, content-oriented goals.

Conclusion

An affective curriculum makes sense when giftedness is considered broadly—beyond just high academic performance, beyond stereotypical assumptions about who gifted youth are and where they come from, and certainly without assumptions that school success precludes social and emotional challenges and distress. This curriculum can be multifaceted, can involve gifted education teachers and classroom teachers and school and other counselors, and can be proactive, reactive, and/or integrative. New skills, such as processing, and new postures, such as nonjudgment and focusing on strengths, can help gifted education personnel, other educators, and parents provide contexts that nurture social and emotional development. A solid affective emphasis in programs for gifted students potentially embraces *all* with high ability, whether they are extreme rebels, underachievers, from nonmainstream backgrounds, contending with disabilities, and/or the highest achievers in the school. It can affirm ability without formally evaluating it—simply by including students in an affectively oriented activity and not judging them or prodding them to be different in order to be "OK." An affective curriculum can embrace them in the present. An affective curriculum might even help some gifted students to survive the school years—literally.

References

Adams, C. (1991). Qualitative age differences in memory for text: A life-span developmental perspective. *Psychology and Aging, 6*, 323–336.

Adderholdt-Elliott, M. (1987). *Perfectionism: What's bad about being too good?* Minneapolis, MN: Free Spirit.

American Counseling Association. (2005). *ACA code of ethics and standards of practice.* Washington DC: Author.

Baldwin, A. Y. (1994). The seven plus story: Developing hidden talent among students in socioeconomically disadvantaged environments. *Gifted Child Quarterly, 38*, 80–84.

Bandura, A. (1994). Self-efficacy. In V. S. Ramachaudran (Ed.), *Encyclopedia of human behavior* (Vol. 4, pp. 71–81). New York: Academic Press.

Barrett, M., & Berman, J. (2001). Is psychotherapy more effective when therapists disclose information about themselves? *Journal of Consulting and Clinical Psychology, 69*, 597–603.

Baumrind, D. (1991). Parenting styles and adolescent development. In J. Brooks-Gunn, R. Lerner, & A. C. Peterson (Eds.), *The encyclopedia of adolescence* (pp. 746–758). New York: Garland.

Cohen, R. J., & Swerdlik, M. E. (1999). *Psychological testing and measurement: An introduction to tests and measurement.* Mountain View, CA: Mayfield.

Cross, T. L., Coleman, L. J., & Stewart, R. A. (1993). The social cognition of gifted adolescents: An exploration of the stigma of giftedness paradigm. *Roeper Review, 16*, 37–40.

DeShazer, S. (1985). *Keys to solution in brief therapy.* New York: W. W. Norton.

Elkind, D. (1981). *The hurried child.* Reading, MA: Addison-Wesley.

Evans, D. R., Hearn, M. T., Uhlemann, M. R., & Ivey, A. E. (1998). *Essential interviewing: A programmed approach to effective communication* (5th ed.). Pacific Grove, CA: Brooks/Cole.

Frasier, M. (1997). Gifted minority students: Reframing approaches to their identification and education. In N. Colangelo & G. A. Davis (Eds.), *Handbook of gifted education* (2nd ed., pp. 498–515). Boston: Allyn & Bacon.

Gardner, H. (1985). *Frames of mind: The theory of multiple intelligences.* New York: Basic Books.

Greenspon, T. S. (2000). "Healthy perfectionism" is an oxymoron! Reflections on the psychology of perfectionism and the sociology of science. *Journal of Secondary Gifted Education, 11*, 197–208.

Hébert, T. P., & Kelly, K. R. (2006). Identity and career development in gifted students. In F. A. Dixon & S. M. Moon (Eds.), *The handbook of secondary gifted education* (pp. 35–64). Waco, TX: Prufrock Press.

Higgins, G. O. (1994). *Resilient adults: Overcoming a cruel past.* San Francisco: Jossey Bass.

Huegel, K. (2003). *GLBTQ: The survival guide for queer and questioning teens.* Minneapolis, MN: Free Spirit.

Ivey, A. E., & Ivey, M. B. (2003). *Intentional interviewing and counseling: Facilitating client development in a multicultural society.* Pacific Grove, CA: Brooks/Cole.

Johnson, L. J., Karnes, M. B., & Carr. V. W. (1997). Providing services to children with gifts and disabilities: A critical need. In N. Colangelo & G. A. Davis (Eds.), *Handbook of gifted education* (2nd ed., pp. 516–527). Boston: Allyn & Bacon.

Kerr, B., & Sodano. S. (2003). Career assessment with intellectually gifted students. *Journal of Career Assessment, 15*, 68–86.

Kitchener, K. S. (1984). Intuition, critical evaluation and ethical principles: The foundation for ethical decisions in counseling psychology. *The Counseling Psychologist, 12*(3), 43–55.

Kottman, T., & Ashby, J. (2000). Perfectionistic children and adolescents: Implications for school counselors. *Professional School Counseling, 3*, 182–188.

Lovecky, D. V. (1992). Exploring social and emotional aspects of giftedness in children. *Roeper Review, 15*, 18–25.

Marcia, J. E. (1980). Identity in adolescence. In J. Adelson (Ed.), *Handbook of adolescent psychology* (pp. 159–187). New York: Wiley.

Masten, A. S., & Coatsworth, J. D. (1998). The development of competence in favorable and unfavorable environments: Lessons from research on successful children. *American Psychologist, 53*, 205–220.

Mendaglio, S. (2003). Heightened multifaceted sensitivity of gifted students: Implications for counseling. *Journal of Secondary Gifted Education, 14*, 73–82.

Murphy, B. C., & Dillon, C. (2003). *Interviewing in action: Relationship, process, and change.* Pacific Grove, CA: Brooks/Cole.

Nichols, M. P. (1995). *The lost art of listening.* New York: Guilford.

Peterson, J. S. (1990). Noon-hour discussion groups: Dealing with the burdens of capability. *Gifted Child Today, 13*(4), 17–22.

Peterson, J. S. (1993). Peeling off the elitist label: Smart politics. *Gifted Child Today, 16*(2), 31–33.

Peterson, J. S. (1997). Bright, troubled, and resilient, and not in a gifted program. *Journal of Secondary Gifted Education, 8*, 121–136.

Peterson, J. S. (1998a). The burdens of capability. *Reclaiming Children and Youth, 6*, 194–198.

Peterson, J. S. (1998b). Six exceptional young women at risk. *Reclaiming Children and Youth, 6*, 233–238.

Peterson, J. S. (1999a). Gifted—through whose cultural lens? An application of the postpositivistic mode of inquiry. *Journal for the Education of the Gifted, 22*, 354–383.

Peterson, J. S. (1999b). When it's hard to leave home. *Reclaiming Children and Youth, 8*, 14–19.

Peterson, J. S. (2000a). A follow-up study of one group of achievers and underachievers four years after high school graduation. *Roeper Review, 22*, 217–224.

Peterson, J. S. (2000b). Preparing for college—beyond the "getting-in" part. *Gifted Child Today, 23*(2), 36–41.

Peterson, J. S. (2001a). Successful adults who were once adolescent underachievers. *Gifted Child Quarterly, 45*, 236–249.

Peterson, J. S. (2001b). Gifted and at risk: Four longitudinal case studies. *Roeper Review, 24*, 31–39.

Peterson, J. S. (2003). An argument for proactive attention to affective concerns of gifted adolescents. *Journal of Secondary Gifted Education, 14*, 62–71.

Peterson, J. S. (2007). A developmental perspective. In S. Mendaglio & J. S. Peterson (Eds.), *Models of counseling gifted children, adolescents, and young adults* (pp. 97–126). Waco, TX: Prufrock Press.

Peterson, J. S. (2008). *The essential guide for talking with gifted teens: Ready-to-use group discussions about identity, stress, relationships, and more.* Minneapolis, MN: Free Spirit.

Peterson, J. S., & Colangelo, N. (1996). Gifted achievers and underachievers: A comparison of patterns found in school files. *Journal of Counseling and Development, 74*, 399–407.

Peterson, J. S., Duncan, N., & Canady, K. (2008). *A longitudinal study of negative life events, stress, and school experiences of gifted youth.* Manuscript in review.

Peterson, J. S., & Ray, K. E. (2006a). Bullying among the gifted: The subjective experience. *Gifted Child Quarterly, 50*, 252–269.

Peterson, J. S., & Ray, K. E. (2006b). Bullying and the gifted: Victims, perpetrators, prevalence, and effects. *Gifted Child Quarterly, 50*, 148–168.

Peterson, J. S., & Rischar, H. (2000). Gifted and gay: A study of the adolescent experience. *Gifted Child Quarterly, 44*, 149–164.

Piechowski, M. M. (1999). Overexcitabilities. In M. A. Runco & S. R. Pritzker (Eds.), *Encyclopedia of creativity* (Vol. 2, pp. 325–334). San Diego, CA: Academic Press.

Plucker, J. A., & Levy, J. J. (2001). The downside of being talented. *American Psychologist, 56*, 75–76.

Rimm, S. B., Rimm-Kaufman, S., & Rimm, I. (1999). *See Jane win: The Rimm report on how 1,000 girls became successful women.* New York: Crown.

Schuler, P. (2001). Perfection and the gifted adolescent. *Journal of Secondary Gifted Education, 11*, 183–196.

Seeley, K. (2004). Gifted and talented students at risk. *Focus on Exceptional Children, 37*, 1–8.

Seligman, M. E., & Csikszentmihalyi, M. (2000). Positive psychology: An introduction. *American Psychologist, 55*, 5–14.

Shore, B. M., Cornell, D. G., Robinson, A., & Ward, V. S. (1991). *Recommended practices in gifted education: A critical analysis.* New York: Teachers College Press.

Taub, D. J. (2006). Understanding the concerns of parents of students with disabilities: Challenges and roles for school counselors. *Professional School Counseling, 10*, 52–57.

Webb, J. T., Meckstroth, E., & Tolan, S. S. (1982). *Guiding the gifted child: A practical source for parents and teachers.* Columbus: Ohio Psychology.

The Role of the Arts in the Socioemotional Development of the Gifted

Joyce VanTassel-Baska, Brandy L. E. Buckingham, & Ariel Baska

"Unless some things are known passionately, they are not known at all."

—Eisner

Psychologists allude to the cross-sectional concepts that apply to all behavior: emotional arousal or intensity, goal direction, and motivation essential to both. Yet, the field of gifted and talented education in general has dichotomized these concepts into emotional intelligence (Goleman, 1997; Salovey, Bedell, Detweiler, & Mayer, 2000) and overexcitabilities (Dabrowski, 1938; Piechowski & Colangelo, 1984) to describe affective issues and triarchal intelligence, governed by executive processing (Sternberg, 1985) or g-factor intelligence governed by speed and complexity (Carroll, 1993) to describe cognitive issues as if they are worlds apart.

We contend that the arts are a bridge to connect these two views of intelligence. Only through the arts can we successfully integrate our cognitive and affective selves and provide a pathway to generative learning, a pathway to creating optimal selves; namely the creation of artists. What is creativity but our capacity to harness emotional and rational abilities toward a productive display of novelty in some form? Thus, the arts should be an

integral part of gifted education programs and services, regardless of the age of the learner, his or her special aptitudes, or the
core subject matter of the curriculum.

Unfortunately, aesthetic aspects of human experience are
considered luxuries, examples of play not work, pleasure not
duty. Therefore, they can be cut from school budgets, forced
to be delivered in strange scheduling configurations like a one-
hour per week specialist model, and given less instructional time
in general than other subjects. Recent studies on allocation of
instructional time suggest that the arts have been reduced 16%
in time allotment in the majority of schools nationwide over the
past 6 years (Center on Education Policy, 2008).

We need to be cognizant of curriculum in schools as a
mind-altering device. The absence of a subject in school signals
a devaluing of it. The content and tasks we assign speak to the
mental skills we wish to develop. Thus, learning to read "aesthetic forms" and being diligent in that inquiry is as consum-
mate an intellectual task as solving a difficult math problem, yet
not routinely practiced.

The arts also provide direct opportunities for rich differentiation for gifted students. They focus on higher level thinking
and feeling; they are open-ended, allowing for creative response.
The arts also are challenging in respect to their complexity and
the invitation to go into greater depth in one's exploration of
any given art form. Finally, they are conceptual and encourage
meaning-making for performer and audience alike.

Aesthetic experiences also lose out in American education because of our view of knowledge as a search for truth,
something to be found through the tools of science, as opposed
to seeing knowledge as something to be created, constructed,
and made, a view in which aesthetic dimensions matter. Plato's
notion of dependable knowledge as being that which moves
away from the senses toward the abstract is very much with us.
As a field, we see intelligence in the manipulation of abstract
ideas, not in making or doing, which we relegate to the lesser
term *talent*.

In life are we searching for meaning out there or creating
ourselves from inside here? The answer is central to the role of

aesthetics in our own lives and how the arts shape our experiences in the world.

Social-Emotional Needs of the Gifted and the Arts

The arts in many students' lives serve as a bridge to deeper levels of cognition. Frequently the students who feel unchallenged by normal academic procedure can revel in the ability to find their own meaning in a subjective piece of art, be it musical, visual, or performance. The idea that something exists beyond the repetitive concretes that too often are emphasized in schools can be a liberating force for the gifted. The revelation of more personal, subjective responses to the world in many ways frees a gifted child's mind to connect with herself and those around her in more meaningful ways.

Why do the arts have such a powerful effect? Beyond the metacognition inherent in the arts, they simultaneously provide us with our own emotional experiences and a certain amount of distance and closure. By converting our own relatable perspective into an art form, it automatically becomes objectified. Every aspect of the arts comes with its own set of criteria, making one's own personal vision in some sense quantified. This act provides many with the psychological distance they need to really understand what it is that they are seeing in the patterns played out within their own lives.

In Stephen Sondheim's Tony and Pulitzer prize–winning musical, *Sunday in the Park With George*, Georges Seurat sits working on his *Sunday Afternoon on the Island of La Grande Jatte*. In essence, the whole musical is really about the artist's struggle to establish meaning both in art and life through "composition, balance, order, harmony." However, one song from that show, "Finishing the Hat," typifies the experience of artistic distance: "Finishing the hat, how you have to finish the hat while you look at the rest of the world through a window, while you finish the hat." In this song, he demonstrates how he works on the details of the painting, locking his vision down to one clear, precise, almost scientific element of his artwork. He goes on to point out that his own mind is always, in some sense, focused on the relation of life to art – "there's a part of you always standing by, mapping out a sky, finishing a hat."

The arts, no matter what form they take, are an extraordinary window into secret selves. They can allow us to purge our own intense emotions, as well as express them to others. They can give us emotional closure. Most importantly though, they allow us insights into the world around us that we've never had before.

Application to Drama

This process of connection to both self and others is perhaps most easily expressed in the example of drama. As an art form that represents in many ways a microcosm of reality or emotion, any audience member will be able to relate on some level to the action or message of the performance. Students can compare the sequence of events and the point of view portrayed to their own conception of life, even if the two are distinctly different. The ancient Greeks defined the same idea of projection of self into staging, though mostly through the vicarious purging of emotions. The whole concept behind catharsis is in many ways another form of introspection—of understanding one's own emotions and actions. This psychological projection can lead students to new ways of thinking about themselves and what matters most to them. The process of identity development, a crucial component in reaching socioemotional maturity, is furthered by personal student reactions to dramatic works.

The other great contribution of the arts to students' socioemotional needs comes in the form of self-expression. Creative work provides a vent for the emotional sensibilities, effectively serving as another kind of therapy. Actors learn to harness and direct their emotions, and in the rehearsal process often create several possible inner worlds in response to a single scene (the process of bibliotherapy can be used with other arts to achieve virtually the same results).

In what could be considered the most important function of the arts, drama encourages creative and meaningful interaction. This interaction can be seen between two actors making an emotional connection, a director working to effectively communicate his or her vision to the actors, or an actor varying a performance in response to the moods of the audience. The arts not only provide self-therapy, but their creation can be a key to communicating the deepest part of the self, just as the evaluation of other forms of artistic work reveals more about how the viewer constructs meaning rather than about the actual piece.

Application to Music

Just as with drama, music forms another parallel to these ideas, albeit on a more abstract level. The method of identification in music comes largely from the emotions elicited by the aesthetics of one piece or another. The jarring, disjointed feeling of dissonance or the satisfaction of complex harmonies elicit strong responses from sensually sensitive learners. The creation of this music through performance in turn adds to an internal sense of accomplishment, having completed a difficult Chopin nocturne or successfully flauted Ravel's *Bolero*. Through playing the music, the player must somehow connect with it in his or her own way as an inevitable by-product of the artistic learning process. By seeing how the abstract colors and shadings of the music elicit individual reactions, musically talented learners frequently begin to identify themselves with one composer or another, or one work or another, providing them a new way to reflect themselves nonverbally.

Music also is a means of self-expression and fulfills many of the same needs that drama does. Music, as well as theatre, creates a close community of players and composers. However, as a more abstract art form, the bonds between musicians draws even more importance from the reliance on each element of music to form a meaningful whole. The focus on the inter-related elements of music, the relationship between the violin players in a string quartet, singers in an a capella group or between the members of a jazz band at a jam session, make music a very social form of artistic expression. Even outside of collaborative musical efforts, the performances of solo artists still provide them with an even greater awareness of and connection to their audience through deep absorption in the music. Conveying meaning and emotion through the structural and stylistic elements of music gives the artist a two-fold means of expressing herself, as can be found in each of the performance arts. The strong relationship with both the material and its representation gives the artist and the audience even more to react to at a personal level.

Application to Literature

Coles (1989) described heightened awareness, moments of understanding the meaning of life, and moral decisions reached after reading a particular book. He refers to this as the consequences of reading and responding to a story:

> Its indirections become ours. Its energy invites our own energetic leap into sadness, delight, resentment, frustration. Psychiatrists use words such as empathy, identification, introspection . . . The whole point of stories is not "solutions" or "resolutions" but a broadening and even a heightening of our struggles—with new protagonists and antagonists introduced, with new sources of concern or apprehension or hope, as one's mental life accommodates itself to a series of arrivals: guests who have a way of staying, but not necessarily staying put. (p. 129)

Literature has the power to help us understand human emotion in others and reflect on what it means to our own lives. Bibliotherapy is a specific use of literature to aid gifted students in their social and emotional development through highlighting eternal conflicts and problems that the self faces in the larger world.

Coles' belief that the point of stories is to broaden and heighten personal struggles also echoes Ogburn-Colangelo's (1979) application of Dabrowski's theory of positive disintegration to counseling the gifted. Ogburn-Colangelo pointed out that it is important not for the client to resolve conflict but to be valued for having it, that emotional conflict is useful to development. Ogburn-Colangelo encouraged a personal quest through counseling; Coles promoted similar personal searching by asking students to respond to stories.

Application to the Visual Arts

As children, most, if not all, students are encouraged to draw or finger paint. In many cases, outside of the realm of picture books, this is their first introduction to visual art, as both creators and evaluators. For many students, the visual images they create and interpret only gain more and more meaning as they mature. Eventually the artistic self makes a clear choice with each work— to be representational or abstract. Both are extremely subjective and in many cases intensely personal to the artist; however, the approaches employed by both are distinctive.

As a gifted child engaged with a painting might notice, all of the visual arts in some sense are representational, even in their abstraction, and in some sense, also abstract. The arts have always been formed as a reaction to life, giving even the robust lines of Piet Mondrian a certain amount of organic reality. The blurring of the distinction between the world we live in and the world that the artist creates instills a sense of the cognitive autonomy every person has, in spite of his or her living conditions. In this realization alone, gifted children can appreciate the power of their own thoughts and emotions, identifying with the artist's desire for creative dominion.

At a more basic level, the gifted child also has the ability to contemplate and reflect on the messages the artist projects into her artwork. Paintings and sculpture that require meaning to be constructed hold a particularly strong appeal for gifted and talented learners. This allows them to evaluate a work in terms of their own personal reaction to it, from which they can construct their own meaning, especially in conversation with others.

Art as a Form of Therapy

Art theorists have long held that all art contains meaning; "even the simplest line expresses visible meaning and is therefore symbolic" (Arnheim, 1974, p. 461). The fact that art both represents and elicits emotion can be inferred simply by the fact that so many types of art are grouped into genres according to the emotion they provoke (Tan, 2000). Arnheim (1966) posited three levels at which either the creator or the consumer of art can become emotionally involved in it; at the third level, the "art product engulfs the self . . . when the actor *becomes* Othello, when the novelist's body is shaken by the pains that torture his poisoned heroine, or when melancholy music moves the listener to tears" (p. 318).

Psychologists have taken note of these theorists, and have been harnessing the emotional power of art in therapy for several decades now. Recent research continues to support the use of art therapy in many very different contexts. Analysis of the colors and features included in paintings can differentiate psychiatric diagnoses (Hacking & Foreman, 2000). Art therapy has been shown to improve the mental well-being of posttraumatic stress disorder patients (Glaister, 2000), help adolescent boys with anger management issues (Groves & Huber, 2003), and decrease dementia in senior citizens (Zeltzer, Stanley, Melo, & LaPorte, 2003). Given that the interpretation of art works is a "cognitively complex" task (Tan, 2000, p. 130), it seems especially fitting as a method of counseling the gifted.

Causes of Social and Emotional Conflict in the Gifted

In addition to their demanding intellectual needs, gifted children have their own set of equally demanding emotional and social needs. Lovecky (1993) identified five traits of gifted children that can cause internal and external conflict: divergent thinking ability, excitability, sensitivity, perceptiveness, and entelechy (a determination to achieve self-actualization).

Although divergent thinking can lead to success in many fields in adulthood, it can cause problems for a gifted child. It often leads to difficulty in organizing thoughts, feelings, and materials (Lovecky, 1993). In addition, its inherent nonconformity often elicits negative responses from both teachers and peers who don't understand the divergent thinker's mind; this can lead to feelings of isolation and a negative self-image in the gifted child.

The reigning theory on counseling gifted learners is Dabrowski's (1938) theory of overexcitabilities (OEs). Dabrowski defines five OEs—psychomotor, emotional, intellectual, imaginative, and sensual. Although these are not entirely unique to gifted people, they are more common in the gifted than in those of average intelligence, especially the emotional, intellectual, and imaginative dimensions of OE. Ackerman (1997) found that in her sample, which included both students who had been identified as gifted by their school district and those who had not been, 70.9% of the students could be correctly classified as identified or unidentified according to their scores on an overexcitability questionnaire for psychomotor, intellectual, and emotional OEs. She also found higher questionnaire scores for all five OEs in gifted children than in the unidentified. Each OE, while giving a gifted child certain advantages, also poses its own problems (Silverman, 1993a). Children with psychomotor OE may be misidentified as having Attention Deficit/Hyperactivity Disorder; those with emotional OE are easily hurt and often seen as too sensitive. Without understanding and properly trained teachers, intellectual and imaginational OEs both can lead to problems in school when gifted children do not approach problems and assignments in the same ways as their peers. Sensual OE, although it is more common in gifted adults than children, often manifests itself as intense reactions to noise or discomfort.

Sensitivity in a gifted child often is linked to emotional OE, but can be seen in many other areas as well. In her analysis of the Gulbenkian study, Freeman (1994) found that children with higher IQs were more sensitive to the differences between them and their peers. In addition, they were more likely to have a pessimistic view of the world's future (in particular, more likely to predict nuclear holocaust), a sign of sensitivity toward world events and problems. Gifted children also are more sensitive when it comes to moral issues such as fairness and honesty (Silverman, 1994a). Because of gifted children's asynchronous development, heightened sensitivity to these issues often comes before a child's ability to deal with the issue emotionally, which can lead them to worry excessively and even become depressed (Robinson, 1996).

Highly perceptive children are adept at taking others' points of view and understanding different layers of an issue (Lovecky, 1993). Although this contributes greatly to their intellectual development and understanding of concepts and theories, the absence of this trait in others can be very frustrating for a gifted child. Left unchecked, this frustration can lead to disillusionment, cynicism, arrogance, and distrust.

Strong-willed behavior, perfectionism, and a tendency to put others' needs before one's own all can be the results of entelechy (Lovecky, 1993). At the same time, children with high entelechy are highly motivated to create their own destiny, and this can help them to surmount the obstacles presented to them.

The Use of the Arts in Counseling the Gifted

In order to understand how to use the arts effectively as a tool for addressing the social-emotional needs of the gifted, teachers and other educators first must have an appreciation for the counseling process and how analogous it is to the way the arts work for individuals engaged in them.

The Counseling Process

A critical aspect of counseling is helping the client become independent through an acceptance of self and through learning how to make changes and adjustments (see Figure 9.1).

For the classroom teacher, an awareness of this process is a first step in being able to use it for meeting the affective needs of gifted students through the arts. The importance of developing rapport with the gifted child is an important beginning stage. Such students respond well to humorous interchange, authen-

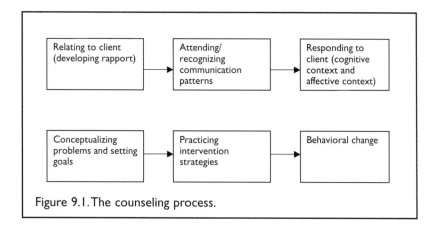

Figure 9.1. The counseling process.

tic dialogue, and open discussion. Silverman (1994b) listed several approaches to establishing rapport with gifted children, all of which are important avenues to explore:
- Invite the person to share his or her feelings.
- Listen.
- Ask for more information—do not assume you understand.
- Respect the problems—do not try to resolve them.
- Withhold judgments.
- Do not agree with the person continuously.
- Be authentic in your responses.
- Empathize—try to enter the student's inner world.
- Encourage the full expression of emotions.
- Support and validate the person's feelings.
- Do not take sides on the issues.
- Share common experiences—no one likes to feel alone.

Attention to a gifted child's communication pattern can yield understanding of how the child thinks and feels about herself as well as about the world. The teacher must be sensitive to both verbal and nonverbal cues and use them to help a child deal with special problems. Just because a child demonstrates a high cognitive ability and displays it confidently in a given context does not mean that affective problems are not present. Many such children betray how they feel in nonverbal ways or through more introspective processes like writing or drawing.

The counseling process is a way to uncover the contextual complexity of the gifted and provide support.

At the level of responding to cognitive and affective cues, the teacher employs appropriate curriculum interventions as the primary tool. This chapter strongly suggests the use of both the writing process and the reading process in various forms as key ways to respond to cognitive and affective needs of the gifted child, a purpose analogous to a counselor employing specific counseling strategies to respond to client content.

Problem finding and goal setting are processes central to effective counseling. Helping a client define his or her own problem, take responsibility for it, and move beyond it through the writing-reading connection, can help a student work through an issue or problem in the context of a discussion or conference, as well as introduce a means of expression that can help students articulate affective concerns.

The importance of practicing behavior in the counseling process is another critical stage. It is not sufficient for a client only to talk about problems; he or she must be able to act on them in some way over time. Again, the teacher of the gifted is in a position to provide appropriate expressive channels to use for problem solving and practicing safe behaviors through constructing hypothetical situations open to the discussion of peers.

The goal of the counseling process, like that of processes in therapy, is positive change in the direction of self-efficacy. Clients emerge from counseling more confident of their abilities to handle problems and more sure of who they are.

The Arts and Counseling Connections

By examining the similarities among the arts and counseling processes, interconnected possibilities emerge for helping gifted students deal with social-emotional concerns. Both processes are student-centered: arts ideas and content are generated from within the student; reading lists are chosen and discussed by the reader; the experiences and issues to be addressed within counseling are expressed by the individual student.

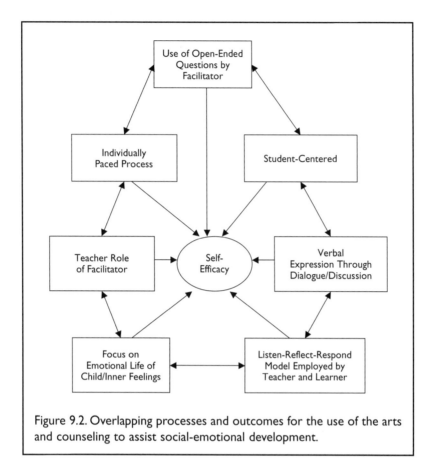

Figure 9.2. Overlapping processes and outcomes for the use of the arts and counseling to assist social-emotional development.

Throughout all of these processes, the teacher or counselor really is a facilitator (Rogers, 1983). The teacher asks the writer, "What do you want to write about?" Questions are open-ended to maximize response. Arts and counseling both draw on the inner feelings of the child by providing appropriate avenues for emotional expression. Moreover, the outcome of both processes is similar: self-efficacy for the learner (see Figure 9.2).

Bibliotherapy

Because gifted children usually are avid readers, literature can be a powerful way to help them deal with their social and emotional problems. Halsted (2002) noted that unlike clinical bibliotherapy, developmental bibliotherapy can be carried out by someone other than a mental health professional, such as a parent or teacher, making it a valuable counseling tool in school and home environments. She outlined four steps in the bibliotherapy process for gifted students: identification, catharsis, insight, and universalization. The facilitator helps guide the student through the four steps while or after reading the book by asking questions focused on identifying with the characters, how they handled the situations in the book, and how the book relates to the student's own life.

Bibliotherapy can be useful in helping students to explore issues of decision making (Friedman & Cataldo, 2002), identity development (Frank & McBee, 2003), emotional intelligence (Sullivan & Strang, 2002), empathy (Ingram, 2003), social problems (Hébert & Kent, 1999), and multiculturalism (Ford, Tyson, Howard, & Harris, 2000), among others. Although the facilitator should choose books based on the goals of the bibliotherapy, if possible, the students involved can be given some choice to increase their interest and thus motivation (Schlicter & Burke, 1994). It may be useful to have a selection of suitable books on hand for students to choose from at any given time (Hébert & Kent, 1999). To increase the effectiveness of the intervention, bibliotherapy can be combined with other art forms through project-based learning to explore the student's relationship to the book (Frank & McBee, 2003; Hébert & Kent, 1999; Sullivan & Strang, 2002).

Videotherapy

The process for videotherapy is much like that for bibliotherapy, but uses movies or television shows rather than books as the vehicle for self-discovery (Milne & Reis, 2000). This process can be applied in many ways; a single movie can be shown in one sitting or in segments over time with questioning after each segment or a series of scenes from different movies and shows revolving around a similar theme can be used (Hébert & Speirs Neumeister, 2002). The movies can be shared with a large group of gifted children, a smaller group needing help with a particular issue, or even gifted students and their parents together. Extroverted students may respond better to the group viewing atmosphere of a movie than to the individual experience of reading a book, and teachers may find it easier to ensure that all students are familiar with the material in this setting (Frank & McBee, 2003). Discussion of films portraying gifted children (whether realistically or in stereotypes) also can be a useful tool in training teachers who are unfamiliar with the characteristics of the gifted (Nugent & Shaunessy, 2003).

Journaling

Journal writing can be a valuable outlet for gifted students to voice their needs and concerns (Hall, 1990). In addition to straight journaling, Hall suggested using journals in conjunction with film viewing, as well as analysis of the journals of other writers for emotional growth. After asking his male adolescent gifted students to write letters to themselves outlining a plan for a positive lifestyle, Lim (1994) found that the letters reflected many of the common traits of gifted students, including introversion and shyness, perfectionism, intense fascination with subjects, high competitiveness, organizational problems, and emotional maturity. Armstrong (1994) found that dialogue journaling between a teacher and student can open lines of communication and facilitate learning for both participants, especially if the teacher approaches the journal as a mode of mutual discourse rather than merely as an opportunity to ask questions.

Writing Process

Perhaps because of the nature of the written word, it is easier to conceptualize writing as a product-oriented subject than as a process. All too often, writing assignments are generated as vehicles to get to an end-product objective; the teacher's emphasis is on the outcome. For the gifted child in particular, an emphasis on product may exacerbate problems with perfectionism or unrealistically high self-expectations.

A process approach to writing shifts the concern from an end-position (product outcome) and spreads it throughout all writing phases. In other words, the *how* and *why* of writing become just as important as the outcome. A linear representation of writing phases demonstrates movement toward the creation of independence in writing.

A writing process program offers some sound practical benefits to gifted learners: students can proceed at their own pace, choose their own topics, use their own vocabulary, and be as creative as they choose. As a therapeutic tool, Salovey et al. (2000) described how writing can facilitate the reflective regulation of emotions. VanTassel-Baska (1994) suggested that writing programs for gifted students begin as soon as they enter school. A process approach enables even very young children to "write," using drawings as the basis of their stories (Gardner, 1980). A writing process program also can span the entire K–12 curriculum. The goal is to create self-directed, independent writers.

Literature

A lifelong commitment or passion for literature seems to develop when students see a personal connection with reading and when they feel competent to interpret the text. A literature program that integrates response, reflection, and presentation shares the counseling components of bibliotherapy: the use of literature to address key counseling needs. In fact, it is sometimes difficult to distinguish one from another.

Such an experiential approach to literature is particularly suited to gifted learners because it:

- presents literature as a system rather than as fragmented skills;
- gives the responsibility for response to the reader and respects the individual's unique interpretation and application;
- presents a body of knowledge for gifted learners to comprehend and to use in writing and in further reading;
- provides a framework for gifted learners to ask the ethical and moral questions that often provoke them; and

- ensures that the results of reading such as critical thinking, introspection, and personal understanding will receive regular attention rather than occasional, sporadic inclusion as a special topic in the curriculum.

Two authors who have described the reading process, Hansen (1987) and Probst (1988), enumerated its essential components. First, readers must be able to choose their own books. Just as writers choose their own content so that they care about it, own it, and can control it, so must readers select their own books in order to care about reading them. Hansen asserted that by selecting their own books, children learn to monitor their own reading strategies, and they become aware of their own reading process. If gifted children are to use literature to probe emotions and universal issues, their books must support that quest. The complexity and ambiguity gifted children face in their lives should be reflected in substantive books they choose to read. Trivial plots and characters with obvious solutions do not support thinking and reflection. Baskin and Harris (1985), Hauser and Nelson (1988), and Halsted (2002) have provided extensive annotated bibliographies for selecting books to offer gifted children.

In order to aid in the connection of literature to social-emotional development, Halsted (2002) has identified a set of social-emotional needs that great books tap into and provided the connections and opportunities for identity development discussed in this section of the chapter. Halsted's social-emotional themes include the following list:

- achievement,
- aloneness,
- arrogance,
- creativity,
- differentness,
- drive to understand,
- identity,
- intensity,
- introversion,
- moral concerns,

- perfectionism,
- relationship with others,
- sensitivity, and
- using ability. (p. 503)

Visual and Performing Arts

The visual and performing arts can help gifted students explore their emotions and values while catering to a wide range of learning styles and preferences (Clark & Zimmerman, 1998). Precocity in visual representation is a common trait in young gifted children. Their ability to symbolically represent emotions and their tendency to reflect common gifted characteristics in their art can make young gifted childrens' drawings a valuable source of information about their concerns and interests (Harrison, 1999). Analyzing the art of another culture can add to students' understanding of that culture and of their own relationship to varied value systems throughout the world (Smutny, 2002). Role-playing can help gifted students, who often dwell on failures (real or perceived), work through past events and learn new coping skills for similar situations in the future (Silverman, 1993b).

Other Strategies for Developing Self-Understanding

Another way to ensure that social-emotional development occurs appropriately is to help students gain understanding of self through various assessment processes. There is a need to understand one's talents and capabilities, interests, values, and personality in order to grow and develop, make good choices, and accrue positive experiences. Thus, using the arts as an avenue to explore these dimensions of self also is important.

Finally, the development of a philosophy of life suggests that a student has integrated self-understanding to a higher level and is able to articulate core beliefs and values. Beyond this level, the student hopefully can demonstrate living one's beliefs and making a commitment to a life theme and career. In order to ensure that social-emotional development occurs in arts domains, as well as in academics, an individual talent development plan may be needed. This plan would outline long-term and short-term goals and outcomes in cognitive, affective, and aesthetic domains. It would identify resources required to activate it, list implementation strategies, and articulate assessment approaches. Through such a plan these ideas of arts infusion and connection with academics becomes vivified.

Use of the Arts Standards by the Gifted Community

In our zealousness around standards, we have ignored a very rich set of standards that emerged in 1994 from the Consortium of National Arts Education Associations. Standards in the arts are a statement of the merger of the cognitive and affective elements of student learning, a merger between doing and making, analyzing and critiquing, and finally connecting the arts to history, to philosophy, and to science. The standards emphasize the value of the arts as both individual and social, practical and personal, formalistic and free, and thinking and feeling. Moreover, they advocate for the importance of integrating ideas in all of the arts into core subjects. A sample template from these standards allows us to see important pathways for curriculum development and integration that would promote both cognitive and affective development (Consortium of National Arts Education Association, 1994). Figure 9.3 depicts a set of such standards in the visual arts.

Teachers of gifted learners may use these standards to integrate the visual arts into their teaching of core content. An example for each standard follows in Table 9.1.

Research in the arts is highly supportive of the orientation of these standards. Bruner (1965) spoke of the nature of art experiences as connective, effortful, engaging, and intellectual, all accomplished through exposure and immersion with art objects. Dudley, Faircy, and Rice (1978) stressed the need to focus on particular art objects to deepen understanding and develop appreciation within and across arts domains.

Aesthetic experiences depend on the reader/viewer/listener's capacity to understand the dynamic properties of art. Music is more than the assembly of pitches and durations but a

1. **Content Standard:** Using knowledge of structure and functions.
    Achievement Standard:
    Students:
    a.   know the differences among visual characteristics and purposes of art in order to convey ideas,
    b.   describe how different expressive features and organizational principles cause different responses, and/or
    c.   use visual structures and functions of art to communicate ideas.

2. **Content Standard:** Choosing and evaluating a range of subject matter, symbols, and ideas.
    Achievement Standard:
    Students:
    a.   explore and understand prospective content for works of art; and/or
    b.   select and use subject matter, symbols, and ideas to communicate meaning.

3. **Content Standard:** Understanding the visual arts in relation to history and cultures.
    Achievement Standard:
    Students:
    a.   know that the visual arts have both a history and specific relationships to various cultures;
    b.   identify specific works of art as belonging to particular cultures, times, and places; and/or
    c.   demonstrate how history, culture, and the visual arts can influence each other in making and studying works of art.

4. **Content Standard:** Reflecting upon and assessing the characteristics and merits of their work and the work of others.
    Achievement Standard:
    Students:
    a.   understand there are various purposes for creating works of visual art,
    b.   describe how people's experiences influence the development of specific artwork, and/or
    c.   understand that there are different responses to specific artwork.

Figure 9.3. Sample visual arts standards.

Table 9.1
Applying and Integrating Standards Into Gifted Curriculum

Standard	Application to Gifted Curriculum
Using knowledge of structure and function in the visual arts.	Use graphic design to develop a presentation of your research project. Delineate the organizational principles you employed to create your presentation. How will you know the design was effective? List criteria you will employ to assess it.
Choosing and evaluating a range of subject matter, symbols, and ideas.	Create a visual montage on the theme of justice. Select art objects for inclusion according to their symbolic value and capacity to communicate the theme to an audience. Write an interpretation of your montage and share it with your classmates in a presentation.
Understanding the visual arts in relation to history and culture.	Study six preselected paintings from the Edo period in Japan. How do these pictures relate to the history and culture of Japan? Now examine six preselected contemporary Japanese paintings. Are they similarly reflective of history and culture? Why or why not, do you think?
Reflecting upon and assessing the characteristics and merits of the work of others.	Create criteria for judging artworks you encounter in any genre. How will you judge how good something is? Apply these criteria to the art of Chagall, Matisse, and Braque. How might you revise your criteria for judgement, based on your application of them to these artists? Now apply your new criteria to a play, movie, or a poem. Write your critique and share with a partner for feedback.

complex interplay of sound and human striving; *Hamlet* is more than words to be dissected but a zigzag course of motivational vectors to be appreciated; and Chagall's painting is more than the manipulation of subject matter and color—rather it is the palpable transformation of the human condition through love. Thus, employing the arts connection systematically through the use of arts standards in curriculum for the gifted provides an important experiential base for aesthetic and emotional development.

The Relationship of the Arts to Cognition

The arts have been known as an avenue for self-expression almost untouched by complex forms of reasoning, yet all of the arts represent higher levels of thought. Affordances of the arts (Eisner, 1996) help us to understand the opportunities to learn at higher levels that the arts teach us and how to perceive relationships, central to understanding analogical reasoning. Understanding how parts relate to the whole, shaping coherence, and seeing the figure-ground dynamic are important skills of both the artist and the scientist.

The arts also require the use of judgment in the absence of rules, developing self-assessment skills, and evaluating several variables, using self-developed criteria. The arts teach us to appreciate nuance, to be more observant, looking for precision and detail. The arts teach us to really see how small differences can have large effects. DeKooning putting tacks on paper to force the viewer to examine a deep reading of a created image is one example of such a nuance. The arts allow us to engage in product-making to create an image, Dewey's (1938) idea of flexible purposing. The arts offer us the opportunity of learning to think within a medium, understanding parameters and special challenges.

Just as these affordances in the arts are cognitive, they also offer opportunities for gifted learners to develop social, emotional, and creative skills in areas like risk-taking, self-trust, identity development, and dealing with perfectionism, and understanding and tolerating individual differences. They suggest that there are multiple solutions to any set of problems and that great art in any medium is the culmination of productive idiosyncrasies over time. Finally, the arts remind us that different representational systems allow different things to be known and that words are not always needed, nor are they always sufficient (Eisner, 1996).

So How Might Gifted Programs Incorporate Aesthetic Experiences More Fully Into Curriculum and Instructional Processes?

Gifted programs, by their very nature, encourage certain creative behaviors in students that an arts curriculum can provide. Gifted programs also desperately want to provide an emphasis on affective development—on helping students become whole individuals. Thus, several of the following techniques satisfy both the goals related to creative thought and those related to self-understanding and development.

Inquiry Techniques

One technique is to treat art as the stimulus for inquiry, asking carefully selected questions about art objects. Key questions developed by Smith (1991) to stimulate thinking and feeling about art include the following:
1. Who made it?
2. How was it made?
3. When was it made?
4. For whom was it made?
5. What is its message or meaning, if any?
6. What is its style?
7. What is the quality of experience it affords?
8. What was its place in the culture in which it was made?
9. What is its place in the culture or society of today?
10. What peculiar problems does it present to understanding and appreciation?

So, for example, by studying the 1952 Matisse cut-out, entitled *Woman With Amphora and Pomegranates*, we can seek answers to these basic questions that allow students to know the art object:

Questions 1–3. The artist Matisse, working with cut paper due to his physical limitations in advanced age, made the piece in the mid-20th century.

Question 4. It was made for the purpose of satisfying Matisse's own internal need to continue to make art.

Question 5. Its meaning is derived from the abstract form of color, shape, and line converging to suggest a simple task of life—carrying an amphora for providing sustenance.

Question 6. Matisse was a part of the Fauvism movement that moved away from impressionism into the use of bold color and more representational forms although abstract work also was a part of his oeuvre.

Question 7. It has goodness of fit—pleasing to the eye because of its simplicity, its appealing color, and the sensuousness of the form.

Question 8. It was made in France and constitutes a similar stylistic approach to that used to create paintings in the Matisse chapel in Vence, with religious artifacts all rendered in similar simplistic forms.

Question 9. Matisse's cut-outs are world-renowned; a whole room is devoted to them at the National Gallery of Art in Washington, DC, and a whole museum houses them in Nice, France. He had the capacity to depict all of life in one color and a few lines.

Question 10. Abstract art requires study and contemplation—the wish of society for quickness of apprehension fights against Matisse's intent to appreciate the essence of experience that is always abstract. One problem is that of "entering the picture" at some point—what do we identify with, the pomegranates, the amphora, or the woman and why? Responses take time and thinking.

Another technique to employ would be to focus on an in-depth understanding of art through careful analysis, asking core questions that explore content, form, meaning, emotional response, history, and value:

1. What is the subject matter?
2. What is it made of?
3. What does it convey?

4. How do you respond to it?
5. What is its context?
6. How good is it?

Teachers may wish to employ art prints, taped musical segments, and poetry as interrelated art forms for students to answer these archetypal questions.

Conceptual and Thematic Techniques

Another tool that gifted educators might use to incorporate the arts into curriculum is a set of interdisciplinary concepts that guide art-making across areas. These concepts include balance (How is coherence achieved?), unity (How does structure, content, and form contribute to meaning?), perspective (What is the point of view of the painting?), color (How does use of color impact the effect of the painting?), theme (What does it say or convey?), and subject matter (What is it?). In literature, authors attempt to connect experiences of character to readers and to all of humankind, including themselves. For example, Mary Oliver's poem "Spring in the Classroom" conveys a special sense of this dynamism through the character transformation of Miss Willow Bangs from narrow, ugly, and seared to a part of the natural world "in the art teacher's arms." In Mary Oliver's prose piece *Blue Pastures,* she speaks of the sense of powerlessness of children and her own redemption through nature and literature as an art form—similar to the transformation of Miss Willow Bangs. Milan Kundera (2003), in *The Art of the Novel,* speaks to the powers of that genre of literature to open up "possibilities" for life, to provide models for thinking about creating a life. He sees teaching novels as "life's little instruction book."

We also can use forms of music to create interdisciplinary understanding. Paul Klee's 1921 *Fugue in Red* illustrates an artist's depiction of musical form, not unlike Mondrian's depiction of *Broadway Boogie Woogie* or many modern artists' appropriation of the jazz idiom to create great art. Music in its structural exactness also provided an analogy for the Bauhaus school of architecture. The fugue with its dialogue between parts, becomes a kind of question and answer in Klee's painting, for example.

Gifted students frequently are concerned about the injustice in their world. A wonderful way for them to understand injustice at a deeper level is to experience how it has been portrayed through the arts. The role of the artist as reformer of society is another great connector of the *arts to history and culture*. Upton Sinclair's literary portrayal and exposé of the Chicago meat packing industry in *The Jungle* led to political action and clean-up of that industry early in the last century. Oscar Hamlin's *The Uprooted* portrayed the abuses of immigrants, leading to reforms in large cities like New York. Depictions of war litter the history of art in all centuries and cultures. Picasso's *Guernica* depicts the horrors of the Spanish Civil War and serves as a world icon for atrocity in a visual medium. Hungarian photographer Robert Capa created modern photojournalism by depicting the suffering of innocent people and the timeless qualities of human conflict.

Project-Based Work

Projects that deliberately ask students to use the arts as the content emphasis for their higher order thinking again reinforces its affective and motivational power. For example, ask students to create a human emotion à la Munch's *The Scream*. Students also can conduct research in literature and the arts—writing original criticism, doing biographical inquiry, and producing significant artistic products themselves. For example, Jacob Lawrence's *Olympics at Munich* highlights the triumphs of Black runners more than 30 years ago. How would students today depict a highlight of the Olympics? Have them create the artistic piece, write about its meaning, and critique its properties.

The Role of Biography

For gifted children historically since the 1920s, biography has served as a model for what they might become as students of eminent personalities of the world over time. Carlyle (1832) once observed that "all history is biography." So, biographical study allows important and unique insights into historical periods, events, and movements and helps us understand humanity in all of its dimensions. Taking a century of great artists like the 20th century and providing biographies for study in the graphic arts, in literature (including poetry, the novel, and the theatre), and in music, we lead students to understand their own potential for greatness in an area. Reading about people who have been eminent provides an identification tool for gifted students, allowing them to connect and dream. More about biographies is included in Chapter 10. By careful choices of artists, we also promote multicultural understanding and appreciation. To read the plays of Soyinka, the novels of Kawabata, and to view the art of Rivera provide students with positive cultural role models and icons.

Conclusion

Perhaps the best way to end our exploration of the importance of aesthetic experiences for the gifted as a bridge to affective development is to acknowledge the unknowns of the creative enterprise, the paradox of inner and outer influences on our understanding of our world. Dali's *Persistence of Memory* is a surrealistic image of these inner and outer landscapes of familiarity and strangeness, so necessary to tap into the emotional developmental potential of the gifted. The arts then have the potential to heal, to excite the imagination, to engage the intellect, and to make people whole. What better antidote to the real world of hurt and pain could gifted students hope for?

References

Ackerman, C. M. (1997). Identifying gifted adolescents using personality characteristics: Dabrowski's overexcitabilities. *Roeper Review, 19*, 229–236.

Armstrong, D. C. (1994). A gifted child's education requires real dialogue: The use of interactive writing for collaborative education. *Gifted Child Quarterly, 38*, 136–145.

Arnheim, R. (1966). *Toward a psychology of art: Collected essays*. Berkeley: University of California.

Arnheim, R. (1974). *Art and visual perception: A psychology of the creative eye* (New version). Berkeley: University of California.

Baskin, B., & Harris, K. H. (1985). *Reading for the gifted*. Reston, VA: ERIC Clearinghouse on Handicapped and Gifted Children.

Bruner, J. S. (1965). *Man: A course of study* (Occasional paper no. 3). Cambridge, MA: Educational Services.

Carroll, J. B. (1993). *Human cognitive abilities: A survey of factor-analytic studies*. Cambridge, England: Cambridge University Press.

Center on Education Policy. (2008). *Instructional time in elementary schools: A closer look at changes for specific subjects*. Washington, DC: Author.

Clark, G., & Zimmerman, E. (1998). Nurturing the arts in programs for gifted and talented students. *Phi Delta Kappan, 79*, 747–752.

Coles, R. (1989). *The call of stories: Teaching and the moral imagination*. Boston: Houghton Mifflin.

Consortium of National Arts Education Associations. (1994). *National standards for arts education*. Reston, VA: Music Educators National Conference.

Dabrowski, K. (1938). Typy wzmozonej pobudliwosci: Psychicnej (Types of increased psychic excitability). *Biul. Inst. Hig. Psychicznej, 1*(3–4), 3–26.

Dewey, J. (1938). *Experience and education*. New York: MacMillan.

Dudley, L., Faircy, A., & Rice, J. G. (1978). *The humanities* (6th ed). New York: McGraw-Hill.

Eisner, E. W. (1996). Qualitative research in music education: Past, present, perils, promise. *Bulletin of the Council for Research in Music Education, 130*, 8–16.

Ford, D. Y., Tyson, C. A., Howard, T. C., & Harris, J. J., III (2000). Multicultural literature and gifted Black students: Promoting self-understanding, awareness, and pride. *Roeper Review, 22*, 235–240.

Frank, A. J., & McBee, M. T. (2003). The use of *Harry Potter and the Sorcerer's Stone* to discuss identity development with gifted adolescents. *Journal of Secondary Gifted Education, 15*, 33–41.

Freeman, J. (1994). Some emotional aspects of being gifted. *Journal for the Education of the Gifted, 17*, 180–197.

Friedman, A. A., & Cataldo, C. A. (2002). Characters at crossroads: Reflective decision makers in contemporary Newbery books: Characters in fine literature serve to model decision-making skills. *The Reading Teacher, 56*, 102–113.

Gardner, H. (1980). *Artful scribbles*. New York: Basic Books.

Glaister, J. A. (2000). Four years later: Clara revisited. *Perspectives in Psychiatric Care, 36*(1), 5–14.

Goleman, D. (1997). *Emotional intelligence*. New York: Bantam.

Groves, J., & Huber, T. (2003). Art and anger management. *The Clearing House, 76*, 186–192.

Hacking, S., & Foreman, D. (2000). The descriptive assessment for psychiatric art (DAPA): Update and further research. *The Journal of Nervous and Mental Disorders, 188*, 525–529.

Hall, E. G. (1990). Strategies for using journal writing in counseling gifted students. *Gifted Child Today, 13*(4), 2–6.

Halsted, J. W. (2002). *Some of my best friends are books: Guiding gifted readers from preschool to high school* (2nd ed.). Scottsdale, AZ: Great Potential.

Hansen, J. (1987). *When writers read*. Portsmouth, NH: Heinemann Educational Books.

Harrison, C. (1999). Visual representation of the young gifted child. *Roeper Review, 21*, 189–194.

Hauser, P., & Nelson, J. A. (1988). *Books for the gifted child* (Vol. 2). Westport, CT: Libraries Unlimited.

Hébert, T. P., & Kent, R. (1999). Nurturing social and emotional development in gifted teenagers through young adult literature. *Roeper Review, 22*, 167–171.

Hébert, T. P., & Speirs Neumeister, K. L. (2002). Fostering the social and emotional development of gifted children through the guided viewing of film. *Roeper Review, 25*, 17–21.

Ingram, M. A. (2003). The use of sociocultural poetry to assist gifted students in developing empathy for the lived experiences of others. *Journal of Secondary Gifted Education, 14*, 83–92.

Kundera, M. (2003). *The art of the novel*. New York: HarperCollins.

Lim, T. K. (1994). Letters to themselves: Gifted students' plans for positive lifestyles. *Roeper Review, 17*, 85–89.

Lovecky, D. V. (1993). The quest for meaning: Counseling issues with gifted children and adolescents. In L. K. Silverman (Ed.), *Counseling the gifted and talented* (pp. 29–50). Denver, CO: Love.

Milne, H. J., & Reis, S. M. (2000). Using video therapy to address the social and emotional needs of gifted children. *Gifted Child Today, 23*(1), 24–29.

Nugent, S. A., & Shaunessy, E. (2003). Using film in teacher training: Viewing the gifted through different lenses. *Roeper Review, 25*, 128–135.

Ogburn-Colangelo, M. K. (1979). Giftedness as multilevel potential: A clinical example. In N. Colangelo & R. T. Zaffrann (Eds.), *New directions in counseling the gifted* (pp. 165–187). Dubuque, IA: Kendall/Hunt.

Piechowski, M., & Colangelo, N. (1984). Developmental potential of the gifted. *Gifted Child Quarterly, 28*, 80–88.

Probst, R. E. (1988). *Response and analysis: Teaching literature in junior and senior high school.* Portsmouth, NH: Heinemann Educational Books.

Rogers, C. R. (1983). *Freedom to learn for the 80's.* Columbus, OH: Charles E. Merrill.

Salovey, P., Bedell, B. T., Detweiler, J. B., & Mayer, J. D. (2000). Current directions in emotional intelligence research. In M. Lewis, & J. M. Haviland-Jones (Eds.), *Handbook of emotions* (2nd ed., pp. 504–520). New York: Guilford Press.

Schlichter, C. L., & Burke, M. (1994). Using books to nurture the social and emotional development of gifted students. *Roeper Review, 16*, 280–283.

Silverman, L. K. (1993a). The gifted individual. In L. K. Silverman (Ed.), *Counseling the gifted and talented* (pp. 3–28). Denver, CO: Love.

Silverman, L. K. (1993b). A developmental model for counseling the gifted. In L. K. Silverman (Ed.), *Counseling the gifted and talented* (pp. 58–78). Denver, CO: Love.

Silverman, L. K. (1994a). The moral sensitivity of gifted children and the evolution of society. *Roeper Review, 17*, 110–116.

Silverman, L. K. (1994b). Affective curriculum for the gifted. In J. VanTassel-Baska (Ed.), *Comprehensive curriculum for gifted learners* (pp. 335–355). Boston: Allyn & Bacon.

Smith, R. A. (1991). An excellent curriculum for arts education. In R. A. Smith & A. Simpson (Eds.), *Aesthetics and arts education* (pp. 245–255). Urbana: University of Illinois Press.

Smutny, J. F. (2002). *Integrating the arts into the curriculum for gifted students* (ERIC Digest No. E631). Arlington, VA: ERIC Clearinghouse on Disabilities and Gifted Education.

Sternberg, R. J. (1985). *Beyond IQ: A triarchic theory of human intelligence.* Cambridge, England: Cambridge University Press.

Sullivan, A. K., & Strang, H. R. (2002). Bibliotherapy in the classroom: Using literature to promote the development of emotional intelligence. *Childhood Education, 79*, 74–81.

Tan, E. S. (2000). Emotion, art, and the humanities. In M. Lewis & J. M. Haviland-Jones (Eds.), *Handbook of emotions* (2nd ed., pp. 116–134). New York: Guilford Press.

VanTassel-Baska, J. (1994). Verbal arts for the gifted. In J. VanTassel-Baska (ed.), *Comprehensive curriculum for gifted learners* (pp. 153–189). Boston: Allyn & Bacon.

Zeltzer, B. B., Stanley, S., Melo, L., & LaPorte, K. M. (2003). Art therapies promote wellness in elders. *Behavioral Healthcare Tomorrow, 12*(2), 7–12.

Guiding Gifted Teenagers to Self-Understanding Through Biography

Thomas P. Hébert

We read to know we're not alone.

—C. S. Lewis

Meg Holmes ended her day of classes at Kirkwood Central High School with her Honors American Literature students. In early November, she stood at the back of her classroom surveying her group. She was relieved that the school's homecoming festivities were over, and she was able to get her students focused on academics again before they left for the holidays. As her students were engaged in reading the assigned selections from their anthology, she enjoyed a few quiet moments from the back of her classroom and reflected on the gifted teenagers in her class.

She noticed that Jorgé looked exhausted again this week and wondered just how many hours he was working at the local movie theater. She paused and wrote a note to herself to explore that issue with Jorgé. She smiled to herself as she took note of Tyler's rather outlandish new hairstyle, perhaps an indication that another chapter of adolescent rebellion was about to begin. She watched as Celia read from her textbook and wrote reflective notes in her calligraphy-like penmanship. Celia seemed to enjoy her class, yet Meg wondered if Celia's conscientious work habits were bordering on perfectionism. Meg spotted Annette passing a note again to Josh. She decided to ignore this move, as it was probably Annette's attempt to make a friendship connection, something that appeared to be lacking in her life. As Meg Holmes walked to the front of her classroom, she stopped at Steve's desk and gently nudged him to wake him from another nap. She was frustrated with Steve and wanted to let him know how she felt about this student with so much potential, the self-proclaimed "Slacker King of Kirkwood Central." Just as she aroused Steve, the school's intercom came alive, and the end of the day announcements concluded the seventh-period class. As her students began to leave, Meg reminded them of the essay assignment she would be collecting the following day and wished them a pleasant evening.

She was happy that her afternoon schedule did not include another school committee meeting as she packed her bags to leave for the day. She was meeting Beth Rogers at a nearby coffee shop and was looking forward to seeing her friend and commiserating with another English teacher. She and Beth had graduated from university together, and Beth was currently teaching at the local middle school. As she waited for her friend to arrive at the downtown coffee shop, she glanced through a magazine featuring a cover story of Oprah Winfrey and the book club she had made popular nationwide. As she read the article describing Oprah's success at emphasizing the importance of reading with young people, Meg became intrigued with Oprah's rationale for creating a national movement supporting reading groups.

The interview with Oprah highlighted how she was a voracious reader as a young woman and believed that biographies had saved her life. Oprah described how she felt she was able to overcome the adversity in her adolescent experience because of significant role models she met in the biographies of gifted women such as Anne Frank and Helen Keller, women who had overcome adverse challenges in their own lives. In reading these women's stories, she discovered that she was not alone, she felt inspired by their courage, and became determined to apply their philosophical approach to her personal situation. When Oprah reached national prominence, she felt compelled to begin Oprah's Book Club in hopes that young people throughout the country would be positively influenced in similar ways.

Beth Rogers arrived just as Meg finished reading the article. While Meg waited for her friend to purchase her cup of coffee, she reflected on her students in her Honors American Literature class and the variety of challenges several of them faced. The article on Oprah had her thinking about how she would approach an important instructional unit in her class. Because she and Beth had always enjoyed exchanging ideas about teaching strategies, she was eager to share her thinking about Oprah's important message and how she might infuse biographies into her curriculum in order to address some of social and emotional issues facing her students. As Beth approached the table, Meg announced with a big smile, "Hi! I'm so glad you're here! I can't wait to share a new idea with you. Believe it or not, I think Oprah may be able to help us this year."

Guiding Gifted Students Using Biographies

Educators have long recognized what Meg Holmes discovered that afternoon in reading the article about Oprah Winfrey. Books have been acknowledged as significant, effective tools to help young people solve personal problems and develop skills necessary for successful living. Bibliotherapy is the use of reading to help understand and resolve personal issues (Halsted, 2002; Lenkowsky, 1987). Educators often see this approach as an attempt to produce affective change and promote personality growth and development. For gifted students, this change occurs when readers see something of themselves in a biography, identify with the person whose life story is being presented, reflect on that identification, and undergo some emotional growth as a result (Hébert, 1995; Hébert, Long, & Speirs Neumeister, 2005).

The bibliotherapeutic process consists of several stages: identification, catharsis, insight, and application (Halsted, 2002; Lenkowsky, 1987). In the case of the biographical genre, *identification* with the person whose life story is being told or with the situations or events in that individual's life would enable intelligent teenagers to see their problems from a different perspective. Consider a teenager reading a biography of Jim Carrey, the talented actor and comedian: "Wow! I never realized that Jim Carrey came from such a poor family with so many problems. His teenage life was so much like mine." This experience of connecting with Jim Carrey's story provides the reader with a sense of *catharsis* when he realizes that others have faced the same situations: "I guess I should feel better knowing that I'm not the only kid whose father can't hold down a job." With the support of a teacher guiding a discussion of the biography and the conversation with classmates, this teenager should reach the third stage in the process—*insight*—and reflect on how the inspirational messages offered in the biography might apply to his life: "I think that Jim Carrey was able to overcome his difficult situation because he developed his sense of humor into something that could protect him from the pain he was feeling. Maybe I should do the same." The final stage of the process involves application, in which the reader leaves the discussion of the biography well-equipped with new strategies that he can apply to his problematic situation the next time the issue occurs: "Next time someone teases me about my hand-me-down clothing being out of style, I'm going to crack a joke. I may even use one of Carrey's quick comebacks. I'll be ready!" This vicarious experience with a biography provides gifted young people opportunities to develop insight into challenges they experience, as well as various approaches to solving their problems.

To highlight the appropriate use of this approach with young people in school settings, a distinction is made between clinical bibliotherapy and developmental bibliotherapy. *Clinical bibliotherapy* necessitates psychotherapeutic methods used by skilled and licensed practitioners with individuals experiencing serious emotional difficulties. *Developmental bibliotherapy* refers to helping young people in their normal emotional health and development and is the focus of this chapter. Proponents of this developmental intervention emphasize that one advantage is that educators can identify the concerns of young people in their classrooms and address the issues before they become serious problems. As seen in the earlier scenario, Meg Holmes took note of students in her classroom searching for friendships, struggling with motivation, or searching for an identity. Through her guided discussions of biographical materials, she should be able to provide her students with an understanding of the issues confronting them and examples of how other gifted teenagers dealt with the same challenges.

Meg Holmes might be pleased to discover that she is in good company. The use of guided discussions of biographies long has been recognized as a viable option for supporting the social and emotional development of gifted adolescents. In the 1920s, Leta Hollingworth, the founder of the Speyer School for highly gifted children in New York City, infused biographical studies into the school's curriculum. Hollingworth's elementary students facilitated discussions of their self-selected biographies for 40-minute periods. Hollingworth discovered that her young students raised so many questions that she decided to provide a depository box for questions not addressed during the seminar time allotted in class (Robinson & Millen, 2006). Following that experience, the dedicated teacher decided that the study of biography would become a permanent component of the Speyer School curriculum. Hollingworth (1926) found that her students discovered that biographies were captivating, inspirational, and showed them how to maintain high aspirations. Hollingworth explained:

> For many reasons, the study of biography would seem to be especially appropriate in the education of gifted children. For adjustment to life as they are capable of living it, they need information as to how persons have found adjustment, as to how careers are made and are related serviceably to civilization, and to all the various kinds of intellectual work required by the world in their day. (pp. 319–320)

Forty years following Hollingworth's seminal work with gifted students, Hildreth (1966) also highlighted the value of biographical studies for gifted students:

> The reading of biography is an illuminating experience in which young people meet personalities they would like to emulate. In biography the young reader comes to identify himself with persons of intelligence and learning. Reading about noble deeds may not of itself produce noble character, but such reading is undoubtedly a source of inspiration. The ambitious young person who is fond of reading finds enchantment in the lives of people who overcame obstacles to achievement through dint of hard effort. (pp. 380–381)

The bibliotherapy process using biographical materials is well-supported in the gifted education literature (Flack, 1992, 1999; Kerr, 1994; Kollof, 1998; Robinson & Butler Schatz, 2002) and contemporary leaders in gifted education continue to advocate such an approach. Robinson and Millen (2006) noted, "By examining a life, students learn about a real person in an historical time and place, but they also learn about themselves. The subjects of biographies can provide role models for their readers" (p. 8). They opined that because biographies often focus on the challenges encountered by individuals, this genre of reading helps students recognize and address problems of their own. Moreover, they maintained that well-crafted biographies could teach "life lessons" in ways that are compelling for intelligent young people.

The Benefits of Using Biographies to Guide Gifted Teenagers Based on Gender

Adolescence is filled with difficult challenges for all young people. It is a developmental period replete with new stresses. This period may be especially difficult for gifted teenagers because of the high levels of emotionality and sensitivity that often accompany high intelligence (Piechowski, 2006), exacerbating the stresses experienced in school and at home. Addressing the emotional needs of gifted teenagers is critical; therefore, facilitating discussions of biographies with students may serve as an important pathway in providing guidance.

The literature indicates that gifted students often are voracious readers (Halsted, 2002), particularly gifted girls. Gifted young women enjoy reading, and addressing affective concerns through guided discussions appeals to their love of literature. The reading preferences of young women also suggest that biographies are an appropriate choice. Langerman (1990) found in her research of reading preferences of boys and girls that young females enjoy delving into literature describing relationships. Because biographies often are filled with descriptions of important relationships in the lives of the central figures, the use of biography is a good match. Moreover, reading biographies with young women is an approach consistent with the empathic qualities evidenced in gifted females. Their need for vicariously experiencing the feelings of others is addressed through enjoying biographies filled with descriptions of the challenges and disappointments other gifted women have experienced, as well as their inspirational achievements (Hébert et al., 2005).

Langerman's (1990) findings on adolescent book selection indicated that reading preferences of boys change as they mature, with young men choosing less fiction and more non-fiction during the middle and high school years. More recently, Cavazos-Kottke (2006) found that talented boys demonstrated a strong interest in reading materials that appealed to adult interests and could increase cultural literacy. As a result, the use of biographies with gifted males also is consistent with their interests. In addition, teachers realize that gifted adolescent males have a need for serious introspection; however, as societal expectations continue to demand that young men constrain their emotionality, the struggle to get young men to express their feelings openly continues (Balswick, 1988; Kindlon & Thompson, 1999; Pollack, 1998). If educators are to help young men in dealing with introspection and learning how to express their emotions through ways in which they feel comfortable, they must create supportive classroom environments where this can happen. Guided discussions of good biographies through which boys can examine their problems through a third-person approach can become an integral part of such a classroom (Hébert, 1991).

Having gifted teenagers delve into biographies may provide them with additional benefits. Through biographies, gifted students are exposed to role models that may not exist in their immediate lives. In addition, biographies expose gifted students to new ways of thinking and different perspectives of the world around them. By reading biographies, gifted teenagers benefit from exposure to a variety of philosophical views of life; various liberal and conservative world views; and a diversity of socioeconomic backgrounds, cultures, and religions. Gifted teenagers also appreciate the realistic portrayal of the lives of gifted men and women, providing them with influential lessons and inspirational messages for succeeding in life. Moreover, many biographies of individuals whose lives were filled with adversity often provide adolescent readers with realistic strategies for developing resilience.

Affective Concerns Addressed by Educators Using Biographies

In the opening scenario, Meg Holmes represented teachers who know their students quite well and are willing to do all they can to support them as gifted young people. Teachers of gifted students often have the opportunity to address the affective concerns of their students through classroom activities, and the success of such affective curriculum in the classroom relies greatly on the attitude and comfort level of the teacher (Nugent, 2005). With this understanding, it is important to consider which issues in the social and emotional lives of gifted teenagers would be appropriate issues to address in classroom settings. Most educators willing to consider such an approach with gifted students will do so if the issues addressed are developmental in nature. Such issues often are concerns that all young people face; however, the interaction of giftedness with the issue may intensify the problem. Therefore, it is important for educators

to plan guided discussions of biographies with thorough attention to detail, sensitivity to the possible responses from their
students, and empathy for their feelings concerning the issues
discussed within the classroom.

Educators who design appropriate lessons using biographies take into account the affective characteristics and the
concomitant social and emotional needs of gifted students.
Several researchers have reviewed the gifted education literature examining the affective development of gifted students and
have delineated lists of social and emotional traits, characteristics, and behaviors evidenced in this population (Clark, 2002;
Nugent, 2005; Reis & Small, 2005; VanTassel-Baska, 1998). In
analyzing the lists, the following characteristics were those that
appeared most consistently across the work of the researchers:
high expectations of self and others—perfectionism; internal
motivation and inner locus of control; emotional sensitivity, intensity, and depth; empathy; highly developed sense of
humor; resilience; and advanced levels of moral maturity with
consistency between values and actions.

With an understanding of those characteristics must come
an appreciation for the concomitant social and emotional
needs. For example, if educators observe an emotional intensity and sensitivity within their students, they soon will realize that there is a need for the students to cognitively process
the emotional meaning of an experience and learn appropriate
ways of expressing their emotions. Should teachers find that
their students maintain high expectations for themselves and
others, then they must understand that these students may need
to learn how to set reasonable goals for themselves and communicate their feelings about those goals. If internal motivation
is evidenced within students, there may be a need to assist students in self-monitoring their motivational issues.

With an understanding and appreciation of these affective
characteristics and concomitant social and emotional needs,
Hébert (2005, 2007) surveyed several groups of secondary educators to determine particular issues they believed were appropriate to address with gifted students through affective activities
in school settings. With more emotionally laden or controver-

sial issues, the educators indicated they would reach for the support of school counselors in their settings. Following thematic analysis of the responses, the following issues were those that middle and high school teachers felt comfortable handling in open class discussions:

- self-expectations, parental expectations, and peer expectations;
- being overwhelmed by competing expectations;
- underachievement;
- developing an internal locus of control, internal motivation;
- multipotentiality;
- heightened emotional intensity and depth;
- understanding and appreciating individual value systems;
- celebrating a sense of idealism;
- appreciating diversity;
- celebrating individual creativity;
- peer pressure;
- gender role expectations;
- nonconformity;
- perfectionism;
- striving for self-actualization;
- finding authentic friendships;
- identity development;
- developing resilience;
- stress and stress management;
- believing in self;
- career exploration; and
- understanding introversion and extraversion.

Strategies for Using Biographies With Gifted Students

Meg Holmes was eager to begin discussing with Beth Rogers the possibilities of using biographies with her gifted students. Their conversation in the coffee shop may have involved a multitude of strategies they would enjoy facilitating as they exposed their students to the fascinating lives of gifted men and women of achievement. As enthusiastic teachers plan to address the affective development of their students, they will want to consider a variety of approaches for such instruction.

Biographical materials can be shared with gifted young people in a variety of ways; however, teachers must recognize the importance of listening closely to the emotional responses of the students. As teachers facilitate discussions centered on biographical lives and draw parallels to the lives of their students, they must be prepared to deal with the emotional responses of the young people involved in the classroom conversation. With a teacher modeling appropriate self-disclosure, students participating in the discussion need to feel comfortable opening up and providing emotional support for each other as they discuss the struggles of the gifted individuals featured in the biographies. For example, students may examine the teenage years of Tom Brokaw and appreciate how his high school experiences were filled with one success after another until his senior year when he became a serious underachiever. As participants hypothesize as to why they believe Brokaw lost his motivation in school, there may be students who compare their personal situations to Brokaw's. Such a discussion will need the guidance of a supportive educator who can direct the conversation appropriately in order to support the young people who may see themselves in Tom Brokaw's story. In any discussion addressing affective issues, the goal is for the young people involved to share their feelings and listen closely to themselves, as well as each other. In a classroom setting, it is important that the students leave the session, having reached an awareness that their classmates have experienced the same feelings they currently are facing. A class discussion should highlight the universality of life experience, an understanding that all of us face struggles in life that may require reaching out to others for support.

The following strategies may be possibilities for designing effective lessons through which biographical materials are used to guide teenagers to self-understanding. Secondary educators considering such an approach may struggle with the notion of dedicating the allotted time it might take for students to read and digest complete biographies. In such a case, teachers may want to consider sharing the single chapter from a biography that typically deals with the individual's childhood and adolescent years. This "slice" of the biography is where many students will identify with the gifted individual featured. Such material enables teachers to facilitate discussions focusing on affective concerns effectively and efficiently. Should the students become intrigued with the life story of the featured individual, they may request to read the entire biography. Teachers might want to consider incorporating a lending library of biographies in their classrooms for such use.

Secondary teachers also may want to organize discussions of biographies according to a focused theme or issue across multiple biographies. For example, having gifted teenagers examine the parental expectations faced by prominent individuals such as Steven Spielberg, Beverly Sills, Madeleine Albright, and Derek Jeter may help to shed understanding on how one issue may have impacted the lives of gifted individuals differently. Other possibilities for focused analyses might be an examination of the chapter describing the early professional careers of the featured individuals or segments of the biographies highlighting the adversity faced by gifted men and women.

Teachers conducting affective discussions using biographies also may want to combine the biography with biographical videos. Supplementing the written biography with an audio-visual component may help to enrich the experience for students. Collections of contemporary biographies are now available in DVD format and can be acquired inexpensively in commercial bookstores, as well as through the Internet. Educators have discovered that such material is thoroughly researched and is consistent with the written biographical materials offered to students.

In addition to combining biographies with audio-visual components, teachers may want to consider combining the biography with a guest speaker. Some teenagers may read the biographies of men and women of achievement whom they perceive as "larger than life" and find it difficult to identify with them. Therefore, it may be beneficial to invite younger individuals as guest speakers, from backgrounds similar to the person featured in the biography yet at an earlier stage of their self-actualization. For example, if students are reading about the political experiences of Christine Todd Whitman, Donna Brazille, Barbara Jordan, and Pat Schroeder, an appropriate guest speaker for the class might be a local female politician who could share her experiences as a member of the community.

Educators may enjoy possibilities beyond the regular classroom. Secondary teachers in gifted education programs also might consider offering elective courses in talent development issues through biographies of gifted individuals. Secondary gifted programs often feature examinations of eminence within the curriculum (Betts & Kercher, 1999). Recently VanTassel-Baska and her colleagues (2005) at the College of William and Mary published a rich collection of comparative analyses of eminent individuals following a semester of graduate students working with biographical materials. Gifted high school students could enjoy and benefit from the same compelling approach.

In addition to elective courses in biographical studies, teachers and school counselors who have been successful in leading discussion sessions with gifted young people also may want to create a biography discussion club and allow the participants to select biographies for the group. Peterson (1996) described significant benefits her gifted students received in a high school poetry club that met regularly for breakfast before their hectic school day. Teenagers interested in biographies may enjoy a similar approach. Teachers or counselors may want to facilitate brown bag luncheons centered on biographies during a school lunch period. It also may be interesting to experiment with a single gender approach for such meetings. A "men's only" or "women's only" series of discussion sessions may allow for increased student comfort, and the young men or women involved may generate other issues that concern them.

Educators must realize that the success of a discussion session focusing on affective concerns is not determined by the quality of the book being read. Instead, the most critical elements often are the activities following the group's discussion of the book. The therapeutic effect of a biography depends on the group discussion facilitated by a teacher who provides follow-up activities such as creative writing, reflective journaling, writing song lyrics, writing raps, designing television commercials, role-playing, creative problem solving, cartooning and other artistic activities, or self-selected options for students to pursue in small groups or individually (Hébert & Kent, 2000).

In conducting the follow-up activities, teachers discover that the more enjoyable they are, the more effective they are. When young people are engaged in something enjoyable, they are more apt to continue discussion amongst themselves, continuing to process the issues that were discussed earlier with the class. During this time students also will continue to provide each other with supportive feedback. For example, as teenage males are engaged in an artistic activity, a teacher may overhear comments such as, "Zack, I didn't realize that your father really gets on your case about the honor roll! I thought he seemed like a really laid-back kind of guy. It really made me feel better to know that I'm not the only one in this class with parents freaking out over grades. Hey man, I felt relieved when you shared that with us."

In facilitating the follow-up activities, teachers may want to consider activities that are either collaborative or private. Providing students a choice of whether they want to work in groups or alone enables them to feel more comfortable and addresses their learning styles. Moreover, when discussions have involved students engaging in serious self-disclosure, private journaling as a follow-up activity is helpful in providing time for teenagers to process through their feelings. The follow-up activities are as important as the class discussion, and the more hands-on the activity, the more the males in the group will talk. Engaging in hands-on activity often is critical for young men to feel comfortable in discussing their feelings (Hébert, 2006). Young women appear to have less difficulty with this issue. With these points in mind, guided discussions centered on affective concerns can be enjoyable while providing a time for serious introspection for gifted young people.

A Sample Lesson

The following discussion presents an example of how educators might facilitate discussions using a biography with gifted middle and high school students. The biography featured in this lesson is Antonia Felix's (2002) work entitled *Condi: The Condoleezza Rice Story*. The author has presented a compelling portrait of an influential leader who broke all barriers to excel as an African American woman in an area dominated by White males. From her childhood in segregated Birmingham, AL, where her parents nurtured her many talents, fostered a love of learning, and encouraged her to strive for excellence, to her rise through the political ranks of the nation's capital, this biography offers a fascinating portrait of one of the most powerful women in American politics.

Secondary educators would want to consider the focus of the discussion accompanying the reading of *Condi* and determine several important issues they would want to highlight in discussion. Key issues that emerge in the biography of Condoleezza Rice are: experiencing racism, the development of resilience, finding emotional support from family, the important roles played by mentors, applying one's intelligence to solve life's challenges, having a strong belief in self, and maintaining a balanced lifestyle.

With the key issues for discussion determined, educators should prepare a menu of discussion questions to pose in facilitating the conversation with students. Care should be taken in writing the questions, making sure to include introductory questions that appear nonthreatening to young people, followed by more sensitive questions that focus on the problematic situations faced by both the central figure of the biography and the teenagers involved in the discussion. Teachers may want to conclude the discussion with a question that helps students to succinctly capture the essence of one significant message delivered through the biography. Such a question may be helpful for students who need to decompress from any emotionally laden discussion that has occurred. A sensitively crafted menu of questions is needed for a cathartic conversation. A menu of discussion questions for use with *Condi: The Condoleezza Rice Story* is provided below:

- What do you like about Condoleezza Rice? What surprises have you discovered in reading her biography?
- What were the challenges Condoleezza Rice faced during her childhood and adolescence? What do you think helped Condoleezza cope with the difficulties she faced?
- Discuss the gifts and talents evidenced in Condoleezza Rice as a young woman. What do you think helped to develop and support her gifts and talents? How are your gifts and talents nurtured and supported? How do you feel about the support systems in your life?
- How did Condoleezza's multipotentiality shape her experience in determining her college major? How might you learn from her story in choosing a college major well-suited for you?
- What important lessons do the parents of Condoleezza Rice have for parents of gifted young people? For parents of gifted young people of color? Would you want to pass these lessons on to your parents? Why or why not?
- What does Condoleezza Rice's life story say about the role of mentors in talent development? Have you had experiences with supportive mentors? How have they influenced you? What impact have they had on the development of your talents?
- What evidence do we have of resilience in Condoleezza's life? How do you think such resilience supports her in her professional domain? Have there been times in your life when you have needed to develop resilience to overcome adversity? How did that occur for you?
- What important message does Antonia Felix's biography of Condoleezza Rice hold for gifted young females? Gifted young women of color?
- What have you found to be most inspirational in the life story of Condoleezza Rice? How might your experience with this biography influence you?

- As you leave this classroom today, what will you remember most about Condoleezza's story that will influence the remainder of your day?

In addition to having a prepared menu of questions that will help guide the conversation with students, a helpful strategy that teachers may want to consider is to select several thought-provoking or inspirational quotes from the biography to use as prompts for discussion. A discussion facilitator should mark these significant passages in their personal copy of the biography to have them readily available. Several examples of thought-provoking passages from *Condi* are provided below.

Condoleezza's childhood in segregated Birmingham, AL:

> "My parents had to try to explain why we wouldn't go to the circus . . . why we had to drive all the way to Washington, D.C., before we could stay in a hotel. And they had to explain why I could not have a hamburger in a restaurant but I could be president anyway, which was the way they chose to handle the situation." (Felix, 2002, p. 45)

> "They explained to me carefully what was going on, and they did so without any bitterness. It was in the very air that we breathed that education was the way out. Among all my friends, the kids I grew up with, there was . . . no doubt in our minds that we would grow up and go on to colleges—integrated colleges—just like other Americans." (Felix, 2002, p. 59)

Condoleezza's experience with a high school guidance counselor:

Another dramatically new aspect that Condi had to digest in her first weeks was that her academic prospects were called into question for the first time. During her first term, a school counselor told the Rices that Condi's standardized test scores showed that she was not college material—never mind her straight-A record or her long list of academic, musical, and athletic accomplishments. Condi was stunned, but her parents—immune to talk of limitation or failure—didn't flinch. They assured her that the assessment was wrong and that she should just ignore it. (Felix, 2002, p. 65)

Condoleezza's experience in a university classroom as a 15-year-old undergraduate:

What went through Condi's mind as the professor described and appeared to support Shockley's view of blacks as "genetically disadvantaged?" Rather than crouch down in her seat and avoid the onslaught, she sprang out of her chair and defended herself. "I'm the one who speaks French!" she said to the professor. "I'm the one who plays Beethoven. I'm better at your culture than you are. This can be taught!" (Felix, 2002, p. 69)

Following healthy, thought-provoking, and therapeutic discussion of the biography, teachers and counselors conducting such a lesson need to conclude the lesson with follow-up activities that enable the students to continue processing through the feelings they have encountered during their reading of the material and the class discussion. The following is a suggested menu of follow-up activities to be used with Felix's (2002) *Condi: The Condoleezza Rice Story:*

• Pretend that you are Condoleezza Rice. Write a poem about overcoming difficult obstacles in life.
• Condoleezza Rice's life story has become a Broadway musical. Write the lyrics to a song to be performed in this new theatrical production.
• Pretend that Condoleezza Rice was visiting your community. As a reporter for your school newspaper, you have been assigned to interview her for a cover story. Design and role-play the interview.
• Design and illustrate a road map of Condi's journey.

- Create an artistic representation of the important lessons learned through reading *Condi: The Condoleezza Rice Story.*
- Write an essay in which you compare and contrast the experiences of Condoleezza Rice with another inspirational woman you admire. How are these two women different? How are they similar? Submit your essay to a young women's journal.
- Imagine that during her high school years Condoleezza Rice wrote a letter to an advice columnist asking for advice. How does her letter read? What advice does the columnist provide Condoleezza? Write both letters.
- Reflect on the following prompt in your journal: What lesson stood out to you in the biography, *Condi: The Condoleezza Rice Story*? How does this apply to your own life?
- Condoleezza Rice often is asked to serve as an inspirational speaker to large audiences of young people throughout the country. Write a speech that Dr. Rice might present to your school.

Suggested Biographies and Autobiographies to Use in Guiding Gifted Students

One may assume that Meg Holmes left her coffee shop meeting with Beth Rogers and went directly to her local public library or bookstore in search of high-quality biographies to pursue with her gifted students. She may have discovered quickly that finding such material can be a challenge. Often the biographies available in commercial bookstores feature individuals whose lives may not serve as appropriate models for teenagers. For example, Hollywood celebrities describing their marital affairs or difficulties with drugs and alcohol is not what secondary educators in any school setting would want to use. For that reason, educators will need to read a biography from cover to cover before determining whether it is material that would benefit their students. Other challenges that educators may discover as they search for high-quality materials is the gender bias of the publishing houses. It is much easier to locate biographies featuring prominent men than women and often the biography collections in commercial bookstores will be dominated by biographies of athletes. Enthusiastic teachers such as Meg Holmes will enjoy the challenge of searching for the best biographical materials available.

The following biographies and autobiographies are recommended for supporting the social and emotional development of gifted young men and women. A collection of biographies of prominent women of achievement is followed by a selection of biographies featuring prominent men of achievement. In addition to whether the biographies were appropriate for use in school settings, several other considerations were taken into account in determining their inclusion in the collection: quality of writing, cultural diversity, potential themes in the life stories to engage students in discussion, and domains of talent featured. The biographies are presented alphabetically and feature many contemporary gifted individuals, as well as more historical figures.

Biographical Materials For Guiding Gifted Teenagers

Biographies of Women of Achievement

The following biographies can be used in a gifted classroom's discussion of women of achievement or to support the social-emotional development of achieving female students.

- **Madeleine Albright** (Secretary of State)
  Albright, M. (2003). *Madam secretary: A memoir.* New York: Hyperion Books.
  Dobbs, M. (1999). *Madeleine Albright: A twentieth century odyssey.* New York: Holt.
- **Maya Angelou** (Author and Poet)
  Angelou, M. (1969). *I know why the caged bird sings.* New York: Bantam Books.
- **Melba Pattillo Beals** (Author and Journalist)
  Beals, M. P. (1994). *Warriors don't cry: A searing memoir of the battle to integrate Little Rock's Central High.* New York: Washington Square Press.

- **Erma Bombeck** (Author and Humorist)
  Edwards, S. (1997). *Erma Bombeck: A life in humor.* New York: Avon.
- **Donna Brazille** (Political Strategist)
  Brazille, D. (2004). *Cooking with grease: Stirring the pots in American politics.* New York: Simon & Schuster.
- **Rachel Carson** (Environmentalist)
  Lear, L. (1997). *Rachel Carson: Witness for nature.* New York: Henry Holt.
- **Sandra Cisneros** (Author)
  Mirriam-Goldberg, C. (1998). *Sandra Cisneros: Latina writer and activist.* Springfield, NJ: Enslow.
- **Amelia Earhart** (Pilot)
  Butler, S. (1997). *East to dawn: The life of Amelia Earhart.* Reading, MA: Addison-Wesley.
- **Anne Frank** (Victim of the Holocaust)
  Gies, M. (1987). *Anne Frank remembered.* New York: Simon & Schuster.
- **Lorraine Hansberry** (Playwright)
  Hansberry, L. (1969). *To be young, gifted and Black: An informal autobiography of Lorraine Hansberry.* New York: Penguin.
- **Leta Hollingworth** (Educator)
  Klein, A. (2002). *A forgotten voice: A biography of Leta Stetter Hollingworth.* Scottsdale, AZ: Great Potential Press.
- **Charlayne Hunter-Gault** (Journalist)
  Hunter-Gault, C. (1992). *In my place.* New York: Farrar Strauss Giroux
- **Barbara Jordan** (Politician)
  Rogers, M. (1998). *Barbara Jordan: An American hero.* New York: Bantam.
- **Helen Keller** (Author and Activist)
  Keller, H. (2003). *The story of my life.* New York: W. W. Norton & Company.
- **Coretta Scott King** (Human Rights Activist)
  Vivian, O. (2006). *Coretta: The story of Coretta Scott King.* Minneapolis, MN: Fortress Press.

- **Rebecca Lobo** (Athlete)
  Lobo, R. A., & Lobo, R. (1996). *The home team: Of mothers, daughters, and American champions.* New York: Kondasha International.
- **Wilma Mankiller** (Leader of the Cherokee Nation)
  Mankiller, W. (1993). *Wilma Mankiller: A chief and her people.* New York: St. Martin's Press.
- **Margaret Mead** (Anthropologist)
  Bateson, M. C. (1985). *With a daughter's eye.* New York: Washington Square Press.
- **Sandra Day O'Connor** (Supreme Court Justice)
  Biskupic, J. (2005). *Sandra Day O'Connor: How the first woman on the Supreme Court became its most influential justice.* New York: Harper Perennial.
  Day O'Connor, S., & Day, A. (2002). *Lazy B: Growing up on a cattle ranch in the American southwest.* New York: Random House.
- **Mary Lou Retton** (Athlete)
  Retton, M. L. (2000). *Mary Lou Retton's gateways to happiness.* New York: Broadway Books.
- **Condoleezza Rice** (Secretary of State)
  Felix, A. (2002). *Condi: The Condoleezza Rice story.* New York: Newmarket Press.
- **J. K. Rowling** (Author)
  Kirk, C. A. (2003). *J. K. Rowling: A biography.* Westport, CT: Greenwood Press.
- **Esmerelda Santiago** (Author and Screenwriter)
  Santiago, E. (1993). *When I was Puerto Rican.* New York: Vintage.
  Santiago, E. (1998). *Almost a Woman.* New York: Vintage.
- **Pat Schroeder** (Politician)
  Schroeder, P. (1998). *24 Years of House work . . . and the place is still a mess: My life in politics.* Kansas City, MO: Andrews McMeel.
- **Beverly Sills** (Opera Singer)
  Sills, B. (1976). *Bubbles: A self-portrait.* New York: Bobbs-Merrill.

Sills, B., & Linderman, L. (1987). *Beverly: An autobiography*. New York: Bantam Books.

- **Barbra Streisand** (Actress and Singer)
Riese, R. (1993). *Her name is Barbra*. New York: St. Martin's.

- **Maria Tallchief** (Ballerina)
Tallchief, M. (1997). *Maria Tallchief: America's prima ballerina*. New York: Holt.

- **Heather Whitestone** (Miss America, Motivational Speaker)
Gray, D. (1995). *Yes, you can, Heather!* Grand Rapids, MI: Zondervan.
Whitestone, H., & Hunt, A. (1998). *Listening with my heart*. New York: Doubleday.

- **Christine Todd Whitman** (Politician)
Beard, P. (1996). *Growing up Republican—Christine Whitman: The politics of character*. New York: HarperCollins.

Biographies of Men of Achievement

The following biographies can be used in a gifted classroom's discussion of men of achievement or to support the social–emotional development of achieving male students.

- **Lance Armstrong** (Athlete)
Armstrong, L., & Jenkins, S. (2000). *It's not about the bike: My journey back to life*. New York: G. P. Putnam's Sons.

- **Neil Armstrong** (Astronaut)
Hansen, J. (2005). *First man: The life of Neil A. Armstrong*. New York: Simon & Schuster.

- **Arthur Ashe** (Athlete)
Ashe, A., & Rampersand, A. (1993). *Days of grace: A memoir*. New York: Alfred A. Knopf.

- **Russell Baker** (Author)
Baker, R. (1982). *Growing up*. New York: Congdon & Weed.

- **Larry Bird** (Athlete)
Bird, L. (1991). *Drive: The story of my life*. New York: Doubleday.

- **Terry Bradshaw** (Athlete, Commentator)
  Bradshaw, T. (1989). *Looking deep*. New York: Contemporary Books.
  Bradshaw, T., & Fisher, D. (2002). *Keep it simple*. New York: Atria Books.
- **Tom Brokaw** (Television Journalist)
  Brokaw, T. (2002). *A long way from home: Growing up in the American heartland*. New York: Random House.
- **Jim Carrey** (Actor)
  Knelman, M. (2000). *Jim Carrey: The joker is wild*. Buffalo, NY: Firefly Books.
- **Ben Carson** (Surgeon)
  Carson, B. (1990). *Gifted hands: The Ben Carson story*. Grand Rapids, MI: Zondervan.
  Carson, B., & Murphy, C. (1992). *Think big: Unleashing your potential for excellence*. Grand Rapids, MI: Zondervan.
- **Jimmy Carter** (President)
  Carter, J. (2001). *An hour before daylight: Memories of a rural boyhood*. New York: Simon & Schuster.
- **Bart Conner** (Athlete)
  Conner, B. (1985). *Winning the gold*. New York: Warner Books.
- **Anderson Cooper** (Television Journalist)
  Cooper, A. (2006). *Dispatches from the edge: A memoir of war, disasters, and survival*. New York: HarperCollins.
- **Bob Dole** (Politician)
  Dole, B. (2005). *One soldier's story: A memoir*. New York: HarperCollins.
- **John Edwards** (Politician)
  Edwards, J. (2004). *Four trials*. New York: Simon & Schuster.
- **Bill Gates** (Entrepreneur)
  Manes, S., & Andrews, P. (1994). *Gates*. New York: Simon & Schuster.
  Wallace, J., & Erickson, J. (1992). *Hard drive: Bill Gates and the making of the Microsoft empire*. New York: John Wiley & Sons.

- **John Glenn** (Astronaut)
  Glenn, J., & Taylor, N. (1999). *John Glenn: A memoir*. New York: Bantam Books.
- **Tony Hawk** (Athlete)
  Hawk, T., & Mortimer, S. (2000). *Hawk: Occupation: Skateboarder*. New York: HarperCollins.
- **Homer Hickam, Jr.** (Aerospace Engineer)
  Hickam, H., Jr. (1998). *October sky*. New York: Dell.
- **Grant Hill** (Athlete)
  Hill, G. (1996). *Change the game: One athlete's thoughts on sports, dreams, and growing up*. New York: Warner.
- **Ron Howard** (Film Director)
  Gray, B. (2003). *Ronnie Howard: From Mayberry to the moon . . . and beyond*. Nashville, TN: Rutledge Hill Press.
- **Derek Jeter** (Athlete)
  Jeter, D., & Curry, J. (2000). *The life you imagine. Life lessons for achieving your dreams*. New York: Three Rivers Press.
- **Michael Jordan** (Athlete)
  Greene, B. (1992). *Hang time: Days and dreams with Michael Jordan*. New York: St. Martin's Press.
- **Bob Kerrey** (Politician)
  Kerrey, B. (2002). *When I was a young man*. New York: Harcourt.
- **Martin Luther King, Jr.** (Civil Rights Leader)
  Carson, C. (Ed.). (1998). *The autobiography of Martin Luther King, Jr.* New York: Warner.
- **Carl Lewis** (Athlete)
  Lewis, C. (1990). *Inside track: My professional life in amateur track and field*. New York: Simon & Schuster.
- **Marcus Mabry** (Journalist)
  Mabry, M. (1995). *White bucks and black-eyed peas*. New York: Scribner.
- **John McCain** (Politician)
  McCain, J. (1999). *Faith of my fathers*. New York: Random House.
- **Ruben Navarette** (Journalist)
  Navarette, R., Jr. (1993). *A darker shade of crimson: Odyssey of a Harvard Chicano*. New York: Bantam.

- **Barack Obama** (Politician)
  Obama, B. (2004). *Dreams from my father: A story of race and inheritance.* New York: Three Rivers Press.
- **Paul O'Neill** (Athlete)
  O'Neill, P., & Rocks, B. (2003). *Me and my dad: A baseball memoir.* New York: William Morrow.
- **Gordon Parks** (Photographer and Film Director)
  Parks, G. (1990). *Voices in the mirror: An autobiography.* New York: Doubleday.
- **Colin Powell** (Secretary of State)
  DeYoung, K. (2006). *Soldier: The life of Colin Powell.* New York: Alfred A. Knopf.
  Powell, C. (1995). *My American journey.* New York: Random House.
  Steins, R. (2003). *Colin Powell: A biography.* Westport, CT: Greenwood Press.
- **Dan Rather** (Television Journalist)
  Rather, D. (1991). *I remember.* Boston: Little, Brown.
  Weisman, A. (2006). *Lone star: The extraordinary life and times of Dan Rather.* Hoboken, NJ: John Wiley & Sons.
- **Richard Rodriguez** (Journalist)
  Rodriguez, R. (1982). *Hunger of memory: The education of Richard Rodriguez.* New York: Bantam.
  Rodriguez, R. (1992). *Days of obligation: An argument with my Mexican father.* New York: Viking.
  Rodriguez, R. (2002). *Brown: The last discovery of America.* New York: Penguin.
- **Carl Rowan** (Journalist)
  Rowan, C. (1991). *Breaking barriers.* Boston: Little, Brown.
- **Tim Russert** (Television Journalist)
  Russert, T. (2004). *Big Russ & me: Father and son—Lessons of life.* New York: Miramax.
- **Carlos Santana** (Musician)
  Shapiro, M. (2000). *Carlos Santana: Back on top.* New York: St. Martin's Press.
- **Jerry Seinfeld** (Comedian)
  Levine, J. (1993). *Jerry Seinfeld: Much ado about nothing.* Toronto, Canada: ECW Press.

Oppenheimer, J. (2002). *Seinfeld: The making of an American icon*. New York: HarperCollins.
- **Steven Spielberg** (Film Director)
McBride, J. (1997). *Steven Spielberg: A biography*. New York: Simon & Schuster.
- **J. C. Watts** (Politician)
Watts, J. C., Jr. (2002). *What color is a conservative?: My life and my politics*. New York: HarperCollins.
- **Carl Yastrzemski** (Athlete)
Yastrzemski, C. (1990). *Yaz: Baseball, the wall, and me*. New York: Warner Books.

Summary

Addressing affective concerns in the lives of teenagers by guiding them through discussions of high-quality biographical materials has the potential to help gifted students develop positive attitudes about their abilities, the world around them, important relationships with others, and their own uniqueness. With the guidance of a supportive teacher or counselor, gifted young people will reach self-understanding, and discover ways for reaching a self-actualized life through biography. Through reading and discussing these real-life stories, they may encounter challenges similar to their own, develop important ideas that will shape the formation of their values, and gain beneficial insights from other gifted men and women who have gone before them.

References

Balswick, J. (1988). *The inexpressive male*. Lexington, MA: Lexington Books.
Betts, G., & Kercher, J. K. (1999). *The Autonomous Learner Model: Optimizing ability*. Greeley, CO: ALPS Publishing.
Cavazos-Kottke, S. (2006). Five readers browsing: The reading interests of talented middle school boys. *Gifted Child Quarterly, 50*, 132–147.
Clark, B. (2002). *Growing up gifted* (6th ed.). Upper Saddle River, NJ: Merrill/Prentice Hall.

Felix, A. (2002). *Condi: The Condoleezza Rice Story*. New York: Newmarket Press.

Flack, J. D. (1992). *Lives of promise: Studies in biography and family history*. Englewood, CO: Teacher Idea Press.

Flack, J. D. (1999, July). *Autobiography and gifted students: Hows and whys*. Paper presented at Confratute Summer Institute on Enrichment Learning and Teaching, University of Connecticut, Storrs.

Halsted, J. W. (2002). *Some of my best friends are books: Guiding gifted readers from pre-school to high school* (2nd ed.). Scottsdale, AZ: Great Potential Press.

Hébert, T. P. (1991). Meeting the affective needs of bright boys through bibliotherapy. *Roeper Review, 13*, 207–212.

Hébert, T. P. (1995). Using biography to counsel gifted young men. *Journal of Secondary Gifted Education, 6*, 208–219.

Hébert, T. P. (2005, July). *Fostering social and emotional development in gifted teens*. Paper presented at the Summer Academy, Fort Worth Independent School District, Fort Worth, TX.

Hébert, T. P. (2006). Counseling gifted males: Lessons learned from Eddie. *Gifted Education Communicator, 33*(4), 16–18.

Hébert, T. P. (2007, February). *Supporting the social and emotional development of gifted secondary students*. Paper presented at Oconee County Public Schools, Watkinsville, GA.

Hébert, T. P., & Kent, R. (2000). Nurturing social and emotional development in gifted teenagers through young adult literature. *Roeper Review, 22*, 167–171.

Hébert, T. P., Long, L. A., & Speirs Neumeister, K. L. (2005). Using biography to counsel gifted young women. In S. K. Johnsen & J. Kendrick (Eds.), *Teaching and counseling gifted girls* (pp. 89–118). Waco, TX: Prufrock Press.

Hildreth, G. H. (1966). *Introduction to the gifted*. New York: McGraw-Hill.

Hollingworth, L. S. (1926). *Gifted children: Their nature and nurture*. New York: Macmillan.

Kerr, B. A. (1994). *Smart girls: A new psychology of girls, women, and giftedness*. Scottsdale, AZ: Gifted Psychology Press.

Kindlon, D., & Thompson, M. (1999). *Raising Cain: Protecting the emotional life of boys*. New York: Ballantine Books.

Kolloff, P. B. (1998, November). *Lessons from gifted lives*. Paper presented at the annual meeting of the National Association for Gifted Children, Louisville, KY.

Langerman, D. (1990, March). Books and boys: Gender preferences and book selection. *School Library Journal*, 132–136.

Lenkowsky, R. S. (1987). Bibliotherapy: A review and analysis of the literature. *The Journal of Special Education, 21*, 123–132.

Nugent, S. A. (2005). Addressing the social and emotional needs of gifted students in the classroom. In F. A. Karnes & S. M. Bean (Eds.), *Methods and materials for teaching the gifted* (2nd ed., pp. 409–438). Waco, TX: Prufrock Press.

Peterson, J. S. (1996). The breakfast club: Poetry and pancakes. *Gifted Child Today, 19*(4), 16–19, 49.

Piechowski, M. M. (2006). *"Mellow out," they say. If only I could: Intensities and sensitivities of the young and bright.* Madison, WI: Yunasa Books.

Pollack, W. (1998). *Real boys: Rescuing our sons from the myths of boyhood.* New York: Henry Holt.

Reis, S. M., & Small, M. A. (2005). The varied and unique characteristics exhibited by diverse gifted and talented students. In F. A. Karnes & S. M. Bean (Eds.), *Methods and materials for teaching the gifted* (2nd ed., pp. 3–36). Waco, TX: Prufrock Press.

Robinson, A., & Butler Schatz, A. (2002). Biography for talented learners: Enriching the curriculum across the disciplines. *Gifted Education Communicator, 33*(3), 12–15, 38–39.

Robinson, A., & Millen, G. (2006). *Blueprints for biography.* Little Rock, AK: Center for Gifted Education at The University of Arkansas at Little Rock.

VanTassel-Baska, J. (1998). Characteristics and needs of talented learners. In J. VanTassel-Baska (Ed.), *Excellence in educating gifted and talented learners* (3rd ed., pp. 173–191). Denver, CO: Love.

VanTassel-Baska, J., French, H., & Worley, B., II. (2005). Talent development and eminence. *Current Issues in Gifted Education, 2*(1), 3–5.

Discussion Groups as a Component of Affective Curriculum for Gifted Students

Jean Sunde Peterson, George Betts, & Terry Bradley

A major goal in the education of gifted children is their development as independent, self-directed learners (Betts & Kercher, 1999; Feldhusen & Treffinger, 1980; Renzulli, 1986; Treffinger, 1983). Attention to affective development offers crucial support for accomplishing that goal. The long and growing emphasis in the field of gifted education on social, emotional, and career development reflects a sense that gifted individuals' *experience* of development is qualitatively different from the experience of others (e.g., Betts, 1985; Betts & Kercher, 1999; Colangelo & Peterson, 1993; Dabrowski, 1967; Dabrowski & Piechowski, 1977; Hébert & Beardsley, 2001; Jackson & Peterson, 2003; Mendaglio, 2008; Mendaglio & Peterson, 2007; Peterson, 2002, 2003; Peterson & Ray, 2006a, 2006b), justifying inclusion of affective curriculum in programs for gifted children and adolescents.

Discussion Groups: Purpose and Function

Discussion groups are an ideal vehicle for attending to social and emotional development. Indeed, groups can be the most significant and effective component of an affective curriculum in gifted education. Certified counselors and educators of the gifted can facilitate discussion groups individually or as cofacilitators, each offering important expertise. Materials developed specifically for working with gifted students are available (e.g., Betts, 1985; Betts & Kercher, 1999; Peterson, 2008), but gifted education teachers and counselors also can create their own. They can learn basic listening and responding skills through workshops, and detailed guidelines (e.g., Peterson, 2008) also can provide instruction.

Affective curriculum in gifted education should provide open-ended experiences that encourage gifted students to explore social and emotional development (Betts, 1985; Betts & Kercher, 1999, Peterson, 2003, 2008). Small-group discussion can momentarily move gifted students out of a potentially competitive, evaluative environment and into an atmosphere where no one dominates, no grades are given, and no one judges them. A skilled facilitator can essentially ensure this kind of atmosphere. Bringing gifted students together for weekly discussion gives them a chance to feel heard, have support for social and emotional development, and enlarge their expressive vocabulary. They also can learn strategies for coping with stressors associated with high ability, including dealing with their own and others' expectations. Developing trust within the social microcosm of small groups allows gifted students to remove protective facades and become vulnerable, complex, and "human" with each other.

In group work, the *process* of learning and developing is as important as the outcome. In small groups, gifted students can make social connections with intellectual peers, feel support in the school environment, and challenge achiever and underachiever stereotypes (Peterson, 2008). In addition, they can recognize and affirm strengths and limitations, learn appropriate behavior for a variety of settings, learn about the self, reduce stress and anxiety, and develop a positive self-concept. Socially, they can develop skills in communication, learn to express their own feelings, and respond to the feelings of others. Both learners and group facilitators can consider the concerns of widely varying high-ability individuals and create topics for discussion (Betts & Kercher, 1999). The following selected goals, reflecting perspectives of Betts (1985) and Peterson (2003, 2008), are appropriate for discussion groups:

I.   Gifted students will have important skills related to present and future well-being.

- They will have an expressive vocabulary for articulating feelings and concerns.
- They will know how to give and receive feedback.
- They will be able to listen and respond appropriately to age peers and adults.
- They will have skills related to coping effectively with complex feelings, perfectionism, stress, isolation, and family and developmental transitions.
- They will know when and how to ask for help.

II. Gifted students will be more aware of and sensitive to nuances related to relationships with age and ability peers and with adults.

- They will recognize shared normal developmental challenges among age peers.
- They will be less likely to think in stereotypes about fellow students and adults.
- They will understand that everyone has strengths and limitations.
- They will better understand and know better how to work with "the system."
- They will appreciate the complexities of teachers' work.

III. Gifted students will better understand themselves.

- They will feel affirmed for their strengths, regardless of school performance, and be comfortable with their limitations.
- They will have insights about themselves related to career development.
- They will have a sense of themselves in regard to the complexities of giftedness.

Because small groups are an efficient mode for delivery of services, they are an especially practical program option, and justifiably a preferred option, when programs are understaffed and when gifted education teachers serve multiple sites and/or school levels. The presence of small-group work in programs for gifted students for addressing social and emotional concerns also encourages school personnel to consider that gifted students are complex individuals. Instead of being perceived as elitist or as inconsequential, a program that includes an affective curriculum with a small-group format sends a message that gifted students have developmental needs and concerns beyond just academic challenge.

Approaches to Group Work With Gifted Students

Group work has been basic to the authors' work in education for gifted children and adolescents. The purpose of this chapter is to raise awareness of the benefits of using groups as an affective tool to enhance development and of the role of facilitators in discussion groups for gifted students. The authors' discussion-group approaches overlap to a considerable extent, most noticeably in regard to the notion of a discussion *facilitator*, rather than *leader*; emphasis on discussion, rather than on counseling, per se; and open-endedness, whether through the use of facilitative questions or through reliance on participants for generating content, rather than an emphasis on psychoeducational presentation of information. Differences are apparent in how discussion topics are generated, whether cognitive concerns are intentionally addressed, whether normal developmental challenges or giftedness are specific foci, and the extent to which basic counseling tenets are applied.

The Peterson Developmental Group Model

Peterson's group model is semistructured, topical, and ability-appropriate. It is skills-oriented and is based on developmental theory, which has been embedded into a curriculum with session objectives. Her model can be used to train school counselors, but it also is detailed enough, with step-by-step instructions, to guide noncounselors as they begin and continue to work with groups. With experience, these group facilitators may need such guidance less and less, but the topics and flexible structure can continue to be useful.

The focus in this model is on increasing expressive vocabulary, making connections with peers, normalizing developmental challenges and experiences, and developing listening and responding skills. Parents, school personnel, and school boards who are skeptical about the purpose and function of group work can be shown the curriculum and be assured that the purpose is not to "air family laundry" or to complain about teachers, two suspicions that may be expressed when groups are initially created. Having some structure helps to ensure that no group member dominates, because there usually is at least one "around-the-circle" response pattern per session, and the facilitator can, if necessary, use the session focus to bring the group back to the main topic of the day.

Peterson's (2008) group-work volume focusing on gifted teens contains 70 topics related to social and emotional development. Many session topics have accompanying activity sheets (e.g., sentence stems related to 14 kinds of loss in "Loss and Transition"; a checklist of 36 roles in "Family Roles"; checklists of needs, personal characteristics, and preferences in "Choosing a Career"). When activity sheets are used, they require only a few minutes for writing brief responses or checking listed items. During the remainder of a session, students explain their responses, which help even the most reticent group members to have something to say. Responses and comments typically generate discussion.

Introductory information at the beginning of each session provides background material for facilitators. When activity sheets are not used, open-ended questions related to the session topic are provided for generating discussion. Courage, stereotypes, strengths and limitations, success and failure, *alone* vs. *lonely*, mistakes, facades, heroes, priorities, sensitivities, change, procrastination, perfectionism, competition, self-harm, and multipotentiality related to career direction are examples of topics that can generate discussion for single meetings of gifted adolescents. However, all ages of gifted children can benefit from topics such as friendship, frustrations, sadness, disappointment, stress, and fears.

These sessions are focused, but also flexible. The open-endedness of both questions and format allows discussions to move in unexpected directions. Nimbly pursuing interesting and engaging discussion strands can reap dividends for a group. If a student is obviously distressed when arriving, it is appropriate to ask the student if he or she wants to talk about whatever has been upsetting. An entire session may, on occasion, be devoted to one group member's concerns. However, it also is possible that one student may have something new and dramatic to share at every meeting. If that student receives major attention in one or more successive weeks, other group members may quickly feel neglected and even bored. With the minimal structure of this model and with effective leadership skills, facilitators can ensure that no one dominates.

The Betts and Kercher Model: Learner-Directed ALM Groups

The Autonomous Learner Model (ALM) for the Gifted and Talented (Betts, 1985; Betts & Kercher, 1999) is a complete approach for addressing the emotional, social, and cognitive needs of the gifted. The Orientation Dimension and the Individual Development Dimension of the ALM provide opportunities for students to be involved in learner-directed discussion groups dealing with topics developed by the learners themselves. The facilitator begins the discussions and activities, but as the group develops, the ownership of the group, the topics to be discussed, and the activities that come from the discussions all come from the learners. After one or two initial meetings, with topics likely planned beforehand, students then brainstorm and choose topics for future meetings. Student input also allows the facilitator to know which topics will hold their interest. Basic premises for this approach are that students should be producers of their own knowledge, and that students engage in the discussions when topics are meaningful to them. The facilitator facilitates the students' learning.

When the ALM first began, the learners developed discussion groups and labeled them "Coping Groups" because coping with giftedness, peers, school, and family were the major topics, but a year later they renamed the groups "Enhancement Groups." The entire group process had changed from reflecting frustration to investment in growth. Ultimately the groups were called discussion groups by the learners. The facilitators were pleased because they had not interfered with the process. The learners had decided direction and emphasis and continued to be responsible for those. *The Autonomous Learner Model: Optimizing Ability* (Betts & Kercher, 1999) contains more than 25 group-building and communication activities that are a foundation for discussion groups. *The Young Child and the Autonomous Learner Model* (Betts, Toy, & Vasquez, 2005) does the same for young children. An essential component of the Autonomous Learner Model is a series of activities known as the Profiles of the Gifted. Facilitators become more knowledgeable about group needs and abilities through this inventory of skills, concepts, and attitudes.

The Bradley Approach: Creative Adaptation

Bradley has adapted both the Peterson and Betts and Kercher models for working with gifted adolescents, employing the facilitation aspect of ALM, the Peterson guidance about how to proceed with sessions, and both models, along with other resources, for ideas for session topics. What distinguishes the Bradley approach is the creative adaptation of format and content to fit the age of the students and the dynamics of the group. This approach may use a student question, insight, common concern, or uncomfortable situation as a teachable moment and then build a session around that incident for the following week.

If students are interested in discussing how they can make more friends, for example, friendship could become a session topic. A specific concern might prompt a discussion about ways to be a friend, how to become a better listener and communicator, how and where to meet new people with similar interests, and what qualities make a good friend. To raise awareness of the importance of being good listeners, students might take turns, in pairs, talking for one minute about a topic determined by group members beforehand without being interrupted by the partner. At the end of each minute, the partner repeats back what has just been said in order to show that he or she listened. Practicing nonverbal, as well as verbal, listening skills helps students gain confidence as listeners. This activity might follow some group members' expressed concerns about feeling lonely. All group members can benefit from this activity, because practicing good listening skills is important to becoming an effective communicator.

During a week with many exams, a conversation about stress-management techniques might be beneficial. Asking students what they do to relieve stress can prompt an interesting discussion about healthy outlets and releases. Students also benefit from hearing what their peers do for stress relief and may be able to use new, effective techniques to manage their own stress. As a lesson in effective self-advocacy, the students might spend a session or two writing down suggestions for how parents and educators can assist them in reducing stress. In Bradley's workshops, these student-generated tips have been well-received by adults who want to parent and/or teach in ways that relieve stress and lessen pressure on the students. At the very least, these suggestions raise awareness of students' feelings and open up communication.

Students appreciate a focus on humor as a stress reducer and enjoy looking through age-appropriate humor books, telling jokes, and playing games during a session. Laughing together as a group is an enjoyable way not only to relieve stress, but also to build group cohesion. Bradley also often uses film, children's books, physical movement, manipulatives, and games when they fit the topic and the needs of the group, particularly with middle school students.

Proactive, Prevention-Oriented Goals

School counselors are currently admonished to devote a significant portion of their time to proactive, prevention-oriented activities. In addition to individual counseling, counselor training programs focus on skills for whole-classroom and small-group work. By intervening before problems begin, or addressing existing problems before they become crises, counselors can help students navigate complex developmental challenges, develop important interpersonal skills, gain support and skills for problem solving, and connect with peers in ways that contribute to ease in the school environment. The focus is on helping students understand, normalize, and manage development-related stressors, interact effectively with others, and plan for the future.

As a component of programming for gifted students, small-group discussion has similar goals. Gifted students, as much as anyone else in schools, deserve a small-group experience, led by a counselor who is comfortable working with gifted students and/or an educator who has some awareness of group process—or both as cofacilitators. Groups provide both well-functioning and poorly functioning students an opportunity to develop skills related to expressing emotion language. For example, they can learn that fear, worry, anxiety, frustration, irritation, sadness, disappointment, and anger can be talked about with others, as well as joy, satisfaction, delight, and intense interest. In addition, adolescent difficulties related to identity, including incorporating giftedness into it, can be seen as "normal" when group members share their confusion and concerns. Discussion also can explore real and potential relationships—with siblings, teachers, peers, persons in authority, and romantic interests. Referrals can be made to a school or community counselor/therapist when a student needs further support and exploration in these or other areas.

Career development also is an important focus, even at early grade levels. Not only are young gifted children imagining themselves in adult career roles, but their future in careers also will be affected by their interpersonal skills, learning aptitudes, and attitudes toward others, all of which are continually developing. Middle-school students might avoid a downturn in achievement (cf. Peterson & Colangelo, 1996) if they can talk about their struggles with identity, change, doubt, peer relationships, and envisioning future direction. Older adolescents can explore relationships with teachers, peers, siblings, coaches, directors, and parents. Seniors can share their concerns about being able to adjust to college life. These are but a few of a multitude of potential discussion topics related to career development (Betts, 1985; Betts & Kercher, 1999; Peterson, 2008).

Students also can discuss how they and their peers do, and do not, fit various stereotypes, including stereotypes of gifted kids. They can anticipate developmental transitions, such as entering puberty, moving to a new school level, establishing romantic relationships, and leaving home after high school. They can share insights about cognitive, physical, social, and emotional development, these topics perhaps discussed only rarely, per se, with their peers. They can dissect stress. Group members can learn about and talk about school structure and culture and consider ways to ask for help when needed and advocate for themselves effectively. Discovering that their peers share many of their concerns about growing up, they feel less lonely and different.

Basic Ethical Concerns

Small-group facilitators need to consider certain ethical and legal issues prior to, and during, group activity. Foremost, because of liability concerns, it is important that educators who are not trained as counselors not claim to be counselors. Currently, nationally accredited preparation programs require that school counselors have at least 48 credit hours of postgraduate coursework, including 700 hours of supervised field work. Skills, thorough knowledge of ethical codes, and special training in group facilitation, assessment, human development, career development, and multicultural concerns, for instance, characterize well-trained school and other counselors. Laws and codes are intended to protect the public, including school children, from untrained persons who claim to have counselor expertise. Like any other clients, students are uniquely vulnerable when interacting about personal concerns.

Therefore, it is important for gifted education personnel and others who are not counselors to use the term *facilitator* or *leader* to refer to their role and to refer to the groups by some term other than *counseling groups*. *Discussion groups* (Peterson, 1990, 2008) or *clubs* (Littrell & Peterson, 2002, 2005) are appropriate terms for school groups, even when facilitated by trained counselors, because these identifiers do not carry the stigma often associated with counseling. Group leaders should be clear to themselves and to group members and their parents that the groups are not meant to be therapy groups. Existing, defensible developmental curriculum should be used selectively, or new curriculum created and followed. Additionally, discussion is greatly enhanced when facilitators are aware of common affective concerns of gifted children and adolescents.

Confidentiality

Confidentiality cannot be guaranteed in group work. A group facilitator can guarantee only his or her own respect for group members' privacy. In individual counseling, a client can choose to talk about a session with anyone, of course, but knows that the ethical code constrains the counselor unless the client has given permission to share information with a third party. A problem about confidentiality arises in group work, because more than just a counselor/facilitator and a client are involved. Group members can control only their own behavior. A facilitator is responsible for clarifying this reality at the outset of a group series, at the same time explaining important limits. For example, for anyone facilitating a group, not only is reporting suspected abuse mandatory (first to a school counselor, if the facilitator is not one), but so is reporting that a student is in imminent danger to self or others (e.g., suicidal or homicidal). If properly informed, when a group member reveals something that fits these categories, he or she already knows that the facilitator has to act on it and is likely hoping to be helped.

Facilitators can establish confidentiality as a norm from the outset, explaining how important privacy and trust are in feeling safe to talk in a group. Some facilitators have group members sign an informal agreement or verbally agree to terms of confidentiality and accepted group behaviors. However, facilitators of discussion groups should not belabor the issue of confidentiality, because the approaches proposed here typically do not encourage discussion of private information. Overplaying the warnings might serve only to raise member, parent, or teacher concerns about privacy and the purpose and function of the groups. For the same reason, any reference to "keeping secrets" is not appropriate. However, with students' comfort and trust in mind, agreeing to some guidelines about confidentiality is an appropriate step that demonstrates good intentions.

Homogeneity

When possible, groups also should be homogeneous according to age. Even 1 or 2 years of age difference can mean a great deal of difference in social and emotional maturity. Cognitively precocious gifted students should not be assumed to be advanced socially or emotionally, although some might be. Regardless of their developmental level, however, it is more likely that concerns related to social and emotional development will be more similar for 5 fourth graders than for 3 fourth graders and 2 sixth graders in the same group. Even when a child is in the same grade as other gifted students, there may be a mismatch of developmental level if the child has been accelerated into a higher grade, and the group dynamic may be affected negatively. Mixing gifted students with students who have not been identified as gifted may have some potential benefits, but ideally gifted students should be grouped homogeneously with other identified gifted students. Their sense of differentness often leads to skepticism about age peers being able to understand their concerns. As a result, in a heterogeneous group, gifted students are less likely to remove their protective façade and reveal doubts, concerns, and frustrations.

However, within a group, a wide variety of gifted students can interact comfortably—achievers and underachievers, students representing various socioeconomic levels, students from a variety of cultural and ethnic groups, rebels, introverts and extroverts, "nerds," star athletes, students with low English proficiency, and students with learning or physical disabilities, for example. All are developing. All are highly able. They usually find that they have more in common developmentally than they anticipated. High achievers may not necessarily be ahead of underachievers in social and emotional development. Some underachievers may be more intellectually advanced than high achievers. Underachievers also may be more able to articulate social and emotional concerns than achievers. Underachieving and other nonstereotypical gifted students' ability can be affirmed simply by being a part of a group. Discussion groups can be one—and perhaps the only—component of a gifted program that embraces all types of gifted students.

Age Differences and Expectations

Group work at the primary level is quite a different enterprise than at older grade levels. There often is a tendency for young children not to talk with each other, and perhaps not even to interact with each other, but to communicate instead with the group facilitator. In addition, because of the probability of the long narratives of some, with other group members becoming impatient because of perceived lack of attention, facilitators need particular expertise maintaining group cohesion.

Developmentally, young gifted children are, by definition, well beyond the level of cognitive development of most their age—insightful and perceptive. However, not all gifted children are highly verbal; they may differ in ability to handle abstract concepts; they may not be ahead of their age peers socially and emotionally; and their small-motor skills may not be advanced. Therefore, facilitators should carefully assess potentially differing development levels within groups when considering topics for discussion or hands-on activities. A brief activity (e.g., six to eight sentence stems to complete or a checklist about learning preferences) often is a good way to engage young children in thinking about a particular topic and a gauge of readiness.

School counselors often have more materials available for working with young children than are needed for their groups or prevention-oriented classroom lessons. These usually work just as well with gifted children as with the general school population because developmental tasks are universal. However, given the vocabulary level and intellectual nimbleness of most the gifted, some adaptations of the materials might be appropriate.

Group Size, Session Length, Scheduling, and Membership Constraints

Group size should vary according to age level. In the interest of giving members attention and opportunity to express themselves, primary-level groups should probably be limited to three students, while intermediate-level groups might have five. Middle school and high school groups should not have more than six to eight students. These group sizes reflect ideal numbers; group size may vary according to student needs and logistical constraints. A small group size, with opportunity for group members to become well-acquainted with peers beyond a superficial level, contributes potentially to a sense of comfort and safety in the group and perhaps in school in general, less perceived competitiveness and evaluation, and feeling heard. Group privacy is essential. A quiet room, preferably smaller than a classroom, with the door closed is best for effective group work.

Facilitators often limit primary-level groups to 20 minutes; however, young gifted children with longer attention spans might be engaged for 30 minutes. Usually the length of group sessions for increasingly older age levels is set by class schedules. Middle school groups easily can be productive for 45 minutes and high school groups for an hour. Groups for older adolescents are best when time accommodates depth of discussion and closure, but should nevertheless usually be limited to a class period in order to set an appropriate boundary and to fit the school structure.

Some facilitators schedule weekly meetings for a specific period of time (e.g., a 6- or 8-week series). Others meet with students for a semester or throughout a school year. Many teachers schedule sessions during the lunch hour, with other group facilitators taking advantage of designated study hall or advisor-advisee periods. Others arrange to meet with students during regular classes, making sure not to cause students to miss the same class more than once during a 6-week period, for instance, by varying the hour of the group meeting. Sometimes gifted students are intentionally grouped together for a regular class-size homeroom so that large-group discussion is possible. However, facilitators should be aware that level of trust and depth of discussion typically do not develop as well in class-size groups as in small groups.

"Closed" membership is preferable to "open" for the discussion groups advocated here. Even though having fluid membership is sometimes warranted, somewhat unavoidable, and even insisted on by a parent or student, stable membership helps group members develop trust and comfort for exploring social and emotional challenges. However, even though steady attendance is ideal, unexpected assignments, suddenly altered activity schedules, and social situations may all interfere with attendance. Students appreciate a flexible facilitator who acknowledges these realities and avoids contributing to more stress by complaining or indicting. However, most students may choose to attend regardless of other demands. When possible, the facilitator and members should remain constant for the life of a group, but, if changes are made, they are best done at the outset of a year, a semester, or series. When a group member will be relocating to another school or city, a facilitator can explore the effect on the group of that change (e.g., "Our group will be changing. I wonder what that will be like for us." "Our group has had a change. How is that for us?"). Asking members about "the present moment" can help them to reflect and gain skills in expressing feelings about social and emotional concerns (e.g., "What was that like for you when she said that?").

Parent Permission and Inclusion

It is important to secure parent permission for children's participation in a group. Some schools view both individual and group work by school counselors as part of the total school curriculum, with no need for parent permission. Others require permission for both group and extended individual work.

Parents certainly have a right to be aware of curriculum and format of instruction and may not wish to have their children involved in anything related to feelings and nonacademic concerns. It is wise to explain the purpose of the proposed groups on either the permission form or in a meeting where information can be disseminated, including possible topics for discussion.

Ideally, facilitators should keep parents informed about discussion topics so that pertinent conversations can continue at home among the family, perhaps at the dinner table, with parents thereby educated about their children's feelings and concerns. According to the authors' collective experience, parents value being included. Without sharing specifics about students' conversations, facilitators might send parents a brief, weekly e-mail as an update about a topic.

Facilitator Posture and Facilitation Skills

Basic counseling tenets apply to group work, whether led by counselors or noncounselors. Besides the important posture of nonjudgment, it is important to resist the "rush to fix" students and problems and to avoid giving advice. It is more effective to ask group members for suggestions than to offer them as a facilitator, and hearing others' thoughts about a common concern often is as powerful as actual problem solving. The purpose of the kind of group work being described here is to allow gifted students to talk with each other, feel heard, find commonalities and make connections, and normalize feelings and concerns. The comments of others may help group members to resolve their own conflicts with peers and family. Encouraging them to listen carefully, validate others' feelings, resist giving advice, and challenge only tactfully and when appropriate helps speakers to feel affirmed for their strengths, resilience, ability to make decisions, and ability to express complex feelings and thoughts.

Gathering information and suggestions, hearing about others' experiences, and thinking about alternatives are valuable processes in themselves. To group members who are wrestling with difficult situations, a question like "Well, what are your options?" puts the responsibility on them and communicates faith in their resilience and in their ability to generate viable alternatives. They can discuss a situation, exploring each possibility, and then perhaps move ahead confidently. Discussing options with other group members can help students explore thoughts and feelings and make an informed decision—even in relatively uncomplicated situations, such as if a high school student says, "I feel terrible. But I can't decide if I should go home or force myself to stay here and go to class so I won't have all the homework to make up."

Counselors-in-training learn that advice-giving does not empower clients, although in discussion groups members may appreciate suggestions from peers now and then. However, facilitators should be aware that their own advice (and the advice of group members as well) may carry some risk. Their advice is based only on their own unique experiences—not necessarily appropriate in other situations. In addition, when a student acts on advice, including from a respected adult, and has a bad outcome, the student may blame the adult and not take responsibility for his or her behaviors. The adult also may be deemed legally liable.

Therefore, it is wise to remember that the role of the facilitator is just that—facilitator of discussion, with group members' comments being the content of the group meetings. Fundamentally, facilitators ensure that group members (1) are psychologically safe in the group (e.g., they prohibit negative comments about group members, bullying in any form, and talking about a member who is absent), (2) have a chance to be heard, (3) consider developmental challenges with each other, and (4) develop important skills related to social and emotional development. Careful adherence to role parameters keeps facilitators from inappropriately or intrusively imposing personal values on students and also disempowering group members by imposing advice.

An important counseling tenet is the concept of being "one down." Rather than being the expert, with a "one-up" position, facilitators are effective when they assume a one-down posture, which puts the client into the position of teacher, feeling empowered and competent. After all, a facilitator cannot know a client's world unless the client teaches the facilitator about it. The client, then, is the expert on his or her life and the experience of it.

The same is true for group members in a school setting. No group facilitator knows more about members' lives and feelings than the members themselves. When students are invited by a listener/facilitator to "teach us," they are usually eager to be known and understood. When facilitation is done smoothly and effectively, students talk comfortably and thoughtfully, taking advantage of a rare opportunity to explain who they are to peers, without fear of judgment. Group members can sort out complex issues by expressing thoughts and feelings and being heard. Groups can provide rare unconditional acceptance, different from most other contexts in their lives where performance or nonperformance may be the focus. They can reflect on others' comments and express feelings and thoughts related to their own development, thus helping them to make connections and normalize developmental experiences.

Setting

From the first meeting, it is important to create a climate that is supportive, respectful, and engaging. It is helpful to provide a meeting area that allows for few interruptions, is comfortable, and is visually appealing. A space that allows room for students to move around is ideal. Making sure they are sitting where they can see all other group members, including if they are seated around a table, potentially helps everyone to feel involved and part of the group. Many group members feel more comfortable, more secure, and less self-conscious when they are seated around a table. Furthermore, if students are meeting over lunch, a table provides a place to eat. If a group meets in a classroom, individual desks can be moved near each other into a circle.

Getting Acquainted

Peterson (2008) emphasized the importance, at the first meeting, of group members experiencing what the group will be like. Whatever the routine in the future will be (e.g., "settling in," introducing a topic with a preliminary activity, discussing the topic, and closure), that format should be obvious at that initial meeting. The group should be engaged in an interactive activity or discussion. If the first meeting is devoted solely to rule-setting and guidelines, students may not return. It is possible that rules may never need to be addressed, especially if the facilitator is careful to model and gently set boundaries and to compliment students for positive and appropriate group behaviors.

Activities such as Betts and Kercher's (1999) "Find Someone Who" encourage group-building, trust, and cohesion. Their "Temperature Readings" activity allows facilitator and group members to regularly check in with a scaled number representing their mood and morale before discussing the topic of the day. When students first come into the room, they may enjoy a few mind-benders or "Thoughts of the Day" on a wall board to focus on until all group members have arrived. At the outset of a series, Bradley uses a "Name Game" ball toss for learning group members' names, a physical activity probably familiar to campers. In this game, students call out another group member's name while tossing a ball to that person. Once the ball has been thrown to everyone, a second ball is added, and two balls are then in play. Students call the name and toss the ball in the original order, with two balls going simultaneously. Additional balls continue to be added, and names are called, again in the same order. The predictability helps the group to focus on learning names quickly. Elementary and middle-school-aged students typically appreciate activities that allow movement. Session formats can be adapted to permit action, when appropriate, keeping in mind that physical activities can be too stimulating, and therefore distracting, for some students.

Discussion Topics

There is no "typical" gifted child or adolescent. All are individuals, with idiosyncratic behaviors, preferences, needs, and emotional responses to situations. However, small-group discussions provide an opportunity for self-exploration in a context that acknowledges and appreciates their shared social and emotional concerns. Facilitators can preselect topics for student discussions or allow the students to self-select from a checklist of possible topics or in an open-ended brainstorming session. Below is a list of topics, adapted from Colangelo and Peterson (1993) and Peterson (2008), that may be used as a checklist at the initial meeting of a group to learn about group members' needs and what their most pressing concerns are. Blank lines at the end for topics of interest that are not on the list may be added. When a topic is added later, the facilitator may monitor where the conversation goes and incorporate activities based on student interests during subsequent meetings. The questions below offer some direction for discussion, but many other activities and questions also are appropriate.

- *Understanding giftedness*: What is it? What are the stereotypes? How do others feel about it? How do you feel about it? What are the positives and negatives of being gifted?
- *Perfectionism*: What is it? What's bad about being so good? What fears are connected to perfectionism? How can perfectionism be harnessed as an asset, rather than letting it be in control?
- *Stress*: What is it? When is it too much? When can stress be good? What are some stress-management techniques that work for you?
- *Friendships*: How do you make new friends? What does it take to be a good friend? What kinds and levels of friendship are there? How might friendships change over the years? If you have experienced changes (e.g., when moving to a new school level), how has that been for you? If you have ever "redefined" a relationship, how did you do that?
- *Sadness and depression*: What do "low times" feel like? When should students tell someone that they are worried about how they are feeling? Who should they tell?
- *Image and popularity*: How do you want others to see you? How do you see yourself? What does it mean to be popular? What helps someone to have good, solid self-esteem? What do you value about yourself?

- *Sensitivity*: Do you ever feel as if you are too much of something—too shy, emotional, odd, impulsive, perfectionistic, talkative, or assertive? What kinds of situations do you respond sensitively to?
- *Self-expectations and expectations of others*: How do you know if your expectations of yourself are realistic? In what ways do you feel pushed by others' expectations of you?
- *Passion areas*: What are you passionate about? What do you want to learn more about? When do you feel especially fulfilled as a learner? What career(s) are connected to your area of passion?
- *Mood swings*: How wide are your mood swings? How much do they affect you and others around you?
- *Being organized*: If you are involved in many activities in and outside of school, how do you manage to keep your life running smoothly when there's so much to do and so much to remember? How much of a concern is organization for you, on a scale of 1–10, with 0 being "not at all"?
- *Advocating for self*: What are some appropriate ways to express a need? How can you be assertive without being arrogant and cocky? What basic skills help us to be good communicators?
- *Dealing with family transitions*: Change can be hard to accept and hard to adjust to. How have you adjusted to major changes in your family?
- *Optimism vs. pessimism*: How would you rate yourself on a scale with optimism at the top end and pessimism at the bottom? What is resilience? How do you think a person becomes resilient?
- *Learning styles*: What is intelligence? Is there more than one kind? How creative are you? What do you think of this statement: It is more important to know how you are smart than how smart you are.
- *Introversion vs. extroversion*: How would you rate yourself on a scale with introversion being at the top and extroversion at the bottom? How does your personality affect how you communicate with others and live your life?

- *Competition*: How do you handle competition? What do you do to cope with it? What makes "healthy" competition? "Unhealthy" competition?
- *Gifted girls*: How much, if at all, does being smart affect your social life? Your relationship with boys?
- *Gifted boys*: How much, if at all, does being smart affect your social life? Your relationship with girls?
- *Careers*: What are your strengths? What are your interests and passions? If you have multiple talents, thinking about focusing on a single career might be confusing, frightening, or discouraging. How much of a problem is that for you, on a scale of 1–10, with 10 being a great problem?
- *Developing leadership ability*: What characteristics make a good leader? How might a person learn to be a leader? How can people make sure they are effective leaders?
- *Helplessness*: National and world problems can seem overwhelming. What do you worry about when you watch and listen to the news? Is there anything you would like to do to make a difference in the world? How do you feel about people who are in need?

Psychoeducational dimensions also lend themselves to development-oriented discussion. Information can be presented by a facilitator or guest speaker about illegal substance use and abuse; puberty, intimacy, and/or sexual orientation; eating disorders and other mental health disorders, such as depression; and self-protection in a university or other environment, for example. Information also can be shared about school clubs and activities and opportunities for community involvement. College freshmen home for a holiday can talk about transitioning into college. A panel of high school students can answer questions from eighth graders about how high school will be different from middle school. A panel of middle school sixth graders can help next year's incoming students similarly. Involving community resources in presentations encourages support, raises awareness, and connects school to community.

Both children and adolescents can learn about the social and emotional side of giftedness by discussing what has been written in gifted education publications. Such information can generate conversation in a safe, nonjudgmental setting with a stable, rational, and compassionate adult, perhaps a rare opportunity even for some of the most high-functioning children and adolescents. Typically, students appreciate being listened to, validated, and understood. Students also appreciate being told they can choose not to participate in an activity they believe will be uncomfortable, feeling allowed to sit and listen, including being able to say "Pass" during roundtable commenting.

Resources to Enhance Discussion

A number of meaningful activities for individuals can be adapted to a group discussion format (See Appendix A for examples). Activities involving physical movement or discussion of song lyrics and media clips usually appeal to all age levels. Such activities can be paired with pertinent discussion topics to promote group interaction—in regard to being labeled *gifted*, coping with stress, or anticipating college, for example. Inventories related to values, personality, and behavior can foster self-reflection.

Many children's books carry powerful messages and address topics that appeal to gifted students of all ages. These books can be used either as an introduction to a discussion topic or as the culmination. Book messages are timeless, and even middle and high school students can relate to experiences of characters in children's books. In a book world, situations may appear easy to explain and resolve. Vicariously, group members can gain hope for resolving their own confusing situations or feel satisfaction for having coped with personal difficulties effectively.

Closure

Near the end of every discussion, it is important to make a habit of protecting time for the students to reflect on how they experienced the meeting and to have a sense of closure.

Asking one or more of them to summarize what was discussed and to offer feelings or thoughts helps to bring the session to a meaningful conclusion. Open-ended questions can ask what they learned, what they experienced, and how they might put the experience or information to use.

Two or three sessions before the end of a group series, especially when the series has been sustained over many weeks, it is important to prepare for termination, recognizing that students may have difficulty with endings. Some group members may have experienced peer support and trust for the first time, as well as a nonjudgmental, unconditionally supportive adult. Therefore it is wise to mention the date for the final session in advance of that time. In addition, at the final meeting, "Endings" or "Changes" might be good session topics, with members encouraged to talk about feelings and memories associated with change and loss.

Planning an activity to elicit mutual affirmation among group members (e.g., inviting group members to write a positive comment and a wish on a paper for each of the other group members or to tell orally what they have appreciated about each) is appropriate for the final meeting. The facilitator also can compliment each group member and model expression of feelings about ending the group. An informal awards ceremony, with each member receiving a certificate celebrating an individual characteristic (e.g., "Most Optimistic Thinker," "Best Jokes," "Most Creative Ideas") also can offer individual validation and punctuate the group experience.

In order to plan effectively for future groups, facilitators often create an evaluation form to gather feedback at the final session about what group members enjoyed and learned. Students usually respond well to scaling questions ("On a scale of 1–10 . . . "), although one or two open-ended requests for comments and suggestions also can suffice. Just the experience of filling out the form can provoke self-reflection about personal growth.

Feedback

Students routinely have given the authors positive feedback about discussion groups in various settings, with some even commenting that the group helped them survive a difficult time or year or helped them realize that growing up is challenging for even those who appear secure and at ease. Sometimes a group member who has been quiet expresses gratitude. The authors have learned not to underestimate the value of groups for individual members, including those who are more inclined to listen than to share. One comment by a ninth grader captured two important dimensions of the group experience: "It's a chance for me to get together regularly with people outside of my normal social circle. It's good to discuss the things that are different for us."

Parents also have commented on the value of the small-group experience for their children—formally in letters and informally as well. One parent wrote the following:

> There are two primary benefits we have observed. First, the group has built a healthy community that allows for a mix of fun, introspection, and trusted discussion. All of these activities yield insight and learning. Second, facilitation by a skilled practitioner allows the group members to work with an adult on difficult issues to support the parents' primary role as advisors for their children. For example, our daughter is comfortable raising some issues with her peers and the facilitator that might be somewhat awkward at home. Achieving the above takes substantial skill by the facilitator and a willingness to invest in this activity over the long term. I assume there are flashes of insight for students at most meetings, but far deeper value is achieved over time.

When facilitating high school and middle school groups for gifted students, the first author routinely invited each principal in her school to attend as the only guest at one group session. "What Do You Wish Teachers Understood about You?" was typically the topic for that session. At the end of thoughtful, insightful interaction, each principal predictably made a comment like "*Every* kid in this school ought to have this experience." It is indeed feasible to accomplish that if school counselors regularly facilitate multiple series throughout the school year, and every student does deserve a group experience. Gifted students can benefit from a group experience as much as anyone else can. For them, too, discussion group work is an effective and efficient way to address affective concerns.

The principals also usually made comments like "You'd never guess that there was so much going on in the heads of these kids." After all, these were generally students who looked good, performed well, behaved well, and appeared to thrive in school. Even the underachievers were usually not "problem students." The principals appeared to become convinced of the value of small discussion groups—including in gifted education.

Conclusion

The authors here encourage gifted education teachers, schools, and skilled and committed parents to consider development- and prevention-oriented small-group work as an important curricular component for meeting the affective needs of gifted school-age individuals. Facilitators need to be aware of appropriate protocol and posture, but student experiences and outcomes also are affected by the topics and activities selected, the length of group series, the frequency of meetings, group size, and who the group members are. When concerned adults move ahead and conduct discussion groups because such groups are needed and valuable, and because they themselves have an interest in serving gifted children and adolescents in this way, students potentially benefit. Paying attention to confidentiality, being willing to learn by doing, being respectful and nonjudgmental, and responding flexibly to whatever emerges during discussion—these usually ensure successful group facilitation. All of these components take practice, *after* taking the first step.

References

Berger, S. (2006). *College planning for gifted students* (3rd ed.). Waco, TX: Prufrock Press.

Betts, G. (1985). *The Autonomous Learner Model for the gifted and talented.* Greeley, CO: ALPS.

Betts, G., & Kercher, J. (1999). *The Autonomous Learner Model: Optimizing ability.* Greeley, CO: ALPS.

Betts, G., Toy, R., & Vasquez, K. (2005). *The young child and the Autonomous Learner Model.* Greeley, CO: ALPS.

Celsi, T. (1990). *The fourth little pig.* Austin, TX: Steck-Vaughn.

Colangelo, N., & Peterson, J. S. (1993). Group counseling with gifted students. In L. K. Silverman (Ed.), *Counseling the gifted and talented* (pp. 111–129). Denver, CO: Love.

Coles, R. (1995). *The story of Ruby Bridges.* New York: Scholastic.

Cooney, B. (1982). *Miss Rumphius.* New York: The Viking Press.

Dabrowski, K. (1967). *Personality-shaping through positive disintegration.* Boston: Little Brown.

Dabrowski, K., & Piechowski, M. M. (1977). *Theory of levels of emotional development: Volume 1–Multilevelness and positive disintegration.* Oceanside, NY: Dabor Science Publications.

Delisle, J., & Galbraith, J. (2002). *When gifted kids don't have all the answers.* Minneapolis, MN: Free Spirit.

Feldhusen, J., & Treffinger, D. (1980). *Creative thinking and problem-solving in gifted education.* Dubuque, IA: Kendall & Hunt.

Fleischman, P. (1999). *Weslandia.* Cambridge, MA: Candlewick Press.

Fox, M. (1988). *Koala Lou.* San Diego, CA: Voyager Books.

Gardner, H. (1993). *Frames of mind: The theory of multiple intelligences.* New York: Basic Books.

Greene, M. J. (2006, November). *Let's do lunch: Using popular media for guided discussion.* Presented at the annual meeting of the National Association for Gifted Children, Charlotte, NC.

Halsted, J. (2002). *Some of my best friends are books.* Scottsdale, AZ: Great Potential Press.

Hébert, T. P., & Beardsley, T. M. (2001). Jermaine: A critical case study of a Black child living in rural poverty. *Gifted Child Quarterly, 45,* 85–103.

Jackson, E. (1994). *CinderEdna.* New York: Lothrop, Lee & Shepard Books.

Jackson, P. S., & Peterson, J. S. (2003). Depressive disorder in highly gifted adolescents. *Journal of Secondary Gifted Education, 14,* 175–186.

Kincher, J. (1995). *Psychology for kids II*. Minneapolis, MN: Free Spirit.

Klise, K. (2006). *Why do you cry?* New York: Henry Holt and Company.

Kraus, R. (1971). *Leo the late bloomer*. New York: Harper Collins.

Leaf, M. (1936). *The story of Ferdinand*. New York: Scholastic.

Lionni, L. (1967). *Frederick*. New York: Dragonfly Books.

Littrell, J. M., & Peterson, J. S. (2002). Establishing a comprehensive group work program in an elementary school: An in-depth case study. *The Journal for Specialists in Group Work, 27*, 161–172.

Littrell, J. M., & Peterson, J. S. (2005). *Portrait and model of a school counselor*. Boston: Houghton Mifflin/Lahaska Press.

Mendaglio, S. (2008). *Dabrowski's theory of positive disintegration*. Scottsdale, AZ: Great Potential Press.

Mendaglio, S., & Peterson, J. S. (2007). *Models of counseling gifted children, adolescents, and young adults*. Waco, TX: Prufrock Press.

Munsch, R. (1980). *The paper bag princess*. New York: Annick Press.

Peterson, J. S. (1990). Noon-hour discussion groups: Dealing with the burdens of capability. *Gifted Child Today, 13*(4), 17–22.

Peterson, J. S. (2002). A longitudinal study of post-high-school development in gifted individuals at risk for poor educational outcomes. *Journal of Secondary Gifted Education, 14*, 6–18.

Peterson, J. S. (2003). An argument for proactive attention to affective concerns of gifted adolescents. *Journal of Secondary Gifted Education, 14*, 62–71.

Peterson, J. S. (2008). *The essential guide to talking with gifted teens: Ready-to-use discussions about identity, stress, relationships, and more*. Minneapolis, MN: Free Spirit.

Peterson, J. S., & Colangelo, N. (1996). Gifted achievers and underachievers: A comparison of patterns found in school files. *Journal of Counseling and Development, 74*, 399–407.

Peterson, J. S., & Ray, K. E. (2006a). Bullying among the gifted: The subjective experience. *Gifted Child Quarterly, 50*, 252–269.

Peterson, J. S., & Ray, K. E. (2006b). Bullying and the gifted: Victims, perpetrators, prevalence, and effects. *Gifted Child Quarterly, 50*, 148–168.

Polacco, P. (1998). *Thank you, Mr. Falker*. New York: Philomel Books.

Rathmann, P. (1991). *Ruby the copycat*. New York: Scholastic.

Renzulli, J. (1986). The three-ring conception of giftedness: A developmental model for creative productivity. In R. J. Sternberg & J.

E. Davidson (Eds.), *Conceptions of giftedness* (pp. 53–92). Cambridge, MA: Cambridge University Press.

Ross, T., & Barron, R. (1994). *Eggbert, the slightly cracked egg.* New York: Putnam & Grosset.

Schmitz, C., & Hipp, E. (1995). *A leader's guide to fighting invisible tigers.* Minneapolis, MN: Free Spirit.

Seligman, M. (1995). *The optimistic child.* New York: HarperCollins.

Shannon, D. (1998). *A bad case of stripes.* New York: The Blue Sky Press.

Silverstein, S. (1964). *The giving tree.* New York: Harper & Row.

Steig, W. (1986). *Brave Irene.* New York: Farrar, Strauss, & Giroux.

Treffinger, D. J. (1983). Fostering effective, independent learning through individualized programming. In J. S. Renzulli (Ed.), *Systems and models for developing programs for the gifted and talented* (pp. 429–460). Mansfield Center, CT: Creative Learning Press.

Wolff, F., & Savitz, H. M. (2005). *Is a worry worrying you?* Terre Haute, IN: Tanglewood Press.

Appendix A
Resources to Enhance Discussion

The books mentioned below provide helpful ideas in addition to the activities that are highlighted as being useful for generating group interaction.

- Delisle and Galbraith (2002) prompt students to consider their personal reactions to being labeled gifted in an activity called "Ups and Downs" and suggest using "Great Gripes" to launch discussions about giftedness.
- Betts and Kercher (1999) offer an Autonomous Learner Multiple Intelligences Inventory, adapted from Gardner (1993), which helps students identify strengths and appreciate similarities to, and differences from, other group members.
- Schmitz and Hipp (1995) offer a "Teen Inventory on Common Stressors" and information on life skills to help students identify what is causing them stress and how to diffuse and control it with stress-management techniques.
- Peterson (2008) suggests "Family Communication," "Family Communication Role-Plays," and "Family Roles" activities, which can help students recognize how their families communicate, be able to ask for what they need, and consider what roles family members play.
- Peterson's (2008) "A Question of Values" helps students note and explore what values are important to them, and "Façade, Image, and Stereotype" allows them to consider the emotional price they may pay for living up to, or protecting, an image.
- Betts and Kercher's (1999) "Six Selves" activity allows students to develop a deeper awareness and appreciation of themselves as lifelong learners.
- Seligman's (1995) "Attributional Style Questionnaire" helps students to assess their levels of optimism and pessimism. A discussion can ensue about how to develop more positive ways to explain and cope with adversity.
- Especially for young students, Kincher's (1995) *Psychology for Kids II* provides various one-page inventories that pro-

mote discussion of concepts such as leadership and person-ality with "Are You a Leader?" and "Are You an Introvert or an Extrovert?" Also appropriate are activities in *The Young Child and the Autonomous Learner Model* (Betts, Toy, & Vasquez, 2005).

- *College Planning for Gifted Students* (Berger, 2006) offers questionnaires to help students identify interests and refine goals in the college search process. Students may have opportunities to speak with career personnel in their high schools, but having a forum for talking with other gifted students about college and careers is a bonus.

- To incorporate movement into the discussion, an enjoyable twist to simply responding to open-ended questions is to write the questions on a large rubber ball. Group members can bounce or throw the ball to each other and answer the question where their left thumb lands.

- Older students can benefit from reading lyrics of popular songs together and discussing the intent and emotions of the songwriter, as well as what the lyrics mean to them. Similarly, students can ponder and discuss pertinent famous quotations on a chalk or dry-erase board, as related to their lives in the present.

- Viewing media clips with content relevant to student con-cerns provides an opportunity for students to connect with a character or idea and discuss insights (Greene, 2006). A helpful collection of videos with gifted characters and gifted issues can be found at http://www.hoagiesgifted.org/movies/htm.

- Halsted (2002) provides a helpful resource related to using books to explore emotional issues. Children's books, such as the following, can be useful for self-reflection even with adolescents.

  - *Weslandia* (Fleischman, 1999) and *Eggbert, The Slightly Cracked Egg* (Ross & Barron, 1994) validate how being different can be isolating.

  - *Is a Worry Worrying You?* (Wolff & Savitz, 2005) addresses how stress manifests itself and confuses thinking.

- *Ruby the Copycat* (Rathmann, 1991) and *A Bad Case of Stripes* (Shannon, 1998) reassure readers that it is best to be an individual and accept oneself.
- *The Giving Tree* (Silverstein, 1964) portrays sensitivity and the satisfaction of caring selflessly about others.
- *Why Do You Cry?* (Klise, 2006) gives permission to cry and encourages discussion about crying.
- *The Story of Ferdinand* (Leaf, 1936) and *The Paper Bag Princess* (Munsch, 1980) demonstrate that others' assumptions are not always accurate.
- *Koala Lou* (Fox, 1988) examines how upsetting and confusing family transitions can be.
- The concept of positive thinking is portrayed in *CinderEdna* (Jackson, 1994).
- *Frederick* (Lionni, 1967) illuminates the concept and importance of multiple intelligences.
- *The Fourth Little Pig* (Celsi, 1990) guides readers to take healthy risks and enjoy what life has to offer.
- *Miss Rumphius* (Cooney, 1982) dignifies altruism and the difference that one person can make in his or her world.
- *Brave Irene* (Steig, 1986) portrays a resilient young girl struggling against adversity, a poignant story about succeeding because of love and courage.
- *The Story of Ruby Bridges* (Coles, 1995) shows how to overcome adversity using bravery, honesty, and kindness.
- For students who are twice-exceptional (being gifted and having a disability), *Leo the Late Bloomer* (Kraus, 1971) and *Thank You, Mr. Falker* (Polacco, 1998) validate the frustration of developmental challenges and not living up to the expectations of self and others.

Preventing Suicide Among Students With Gifts and Talents

Tracy L. Cross, Andrea D. Frazier, & Samantha M. McKay

In the face of rising suicide prevalence rates in children and adolescents in general, and by extension, gifted and talented students, it is critical that concerned individuals take action and intercede in the lives of young people who are endangered. Yet, how does one proceed? At present, much of what is known about suicide in gifted students is based on work exploring suicide in the general population. The following chapter describes seminal theories that have great potential for explaining suicide in gifted adolescents and reports the findings of research aimed at exploring suicide in this special population. Moreover, recommended best practices for intervening with gifted adolescents by schools, peers, and parents are discussed.

According to the American Association of Suicidology (2007), suicide is the third leading cause of death among adolescents and young adults in the United States. Prevalence rates increased significantly (240%) between 1950 and 1995 in this population. Another group that saw significant increases was the under-14 age group. Although there was a decline in suicide rates between 1994 and 2002 (from 13.8 per 100,000 in 1994 to 9.9 per 100,000 in 2002) among adolescents and young adults, a sharp increase ensued in 2006 (American Association of Suicidology, 2007).

Troubling suicide rates in adolescents and young adults (ages 15 to 24) are a phenomenon that reaches beyond the borders of this country. Based on data supplied by Pelkonen and Martunnen (2003), suicide rates in this age group and particularly among young men has been increasing in Australia, New Zealand, and some European countries. The suicide rate of young women in Estonia from 1998 to 1999 went from 3.8 per 100,000 to 11.4. In Iceland, between 1996 and 1997, the suicide rate among young women between 15 and 19 went from 0.00 per 100,000 to 9.6. Portzky, Audenaert, and van Heeringen (2005) reported that the suicide rate in Belgium doubled over the past decade for 15–24-year-old young men.

Suicide rates increased by 51% for young people between the ages of 10 and 14 (American Association of Suicidology, 2007). Suicide rates in this age group increased the most for African American children (American Association of Suicidology, 2007). At the same time, White children in this age group were more likely to successfully complete a suicide attempt than African American children (American Association of Suicidology, 2007). The methods used to complete suicide in children include the use of firearms and suffocation. Suffocation as a deadly suicide method has been on the rise since 1999 (American Association of Suicidology, 2007).

What do these patterns tell us about suicide prevalence rates among students with gifts and talents? Actual prevalence rates for these age groups of gifted students are not known for a variety of reasons, including the lack of national clarity about the definition of giftedness precluding identifying youth who have completed suicide as gifted, limited access to information about youth who have completed suicide, and nondisaggregated national data on youth suicide based on whether suicide completers were nongifted or gifted (Cross, Cassady, & Miller, 2006). It is reasonable, however, to assume that the rates for gifted students have followed that of the general population of the same age groups. Understanding and preventing suicidal behaviors of students with gifts and talents is of great importance, especially given that the prevalence rates have begun to climb once again (American Association of Suicidology, 2007).

Due to the limited amount of research devoted to exploring suicide in gifted and talented youth, an overview of the research on the suicidal behavior of the general population of children will be reported first. The overview will highlight a few particularly important works that set the stage for understanding suicide and suicidal behavior in the general population and thus in gifted students. A series of elaborated recommendations for how to prevent suicidal behavior in the gifted and talented completes this chapter. Included in the recommendations is a summary of suicide research that illustrates many of the known factors associated with suicidal behavior. Those factors that can be affected will serve as the conceptual frame for the recommendations for gifted and talented youth.

Ultimately, this chapter will problematize several myths about suicide in gifted and talented young people (King, 1999):

1. Suicide occurs without warning.
2. Gifted and talented youth who talk about suicide are not serious about committing suicide.
3. Educating gifted students about suicide can lead to an increase in suicide ideation among this population coupled with more knowledge about ways of being successful in their suicide attempts.
4. If a gifted young person wants to commit suicide, very little can stop her or him.
5. Only trained counselors or mental health professionals are capable of intervening with suicidal gifted youth.

Suicide in the General Population

Suicidal behavior includes four categories of behaviors. The first category is called *suicide ideation*. Suicide ideators think about killing themselves. The second category is *gestures*. Gesturors utilize efforts that are not-so-serious attempts to end their lives (gestures). The third group of behaviors is characterized by bona fide but failed efforts to commit suicide. These behaviors are labeled suicide attempts and those who engage in them are *attemptors*. The last set of behaviors end in death. Individuals in this group are called *completers*.

In order to best understand suicide in gifted and talented children and adolescents, it is important to identify the factors that make certain young people susceptible to suicide. Pelkonen and Martunnen (2003) stated that suicide is more of an issue for older adolescents than younger children. Adolescents are more likely to turn anger and self-loathing on themselves. Children expend their anger on the people around them (Cross, Gust-Brey, & Ball, 2002). As proof they offer that global suicide rates for 5–14-year-old children are 0.5 per 100,000 for males and 0.9 for females, but 12 per 100,000 for females and 14.2 per 100,000 for males for 15- to 24-year-olds. Davidson and Linnoila (1991) listed several risk factors associated with suicides in adolescents:

1. psychiatric disorders such as depression and anxiety,
2. drug and alcohol abuse,
3. genetic factors,
4. family loss or disruption,
5. friend or family member of suicide victim,
6. homosexuality,
7. rapid sociocultural change,
8. media emphasis on suicide,
9. impulsiveness and aggressiveness, and
10. ready access to lethal methods.

Bae, Ye, Chen, and Rivers (2005) identified factors such as being harmed by a weapon, obesity, and abuse by a boyfriend or girlfriend. Other risk factors include prior suicide attempts and poor communication with parents (Pelkonen & Martunnen, 2003).

Some researchers have included perfectionism, personal crises, "supersensitivity," and anxiety (Hayes & Sloat, 1989; Leroux, 1986) as risk factors for suicide among young people with gifts and talents. These would be in addition to the afore-mentioned factors. Moreover, it is probable that the factors identified for students with gifts and talents are risk factors for the general population. That being said, research that has iden-tified specific risk factors for gifted and talented youth will be covered later in this chapter.

Much of the research about suicide risks have sought to establish the relationship between demographic factors like race, age, sexual orientation, socioeconomic status, and the like with thoughts of suicide or suicide attempts. Although these studies have done the important job of identifying who could potentially be at risk for suicide, these studies do not explain why some people decide to take their own lives. This approach also permits consumers of this research to assume that some people are more prone to suicide attempts and completions than others. This blind spot could lead to the misidentification of some and the underidentification of others who are at risk for suicide. This also could lead to ineffective intervention strategies (Rutter & Behrendt, 2004).

For example, although suicide rates traditionally have been low among African Americans, Native Americans, and Latinos/as, there has been an increase in suicide completions in these populations of youth over the last 10 years. Much of the research and intervention strategies that have been useful with White students have not been as successful with Native American, Latino, and African American students. Moreover, these populations may not be assessed or assessed correctly (Rutter & Behrendt, 2004).

For these reasons, Rutter and Behrendt (2004) advocated for the inclusion of context in determining risk for suicide. They forward the argument that the psychosocial characteristics of hopelessness, isolation, a negative self-concept, and hostility may be just as effective in identifying young people at risk for suicide. This argument has an intuitive appeal due to the large numbers of people who are impulsive, for example, yet not suicidal. Below are models of suicidal behavior that attempt to explain and predict those who complete suicide.

Models of Suicidal Behavior

Several suicidologists, or researchers who study suicide, have attempted to determine what places individuals at greater risk of suicide. Stillion and McDowell's (1996) suicide trajectory model combined several communities of thought in psychology that explain and predict suicide risk. Their model summarized four primary categories of risk factors: (a) biological (e.g., depression, gender, genetics); (b) psychological (e.g., self-esteem, depression, feelings of hopelessness); (c) cognitive (e.g., poor problem solving, inflexible thinking, low coping strategies); and (d) environmental (e.g., family experiences, life events, presence of deadly weapons). Stillion and McDowell argued that interactions among these factors are important when determining the likelihood of suicidal risk.

In the next theory, the researcher makes the transition from a characteristics-based model to one that places the experience of the person at its center. Holmes (1991) claimed that, in the face of extreme perceived stress (environmental/psychological), adolescents often would view suicide as an escape. Poor problem-solving strategies (cognitive) are typically displayed, leading to inflexible thinking and fixation on a limited selection of potential solutions to the problem. Once suicide is generated as a possible solution to the perceived problem, the individual is likely to perseverate on suicidal thoughts and tendencies until an attempt is made. Consequently, the probability of suicide completion is heightened when firearms are readily available (environmental), particularly for adolescents with depression (biological).

Shneidman (1981) offered an alternative to the suicide trajectory model. In his classic work, Shneidman described four elements of suicide: (a) heightened inimicality, (b) exacerbation of perturbation, (c) increased constriction of intellectual focus (tunneling or narrowing of the mind's content), and (d) cessation. According to Shneidman, inimicality involves "qualities within the individual that are unfriendly toward the self" (p. 222). He described the individual as becoming one's own enemy, often engaging in self-destructive behaviors. Perturbation reflects "how disturbed, 'shook up,' ill at ease, or mentally upset a person is" (p. 223). Constriction manifests itself in dichotomous thinking, blocking out memories of the past, or avoiding thought about how others would be affected by killing oneself. He described cessation as the "spark that ignites the above potentially explosive mixture" (p. 224). Cessation involves the belief that one can put a stop to his or her pain.

This awareness allows suicide to become the ultimate solution for a desperate individual.

When taken in tandem, the models and the risk factors suggest that the path to suicide in gifted and talented young people is strewn with psychological and/or emotional turmoil. Coupled with this personal turmoil is constriction in how one approaches problem solving. Extreme mental unease, problem areas in one's life, an inability to adequately resolve the problems, and the means in the environment to take one's life as the ultimate solution can make suicide a more viable option. These two models along with the risk factors associated with adolescent suicide serve as the foundation for understanding, and to some extent, predicting suicide. The next section reviews research about personality variables and suicidal behavior as a further means of detailing which gifted youth may be more at risk for suicide.

Personality and Suicidal Behavior

Several studies using the Myers–Briggs Type Indicator (MBTI), a widely used instrument that measures personality, have explored the possibility of personality types being related to suicidal behavior. Before moving on to studies that provide some evidence of a link between MBTI types and suicide, a brief overview of the instrument will be presented. The MBTI conceptualizes personality along four dimensions: Introversion (I)/Extroversion (E), Sensing (S)/Intuition (N), Feeling (F)/Thinking (T), and Judging (J)/Perceiving (P). All of the dimensions are continuous such that a person can be more introverted than extroverted, equally a sensor and a perceiver, more of a thinker than a feeler, and so on. Preferences along the four dimensions are combined to form MBTI-type combinations. There are 16 personality combination types in all. Some possible personality combinations types include Introversion-Sensing-Feeling-Perceiving (ISFP), Extroversion-Sensing-Thinking-Judging (ESTJ), Extroversion-Intuition-Feeling-Perceiving (ENFP), and Introversion-Sensing-Thinking-Perceiving (ISTP) to name a few (Cross, Speirs Neumeister, & Cassady, 2007).

Myers and McCaulley (1985) cited several studies that have linked suicidal behavior to introversion, sensitivity, affectivity, intelligence, and tender-mindedness, which are associated with preferences for Introversion (I), Intuitive (N), Feeling (F), and Perceiving (P) types of the MBTI. Lester's (1989) study found similar results, with the Perceiving and Intuitive dimensions being most correlated with suicidal ideation or behavior. Three additional studies comparing MBTI data with suicidal ideation and suicidal behavior measures have generated some consistent results. Lacy (1990), reporting on a longitudinal study of college freshmen, identified Introversion-Intuitive-Feeling-Perceiving (INFP) and Introversion-Intuitive-Thinking-Perceiving (INTP) as the personality types that appear most at risk for suicidal ideation. Street and Kromney (1994) reported four personality-type combinations that demonstrated the highest risk for suicidal behavior in a sample of college students: Introverted-Perceiving (IP) females, Introverted-Sensing-Feeling (ISF) males, Introverted-Intuitive-Perceiving (INP) males, and Extroverted-Intuitive-Judging (ENJ) males. Komisin (1992) concluded that individuals with an Introversion-Intuitive-Feeling-Perceiving (INFP) type were more likely to engage in suicidal behavior than other types.

Research on Personality and Suicidal Behavior Among Students With Gifts and Talents

The associations among personality types and suicidal thoughts and behaviors are of particular interest to the gifted community for several reasons. Although there are no studies that clearly link giftedness to increased rates in suicide (Cross et al., 2002), prudence demands concerned adults remain vigilant, nonetheless. With half of gifted students expressing introverted tendencies and with two of the reported "at risk" types being both introversion and common MBTI gifted types (Introversion-Intuitive-Feeling-Perceiving [INFP] and Introversion-Intuitive-Thinking-Perceiving [INTP]; Cross et al., 2007), there may be a high likelihood these students could experience more psychological distress and should therefore be screened for depression and/or suicidal ideation. Other MBTI-type combinations found in gifted individuals (Introversion-Perceiving [IP], Introversion-Sensing-Feeling [ISF], Introversion-Intuitive-Perceiving [INP], and Extroversion-Intuitive-Judging [ENJ]; Street & Kromney, 1994) also have been implicated in suicidal ideation or behavior, which suggests these individuals also warrant a careful assessment.

Combining Theory and Practice

Having good theories (Lacy, 1990; Shneidman, 1981; Stillion & McDowell, 1996; Street & Kromney, 1994) with which to frame suicidal behavior among gifted and talented students provides concerned individuals with the tools necessary to prevent premature deaths due to suicide. The next section provides recommendations about how to address and prevent suicidal behavior among students with gifts and talents. Recommendations for the general population will be reviewed as a means of grounding recommendations for gifted students. As mentioned previously, these recommendations are centered on factors that have been reported as most amenable to change.

Toward a Curriculum for Preventing Suicide in School Environments

For the most part, prevention recommendations for the general population of children and adolescents serve as a guide for suicide prevention in students with gifts and talents. This mandates discussion of which prevention strategies have realized some success in the general population. Involving schools seems a common-sense means of addressing suicide. The literature regarding the prevention of adolescent suicide offers several suggestions to improve overall school environment, such as increasing supportive resources for students, educating school personnel about adolescent suicide and the warning signals, and actively addressing students' mental health needs. These types of suggestions would best be described as primary preventions that aim to assist all students to some degree. The following section compiles and details some of the recommendations from the literature regarding school environment.

First, schools can provide training and resources on suicide prevention to school personnel. School staff should be prepared and know specifically how to act should a suicide, or an attempt, occur during school (Delisle, 1990). One way this can be accomplished is through in-service training that would include instructions on how to identify potentially suicidal adolescents, discussions of sample cases, and information regarding referral procedures (Garland & Zigler, 1993). Although limited, the initial research on the effectiveness and acceptability of in-service training seems positive (Eckert, Miller, DuPaul, & Riley-Tillman, 2003).

Likewise, schools can create a task force for responding to and preventing suicide. Adams (1996) reported that part of one school's response to multiple suicides was to create a task force whose goals included developing an admissions/screening procedure for psychological problems, assisting in the design of a prevention program, and gathering information about adolescent suicide to distribute. The task force produced several recommendations for its school including hiring a school, counseling, or clinical psychologist with school experience; planning a postvention for faculty and staff; and establishing a schoolwide crisis prevention plan. Educators are dissuaded from waiting until a suicide attempt or completion occurs before implementing a suicide prevention program (Delisle, 1990).

Additionally, the task force advised putting into action a prevention program with primary, secondary, and tertiary levels. Primary prevention would focus on individual wellness and appropriate social competency. Secondary prevention would focus on identification of and programming for at-risk groups, such as students dealing with issues associated with sexual orientation, eating disorders, low self-esteem, or cultural differences. Tertiary prevention would involve referral to outside agencies such as private mental health clinics or psychologists in private practice (Adams, 1996).

Several recommendations involve modifications or additions to the school curriculum. Schools may wish to consider including a unit on suicide prevention as a part of a mental health curriculum, beginning as early as junior high school. The mental health curriculum should consider strategies that incorporate common needs of students, including their need for acceptance, companionship, and self-understanding. Students play a crucial role in recognizing other adolescents who are suicidal (Delisle, 1990), and the more educated they are about suicide, the more of an asset they become. Eckert et al. (2003) discussed curriculum programs that are presented to students with the primary goals of (a) heightening student awareness regarding suicide, (b) training students to recognize possible signs of suicidal behavior in order to assist others, and (c) providing students with information about various school and community resources. Although research suggests proceeding sensitively and cautiously with suicide awareness curriculum programs, it has been shown to be an acceptable approach for intervening in some school settings (Eckert et al.).

A two-staged screening and assessment process such as Reynolds' model (as discussed in Eckert et al., 2003) that identifies potentially suicidal students could serve as another schoolwide practice for suicide prevention. The first stage uses a classwide or schoolwide screening in which all students complete a brief self-report measure to identify those who may be at risk for suicide. The second stage involves doing individual interviews with all students who score above clinically significant levels. Although initial research is promising, the acceptability of this technique is questionable (Eckert et al., 2003). This is in part due to screening tools reporting false positives for some young people and missing others who are at risk. Educators are encouraged to employ a screening tool multiple times. However, no recommendations were offered for working with youth (and their parents) who are falsely identified as suicidal (Jerry, 2007).

A final recommendation for school involvement in suicide prevention includes schools creating an educational environment that promotes conditions that stimulate and reinforce positive social relationships (Fleith, 1998), whereby students feel comfortable talking about their difficulties and are encouraged to dream and use their imagination. Schools should implement activities that nurture and highlight students' interests, strengths, and abilities (Fleith, 2001).

Some researchers argue that suicidal thoughts and suicide completion are not typical of youth working through difficulties in their life. Instead, suicidal behaviors are more of a possibility for young people struggling with some form of mental illness (Jerry, 2007; Pelkonen & Martunnen, 2003). This is an important observation to consider when deciding what facets to include in a schoolwide prevention program. Jerry argued that "presenting suicide 'as an understandable response to common adolescent problems could inadvertently facilitate the expression of suicidal ideas'" (p. 3). Essentially, educators must be wary of normalizing suicide as an option when students experience stress in their lives.

Additionally, schoolwide prevention programs run the risk of alienating potentially noncompliant young people considering suicide by equating suicidal ideation with mental illness. Although challenging youth who ideate about suicide can have the positive benefit of adolescents experiencing dissonance such that they seek help for their problems, other students could go underground and not pursue the help they need (Jerry, 2007). Educators and parents who advocate for this type of intervention need take this concern into consideration as well.

Jerry (2007) advocated proceeding with this message despite the risks. It is important that people in the community begin to see that suicidal ideation "is a manifestation of mental illness that results from, includes, or exacerbates certain thinking errors" (Jerry, 2007, p. 4), rather than an understandable response to difficulties one experiences. This clearer understanding about the nature of suicide ideation may create greater pressure to seek help for one's self or for others. He reported that a school-based prevention program that utilized this type of message realized a change in attitudes about suicide and encouraged more members in the school community to seek help for themselves or others.

Toward a Curriculum of Prevention Strategies for Individuals

Although the above schoolwide recommendations may impact a majority of students, other strategies are required for those individual students who are at risk for suicide. These suggestions would be characterized as secondary preventions because they apply to individuals who need additional and specialized assistance.

First, it is important that school personnel be aware of the significant risk factors associated with youth suicide. Again, some of those risk factors include psychiatric disorders such as depression and anxiety, drug and alcohol abuse, family loss or disruption, being a friend or family member of a suicide victim, homosexuality, rapid sociocultural change, media emphasis on suicide, impulsiveness or aggressiveness, and ready access to lethal methods (Davidson & Linnoila, 1991).

Once a student has been identified as at risk, the literature offers several prevention strategies. Delisle (1990) discussed the positive self-talk strategy. This strategy requires an adult to guide the student to see the link between inner thoughts and behaviors so the student may evaluate the validity of his or her beliefs and the behaviors related to those beliefs. Similar self-disclosure or self-concept activities can be applied in the classroom through group-building activities that allow students to express important intellectual, social, or emotional issues through discussion, role-playing, or role reversal (Delisle, 1990).

Helping students learn appropriate adaptive skills can help them to better handle stressful situations. Silverman (1993b) suggested it may be beneficial if students can learn to set priorities; avoid overcommitment; understand their strengths, weaknesses, and limitations; develop a sense of meaning and self-actualization; view mistakes as learning experiences; and be able to communicate and solve problems.

We would be remiss in not stressing the pivotal role friends and family play in suicide prevention. Pelkonen and Martunnen (2003) reported that youth sought help from friends and parents rather than professional adults before nearly fatal suicide attempts. Likewise, due to a reluctance or inability to seek help from professionals, concerned family members were the ones who helped young people attain the necessary counseling (O'Donnell, Stueve, Wardlaw, & O'Donnell, 2003). In a study of 13 young women who had reported being suicidal, loving and supportive contact with others helped them turn things around (Everall, Altrows, & Paulson, 2006). Rutter and Behrendt (2004) reported that sexual orientation alone is not enough to determine suicide risk. Youth, irrespective of sexual orientation, who could cite support from friends and/or family were at less risk for suicide. These examples illustrate that it is critical young people considering suicide be surrounded by people who care for them and who believe them when they share they are wrestling with profound sadness, anger, or desperation.

Some of the more heartbreaking stories in the literature are those told by professionals who worked with suicidal youth whose voices were ignored by parents or dismissed by school officials (Willings, 1994). Parents who have lost a child to suicide lament not becoming more active when their child came to them seeking help and urge others not to fall into the trap of assuming a child will not follow through with suicide (Stanley, 2005). Feeling reluctant or hesitant to talk about suicide can stand in the way of positive action aimed at interceding in the life of a young person wrestling with finding meaning for her or his life.

Communication and intervention by schools, parents, and friends thus seem the keys to preventing the loss of life to suicide (Cross et al., 2002). Schools, friends, and parents can partner with each other in ways that safeguard the emotional well-being of gifted and talented students and especially those young people who exhibit consistency in behaviors that we have detailed as red flags.

Toward a Curriculum of Prevention Strategies for Gifted Individuals and Schools

At present, there is a debate concerning whether giftedness protects people against psychological difficulties or makes people vulnerable to such problem areas in their lives. Versteynen

(2001) noted that some researchers have argued that higher IQs allow people to create avenues that promote better coping with life's stressors and that "gifted students overall are characterized by mental flexibility, emotional resilience, and an ability to think positively" (p. 5), characteristics that would promote healthier psychological functioning. Lehman and Erdwins (1981) reported that gifted and talented youth who took part in their sample were more positive, more mature, and enjoyed superior relationships with family members and peers.

Researchers who oppose the belief that giftedness ensures a more positive mental well-being argue that people with gifts and talents are more prone to psychological problems because they may experience alienation, isolation, and higher levels of psychological upheaval due to exceptional levels of emotional sensitivity. Some researchers contend that students who are profoundly gifted may experience more difficulties. Hollingsworth (as cited in Versteynen, 2001) felt that people with IQs of 125 to 155 could share enough common ground with peers of average intellect to permit them to fit in more effectively. Children and adolescents with IQs above that range could feel isolated (Versteynen, 2001).

Both perspectives require more research to substantiate. However, the former perspective may encourage the belief that young people with gifts and talents do not require any particular attention to their psychological well-being. Their IQs will in some way guarantee that they will land on their feet if they struggle emotionally. This expectation is contrary to the experiences educators, counselors, and others have had with gifted and talented youth (Versteynen, 2001). The former perspective also does not address what may be occurring with young people who are gifted and talented in other ways not captured by IQ tests. Although there are an abundance of gifted and talented youth who are doing fine psychologically, others have struggled, do struggle, and will struggle.

Research over the past several decades has investigated more closely the relationship between gifted students and suicide. Although gifted students have not proven more prone to committing suicide than their nongifted peers (Cross, 1996), several studies have looked at prevention strategies specifically for gifted youth. The following section looks at some of the recommendations for preventing suicide among the gifted population.

The risk factors that apply to the general population of children and adolescents holds true for gifted young people until proven otherwise; thus, it is important that adults be aware of the risk factors associated with suicide. Further, several researchers (Cross et al., 2002; Dixon & Scheckel, 1996; Fleith, 1998) have discussed and summarized some characteristics of gifted young people that often are associated with risk of suicide. These characteristics include perfectionism (Blatt, 1995), isolation related to extreme introversion (Kaiser & Berndt, 1985), unusual sensitivity (Delisle, 1986), severe self-criticism (Blatt, 1995), severe identity problems (Davis & Rimm, 1994), dyssynchrony in development (Hayes & Sloat, 1989) and Dabrowski's five overexcitabilities: psychomotor, sensual, intellectual, imaginational, and emotional (Dabrowski, 1964; Piechowski, 1979). Cross et al. (2002) identified similarities among four psychological autopsies of gifted young men, which included intense emotional overexcitability and a difficulty separating fiction from reality; a value system that was ego-driven, hierarchical, and polarized; group discussions that glamorized and romanticized suicide; and behaviors consistent with Levels II or III of Dabrowski's positive disintegration.

In addition to identifying at-risk characteristics, there are several warning signs that may alert others of a gifted student's suicidal intentions. Delisle (1982) included the following signs: lack of friendships, self-deprecation, a sudden shift in school performance, total absorption in schoolwork, and frequent mood shifts. Cross, Cook, and Dixon (1996) suggested being watchful for the following in gifted students: emotional difficulties, especially anger or depression; lack of involvement in prosocial activities; a dissatisfaction with place, situation, school, peers, family, or self; difficulties in romantic or social relationships, especially with peers of similar abilities; nonnormative expression of overexcitabilities; and difficulty separating fact from fiction. Importantly, although cutting and scratching portend emotional distress, self-injurious behavior demonstrates coping behaviors rather than suicide ideation (Cross, 2007).

The literature provides several suggestions to protect gifted children from suicide, suggestions that are particularly valuable for those children whose behavior already evinces several risk factors or warning signs. Preventative practices can and do start at home. Fleith (2001) summarized the literature's recommendations for parents of children with gifts and talents including Silverman's (1993a) suggestions that parents support their child's interest and value his or her creative and intellectual endeavors. Parents should make quality time to communicate with their child and be sensitive to his or her needs; they also should become active in educating themselves about suicide in gifted and talented youth in particular or adolescents in general and intervene to prevent suicide (Nelson & Galas, 1994).

Prevention strategies for schools with gifted students include vigorously meeting the educative needs of gifted and talented students and possibly scheduling individual or group counseling as a part of the educational gifted curriculum. Schools can provide suicide prevention training to students who can serve as helpers to their peers (Fleith, 2001). The schools should be aware of sources of stress for gifted students and help them to identify and cope with these stressors (Nelson & Galas, 1994). Cross et al. (1996) suggested that schools strive for a balance of positive and negative themes and characters in the curriculum.

Delisle (1990) noted that educators of gifted and talented students need to understand the unique social and emotional needs of gifted students and should be prepared to react to warning signs of suicide ideation. For example, many gifted students strive for perfection (Nugent, 2000). This is not a harmful endeavor in and of itself. However, when a gifted young person is never satisfied with her effort or sets unreachable goals that she bemoans meeting, perfectionism becomes a problem. If left unchecked, the drive for perfection can express itself in eating disorders, underachievement, depression, substance abuse, and suicidal ideation. To combat crippling perfectionism, educators should help youth delineate the difference between the pursuit of excellence that can facilitate a feeling of accomplishment and the relentless, unrewarding pursuit of unreachable flawlessness. Educators are further encouraged to help youth focus on improvement and to be more student-centered than evaluator-centered (Nugent, 2000).

Adults in the lives of gifted and talented youth should be willing to offer a listening ear, a guiding hand, or a caring reaffirmation of the similarities we share as human beings. Educators of gifted students should offer guidance that legitimizes the students' right to see their world from an atypical vantage point. Professionals and parents should create safe environments for gifted and talented students to learn and grow while providing support for their mental health needs (Cross et al., 2002). Gifted youth can face severe identity problems when they feel overly isolated and focus on how unusual they are from others around them (Fleith, 1998).

A specific prevention strategy mentioned in the literature that may work with gifted students is bibliotherapy (Delisle, 1990; Spreddmann-Dreyer, 1989). Bibliotherapy uses reading material containing characters who are similarly troubled as a way to model problem solving and address mental health concerns. Students may learn they are not the only ones with problems, gain insights into their own problems by analyzing the difficulties of a fictional character, or reduce their own anxieties and tensions by vicariously sharing the feelings of a character.

A precursor to bibliotherapy being an effective preventative tool in schools is the creation of classroom cultures that respect difference and are warm and welcoming. This type of classroom climate has its own benefits that go beyond helping protect youth socially and emotionally. Moreover, teachers should remain cognizant of their limitations when it comes to implementing counseling protocols through the curriculum. They should not be afraid to advocate that a youth seek professional counseling should that seem necessary.

Cross et al. (1996) concluded that it is better to err on the side of caution when dealing with potentially suicidal gifted students. They recommend not overlooking the potential signs of distress by construing the troubling behavior as indicative of giftedness. When in doubt, they encouraged adults to do something proactive. Proactive actions include helping gifted students to understand their emotional experience and needs and helping a troubled young person attain counseling. Moreover, Cross et al. (1996) encouraged keeping the lines of communication open with gifted students and challenging any ideas that equate suicide with honor.

We understand that being mindful of the possibility of suicide in gifted youth is no easy request. Yet, it is not uncommon to be surprised by the depth gifted youth can bring to everyday concerns like friendship or love or not-so-everyday concerns like world hunger or war. We are a society that can be biased against the young. We also can be overly accepting of the status quo. As a result, it can be harder for young people who want to enact change to do so in significant ways. This powerlessness to make a difference can generate a sense of helplessness that seems strange in young people capable of making a difference in the future.

It also is difficult for each of us to continually put ourselves in the shoes of others. Generally when it happens, we, unintentionally at times, expect people to be as we are. Consequently, the vigilance we must employ to make sure that there is room for children to be all that they are without conforming to our own sense of what is appropriate or right is a battle to maintain.

Even in our most gracious and giving moments, we have blind spots. We make mistakes. We do not hear. We dismiss. Our task, then, is to learn to listen more effectively. To consider possibilities that may seem unusual to us at the offset. To awaken even more to the world around us. This is a profoundly human endeavor that we, hopefully, grow into as time passes. Being mindful of the possibility of suicide in gifted and talented children and adolescents is no easy task but one we must undertake nonetheless. It makes us more humane and provides space for gifted youth in particular and youth in general to be all that they can.

Conclusion

This chapter has presented risk factors associated with suicide in the general and gifted populations and two models, the suicide trajectory model and Shneidman's (1981) elements of suicide, to explain how a youth comes to consider and ultimately carry out a suicide attempt. Moreover, research exploring the link between personality types, as defined by the MBTI, was presented, and the connection between personality types and suicide in general and gifted students were discussed. Finally, recommendations for suicide prevention for schools, friends, and parents were provided.

There is a great deal of potential for making positive impacts in the lives of gifted suicidal youth in school settings. Teens are more apt to talk with their peers rather than adults about suicide, and youth considering suicide are in touch with a consistent body of adults, classroom teachers, for a significant amount of time during the course of a day. These two factors encourage the education of peers and teachers in school settings (King, 2001). As Pelkonen and Martunnen (2003) reported, children who are not working or in school may be at a very high risk for suicide. However, the difficulties concomitant with schoolwide intervention strategies complicate their reception by many (Jerry, 2007). Because of these difficulties, Pelkonen and Martunnen urged schools to consider skills-based programs that bolster student self-esteem, coping and problem-solving strategies, and communication skills. Others advocate for multidimensional programs that focus on enhancing a sense of connectedness between schools, students, and parents; building adult awareness about adolescent suicide; and creating task forces for crisis intervention (King, 2001).

Certain behavioral characteristics like absolute self-absorption, friendlessness, and extremes in mood swings, to name a few characteristics of suicidal youth, are not healthy (especially in combination). Behaviors such as these should not be dismissed as typical of a gifted child.

Because young people and their stories are unique, individual cases of youth considering suicide may or may not be included in the aforementioned theories, definitions, or descriptions. Context matters. The research and recommendations presented are meant to supply some means for which to interpret context and to help with a systematic search of a school environment for this problem area.

In the end, the old standbys of communication, care, and involvement are the foundational principles for the recommendations presented. Interestingly enough, these three serve as the building blocks for good schooling, good parenting, and strong friendships. Considering the upswing in suicide rates in children and adolescents in general, and by extension until proven otherwise, gifted youth, learning that the best way to stay suicide involves behaviors we can engage in naturally feels comforting. As Maslow (as cited in Delisle, 1990) stated:

> Let people realize clearly that every time they threaten someone or humiliate or hurt unnecessarily or dominate or reject another human being, they become forces for the creation of psychopathology, even if these be small forces. Let them recognize that every [person] who is kind, helpful, decent, psychologically democratic, affectionate, and warm is a psychotherapeutic force, even though a small one. (p. 218)

Our responsibility, then, is to be ever vigilant in our efforts to look after the well-being of all children—including those with gifts and talents.

References

American Association of Suicidology. (2007). *Youth suicide fact sheet*. Retrieved July 17, 2007, from http://www.suicidology.org/associations/1045/files/Youth2004.pdf

Adams, C. M. (1996). Adolescent suicide: One school's response. *Journal of Secondary Gifted Education, 7*, 410–417.

Bae, S., Ye, R., Chen, S., & Rivers, P. A. (2005). New risk factors associated with suicide in adolescents. *The Brown University Child and Adolescent Letter, 21*(5), 3–4.

Blatt, S. J. (1995). The destructiveness of perfectionism: Implications for the treatment of depression. *American Psychologist, 50*, 1003–1020.

Cross, T. L. (1996). Examining claims about gifted children and suicide. *Gifted Child Today, 18*(3), 46–48.

Cross, T. L. (2007). Self-mutilation and gifted children. *Gifted Child Today, 30*(3), 49–50, 65.

Cross, T. L., Cassady, J. C., & Miller, K. A. (2006). Suicide ideation and personality characteristics among gifted adolescents. *Gifted Child Quarterly, 50*, 295–306.

Cross, T. L., Cook, R. S., & Dixon, D. N. (1996). Psychological autopsies of three academically talented adolescents who committed suicide. *Journal of Secondary Gifted Education, 7*, 403–409.

Cross, T. L., Gust-Brey, K., & Ball, P. B. (2002). A psychological autopsy of the suicide of an academically gifted student: Researchers' and parents' perspectives. *Gifted Child Quarterly, 46*, 247–264.

Cross, T. L., Speirs Neumeister, K. L., & Cassady, J. C. (2007). Psychological types of academically gifted adolescents. *Gifted Child Quarterly, 51*, 285–294.

Dabrowski, K. (1964). *Positive disintegration*. Boston: Little, Brown.

Davidson, L., & Linnoila, M. (Eds.). (1991). *Risk factors for youth suicide*. New York: Hemisphere.

Davis, G. A., & Rimm, S. B. (1994). *Education of the gifted and talented* (3rd ed.). Needham Heights, MA: Allyn & Bacon.

Delisle, J. R. (1982). Striking out: Suicide and the gifted adolescent. *G/C/T, 13*, 16–19.

Delisle, J. R. (1986). Death with honors: Suicide among gifted adolescents. *Journal of Counseling and Development, 64*, 558–560.

Delisle, J. R. (1990). The gifted adolescent at risk: Strategies and resources for suicide prevention among gifted youth. *Journal for the Education of the Gifted, 13*, 212–228.

Dixon, D. N., & Scheckel, J. R. (1996). Gifted adolescent suicide: The empirical base. *Journal of Secondary Gifted Education, 7*, 386–392.

Eckert, T. L., Miller, D. N., DuPaul, G. J., & Riley-Tillman, T. C. (2003). Adolescent suicide prevention: School psychologists' acceptability of school-based programs. *School Psychology Review, 32*, 57–76.

Everall, R. D., Altrows, K. J., & Paulson, B. L. (2006). Creating a future: A study of resilience in suicidal female adolescents. *Journal of Counseling & Development, 84*, 461–470.

Fleith, D. S. (1998). Suicide among talented youngsters: A sociocultural perspective. *Gifted Education International, 13*, 113–120.

Fleith, D. S. (2001). *Suicide among gifted adolescents: How to prevent it*. Retrieved March 5, 2007, from http://www.gifted.uconn.edu/nrcgt/newsletter/spring01/sprng012.html

Garland, A. F., & Zigler, E. (1993). Adolescent suicide prevention: Current research and social policy implication. *American Psychologist, 48*, 169–182.

Hayes, M. L., & Sloat, R. S. (1989). Gifted students at risk for suicide [Abstract]. *Roeper Review, 12*, 102

Holmes, D. (1991). *Abnormal psychology*. New York: HarperCollins.

Jerry, C. (2007). Suicide prevention: An analysis and replication of a curriculum-based high school program. *Social Work, 52*, 41–49.

Kaiser, C. F., & Berndt, D. J. (1985). Predictors of loneliness in the gifted adolescent. *Gifted Child Quarterly, 29*, 74–77.

King, K. A. (1999). 15 myths about suicide. *Education Digest, 65*, 68–70.

King, K. A. (2001). Developing a comprehensive school suicide prevention program. *Journal of School Health, 71*, 132–138.

Komisin, L. K. (1992). Personality type and suicidal behaviors in college students. *Journal of Psychological Type, 24*, 24–32.

Lacy, O. W. (1990). Nonthreatening, objective psychometric identification of students at risk for depression and/or suicidal behavior. *Journal of College Student Psychotherapy, 4*, 141–163.

Lehman, E. B., & Erdwins, C. J. (1981). The social and emotional adjustment of young, intellectually gifted children. *Gifted Child Quarterly, 25*, 134–137.

Leroux, J. (1986). Suicidal behavior and gifted adolescents. [Abstract]. *Roeper Review, 9*, 77.

Lester, D. (1989). Jungian dimensions of personality, sub-clinical depression and suicide ideation. *Personality and Individual Difference, 10*, 1009.

Myers, I. B., & McCaulley, M. H. (1985). *Manual: A guide to the development and use of the Myers-Briggs Type Indicator*. Palo Alto, CA: Counseling Psychological Press.

Nelson, R. E., & Galas, J. C. (1994). *The power to prevent suicide: A guide for teens helping teens*. Minneapolis, MN: Free Spirit.

Nugent, S. A. (2000). Perfectionism: Its manifestations and classroom-based interventions. *Journal of Secondary Gifted Education, 11*, 215–222.

O'Donnell, L., Stueve, A., Wardlaw, D., & O'Donnell, C. (2003). Adolescent suicidality and adult support: The Reach for Health study of urban youth. *American Journal of Health Behavior, 27*, 633–644.

Pelkonen, M., & Martunnen, M. (2003). Child and adolescent suicide: Epidemiology, risk factors, and approaches to prevention. *Pediatric Drugs, 5*, 243–263.

Piechowski, M. (1979). Developmental potential. In N. Colangelo & T. Zaffran (Eds.), *New voices in counseling the gifted* (pp. 25–57). Dubuque, IA: Kendall/Hunt.

Portzky, G., Audenaert, K., & van Heeringen, K. (2005). Suicide among adolescents: A psychological autopsy study of psychiatric, psychosocial and personality-related risk factors. *Social Psychiatry & Psychiatric Epidemiology, 40,* 922–930.

Rutter, P. A., & Behrendt, A. E. (2004). Adolescent suicide risk: Four psychosocial factors. *Adolescence, 39,* 295–302.

Shneidman, E. (1981). Suicide thoughts and reflections. *Suicide and Life-Threatening Behavior, 11,* 198–231.

Silverman, L. K. (1993a). Counseling families. In L. K. Silverman (Ed.), *Counseling the gifted and talented* (pp. 151–178). Denver, CO: Love.

Silverman, L. K. (1993b). Techniques for preventing counseling. In L. K. Silverman (Ed.), *Counseling the gifted and talented* (pp. 81–109). Denver, CO: Love.

Spreddmann-Dreyer, S. (1989). *The bookfinder: Volume 4.* Circle Press, MN: American Guidance Services.

Stanley, N. (2005). Parent's perspectives on young suicide. *Children & Society, 19,* 304–315.

Stillion, J. M., & McDowell, E. E. (1996). *Suicide across the life span.* Washington, DC: Taylor & Francis.

Street, S., & Kromney, J. D. (1994). Relationship between suicidal behavior and personality types. *Suicide and Life-Threatening Behavior, 24,* 282–292.

Versteynen, L. (2001). Issues in the social and emotional adjustment of gifted children: What does the literature say? *The New Zealand Journal of Gifted Education, 13*(1). Retrieved July 10, 2007, from http://www.giftedchildren.org.nz/apex/v13art04.php

Willings, D. (1994). A mine of talent caved in. *Gifted Education International, 10*(1), 16–20.

Professional Development for Promoting the Social and Emotional Development of Gifted Children

Elissa F. Brown

To carry out the demands of education reform, teachers, guidance counselors, and administrators must know and understand the subjects they teach, the students with whom they interact, and the local context in which they collaborate. The success of school reform hinges, in large part, on the qualifications and effectiveness of these educators. One way to address the elements of school reform is through professional development because it allows individuals to update their skills, socialize to new district initiatives, and provide a mechanism for implementing curriculum and school reform in a particular school and/or district (Van Tassel-Baska, 2002). The importance of professional development also has clearly been emphasized as a key component in national educational agendas (No Child Left Behind [NCLB] Act, 2001).

The National Staff Development Council (NSDC; 2001) created a set of context, process, and content standards to support professional development efforts targeted at increasing student achievement. The NSDC standards provide a framework for schools and school districts to employ as they plan professional development sessions.

This chapter will explore the role of professional development in providing a mechanism for developing the social and emotional aspects of gifted students. Just as it is seen as the "savior" for implementing broader-based reforms, it also may be seen as an important approach to emphasizing the affective needs of gifted learners in contexts that may only value their cognitive assets.

Review of Related Research on Professional Development

During the past decade, an increasing amount of literature has emerged on professional development and its effect on teacher change, classroom practices, and student achievement. Some recent studies suggest that the duration of professional development is related to the depth of teacher change and school reform (Shields & Knapp, 1997). Other studies suggest that professional development that focuses on specific content areas such as mathematics or science has been effective in promoting teacher change (Cohen & Hill, 1998). Another study, looking at teachers' influence on student adjustment in the middle school, examined parent socialization models for understanding teacher influences. Wentzel (2002) found that parental high expectations was a consistent positive predictor of students' goals and interests, and negative feedback was the most consistent negative predictor of academic performance and social behavior, regardless of gender and ethnicity.

In gifted education, one of the key directives from the U.S. Department of Education's *National Excellence* report (1993), was to increase emphasis on teacher development in order that all children are challenged. According to Westberg, Archambault, Dobyns, and Salvin (1993) classroom teachers with minimal or no training in gifted education implemented little to no differentiation in instruction or curricular modifications in which gifted learners participated. Another study by Westberg, Archambault, and Brown (1997) confirmed earlier study results. The researchers surmised that the responsibility for providing appropriate learning contexts should not rest solely with classroom teachers.

In the mid-1990s, the National Research Center on the Gifted and Talented randomly administered a comprehensive survey to investigate the scope and nature of professional development practices in gifted education used in school districts. The overall findings indicated that professional development practices in gifted education provided throughout the country were limited in nature, degree, and scope. The researchers concluded that school districts were limited in their employment of peer or collegial coaching as a practice and resorted instead to a "one-size-fits-all" approach to dealing with teachers (Westberg et al., 1998).

There is consensus in the literature that providing ongoing, consistent, systematic professional development positively affects teachers and students. Yet, a paltry of literature exists on the impact of professional development on the social-emotional welfare of students. Administrators, school counselors, other support personnel, teachers, and parents all share responsibility for what happens in the classroom to enhance the academic and social-emotional well-being for all learners.

Review of Research on Social-Emotional Needs of Gifted Learners

Gifted learners have similar emotional problems when compared with groups of nongifted children. It is reasonable to assert that gifted learners as an aggregate are well-adjusted and happy (Coleman & Cross, 2005; Neihart, Reis, Robinson, & Moon, 2002). Yet, it is still useful to focus on the social-emotional development of gifted learners. The social and emotional problems that gifted learners may encounter often are assumed to be the result of incongruity between their cognitive abilities and their emotional capacity to handle society's expectations (Coleman & Cross, 2005). Social-emotional issues can emerge from a variety of considerations such as the mismatch of educational experiences and the ability level of the student, the difficulty of finding like-ability peers, or the mismatch of self-expectations as compared to other's (e.g., parents, teachers) expectations (Neihart et al., 2002). These incongruous situations leave gifted learners feeling emotionally vulnerable and frequently ill-equipped to handle situations. The responsibility for helping students reconcile some of these differences rests with educators and other professionals. Thus, educators require targeted professional development opportunities to prepare them to work with students on social-emotional issues.

Dispelling Myths

Planning professional development sessions targeted for gifted education creates an additional layer of complexity because of the unique cognitive and affective needs of gifted children. For example, teachers may hold certain myths or false assumptions about gifted learners being socially and emotionally balanced by virtue of the label or through assumptions about emotional and social levels being concomitant with cognitive levels (e.g., if they are advanced in abstract thinking, then they must be advanced in their ability to interact with others). Yet, according to Silverman (1993), cognitive complexity gives rise to emotional depth, and gifted learners are not exempt from the emotional issues that emerge from this mix of cognition and affect. Educators need to be increasingly aware of the emotional and social needs of the gifted because of the implications for the classroom, school, and community. Other false assumptions held by educators may include:

- *Issues of perceived student maturity*: Gifted learners often employ an advanced vocabulary, giving the appearance of maturity (VanTassel Baska, Johnson, & Boyce, 1996).
- *Ability to work independently or in groups*: Gifted learners enjoy choice and like to work on in-depth projects based on their interests and aptitude, but interest and aptitude do not imply organization skills or self-regulation.
- *Ability to effectively cope with multiple stressors*: Due to the asynchronous development of many gifted learners (Silverman, 1993), they can handle cognitive complexities, but not necessarily emotional ones.
- *Ability to make long-term goals*: Many gifted learners have multiple talent areas that they are passionate about and may

not have a single-minded pursuit of one domain. Child precocity does not ensure adult productivity (Subotnik & Olszewski-Kubilius, 1997).

- *Ability to make and keep friends*: Gifted learners appear to be socially competent yet the research on emotional overexcitabilities (Piechowski, 1999) highlights the sensitivities and concerns that gifted learners experience in deep friendships and attachments.

Consider the following teacher profile highlighting some false assumptions from both the administrator's and teacher's point of view:

> I have been teaching eighth-grade language arts in our middle school for 12 years. This year, my principal put the identified gifted students in my class because he said it was my turn to have the "good" kids. Besides, he added, because I had some of the more difficult students in my other classes, having the gifted students would help balance my teaching load this year. I thought it would be easy because these students are smart and leaders in the classroom. I didn't realize that just because they're smart, they weren't necessarily mature.—B. McGuire

Many teachers are simply not prepared to implement effective strategies to promote social and emotional growth in gifted children. Professional development planners or committees cannot predict the level of knowledge or skills that teachers, school counselors, and administrators in a school district already possess in terms of working with gifted children (Dettmer & Landrum, 1998).

Overcoming Potential Barriers

Many teachers feel pressure from local, state, and federal mandates to only teach students the material that will be assessed on state and national measures; anything else is superfluous. Professional development is an integral part of teaching and learning. Teachers, school counselors, and administrators must be able to plan, implement, and evaluate these experiences in order to promote social-emotional well-being in gifted learners. Stakeholders need to consider the potential barriers that might preclude effective professional development from being implemented at the school or within the school district. Barriers can include psychological, fiscal, time, lack of training, or role constraints, and they may be caused by a myriad of factors. Once barriers can be identified, individuals can begin to implement necessary changes through targeting levers for change.

It is helpful, therefore, to consider the potential barriers to promoting professional development for the social and emotional growth in gifted children, the necessary changes that need to occur for optimal professional development sessions and the levers for supporting and sustaining change over time that promotes professional development opportunities. Table 13.1 displays the relationship of barriers to necessary changes to levers for facilitating those changes. The levers that will matter the most involve collaboration in planning among counselors, teachers, and administrators for roles, time allotments and specific tasks to be completed in providing a year's professional development program. A planning team composed of these personnel could develop a series of opportunities to be provided, using traditional or alternative delivery modes, based on the district's assessment of greatest need. Once they have determined content and mode of delivery, they will need to decide who will facilitate each planned session. Using an outside resource to kick off a series usually is a good idea, followed by internal expertise being used for further capacity building. Again, having a team of people who can be called in to do sessions is preferable to having only one expert.

Once a district can determine potential barriers and put in place necessary changes to mitigate against barriers, then meaningful professional development can occur.

Table 13.1
An Action Plan for Understanding Needed Changes in Professional Development

Barriers	Necessary Changes	Levers for Change
• State assessments are focused on acquisition of content knowledge.	• The cognitive domain is inextricably linked to the social-emotional well-being of an individual. • Performance is based on cognitive and emotional preparation, readiness, and potential.	• Have teachers work with gifted students on test-taking comfort strategies. • Have counselors work with teachers and students on issues of perfectionism and fear of failure. • Have administrators support personnel through flexibility in scheduling.
• Lack of knowledge, skills, or predispositions in teachers, school counselors, and administrators in the social-emotional development of gifted learners.	• Promotion of collegiality and collaborative exchange among staff. • Recognize that social-emotional development is not just a "gifted thing"—it's a "child thing."	• Employ outside speakers for professional development to relevant stakeholder groups. • Invest in the development of 1–2 inside experts on the topic.
• School districts do not have adequate resources to provide specialized training.	• Promote collegiality and collaborative exchange of ideas and strategies.	• Employ a trainer of trainer model for exchanging ideas. • Employ suggested alternative modes of service for professional development.
• Lack of flexibility in the classroom for accommodating social-emotional needs of gifted.	• Change teacher perception of gifted students' social-emotional needs.	• Include education on dispelling myths. • Integrate affective with content-based strategies in classroom.

Table 13.1, Continued

Barriers	Necessary Changes	Levers for Change
• School counselors are increasingly serving in the role of test coordinators.	• Broaden the conceptualization of the function of school counselors.	• Allow others to assist in the role of test coordinators. • Include school counselors in planning, implementing, and evaluating professional development experiences.
• Lack of linkage between school counseling, academic curricula, and career counseling.	• Shore up connections among the main areas. • Recognize that career counseling is a logical extension of talent development.	• Promote joint planning among teachers, school counselors, and administrators for student scheduling. • Afford opportunities for career exploration, decision making, and development of identity.
• Parents perceive that the social-emotional needs of gifted learners is a home function.	• Promote collaboration efforts between school and home.	• Communicate with parents on social-emotional activities in the school. • Create "parents-as-partners" network.
• Social and emotional characteristics of gifted children that pose challenges or maladjustment.	• Intervene in moving children toward more positive aspects of social-emotional development.	• Provide bibliotherapy, discussion groups, creative productive outlets, sociodrama, and so forth on a regular basis.

Planning for Professional Development on Social and Emotional Needs

Schools and school districts need to consider the following key points before professional development goes forward:

- *Conduct a preassessment (formal or informal) to determine prerequisite knowledge of individuals who will be attending*: A preassessment tailors professional development to the needs of the participants. In addition, participants feel some ownership in shaping the content and venue of the opportunity.

- *Determine how conducting ongoing professional development on social-emotional needs of gifted learners aligns with the district's initiatives*: Any professional development should support and align with the school district's needs in order to support the local educational context. Determining ahead of time how this occurs facilitates and creates an implicit value.

- *Recognize that teachers will not change their attitudes, beliefs, or practices unless they see students change* (Guskey, 2000): In order for teachers to internalize and ultimately change instructional practices, they must experience student changes.

- *Approach professional development from the lens that social-emotional needs of gifted students is a new construct, and therefore, teachers (and others) are learning a content area*: The degree to which the participants can understand the importance of developing optimal experiences for gifted learners that respond to their social-emotional needs will determine the degree to which teachers respect the validity of a social-emotional topic as a content area that should be mastered.

- *Understand that change is incremental* (Fullan, 1993): Every experience builds upon its predecessor and is integrated into the larger educational context. Change occurs in incremental steps, and even though an individual is anxious for change to occur as a direct result of professional development, it may occur and evolve over time.

- *Establish up front the purpose of the professional development*: Most professional development experiences have a title or topic but many lack the purpose or targeted outcome of what is to be expected.

- *Develop a system of monitoring implementation of professional development work and be prepared to provide follow-up support:* Success and ultimate fidelity of implementation rests with the degree to which teachers and others can implement the approaches and content garnered from the professional development into classroom practices.
- *Create a concept map or outline linking the professional development on social-emotional needs of the gifted with the following: curriculum implementation, instructional approaches, assessment techniques, and talent development:* Professional development to promote the social-emotional development of gifted learners must be integrated within the larger educational program and not be an add on. Determining how it fits with teachers' instructional approaches, curriculum employed, and assessment techniques affords the opportunity for the professional development to be embedded within the overall instructional program.
- *Realize that your best efforts cannot prevent all of the struggles and turmoil from occurring in a child's life. Your efforts, therefore, should be focused on assisting others who work with students with ideas, strategies, and support for equipping gifted learners* (Cross, 2001): Professional development to promote social-emotional development of gifted learners should be ongoing and systemic. There are multiple variables that impede or facilitate that development, and administrators should maintain a balanced perspective of what they can and cannot do.

Professional development experiences geared to address the differentiated emotional and social learning needs of gifted learners must be carefully and deliberately planned so that the experiences can give way to student growth and well-being.

Strategies for Implementing Effective Professional Development

Ideas for facilitating professional development opportunities for teachers, guidance counselors, and administrators on the social and emotional development of gifted students can come in different venues. They do not have to be structured in a typical in-service style. Table 13.2 displays traditional and alternative modes of delivery for professional development. Each school and/or school district will need to decide which of the following options is the best fit, based upon local context, expertise levels, student populations, and available resources. Regardless of the approach taken, teachers, guidance counselors, and administrators stand to benefit. Schools may decide to select a few ideas from each column and design a menu of overall options for an academic year.

Measuring the Effectiveness of Professional Development

Evaluating the effectiveness of professional development in promoting the social-emotional needs of gifted children is a neglected area. In fact, evaluation of any type of professional development often is overlooked. There is no single approach to evaluation of professional development or student needs, and differences in evaluation approaches may be based in philosophies or more pragmatic concerns. Regardless of the methodology utilized, evaluation should focus both on immediate concerns and on long-range goals for improvement and continuation (Dettmer & Landrum, 1998).

Designing and Evaluating Professional Development on Social-Emotional Developmental Needs of Gifted Learners

Using Guskey's (2000) model as a framework for evaluating professional development, VanTassel-Baska (2002) developed a set of guiding questions that have applicability to this context for both design and evaluation of professional development. The questions are as follows:

- What knowledge and skills do you want educators to acquire about gifted students' social-emotional development and their learning?

Table 13.2
Traditional and Alternative Modes of Delivery for Professional Development

Traditional Modes for Professional Development	Alternative Modes for Professional Development
Conference attendance.	Discussion groups formed around the following: selected books, themes/issues (e.g., perfectionism), or analyzing a movie for subtext (Nugent & Shaunessy, 2002).
Conference presentation.	Teachers conduct action research on a targeted topic in social-emotional development.
District hires an external consultant to conduct a workshop or a series of workshops over the year.	District hires an external consultant to observe classrooms and specifically focus on social-emotional behaviors and provide authentic feedback.
District conducts a one-day preservice professional development prior to the school year for entire district personnel.	District establishes professional learning communities (PLC) to focus on specific needs as determined by members of the group.
Teachers take graduate or licensure courses.	Teachers interview a sample of gifted students to make instructional changes based on student perceptions.
Teachers attend summer institutes and seminars.	Teachers employ online resources (e.g., discussion boards) with other professionals.
School personnel conduct a staff meeting.	School personnel give presentations to the school board, at a principal's meeting, or at a strategic retreat for capacity-building.
School personnel conduct a half-day workshop after school.	School personnel embed social-emotional development of the gifted as part of their Professional Development Plan (PDP).
School personnel develop curriculum units for gifted enrichment.	School personnel embed affective strategies within and across all content areas.
Teachers take courses online through distance learning opportunities.	Apply for mini-grants for self-directed research or coaching.
Teachers employ a trainer of trainer model.	Teachers engage in peer coaching and/or mentorships.

- Under what delivery mode (see Table 13.2) will educators, school counselors, or administrators best acquire these understandings?
- What organizational support structures are in place to facilitate, support, and continue any changes that are made as a result of the professional development?
- Are adequate resources available for classroom implementation?
- Is the school climate supportive of experimentation?
- What was the impact on gifted students of educators, school counselors, and administrators acquiring new knowledge and skills?
- In what ways did the professional development support the school (school district) initiatives?

Another approach to evaluating professional development and its influence on both the teachers participating and the students with whom they interact, is to use the National Association for Gifted Children (NAGC; 1998) program standards. The NAGC standards represent requisite and exemplary standards for gifted education programming. They may serve as benchmarks for measuring program effectiveness. It may be useful to schools and school districts to consider employing the standards as a formative tool in self-assessing the impact of professional development in the categories of socioemotional guidance and counseling, professional development, program design, program administration, and curriculum and instruction.

For example, a district could form a small task force of individuals who have just benefited from some form of professional development. The task force could rate themselves in respect to the criteria in the NAGC standards and share their ratings and perspectives with the group in order to reach a consensus and potentially draft an improvement plan. One focus of these evaluation systems should be on improvement of gifted learners' social-emotional development over time rather than merely documenting that a scheduled professional development session occurred. Evaluating the effectiveness of professional development geared to address the social-emotional needs of gifted children must be conducted in order to give way to long-term program, professional, and student improvement.

Teacher Standards

A collaborative effort began several years ago between the Council for Exceptional Children (CEC), the National Association for Gifted Children (NAGC), and the National Council for the Accreditation of Teacher Education (NCATE) to create a set of standards in which institutions of higher education offering coursework and/or degrees in gifted education could implement within their respective institutions. Colleges and university programs undergoing NCATE accreditation ultimately would be judged on teacher candidates' proficiencies based upon the gifted standards endorsed by both national organizations. Embedded within the NCATE gifted standards are multiple standards reflecting teachers' knowledge and skills with regard to meeting the social and emotional needs of gifted learners. This ensures that teachers graduating from schools of education at both the undergraduate and graduate levels have demonstrated mastery of the NCATE standards in gifted education, of which social-emotional is embedded, within the larger framework of course offerings. In some institutions a separate course is offered on the social-emotional needs of gifted students. In addition, an implementation guidebook (Kitano, Montgomery, VanTassel-Baska, & Johnsen, 2008) suggests best practices for translating the teacher standards for higher education into enhancing professional development at K–12 levels in order to ensure measures of quality that are consistent nationally. A school district or school could use these standards as benchmarks for determining the level of expertise that teachers need and then provide the subsequent training or target professional development on a particular standard. Implications for employing the NCATE standards in gifted are for curriculum planning and design, professional development for different stakeholder groups, policies on social-emotional needs that support program improvement, and program evaluation.

Conclusion

Planning, implementing, and evaluating professional development to promote social-emotional development in gifted learners requires extraordinary effort, a clear sense of direction, ability to deal with failure, creative approaches to problem solving, and refusal to be complacent with success. No single strategy or setting will fit the needs of every school because of the great diversity among K–12 educational institutions, professional expertise, and the structures inherent in the educational system. We can, however, develop a continuum of professional development options as part of our school goals. Just as gifted learners have the potential to create a better society for all, so do we have the potential to create a better social-emotional context within which these students can learn, respond, and develop.

References

Cohen, D. K., & Hill, H. C. (1998). *State policy and classroom performance: Mathematics reform in California.* Philadelphia: Consortium for Policy Research in Education (CPRE).

Coleman, L., & Cross, T. (2005). *Being gifted in school* (2nd ed.). Waco, TX: Prufrock Press.

Cross, T. L. (2001). *On the social and emotional lives of gifted children.* Waco, TX: Prufrock Press.

Dettmer, P., & Landrum. M. (1998). *Staff development: The key to effective gifted education programs.* Washington, DC: National Association for Gifted Children.

Fullan, M. G. (1993). *Change forces: Probing the depths of education reform.* Bristol, PA: Falmer Press.

Guskey, T. R. (2000). *Evaluating professional development.* Thousand Oaks, CA: Corwin Press.

Kitano, M., Montgomery, D., VanTassel-Baska, J., & Johnsen, S. K. (2008). *Using the national gifted education standards for pre-K professional development.* Thousand Oaks, CA: Corwin Press.

National Association for Gifted Children. (1998). *Gifted education program standards.* Washington, DC: Author.

National Staff Development Council. (2001). *Standards for staff development.* Washington, DC: Author.

Neihart, M., Reis, S. M., Robinson, N. M., & Moon, S. M. (2002). *The social and emotional development of gifted children: What do we know?* Waco, TX: Prufrock Press.

No Child Left Behind Act, 20 U.S.C. §6301 (2001).

Nugent, S. A., & Shaunessy, E. (2002). Using film in teacher training: Viewing the gifted through different lenses. *Roeper Review, 25*, 128–134.

Piechowski, M. (1999). Overexcitabilities. In M. A. Runco & S. R. Pritzker (Eds.), *Handbook of creativity* (Vol. 2, pp. 325–334). San Diego, CA: Academic Press.

Shields, P., & Knapp, M. (1997). The promise and limits of school-based reform: A national snapshot. *Phi Delta Kappan, 79*, 288–294.

Silverman, L. K. (1993). *Counseling the gifted and talented.* Denver, CO: Love.

Subotnik, R., & Olszewski-Kubilius, P. (1997). Restructuring special programs to reflect the distinctions between children's and adult's experiences with giftedness. *Peabody Journal of Education, 72*, 101–116.

VanTassel-Baska, J. (2002, Fall). Planning professional development experiences in gifted education. *Virginia Association for the Gifted, 24*(1), 1–4

VanTassel-Baska, J., Johnson, D., & Boyce, L. (Eds.). (1996). *Developing verbal talent: Ideas and strategies for teachers of elementary and middle school students.* Boston: Allyn & Bacon.

Wentzel, K. R. (2002). Are effective teachers like good parents? Teaching styles and student adjustment in early adolescence. *Child Development, 73*, 287–301.

Westberg, K. L., Archambault, F. X., Jr., & Brown, S. W. (1997). A survey of classroom practices with third and fourth grade students in the United States. *Gifted Education International, 12*(1), 29–33

Westberg, K. L., Archambault, F. X., Jr., Dobyns, S. M., & Salvin, T. J. (1993). *An observational study of instructional and curricular practices used with gifted and talented students in regular classrooms.* Storrs: National Research Center on the Gifted and Talented, University of Connecticut.

Westberg, K. L., Burns, D., Gubbins, E., Reis, S., Park, S., & Maxfield, L. (1998). *Professional development practices in gifted education: Results of a national survey.* Storrs: National Research Center on the Gifted and Talented, University of Connecticut.

Creating Gifted Lives: Concluding Thoughts

Tracy L. Cross, Joyce L. VanTassel-Baska, & F. Richard Olenchak

On some positions, Cowardice asks the question, "Is it safe?" Expediency asks the question, "Is it politic?" And Vanity comes along and asks the question, "Is it popular?" But Conscience asks the question, "Is it right?" And there comes a time when one must take a position that is neither safe, nor politic, nor popular, but he must do it because Conscience tells him it is right.
    —Martin Luther King, Jr., Address delivered at the
        National Cathedral, Washington, DC, March, 31,
            1968. Congressional Record, April 9, 1968.

Amidst a daunting educational environment driven more by quantitative test results than by other, more desirable outcomes, this book represents an undertaking that is neither safe, nor politic, nor popular, yet cast against a backdrop of research and theory, seems ethically right. Creating this book, targeted to teachers and counselors who will assist students with gifts and talents develop their social and emotional selves from kindergarten through 12th grade, was inherently a complicated and multifaceted task. It required authors to establish the affective needs of the general population of students with gifts and talents or for specific groups and then offer specific curricula associated with those need areas. To that end, both traditional and contemporary theories were used to establish intellectual underpinnings for the topics discussed.

This book attempts to inform the reader by giving voice to authors who are experts in these important topics. It also provides information critical to teachers and counselors in their roles as mentors and guides in the social and emotional lives of students with gifts and talents. The final product has become a significant offering for the field as it provides important information for teachers and counselors to consider as they work on behalf of those with gifts and talents.

Internal Themes Emerging Across Authors

From the diverse topics included, several themes emerged from the chapters of this book: (1) the primacy of experience, both for those authoring the chapters and those being written about; (2) the importance of the concept of self as an essential construct from which to understand the social and emotional nature and needs of students with gifts and talents; and (3) the developmental backdrop against which issues in the social and emotional realm for students with gifts and talents must be explored. In the concluding chapter to this book, we try to summarize some of the most important points made by the authors and to synthesize an overarching direction for strengthening gifted and talented education as a field as it matures.

The Primacy of Experience

When establishing the nature and needs of students with gifts and talents, the authors grounded their chapters in prior research. Many also brought to bear aspects of their own lived experience that informed their writing, as well as the lived experiences of the gifted students being written about. The strength that this primacy of lived experience creates was described by Rollo May (1969) as the difference between knowing something and knowing about something. Several of the chapters are underpinned by both the literature that preceded the work and the authors' intimate knowledge of the topic of the chapter. This not only informs the author when writing, but also informs the writing in a manner not possible when one merely knows about a topic. As examples, Day-Vines, Patton, Quek, and Woods offered a chapter that is culturally specific and informed by lived experience, while Kwan focused more on a variety of minority groups and the interventions likely to be successful.

The Importance of Self

When editing the chapters in this book, the critical importance of the development of one's sense of self became evident. Although it is not surprising that it appeared in a book about affective curriculum, it is noteworthy the extent to which it emerged as a significant factor for much of the book. Many in the field of gifted education have written about the essential nature of self when trying to understand the social and emotional aspects of children with gifts and talents. In a recent interview Annemarie Roeper said,

> . . . My interest [in gifted children] is because I truly feel that the motivation, the impetus for action in human beings' lives, comes from their own inner agenda. And that if we want to change the world (and we know the world is not going where everybody hopes it will go) we need to understand the underlying motivation of people's behavior. (Kane, 2003)

In this example, the self was operationalized as the origin of motivation. In this book, other very important insights into differing conceptions of self underpin the major treatise of respective chapters. The Moon chapter outlines the major theories of self that impact our thinking about the social and emotional development of the gifted in the beginning of the book. This view is built on by other authors throughout the text. From the Olenchak chapter outlining his Bull's Eye Model for first conceptualizing and then serving psychosocial growth in accordance with each individual student's personal pace of affective development, to the Hébert chapter on the use of biography, to the Renzulli chapter on his Houndstooth theory, the importance of self in the construct of being is evident. If Roeper is correct and action comes from the motivation that is rooted in the person's self, then understanding the "agenda" of the individual, the life theme, is critical to having positive effects on his or her life.

Developmental Backdrop

Arguably the most fundamental aspect of this book across virtually all of its chapters is the basic construct of human development. Whether it is the Peterson, Betts, and Bradley chapter on the importance of discussion groups, or the Cross, Frazier, and McKay chapter emphasizing the prevention of suicide, the development of the student with gifts and talents is a crucial component. In some chapters this important assumption is not as obvious as in other chapters, but it is clear that when considering the affective curriculum of students, the development of the student is a necessary ingredient. At the most basic level, agreeing that our role in working with students with gifts and talents is based on the assumption that they develop over time and that our work must be congruent with universal and nonuniversal aspects of their development is very important. It pushes our field in the direction of a conception of giftedness that is neither entity-based nor static in nature. Rather, it moves us to a position in the field that the manifestations of giftedness have inherent developmental steps, stages with needs preceding them. For a field that has dozens of conceptions, acknowledging the importance of development has the potential to coalesce the entire field.

External Facilitation of Emotional Growth

In addition to the internal thematics just explored, there also is a need to describe the environmental concerns mentioned in several chapters. Peterson worries about the training and background of the facilitators who will conduct discussion sessions with gifted students, sensitive to the strategies they may use to elicit commentary. VanTassel–Baska views the propitious intervention at the right time as a key factor in meeting needs, whether through bibliotherapy or the arts. Brown constructs a system of support for ensuring that interventions occur in school settings, providing the planning direction necessary to be sure it happens.

Our collective view as editors is that environmental catalysts can interact successfully with internal motivations to help students develop healthy selves and create the persons they want to become. This powerful interaction effect is dependent, however, on knowledgeable teachers and counselors and parents who see the possibilities in children, those who will take the time to encourage, guide, and nurture such children on a life path toward greater understanding of self and others. In fact, without the critical and appropriate involvement of adults important in each child's life, there is ample reason to believe that development approaching the optimum in *both* the cognitive and the affective domains is unlikely. Moreover, the potential for educational services less suitable to maximizing one's sense of self and ultimately for developing one's gifts and talents serves as a barometer for misidentification of an array of troublesome issues that may not be real beyond the need to make each child "fit" the ever-increasing prescriptive nature of schooling (Webb et al., 2005). In crystallizing the works of the various authors herein, the editors deduce that prescriptive, single-size educational services inhibit rather than promote affective development and, in turn, may marginalize a child's sense of self and delimit advantageous cognitive application. In other words, talent development and affective development are codependent.

The Preparation and Role of Counselors and Teachers in Schools

However, in order for human external influences to be productive in children's lives, adults must be trained in relevant skills, select interventions with care at propitious times, and ensure that the systems within which they function are attuned to the need for flexibility in implementation. Each of these important preparatory aspects must be adapted in accordance with both general theories of human development and those addressing psychosocial development of gifted and talented populations specifically.

The preparation of counselors and teachers in schools is no small matter, given the current emphases in schools on students who are not performing at appropriate levels of achievement. Counselor preparation does not acknowledge a required course or even an emphasis on the importance of working with the gifted, and even advanced graduate training programs in counseling psychology embrace little if any training aimed at effecting affective growth among the gifted as a special population. Nor is there a common acceptance among counselors and counseling psychologists of specialized affective needs of gifted students. Little meaningful involvement of counselors with gifted programs has occurred. Thus, we are faced with barren ground that needs to be plowed if the needs of this population are to be met.

There are a variety of strategies that school districts may try to involve counselors and counseling psychologists effectively with this population. Some of these ideas include the following:

- At the secondary level, selecting one counselor in a building who becomes the expert on gifted students and their levels of affective development and who then is assigned to work with these learners on social and emotional issues that emerge but also addresses needs in a preventive mode through small-group sessions.

- At the elementary level, where counseling services may be less accessible, training the administrator or his or her designee in the social and emotional needs of gifted and talented students, as well as equipping that professional with skills to address them, will provide at least a frontline opportunity for promoting self-efficacy, self-esteem, and self-assuredness early in the educational process.

- Involving counselors in the professional development sessions about working with gifted learners, especially those that focus on affective needs, development of the self, and understanding of general human development research, as well as that specific to students with high potential.

- Developing collaborative teams to address the needs of the gifted in schools that include counselors who would take responsibility for building not only the talent development plan but for determining a fundamental philosophical model to which affective development will adhere school-wide.

The development of skills and attitudes among teachers in school settings that will foster the social-emotional growth of the gifted again will require hard work by coordinators of gifted programs. They will need to ensure on an annual basis that teachers who work with gifted learners:

- Have the appropriate knowledge and skills in affective development designated in the teacher education standards delineated in Chapter 1 of this book.
- Receive instructional coaching and support in the execution of various strategies like bibliotherapy, emotional intelligence lesson design, and question asking.
- Participate in special seminars that focus on selected case studies of gifted students that build competence in dealing with issues like uneven development, emotional lability, and at-risk factors.

The Need to Include
Social and Emotional Curriculum in Schools

Beyond just the preparation of counselors and teachers lies the bigger issue of sensitizing schools to the need to weave the affective strand into all of their work for these learners, as well as others in the school system who stand to benefit. Just as we now understand that open-ended and inquiry-based activities aimed at enhancing critical thinking designed for the gifted can be used successfully with all learners (see VanTassel-Baska, Stambaugh, & Bracken, 2008), so we too should be promoting the same strategy on the affective side. Social and emotional curriculum designed for the gifted can be applied successfully in the following ways:

- It can be embedded in core content, allowing lessons to be enriched in all subject areas. Students can read about eminent scientists and mathematicians, their struggles, and their talent development process and come together to discuss the common and uncommon features of each life. Such a technique can be replicated in other subject domains as well.

- It can be integrated through the arts. Teachers can bring art forms and functions into the classroom as different symbol systems that define concepts, issues, and themes studied in the core subjects. Escher's visual works can help students understand how geometric forms can be used for artistic effect. Conceptual poetry can help students understand how to weave idea and form together for creative projects in language arts. The music of Debussy can provide an outlet for understanding mood, tone, and feeling in a human creation and how to use such tools in their own creative work in any area of learning. The dance of Baryshnikov may offer students an opportunity to frame how physical movement, ideas, and feelings can be intertwined for expression and ways for integrating, body, mind, and heart as they undertake their own pursuits.

- It can deliberately focus on emotion as a topic for learning in its own right. All great literature has a protagonist caught in a set of circumstances that require resolution through the use of emotional intelligence. Students can come to understand how emotions can be a help and hindrance to problem solving. They can reflect on the emotions of historical figures caught in the throes of events beyond their control, and on the emotions of the lonely creator, working on problems too intractable to solve.

What Is Realistic, Given the Climate?

If educators have the conscience to do the right thing by gifted students, then the above ideas are achievable in schools across the country. Yet, the current climate persists to push aside the needs of the gifted in favor of other groups, even to the point of scapegoating, bullying, and manipulating them to serve as second instructors in the room in addition to just ignoring them and their needs. How do we successfully combat the image of the gifted as self-sufficient learners who do not require help with their development in either cognitive or affective areas? We believe that the lack of attention to their affective development is an extension of the myth that gifted students can make it on their own in the cognitive sphere as well. This belief is further exacerbated by a frenzied climate of high-stakes assessment on low-level instruments in most states. Yet, the climate in schools has never been receptive to the social-emotional development of the gifted, even before No Child Left Behind. Data from evaluations for the last 12 years suggest that schools have no system in place to provide guidance and counseling to their gifted populations (VanTassel-Baska, 2006).

So, how can the agenda be built that is suggested by these chapters, an agenda that acknowledges the social and emotional needs of the gifted; that outlines theories, research, and applications in practice that are successful in enhancing affective growth; and that defines the knowledge and skills needed by teachers, counselors, and others to facilitate progress? We argue that the agenda must be attempted through the goodwill and acumen of the few in schools who understand its grave importance in reclaiming lives that are already damaged and in helping others create satisfying and productive lives in their future. Meanwhile, there is an urgent need for community health care groups, universities, and other purveyors of programs and services to the gifted to become aware of these needs as well and educate themselves to the most effective strategies for reaching this population. Parents, too, need to become well-versed in the counseling and guidance needs of their children and to seek outside assistance from experts who can provide what the schools may not be providing—individual assistance, small-group opportunities, and curriculum interventions that touch gifted children's lives.

An important finding of the analysis of the themes emerging from the chapters of this book is that internal mechanisms involving the primacy of experience, importance of self, and developmental backdrop are essential components for social-emotional development to occur. Moreover, external mechanisms involving the role of knowledgeable and skilled teachers and counselors in the drama of providing curriculum sensitive to gifted students' needs at different stages of development also are essential interactive aspects with the self to produce growth in the affective dimension.

So What? Why Did We Bother With This and Why Should You?

The collective view of experts assembled in this publication is that gifted and talented persons do not magically emerge as fully developed, well-adjusted individuals who ply their abilities in a fashion pleasing not only to themselves but also to others. Explicit advice for improving education for gifted students is provided in each chapter, but perhaps just as important and more likely to be overlooked are some implicit messages:

- Gifted children come into the world with social and emotional equipment that distinguishes them markedly from other groups of young people and, as a result are likely to manifest affective needs that are distinctive. Given that cognitive and affective development are not as separable as perhaps once believed, educational services provided for students with gifts and talents demand not only attention but attention to detail. While educational pundits raise concerns about the nationwide need to improve schools, efforts to do anything substantive to improve schools for *all* students have not embraced the gifted population in an integrated fashion to attend to cognitive and affective growth concurrently as codependent features of each individual student's education.

- Just as society searches for scientifically based evidence to undergird what schools do, accountability systems have been myopic in not considering students who not only think efficiently and effectively but who know how to apply and regulate emotional and social skills. As a result, embedding affective curriculum and instruction into the overall school plan appears to be critical for the optimal development of each gifted learner.

In a culture that seems to wish for quick answers to intractable problems, the experts in this book also offer some cautions. Only through a comprehensive, purposeful approach in which teachers, counselors, psychologists, administrators, and parents come together will schools begin to demonstrate their collective conscience for talent development. Another willy-nilly program of isolated activities cannot and will not suffice if we as a society are serious about developing each individual student optimally; attention to affective curriculum and instruction is as foundational to the growth of each individual student as are the enormous efforts aimed at cognitive success in today's schools. Negative statistics such as rising drop-out rates (McNeil, Coppola, Radigan, & Vasquez-Heileg, 2008) and increasing school discipline concerns (Skiba, Michael, Nardo, & Peterson, 2002) seem to guide educational policy, and decision makers veer toward curriculum and instruction that are quick fixes in the context of cognitive development where many educators feel more comfortable. However, little attention has been paid to affective development amidst this reactive approach to educational improvement (McNeil et al., 2008). When one considers that human beings do not create cognitive or affective habits of mind and heart overnight, the imminent need for more thorough, well-planned approaches to educational improvement emerges suddenly as the only hope for enhancing learning.

School reforms must begin to embrace not only cognitive growth programs and their assessments but also attention paid to pupils' affective needs and evaluation systems helpful in shaping programs to address those needs. Until such time as the United States awakens to the need for comprehensive curricular and instructional planning and implementation that includes *both* cognitive and affective curriculum, the research, theories, and applied practices expounded in this book will remain simply as passive reminders. If, however, the ideas are acted upon, schooling in the United States, like a freshly painted oil canvas, will glow in newfound and authentic achievement, optimizing individual student growth and holistic development based on a foundation of equal attention to both affective and cognitive learning.

References

Kane, M. (2003). A conversation with Annemarie Roeper: A view from the self. *Roeper Review, 26,* 5–11.

May, R. (1969). The emergence of existential psychology. In R. May (Ed.), *Existential psychology* (pp. 1–48). New York: Random House.

McNeil, L. M., Coppola, E., Radigan, J., & Vasquez-Heileg, J. (2008). Avoidable losses: High-stakes accountability and the dropout crisis. *Education Policy Analysis Archives, 16*(3). Retrieved April 23, 2008, from http://epaa.asu.edu/epaa/v16n3

Skiba, R. J., Michael, R. S., Nardo, A. C., & Peterson, R. L. (2002). The color of discipline: Sources of racial and gender disproportionality in school punishment. *The Urban Review, 34,* 317–342.

Webb, J. T., Amend, E. R., Webb, N. E., Goerss, J., Beljan, P., & Olenchak, F. R. (2005). *Misdiagnosis and dual diagnoses of gifted children and adults.* Scottsdale, AZ: Great Potential Press.

VanTassel-Baska, J. (2006). A content analysis of evaluation findings across 20 gifted programs: A clarion call to enhance gifted program development. *Gifted Child Quarterly, 50,* 199–215.

VanTassel-Baska, J., & Stambaugh, T. (Eds.). (2008). *What works: 20 years of curriculum development and research for advanced learners.* Waco, TX: Prufrock Press.

About the Editors

Joyce VanTassel-Baska is the Jody and Layton Smith Professor of Education and Executive Director of the Center for Gifted Education at The College of William and Mary in Virginia (http://www.cfge.wm.edu). Formerly, she initiated and directed the Center for Talent Development at Northwestern University and also has served as a state director of gifted programs, a district coordinator, and a teacher of high school students. Dr. VanTassel-Baska has published widely, including 26 books and more than 500 refereed journal articles, book chapters, and scholarly reports. She is the editor of the Equity and Excellence in Gifted Education Series, of which this is the third volume. She also served for 7 years as the editor of *Gifted and Talented International*, a publication of the World Council on Gifted and Talented. Dr. VanTassel-Baska is the past-president of the National Association for Gifted Children (NAGC). Her research interests are on the talent development process of gifted learners and affective curriculum and instructional interventions for them.

Tracy L. Cross, George and Frances Ball Distinguished Professor of Gifted Studies, is the Associate Dean for Graduate Studies, Research, and Assessment for Teachers College at

Ball State University (BSU). For 9 years he served BSU as the Executive Director of the Indiana Academy for Science, Mathematics and Humanities, a public residential school for academically gifted adolescents. He received his graduate degrees in educational psychology from the University of Tennessee. Dr. Cross has published more than 100 articles, columns, and book chapters; a coauthored textbook, *Being Gifted in School: An Introduction to Development, Guidance, and Teaching*; and a supplemental book entitled *On the Social and Emotional Lives of Gifted Children*. He is the editor of the *Journal for the Education of the Gifted* and editor emeritus of *Roeper Review*, *Gifted Child Quarterly*, *Journal of Secondary Gifted Education*, *Research Briefs*, and others. He served as president of The Association for the Gifted of the Council for Exceptional Children and has served on the executive committee and the board of the National Association for Gifted Children.

F. Richard "Rick" Olenchak serves as professor, psychologist, and codirector of the Urban Talent Research Institute at the University of Houston. Prior to his research career, he was a teacher, principal, and consulting psychologist. Having served in a number of ancillary professional roles, including the presidency of the National Association for Gifted Children, as well as that of the Future Problem Solving Program International, he is most concerned about investigating the relationships between the cognitive and affective domains, focusing particularly on increasing optimal development of young people. Publications that he has either authored or coauthored number approximately 100; among them is the 2005 book *Misdiagnosis and Dual Diagnoses of Gifted Children and Adults*, named as *ForeWord* magazine's Psychology Book of the Year in 2005. He currently is at work on a number of chapters and articles about the social and emotional aspects of giftedness and talent development, including a significant examination of the construct of "hope" and its implications on the holistic development of each student.

About the Authors

Ariel Baska graduated with a degree in classics from The College of William and Mary, where she received a scholarship to produce and direct her own adaptations of classical plays. She is a master's student in gifted education at George Mason University. From an early age, she was lucky enough to watch many professional theatrical productions, as well as perform in, stage manage, produce, direct, and publish reviews of a wide variety of forms of theatre. She has written two *Navigators* (curriculum related to the teaching of literature) with the Center for Gifted Education, and a published article in the *Gifted Education Communicator*. She currently teaches Latin, introduction to foreign languages, and theatre in Fairfax County Public Schools in Virginia.

George Betts is a professor and director of the Center for the Education and Study of the Gifted, Talented, and Creative, as well as director of the Summer Enrichment Program (SEP) at the University of Northern Colorado. He is an internationally acclaimed speaker and consultant who specializes in assisting schools, districts, states, and national organizations to implement and refine programs for gifted and talented learners. He has worked extensively in the United States, Canada,

Germany, Australia, New Zealand, Singapore, and Taiwan. He is currently on the board of the National Association for Gifted Children (NAGC). He received the 1990–1991 Distinguished Service Award from NAGC and was honored with the Lifetime Achievement Award by the Colorado Association for Gifted and Talented (CAGT) in 1996.

Terry Bradley is an advisor for gifted students at Fairview High School in Boulder, CO. She facilitates discussion groups with students and also with parents of gifted students in the community. She is a trainer for Supporting Emotional Needs of the Gifted (SENG), and officiates in state- and district-level advocacy organizations. Her special interests include identifying factors that cause stress in gifted youth, encouraging students' self-awareness through discussion groups, and promoting effective strategies for parenting gifted children.

Elissa F. Brown is the State Consultant for Gifted Education with the North Carolina Department of Public Instruction. Previously she served as director of the Center for Gifted Education at The College of William and Mary, where she also taught graduate courses in gifted education. Dr. Brown received her bachelor's degree from the University of Georgia, her master's degree from Western Carolina University, and her doctorate in educational planning, policy, and leadership with an emphasis in gifted education from The College of William and Mary. Dr. Brown has served on the executive board of the Virginia Association of the Gifted and the North Carolina Association for Gifted and Talented. She received the National Association of Gifted Children's 2004 Early Leader award.

Brandy L. E. Buckingham is a doctoral student in learning sciences at Northwestern University. She holds a bachelor's degree in cognitive science and theater from Massachusetts Institute of Technology, as well as a master's degree in curriculum and instruction with an emphasis in gifted education from The College of William and Mary. Her broad research interests include the design of informal learning environments; the cognitive differences in learning from different media, artifacts, and environments; and the nature of intelligence and its impact on the design of learning environments. Her current research involves documenting the trajectory of learners' understanding of modeling as a scientific process, as well as exploring the information young children can extract from photographs.

Norma L. Day-Vines is an associate professor in the Counselor Education Program at Virginia Polytechnic Institute and State University. She writes extensively about culturally responsive strategies for working more effectively with ethnic minority students in general and African American students in particular. Her work has appeared in the *Journal of Counseling and Development*, *Professional School Counseling*, *Remedial and Special Education*, as well as *Teacher Education and Special Education*.

Andrea D. Frazier is a doctoral student in the educational psychology program at Ball State University. Before attending Ball State, she was an employee of the Illinois Mathematics and Science Academy, a residential academy for students gifted and/or talented in math, science and/or technology. Her research interests center around investigating the educative experience for students of color and girls.

Thomas P. Hébert is professor of educational psychology in the College of Education at The University of Georgia in Athens, where he teaches graduate courses in gifted education and qualitative research methods. He has been a teacher for 13 years, 10 of which were spent working with gifted students at the elementary, middle, and high school levels. Dr. Hébert is a member of the Board of Directors of the National Association for Gifted Children (NAGC). His research interests include the social and emotional development of gifted students, underachievement, and counseling concerns faced by gifted young men.

Wayne J. Hilson, Jr., is director of the Teacher's Resource Center at the Indiana University School of Education

(Indianapolis), as well as a doctoral student in higher education and student affairs with a minor in mathematics education at Indiana University (Bloomington). His bachelor's and master's degrees were completed at Purdue University (West Lafayette) in mechanical engineering and education respectively. After a stint in industry following the completion of his bachelor's degree, he served as both an assistant and interim director of Minority Engineering Programs at Purdue University.

Kwong-Liem Karl Kwan is a faculty member in the Department of Counseling at San Francisco State University. He previously was a tenured faculty member at Purdue University and the University of Missouri at Columbia. He received his doctorate in counseling psychology at the University of Nebraska at Lincoln. His research and consulting interests focus on racial and cultural issues in psychological assessment, identity development, career development, and cross-racial helping process.

Samantha M. McKay is a graduate student in the educational specialist program in school psychology at Ball State University. Her undergraduate degree is from Marietta College in Ohio.

Sidney M. Moon is professor of Gifted, Creative, and Talented Studies and Associate Dean for Learning and Engagement in the College of Education at Purdue University. She has been active in the field of gifted education for almost 25 years. In that time, she has contributed more than 60 books, articles, and chapters to the field. Her most recent book is *The Handbook of Secondary Gifted Education.* Sidney is active in the National Association for Gifted Children, where she has served as Chair of the Research and Evaluation Division and a member of the Board of Directors. Her research interests include talent development in the STEM disciplines (science, technology, engineering, and mathematics), underserved populations of gifted students, and personal talent development.

James M. Patton is professor of Leadership and Special Education at The College of William and Mary. He was formerly Associate Dean of Academic Programs and Director of Project Mandala, a federally funded research and development project aimed at developing culturally responsive systems for identifying and serving selected culturally, linguistically, and socioeconomically diverse students and their families who exhibit at-risk and at-promise characteristics. Dr. Patton has taught special education in the public schools of Louisville, KY, where he also directed the Career Opportunities Program, a federally funded effort to increase the number of indigenous inner-city ethnically and culturally diverse teachers in the Louisville Public Schools. Dr. Patton has authored or coauthored more than 55 articles in referred publications and three books.

Jean Sunde Peterson, coordinator of school counselor preparation at Purdue University, was previously involved in K–12 education, including gifted education, for many years. As a licensed mental health counselor, she has worked with gifted youth and their families and also conducts workshops related to the social and emotional development of high-ability individuals, underachievement, small-group work, and listening skills for teachers. She has received national research awards, a national group-work award, and teaching, research, and service awards at Purdue. She is author of *The Essential Guide to Talking with Gifted Teens* and coeditor of *Models of Counseling Gifted Children, Adolescents, and Young Adults* and is on the NAGC Board of Directors.

Chwee G. Quek has been involved in gifted education in Singapore in different capacities. She began as a teacher in the Gifted Education Programme, and worked as a curriculum specialist before becoming an administrator. She served as assistant editor of *Gifted and Talented International* for 3 years. She received her doctorate from The College of William and Mary and is now a Senior Specialist in the Gifted Education Branch, Ministry of Education, Singapore.

Joseph Renzulli is professor of educational psychology at the University of Connecticut, where he also serves as director of the National Research Center on the Gifted and Talented. His research has focused on the identification and development of creativity and giftedness in young people, and on organizational models and curricular strategies for differentiated learning environments that contribute to total school improvement. His most recent books include the second edition of *The Schoolwide Enrichment Model, The Multiple Menu Model for Developing Differentiated Curriculum*, and *Enriching Curriculum for All Students* (2nd edition). He was designated a Board of Trustees Distinguished Professor at the University of Connecticut in 2000, and in 2003 was awarded an Honorary Doctor of Laws Degree from McGill University in Montreal, Canada.

Susannah Wood is assistant professor at the University of Iowa in the Counselor Education and Supervision Program and has an appointment in The Belin-Blank Center. She teaches a variety of school counseling courses such as school counseling and leadership and counseling children and adolescents to master's students in order to prepare them to work with K–12 students, with an emphasis on counseling the gifted and talented. Her research encompasses examining school counseling services for the gifted student, and preparing school counselors to work with this population, including collaborative efforts with educators of the gifted. She completed her doctorate in counselor education with a cognate in gifted education at The College of William and Mary, focusing on gifted adolescents' experiences in school counseling.